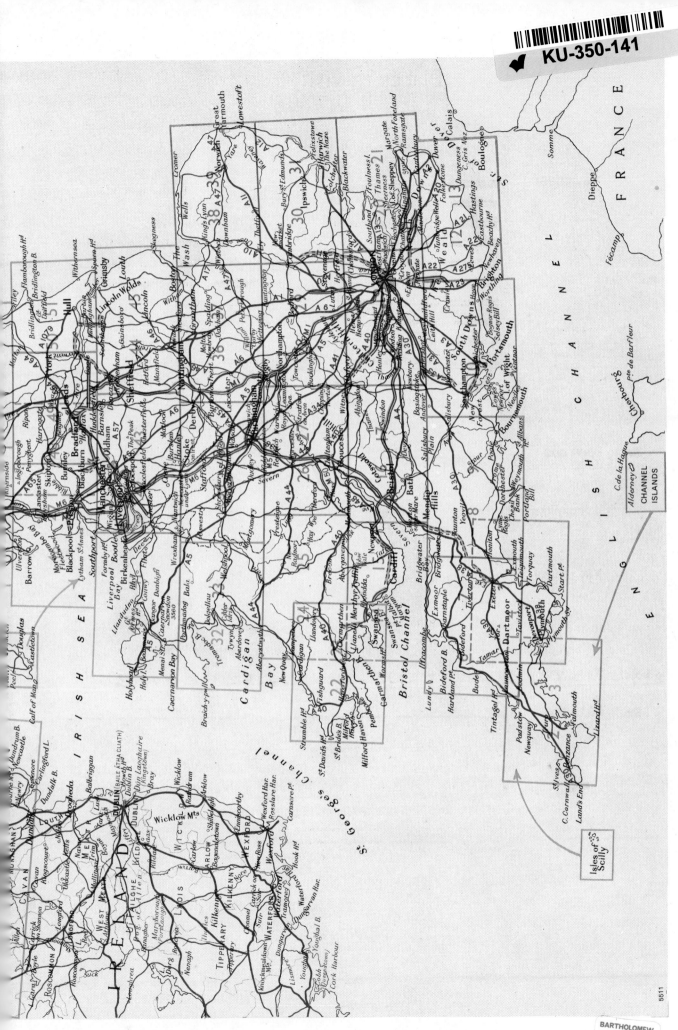

Places to visit

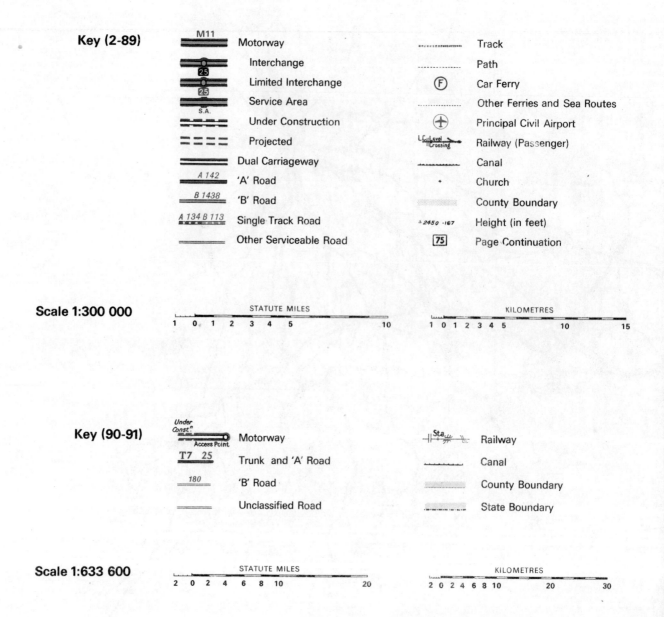

M11	Motorway		Track
	Interchange		Path
25	Limited Interchange	(F)	Car Ferry
25	Service Area		Other Ferries and Sea Routes
S.A.	Under Construction	(airplane)	Principal Civil Airport
	Projected	L.C. Level Crossing	Railway (Passenger)
	Dual Carriageway		Canal
A 142	'A' Road	+	Church
B 1438	'B' Road		County Boundary
A 134 B 113	Single Track Road	△2450 ·167	Height (in feet)
	Other Serviceable Road	75	Page Continuation

Scale 1:300 000

STATUTE MILES
1 0 1 2 3 4 5 10

KILOMETRES
1 0 1 2 3 4 5 10 15

Key (90-91)

Under Const.ⁿ Access Point	Motorway	Sta.	Railway
T7 25	Trunk and 'A' Road		Canal
180	'B' Road		County Boundary
	Unclassified Road		State Boundary

Scale 1:633 600

STATUTE MILES
2 0 2 4 6 8 10 20

KILOMETRES
2 0 2 4 6 8 10 20 30

Maps printed and copyright
© John Bartholomew & Son Ltd., Duncan Street, Edinburgh, EH9 1TA
5150

Explanatory Notes

1. This is an Atlas—a guide to *situation*, not a Guide Book. It is so designed that the traveller consulting it is able to discover *at a glance* what interesting places lie within his reach.

   Wherever practicable the exact positions of these places are marked on the map; but one symbol may indicate several widely spaced items of interest within a town or city (excepting London which is not treated in this volume).

2. Each double page map section is followed by its own gazetteer so that the numbered sites can be quickly identified. (N.B. There is identical site-numbering in all cases where map sections overlap.)

   There is also an alphabetical index at the end of the book.

3. Places which are open to the public on certain days only or by appointment are distinguished by *italics* in the gazetteer and index. This serves as a warning to the intending visitor that opening times should be checked in advance.

   In the main, privately-owned houses which are not open to the public are excluded, however notable they may be; but exceptions have been made where such a house provides an important element in a view, a grouping or a town landscape.

4. The needs of a quick reference system greatly restrict the amount of information which can be given in the gazetteers.

   In cases where public access is controlled, information about opening arrangements, together with a fuller description of the properties concerned, will be found in the following publications:—

   Historic Houses, Castles & Gardens in Great Britain & Ireland (ABC Historic Publications)

   Museums & Galleries in Great Britain & Ireland (ABC Historic Publications)

   Historic Monuments Open to the Public (Department of the Environment)

Ancient Monuments of Northern Ireland (H.M. Stationery Office, Belfast)

National Trust publications obtainable from 42 Queen Anne's Gate, London, SW1H 9AS

National Trust for Scotland publications obtainable from 5 Charlotte Square, Edinburgh EH2 4DU

Information about Almshouses, some of which are open to the public, is obtainable from The National Association of Almshouses, Billingbear Lodge, Wokingham, Berks.

The Council for Nature, Zoological Gardens, Regents Park, London, NW1 4RY, can give information about Nature Reserves.

Other works to which the compilers are indebted are given below. In them will be found descriptions of a great many of the listed places.

The Buildings of England by Nikolaus Pevsner (Penguin Books)

The Shell Guides

The Blue Guides (ed. L. Russell Muirhead. Ernest Benn Ltd.)

Collins Guide to English Parish Churches (ed. John Betjeman)

Notes on the Older Churches in the Four Welsh Dioceses by Sir Stephen R. Glynne (Chas. J. Clark, 1903)

5. Although we have listed over six thousand places it is likely that many users of the Atlas will know of others which they consider worthy of inclusion. We should be most grateful if they would tell us of these and of any mistakes in the text, so that the next edition may be improved.

   Meanwhile, space will be found on most of the gazetteer pages for users of the Atlas to note down their own additions.

Abbreviations

FC	Forestry Commission
BTO	British Trust for Ornithology
FSC	Field Studies Council
NC	The Nature Conservancy
NT/S	The National Trust/Scotland
RSPB	Royal Society for the Protection of Birds
C16	Sixteenth Century

Map Symbols

Nature Reserve		Historic Buildings	
Ecclesiastical		NT/NTS Property	
Archaeological		Beauty Spot	
Viewpoint		Scenic Area	
Garden		General Interest	

First Edition 1975

ISBN 0 7078 0019 6

PRINTED IN GREAT BRITAIN BY

JOHN BARTHOLOMEW & SON LTD

EDINBURGH EH9 1TA

PUBLISHED BY

THE NATIONAL TRUST

42 QUEEN ANNE'S GATE, LONDON SW1H 9AS

5150

An Atlas of **Places to Visit** in England, Scotland, Wales & Northern Ireland

COMPILED BY

THE NATIONAL TRUST

42 QUEEN ANNE'S GATE, LONDON SWIH 9AS

AND

THE NATIONAL TRUST FOR SCOTLAND

5 CHARLOTTE SQUARE, EDINBURGH EH2 4DU

1975

Map 2

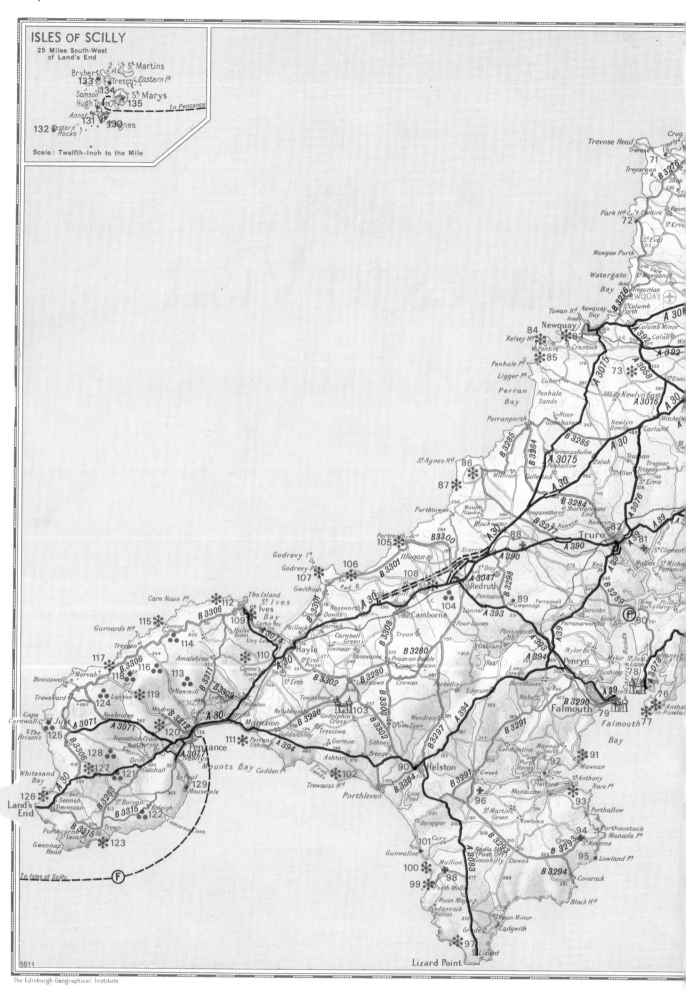

ISLES OF SCILLY
25 Miles South-West of Land's End

St Martins
Bryher 133 · Tresco Eastern Is
134 St Marys
Samson 135 To Penzance
Hugh Town
Annet 131 130 nes
132 Western Rocks

Scale: Twelfth-Inch to the Mile

5511
The Edinburgh Geographical Institute

Map 3

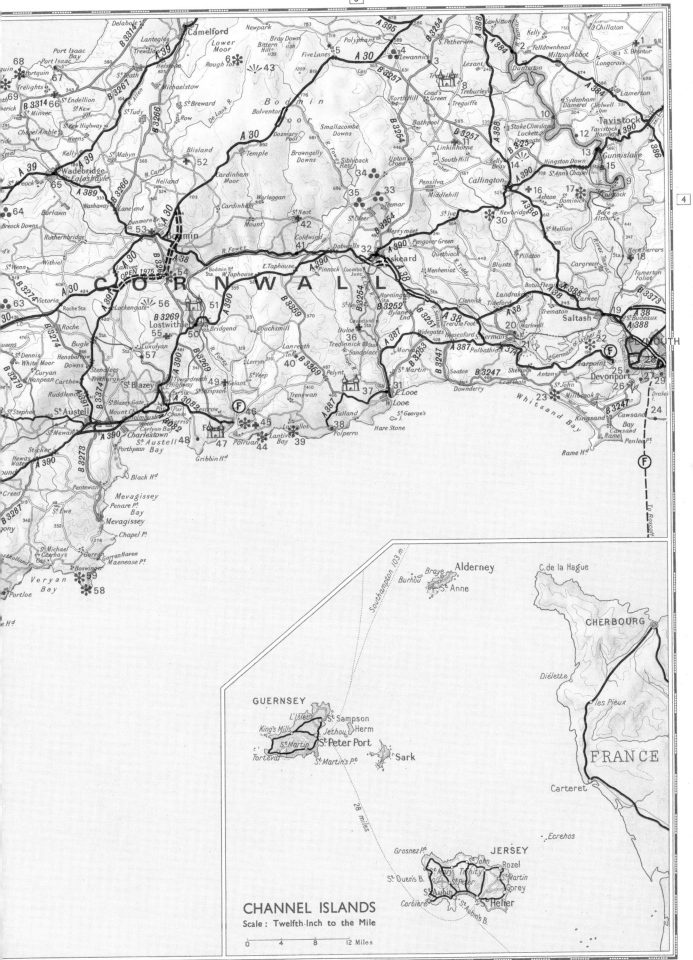

CHANNEL ISLANDS

Scale : Twelfth-Inch to the Mile

0   4   8   12 Miles

© — John Bartholomew & Son Ltd.

2   3   4   5 Miles

Gazetteer to Maps 2·3

1. Brentor Church
2. Greystone Bridge (C14)
3. Trekelland Bridge (C16)
4. Inscribed Stones (C5–6), Lewannick
5. Altarnun Church & Village
6. Rough Tor (moorland, views, Bronze Age village site) (NT)
7. Town Hall (C18; *Borough chattels*), Camelford
8. *Trecarrel Manor* (mediaeval hall & chapel)
9. *Morwellham Quay Museum*
10. Horsebridge (mediaeval bridge)
11. Linkinhorne Church
12. Devon Great Consuls Mine (disused), Tavistock
13. New Bridge (C16), Gunnislake
14. Kit Hill (1094 ft; view)
15. Weir Head (gorge, r. Tamar)
    Morwell Rocks
16. Dupath Well Chapel (c. 1500)
17. *Cotehele House & Gardens* (NT), Calstock
18. Bere Ferrers Church
19. Royal Albert Bridge (Brunel, 1859), Saltash
20. St. Germans Church
    Moyle's Almshouses
21. Lynher Estuary (scenery)
22. *Antony House* (NT)
23. Sharrow Point (cliff views) (NT), Whitesand Bay
    Sharrow Grot (C18 rock chamber)
24. Breakwater (Rennie, 1841), Plymouth
25. Devonport Guildhall & Naval Column (Foulston, 1822–24)
    Oddfellows' Hall (Foulston, 1824)
    St. Aubyn Street (C18 houses)
    Naval Dockyards (C18 buildings)
26. *Mount Edgcumbe* (C18 park, views of Plymouth Sound)
27. Royal William Victualling Yard (Rennie, 1835), Stonehouse
28. St. Andrew's Church, Plymouth
    32, New Street (C16)
    City Museum & Art Gallery
29. Plymouth Hoe (promenade, view)
    Royal Citadel Gate (1670 & later)
    Old Eddystone Lighthouse (Smeaton, 1759, rebuilt)
30. Cadsonbury (Hillfort) (NT)
31. East & West Looe (fishing towns)
    Old Guildhall (C16), East Looe
    The Cornish Museum, East Looe
32. St. Martin's Church, Liskeard
33. Trethevy Quoit (burial chamber)
34. The Hurlers (stone circles), Minions
35. King Doniert's Stone (C9, inscribed), St. Cleer
36. Duloe Church
    Stone Circle
37. *Trelawne* (C16 & earlier; Country Club)
38. Polperro (fishing village)
    The Warren (cliffland, east side) (NT)
    Chapel Cliff (west side) (NT)
39. Lansallos Cliff (NT), Lantivet Bay
40. Lanreath Church & Village
41. Treverbyn Bridge (glen, r. Fowey)
42. St. Neot Church
43. Brown Willy (1375 ft; views), Bodmin Moor
44. Pencarrow Head (NT), Polruan
    Lantic Bay (NT)
    Blackbottle Rock (NT)
45. Lanteglos-by-Fowey Church
46. Pont Pill Creek (NT)
    Hall Walk (cliff walk) (NT)
47. St. Catherine's Castle (Henry VIII coastal fort), Fowey

48. Castle d'Or Stone (C6, inscribed), Menabilly
    The Grotto (c. 1800)
    The Gribbin & Polridmouth (NT)
49. St. Sampson's Church, Golant
50. St. Bartholomew's Church, Lostwithiel
    Mediaeval Bridge
51. Restormel Castle (C12–13 remains)
52. Blisland Church
53. St. Petrock's Church, Bodmin
54. *Lanhydrock, picture gallery & garden* (NT)
55. Lanlivery Church
56. Helman Tor (view)
57. Treffry Viaduct, Luxulian Valley
58. The Dodman (headland, views, Iron Age fort) (NT)
59. Hemmick Beach & Cove (NT), Veryan Bay
60. Portloe (fishing village)
61. Nare Head (views) (NT)
62. *Trewithen* (early C18 house), Probus
63. Castle-an-Dinas (hillfort)
64. St. Breock Monolith (Bronze Age)
65. Mediaeval Bridge, Wadebridge
66. St. Endellion Church
67. Port Isaac (fishing village)
68. Portquin Harbour (NT)
    Doyden Castle (C19 folly) (NT)
69. Carnweather Point (NT), Portquin Bay
    Lundy Bay (NT)
70. Pentire Point & The Rumps (rocks & cliff castle remains) (NT)
71. *Harlyn Bay Museum* (prehistory), Padstow
72. Pendarves Point (views) (NT)
    Bedruthan Steps (cliff rock formation)
73. *Trerice* (manor house)(NT)
74. Probus Church
75. Pendower Beach (NT), Veryan
76. St. Anthony-in-Roseland (coastal & estuarial scenery) (NT)
77. St. Anthony Head (views) (NT)
78. St. Mawes Castle (Henry VIII coastal fort)
79. Pendennis Castle (Henry VIII coastal fort), Falmouth
80. *Trelissick, Gardens, Park & woodlands* (NT)
    King Harry Passage (r. Fal), Carrick Roads
81. St. Clement Church
82. Truro Cathedral
    Lemon Street (Georgian houses)
    County Museum
83. The Gannel (estuary) (NT), Newquay
    The Rushy Green (sandhills) (NT)
84. Kelsey Head (views) (NT)
    Porth Joke (cove) (NT)
85. Cubert Common (NT)
    Holywell Beach (NT)
86. St. Agnes Beacon (views) (NT)
87. Chapel Porth (cove, tin & copper mine ruins) (NT)
88. Chacewater Church
89. Gwennap Pit (Wesleyan amphitheatre)
90. Helston (Georgian town)
    St. Michael's Church
91. Rosemullion Head (views) (NT)
92. Helford River (wooded estuary scenery)
    Glendurgan, Gardens (NT)
93. Trewarnevas Cliff (NT)
    Coneysburrow Cove (NT)
94. St. Keverne Church
95. Lowland Point (Ice Age raised beach) (NT)

    Manacles Rocks
96. Mawgan-in-Meneage Church
97. Lizard Downs (views, flora & geology) (NT)
    Kynance Cove (NT)
98. St. Melan's Church, Mullion
99. Mullion Cove (fishing harbour) (NT)
    Mullion Island (NT)
100. Polurrian Cove & Cliffland (NT)
     Carrag-Luz (viewpoint) (NT)
     Marconi Memorial (NT)
101. Gunwalloe Towans (cliffland) (NT)
     St. Winwalloe's Church
     Church Cove (NT)
     Poldhu Cove (NT)
102. Rinsey Cliff (NT)
103. *Godolphin House*
104. Carn Brea (hillfort), Pool
105. Carvannel Downs (NT)
     Ralph's Cupboard (gully) (NT)
106. Reskajeage Down (cliffland) (NT)
     Hell's Mouth (cliff chasm) (NT)
107. Godrevy Point (headland) (NT)
     The Knavocks (sandhills) (NT)
108. *Beam Mine Engines* (1887–92), Pool (NT)
109. Porthminster Point (cliffland) (NT), St. Ives
110. Trencrom Hill (hillfort, view) (NT)
     Bowl Rock (NT)
111. *St. Michael's Mount* (island castle) (NT)
112. Hor Point (views) (NT)
     Hellesveor Cliff (NT)
113. *Chysauster* (Iron Age village)
114. Zennor Quoit (burial chamber)
115. Zennor Head (views) (NT)
116. Mulfra Quoit (burial chamber)
117. Rosemary Cliffs (NT)
     Trevean Cliffs (NT)
118. Men Scryfa (C5 inscribed stone)
119. Lanyon Quoit (burial chamber) (NT)
120. *Trengwainton, Gardens* (NT)
121. Boscawen-un Stone Circle
122. Merry Maidens (stone circle), St. Buryan
123. Penberth Cove (NT)
     Logan Rock (rocking stone) (NT)
     Treen Castle (Cornish cliff castle) (NT)
124. Chun Castle (hillfort)
125. Ballowal Barrow, St. Just
126. Mayon Cliff (NT), Sennen Cove
     Maen Castle (Cornish cliff castle) (NT)
127. Chapel Carn Brea (657 ft; views) (NT)
128. *Carn Euny* (Iron Age village), Sancreed
129. Mousehole (fishing harbour)
130. St. Agnes (island)
     Old Lighthouse (1680)
     Bird Observatory (BTO)
     The Punch Bowl (perched boulder)
     Troy Town (ancient maze)
131. *Annet Sea Bird Sanctuary* (RSPB)
132. Bishop Rock Lighthouse
133. Bryher (island)
     Shipman Head
     Hell Bay
134. Tresco (island)
     Tresco Abbey, sub-tropical gardens
     Cromwell's Castle (C16)
     Piper's Hole (cavern)
135. St. Mary's (island)
     Giant's Castle (cliff-fort), Porth Hellick
     Star Castle (1593), Garrison Hill (viewpoint)
     Telegraph Hill (viewpoint)
     Pulpit Rock & Peninnis Point (logan rock)

Map 4

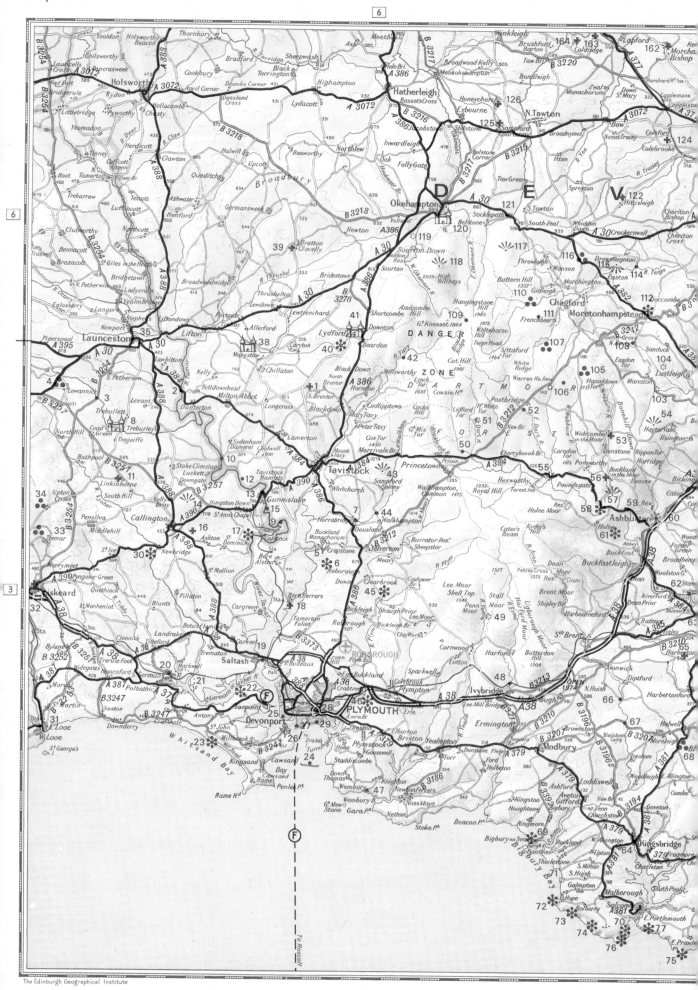

Map 5

Gazetteer to Maps 4·5

1. Brentor Church
2. Greystone Bridge (C14)
3. Trekelland Bridge (C16)
4. Inscribed Stones (C5–6), Lewannick
5. *The Garden House, Gardens,* Buckland Monarchorum
6. *Buckland Abbey* (NT)
7. Horrabridge (C15 bridge)
8. *Trecarrel Manor* (mediaeval hall & chapel)
9. *Morwellham Quay Museum*
10. Horsebridge (mediaeval bridge)
11. Linkinhorne Church
12. Devon Great Consuls Mine (disused), Tavistock
13. New Bridge (C16), Gunnislake
14. Kit Hill (1094 ft; view)
15. Weir Head (gorge, r. Tamar) Morwell Rocks
16. Dupath Well Chapel (c. 1500)
17. *Cotehele House & Gardens* (NT), Calstock
18. Bere Ferrers Church
19. Royal Albert Bridge (Brunel, 1859), Saltash
20. St. Germans Church Moyles Almshouses
21. Lynher Estuary (scenery)
22. *Antony House* (NT)
23. Sharrow Point (cliff views) (NT), Whitesand Bay Sharrow Grot (C18 rock chamber)
24. Breakwater (Rennie, 1841), Plymouth
25. Devonport Guildhall & Naval Column (Foulston, 1822–24) Oddfellows Hall (Foulston, 1824) St. Aubyn Street (C18 houses) *Naval Dockyards* (C18 buildings)
26. *Mount Edgcumbe* (C18 park, views of Plymouth Sound)
27. Royal William Victualling Yard (Rennie, 1835), Stonehouse
28. St. Andrew's Church, Plymouth *32, New Street* (C16) *City Museum & Art Gallery*
29. Plymouth Hoe (promenade, view) Royal Citadel Gate (1670 & later) Old Eddystone Lighthouse (Smeaton, 1759, rebuilt)
30. Cadsonbury (hillfort) (NT)
31. East & West Looe (fishing towns) Old Guildhall (C16), East Looe *The Cornish Museum,* East Looe
32. St. Martin's Church, Liskeard
33. Trethevy Quoit (burial chamber)
34. The Hurlers (stone circles), Minions
35. Launceston Castle (C12–13 remains) St. Mary Magdalene's Church Castle Street (Georgian houses)
38. *Sydenham House,* Lewdown
39. Bratton Clovelly Church
40. *Lydford Gorge & Waterfall* (NT)
41. Lydford Castle (C12–13 remains)
42. Tavy Cleave (gorge) Bronze Age Village, Standon Down
43. Pew Tor (views)
44. Huckworthy Bridge (C16)
45. Goodameavy (river, woods & moorland) (NT) Dewerstone Rock (NT) Wigford Down (hut circles, views) (NT)
46. *Saltram House & Park* (NT)
47. Wembury Bay (coastland) (NT) St. Werburgh's Church Hele's Almshouses (C17)
48. Ivybridge Viaduct (Brunel)
49. Dendles Wood Fall, Cornwood Stone Circles & Rows
50. Clapper Bridge, Beardown
51. Wistman's Wood (ancient oaks), Two Bridges
52. Clapper Bridge, Postbridge
53. Widecombe-in-the-Moor Church Church House (C15) (NT)
54. Haytor Rocks (views)
55. Dartmeet (viewpoint, clapper bridge)
56. Buckland-in-the-Moor Church
57. Holne Chase (views, earthwork)
58. Holne Woods (Dart valley walks) (NT), access by: New Bridge (mediaeval)

59. Holne Bridge (C15)
60. Ashburton Church & Town
61. Hembury Castle (hillfort, views) (NT) Woodlands in Dart Valley (NT)
62. Staverton Bridge (C15) & Mill
63. *Dartington Hall* (part C14; school & estate)
64. The Shambles (C16 market arcade), Kingsbridge
65. Harberton Church
66. Bickham Bridge (C17)
67. Gara Bridge (part C16)
68. Stanborough Camp (hillfort, views) Ancient Ridgeway
69. Clematon Hill (views) (NT), Bigbury-on-Sea
70. *Sharpitor, Gardens & Museum* (views) (NT)
71. Thurlestone Rock (sea-eroded arch)
72. Bolt Tail to Bolt Head (6 miles of cliffland) (NT)
73. Bolberry Down (views) (NT)
74. Cathole Cliffs (NT) Soar Mill Cove (NT)
75. Prawle Point (NT)
76. Bolt Head to Bolt Tail (6 miles of cliffland) (NT)
77. Portlemouth Down (views) (NT)
78. Start Point (views)
79. Slapton Ley (Bird Observatory (BTO), insects & flora (FSC))
80. Dart Estuary (scenery) Dartmouth Castle (coastal fort, 1481) St. Petrock's Church
81. Kingswear Castle (Tudor fort remains)
82. St. Saviour's Church, Dartmouth Shambles House (Tudor) The Butterwalk (1635–40; *maritime museum*) *The Mansion House* (C18) *Newcomen Engine* (working C18 beam engine)
83. Cornworthy Church
84. Brixham Harbour Windmill Cavern
85. Berry Head (view)
86. St. John Baptist's Church, Paignton *Kirkham House* (C15) Oldway (1874)
87. *Berry Pomeroy Castle* (C13 & Tudor remains)
88. Kent's Cavern, Torquay *Torre Abbey* (mediaeval remains & early C18 mansion)
89. *Totnes Castle* (C13–14 remains) St. Mary's Church Mediaeval Town Gates Guildhall (C16 & mediaeval) Fore & High Streets (colonnaded houses) *70, Fore Street* (C16; museum) Grammar School (C18) Dart Bridge (Fowler, 1828)
90. *Compton Castle* (NT)
91. St. Marychurch Church
92. Torbryan Church
93. West Ogwell Church
94. *Bradley Manor* (NT)
95. *Bickleigh Castle* (house & gardens)
96. *Ford House* (1610), Newton Abbot
97. The Ness (view), Shaldon
98. Little Haldon (views) (NT)
99. Dawlish (Regency watering-place) Brunel's Atmospheric Railway (1844)
100. High Land of Orcombe (cliffland) (NT), Exmouth
101. Ashcombe Church
102. *Hazelwood, Gardens,* Hennock
103. Becka Falls
104. Lustleigh Cleave (gorge, r. Bovey)
105. Grimspound (Bronze Age village)
106. Vitifer Tin Mines (mediaeval)
107. Chagford Common (hut circles)
108. North Bovey (village & church)
109. Cranmere Pool Post Box
110. Scorhill Stone Circle Walla Brook Clam Bridge
111. Shovel Down (hut circles), Chagford Kestor Rock (views)
112. Moretonhampstead Almshouses (1637) (NT)

113. Bridford Church
114. Fingle Bridge (C17) Prestonbury Castle (hillfort)
115. Drewsteignton, Sharp Tor (views) View of Castle Drogo (Lutyens, 1910–30)
116. Spinsters Rock (burial chamber) Bradford Pool
117. Cawsand Beacon (views)
118. Yes Tor (2028 ft; views)
119. Meldon Gorge & Viaduct
120. Okehampton Castle (C13 & C14 remains)
121. Old Grist & Serge Mills, Sticklepath Methodist Chapel (1816)
122. Hittisleigh Church
123. Posbury Camp (hillfort)
124. Colebrooke Church
125. Sampford Courtenay Church
126. Honeychurch Church
127. Upton Hellions Church
128. Crediton Church
129. Ashton Church & Village
130. Haldon Belvedere (C18 folly, views)
131. Kenton Church
132. *Powderham Castle*
133. Topsham (old Dutch seaport)
134. Exeter Cathedral *Cathedral Library* St. Mary Arches Church *St. Nicholas Priory* (C11–15) *Guildhall* (C14–16) *Law Library* (C14 hall) *Tuckers' Hall* (C15–17) *Mediaeval Underground Passages* Wynard's Hospital (restored C15 almshouses) Custom House (1689) Devon & Exeter Hospital (1741) County Court (1773) Southernhay (Georgian houses, 1800–06) Barnfield Crescent (c. 1800) Colleton Crescent (c. 1800) Rougemont House (1820) & Grounds *Royal Albert Memorial Museum*
135. Newton St. Cyres Church & Village
136. Cadbury Castle (hillfort)
137. Killerton Park (woods, heronry, hillfort) (NT) *Killerton, Gardens* (NT)
138. Cullompton Church
139. Broad Clyst Church Burrough's Almshouses (rebuilt 1854)
140. *A-la-Ronde* (C18 copy of San Vitale, Ravenna)
141. *Hayes Barton* (Raleigh's birthplace)
142. East Budleigh Church
143. Ladram Bay (views), Otterton
144. *Bicton Gardens* (Le Notre)
145. *Cadhay* (Elizabethan manor house)
146. Ottery St. Mary Church
147. Hembury Fort (hillfort, view)
148. Sidmouth (Regency watering-place) Esplanade & Fortfield Terrace (c. 1805) Sid Meadows (river walk) (NT) *Woolcombe House* (mediaeval hall; museum)
149. Gittisham Church
150. Dumpdon Hill (view)
151. Blackbury Castle (hillfort)
152. Branscombe Church
153. Beer Head (views)
154. *Shute Barton* (C13–16 manor house) (NT)
155. Hawksdown Hill (hillfort, views)
156. *Bindon House* (C15–17), Axmouth
157. Dowlands Cliff & Landslip
158. St. Michael's Church, Lyme Regis The Cobb (old quay, rebuilt 1825)
159. *Forde Abbey & Gardens*
160. Lamberts Castle Hill (hillfort, views) (NT)
161. Stonebarrow Hill (NT) to Golden Cap (cliffland, views) (NT)
162. Morchard Bishop Church
163. Nymet Rowland Church
164. Coldridge Church
165. Haccombe Church
166. Loughwood Meeting House (C17) (NT)

Map 6

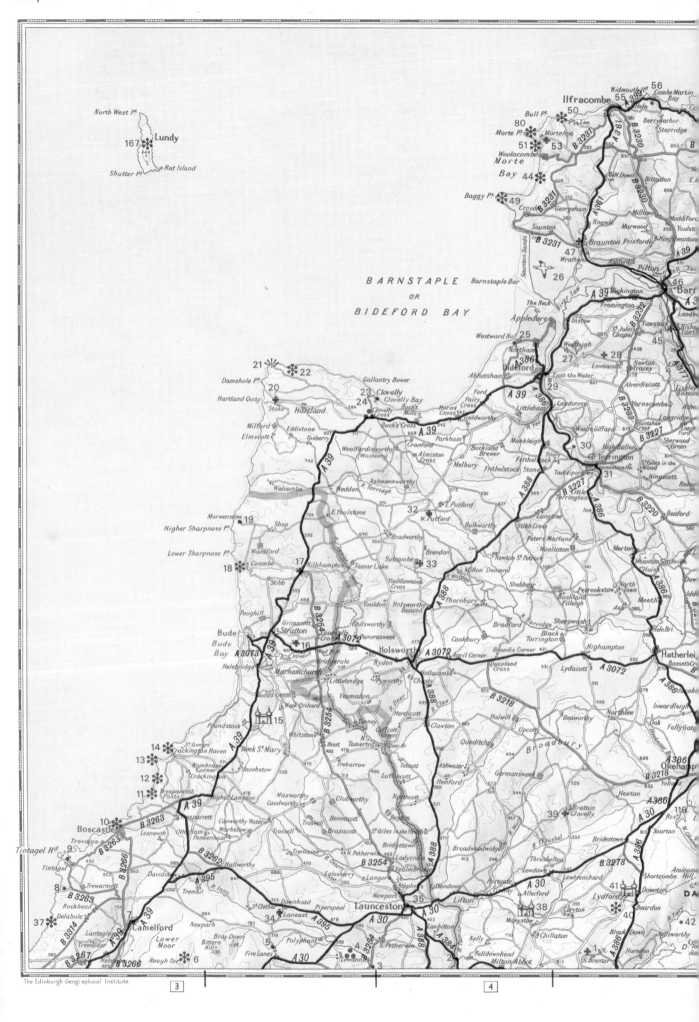

Map 7

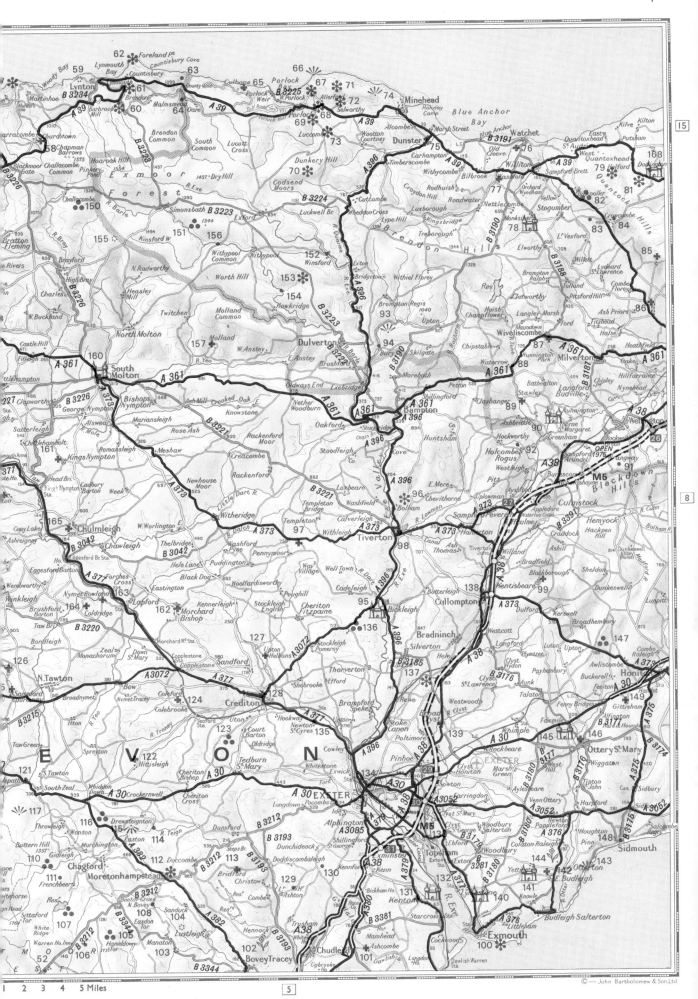

© — John Bartholomew & Son, Ltd.

1 2 3 4 5 Miles

Gazetteer to Maps 6·7

1. Brentor Church
2. Greystone Bridge (C14)
3. Trekelland Bridge (C16)
4. Inscribed Stones (C5–6), Lewannick
5. Altarnun Church & Village
6. Rough Tor (moorland, views, Bronze Age village site) (NT)
7. Town Hall (C18; *Borough chattels*), Camelford
8. Treknow & Bagalow Cliffs (NT) Trebarwith Strand (beach)
9. Tintagel Castle (C13 remains) Celtic Monastery remains (c. 500) St. Materiana's Church *The Old Post Office* (C14) (NT) Barras Nose (headland, views) (NT) Glebe Cliff (views) (NT) Penhallick Point (views) (NT)
10. Boscastle Harbour (NT) Valency Valley (NT) Forrabury Common (Celtic 'stitchmeal' survival) (NT)
11. High Cliff (731 ft) (NT), Crackington
12. Strangles Beach (NT), Crackington
13. Cambeak (headland) (NT)
14. Pencarrow Point (NT), Crackington Haven
15. *Penfound Manor*, Poundstock
16. Launcells Church
17. Kilkhampton Church
18. Steeple Point (views) (NT), Coombe Duckpool Beach (NT)
19. Morwenstow Church Vicarage Cliff (cliffland, 'Hawker's Hut') (NT)
20. St. Nectan's Church, Stoke
21. Hartland Point (views)
22. Shipload Bay (NT), Titchberry
23. Clovelly (fishing village) Hobby Drive (cliff walk)
24. Clovelly Dykes (earthwork)
25. Kipling Tors (scene of Stalky & Co.) (NT), Westward Ho! Pebble Ridge (2 miles long)
26. Braunton Burrows (sand dunes flora & fauna) (NC)
27. *Tapeley Park, Gardens*
28. Horwood Church
29. Bideford Bridge (restored mediaeval) Bridgeland Street (C17 houses) Royal Hotel (part C17)
30. Beam Aqueduct (c. 1824) Rothern Bridge (C15)
31. Great Torrington (hill town) Palmer House (c. 1752)
32. West Putford Church
33. Sutcombe Church
34. Laneast Church
35. Launceston Castle (C12–13 remains) St. Mary Magdalene's Church Castle Street (Georgian houses)
36. Atherington Church
37. Tregardock Beach (NT)
38. *Sydenham House*, Lewdown
39. Bratton Clovelly Church
40. *Lydford Gorge & Waterfall* (NT)
41. Lydford Castle (C12–13 remains)
42. Tavy Cleave (gorge) Bronze Age Village, Standon Down
43. High Bickington Church
44. Woolacombe Warren (sand dunes, surf bathing) (NT) Potters Hill (views) (NT)
45. Tawstock Church
46. Mediaeval Bridge, Barnstaple Queen Anne's Walk (C17–18 market) Westminster Bank (C17 merchant's house) *Penrose Almshouses* (1627) *North Devon Athenaeum Museum*
47. Braunton Church
48. *Arlington Court, House & Grounds* (NT)
49. Baggy Point (headland) (NT), Morte Bay
50. Damage Cliffs (NT)
51. Combegate Beach (NT), Woolacombe
52. Clapper Bridge, Postbridge
53. Mortehoe Church
54. Great Hangman (1043 ft) (NT)
55. Ilfracombe, Torrs Walks (NT) *Chambercombe Manor* (C14–15)
56. *Watermouth Castle* (1825 Gothick) *& Gardens* Golden Cove (NT)
57. Heddon's Mouth (cove & cliffs) (NT) Trentishoe Down (views) (NT)

58. St. Petrock's Church, Parracombe
59. Valley of the Rocks, Lynton
60. Combe Park (Hoar Oak Water woods) (NT)
61. Watersmeet (East Lyn river gorge) (NT), Lynmouth
62. The Foreland & Countisbury Hill (NT)
63. Old Barrow Hill (views), Countisbury Roman Signal Station (C4 earthwork)
64. Malmsmead Bridge, Badgworthy Valley
65. Culbone Church, Porlock
66. Hurlstone Point (views)
67. Bossington (village) (NT)
68. Allerford (village & packhorse bridge) (NT)
69. Horner Water Valley (West Luccombe to Cloutsham) (NT) Horner & West Luccombe Packhorse Bridges
70. Dunkery Beacon (views) (NT)
71. Bossington Hill (NT) Selworthy Beacon (views) (NT)
72. Selworthy Church & Village (NT) Tithe Barn (C15) Bury Castle (earthwork)
73. Luccombe (village) (NT)
74. North Hill (views & ruined chapel), Minehead
75. Dunster (village) St. George's Church & Priory remains Butter Cross (mediaeval) Luttrell Arms Hotel (C16 & C17) Yarn Market (c. 1589, repaired 1647) Gallox Bridge (packhorse) *Dunster Castle* (C13–18) *& Grounds*
76. St. Decuman's Church, Watchet
77. Cleeve Abbey (C12 remains)
78. *Combe Sydenham Hall* (mediaeval & C16)
79. Longstone Hill (views) (NT), Quantock Hills Willoughby Cleeve (moor & woodland) (NT)
80. Morte Point (cliffland, views) (NT)
81. Shervage Wood (views) (NT), Quantock Hills Dowsborough Camp (hillfort)
82. Trendle Ring (hillfort), Bicknoller
83. Heddon Oak
84. Crowcombe Church Churchyard & Village Crosses (mediaeval) Church House (mediaeval)
85. St. Pancras' Church, West Bagborough
86. Bishop's Lydeard Church Churchyard Cross (C14)
87. Wiveliscombe Church
88. Waterrow (hamlet), Tone Valley
89. Stawley Church
90. *Cothay Manor*
91. Blackdown Hills (view to Welsh mountains) Wellington Monument (obelisk, 1818) (NT)
92. Holcombe Rogus Church (Bluett pew) *Holcombe Court, House & Gardens*
93. Haddon Hill (views)
94. Bury Bridge, Dulverton
95. *Bickleigh Castle* (house & gardens)
96. *Knightshayes Court, Gardens* (NT)
97. Cruwys Morchard Church
98. St. Peter's Church, Tiverton St. George's Church Castle Gateway (C14) *Old Blundell's School* (1604) (NT) Greenway's Almshouses (rebuilt 1732, Tudor chapel)
99. Kentisbeare Church *The Old Priest's House* (mediaeval)
100. High Land of Orcombe (cliffland) (NT), Exmouth
101. Ashcombe Church
102. *Hazelwood, Gardens*, Hennock
103. Becka Falls
104. Lustleigh Cleave (gorge, r. Bovey)
105. Grimspound (Bronze Age village)
106. Vitifer Tin Mines (mediaeval)
107. Chagford Common (hut circles)
108. North Bovey (village & church)
109. Cranmere Pool Post Box
110. Scorhill Stone Circle Walla Brook Clam Bridge

111. Shovel Down (hut circles), Chagford Kestor Rock (views)
112. Moretonhampstead Almshouses (1637) (NT)
113. Bridford Church
114. Fingle Bridge (C17) Prestonbury Castle (hillfort)
115. Drewsteignton, Sharp Tor (views) View of Castle Drogo (Lutyens, 1910–30)
116. Spinsters Rock (burial chamber) Bradford Pool
117. Cawsand Beacon (views)
118. Yes Tor (2028 ft) (views)
119. Meldon Gorge & Viaduct
120. Okehampton Castle (C13 & C14 remains)
121. Old Grist & Serge Mills, Sticklepath Methodist Chapel (1816)
122. Hittisleigh Church
123. Posbury Camp (hillfort)
124. Colebrooke Church
125. Sampford Courtenay Church
126. Honeychurch Church
127. Upton Hellions Church
128. Crediton Church
129. Ashton Church & Village
130. Haldon Belvedere (C18 folly, views)
131. Kenton Church
132. *Powderham Castle*
133. Topsham (old Dutch seaport)
134. Exeter Cathedral *Cathedral Library* St. Mary Arches Church *St. Nicholas Priory* (C11–15) Guildhall (C14–16) *Law Library* (C14 hall) *Tuckers' Hall* (C15–17) *Mediaeval Underground Passages* Wynard's Hospital (restored C15 almshouses) Custom House (1689) Devon & Exeter Hospital (1741) County Court (1773) Southernhay (Georgian houses, 1800–06) Barnfield Crescent (c. 1800) Colleton Crescent (c. 1800) Rougemont House (1820) & Grounds *Royal Albert Memorial Museum*
135. Newton St. Cyres Church & Village
136. Cadbury Castle (hillfort)
137. Killerton Park (woods, heronry, hillfort) (NT) *Killerton, Gardens* (NT)
138. Cullompton Church
139. Broad Clyst Church Burrough's Almshouses (rebuilt 1854)
140. *A-la-Ronde* (C18 copy of San Vitale, Ravenna)
141. *Hayes Barton* (Raleigh's birthplace)
142. East Budleigh Church
143. Ladram Bay (views), Otterton
144. *Bicton Gardens* (Le Notre)
145. *Cadhay* (Elizabethan manor house)
146. Ottery St. Mary Church
147. Hembury Fort (hillfort, view)
148. Sidmouth (Regency watering-place) Esplanade & Fortfield Terrace (c. 1805) Sid Meadows (river walk) (NT) *Woolcombe House* (mediaeval hall; museum)
149. Gittisham Church
150. Shoulsbarrow Castle (hillfort)
151. Cow Castle (hillfort)
152. Winsford (village)
153. Winsford Hill (moorland, views) (NT) Wam Barrows (NT) Caratacus Stone (long stone) (NT)
154. Tarr Steps (clapper bridge)
155. Span Head (1618 ft)
156. Landacre Bridge (mediaeval)
157. Molland Church
158. Swimbridge Church
159. Chittlehampton Church
160. Guildhall (1743), South Molton
161. King's Nympton Church
162. Morchard Bishop Church
163. Nymet Rowland Church
164. Coldridge Church
165. Chulmleigh Church
166. Burrington Church
167. Lundy Island (scenery, castle ruin, seabirds) (NT) *Bird Observatory* (BTO)
168. Dodington Hall

Map 8

The Edinburgh Geographical Institute

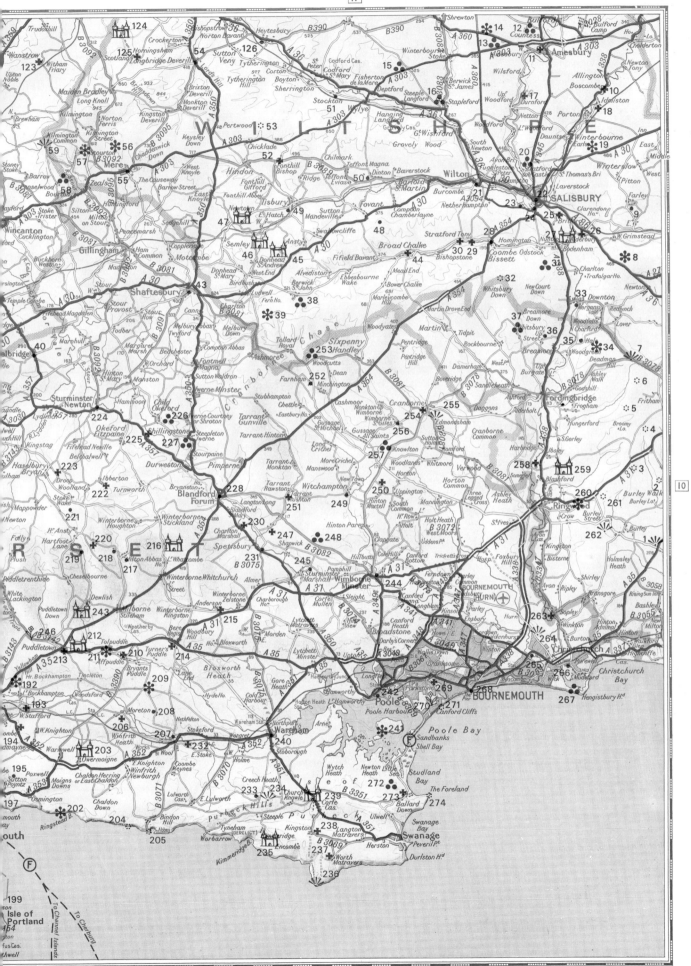

Map 9

Gazetteer to Maps 8·9

1. Wilverley Post (New Forest viewpoint)
2. Mark Ash Wood (beech), Bolderwood
3. Bushey Bratley (beech wood), Bolderwood
4. Ocknell Inclosure & Dewpond
5. Sloden Inclosure (yew)
6. Eyeworth Wood (beech)
7. Bramshaw Telegraph (New Forest viewpoint)
8. Pepperbox Hill (views, C17 folly) (NT) Grimstead Beeches (NT)
9. Farley Church Fox's Hospital (almshouses, 1682)
10. Boscombe Church
11. Amesbury Church
12. Woodhenge (Bronze Age ritual site)
13. Stonehenge (Bronze Age stone circle) The Avenue (Chalcolithic)
14. Stonehenge Down (Bronze Age barrows) (NT) The Cursus (neolithic ritual site) (NT)
15. Yarnbury Castle (hillfort)
16. Stapleford Castle (earthwork)
17. Durnford Church
18. Idmiston Church
19. Figsbury Ring (hillfort, views) (NT)
20. Old Sarum (earthwork, site of Norman cathedral town)
21. St. Mary's Church, Wilton *Wilton House*
22. Salisbury Cathedral Cathedral Close (notable houses include: *The Old Deanery* (C13) King's House (C14–15) *Old Bishop's Palace* (part C14) The Wardrobe (C15) College of Matrons (1682) *Mompesson House* (1701) (NT) Old Chorister's School (1717) *68, The Close* (c. 1720)) Poultry Cross (C14) John Halle's Hall (1470), Gaumont Cinema *Church House* (C15), Crane Street Joiners' Hall (facade c. 1550) (NT) St. Thomas's Church Trinity Hospital (almshouses, 1702) Frowd's Almshouses (1750) Council House (1794) *Salisbury & South Wiltshire Museum*
23. Harnham Mill (mediaeval)
24. Harnham Bridge (1244) St. Nicholas Hospital (almshouse, 1227)
25. Britford Church
26. Ivy Church Priory remains (C12), Alderbury
27. *Longford Castle*
28. Coombe Bissett Bridge (C18) Packhorse Bridge
29. Stratford Tony Church
30. Bishopstone Church
31. Clearbury Ring (Roman camp, views)
32. Great Yews (ancient plantation), Odstock
33. Downton Church The Moot (ancient mound)
34. Hale Purlieu (heath) (NT) Millersford Plantation (NT)
35. *Hale Park, House & Garden* Hale Church
36. *Breamore House* Breamore Church (Saxon)
37. Whitsbury Camp (hillfort, view)
38. Winklebury Camp (hillfort, view)
39. Win Green Hill (views) (NT)
40. Market Cross (C14), Stalbridge
41. *Purse Caundle Manor, House & Garden*

42. Sherborne Abbey Church Sherborne School (part C15) Hospital of St. John (C15 almshouse) *Sherborne Castle* (C16 mansion) Conduit (C14)
43. St. Peter's Church, Shaftesbury Gold Hill (street) *Shaftesbury Abbey Ruins & Museum*
44. Broad Chalke Church
45. Old Wardour Castle (C14–16 remains)
46. *Wardour Castle*
47. *Pyt House*, Tisbury
48. Regimental Badges (turf-cut), Fovant
49. Tisbury Church Place Tithe Barn (C15)
50. *Philipps House* (1816), *Dinton Park* (NT) Hyde's House (c. 1725 & Tudor) *Little Clarendon* (C15 house) (NT) Lawes Cottage (C17)
51. Stockton Church & Village Topp Almshouses (C17)
52. Fonthill Abbey Entrance Gates (C17 or C18)
53. Great Ridge Wood, Hindon
54. Longbridge Deverill Church & Village Thynne Almshouses (1665)
55. St. Michael's Church, Mere Chantry House (C15) Ship Inn (C17)
56. White Sheet Castle (hillfort) (NT)
57. Stourton (village) (NT) Bristol High Cross (C14) *Stourhead, House & Grounds* (NT)
58. Pen Pits (Romano-British quern-quarries), Penselwood
59. Alfred's Tower (view), Kingsettle Hill
60. Batcombe Church
61. St. Mary's Church, Bruton Hugh Sexey's Hospital (almshouse, 1638) Old School (C16), King's School Bruton Bow (C15 Packhorse bridge)
62. Bruton Dovecote (C16) (NT)
63. Wyke Champflower Church
64. Evercreech Church
65. Ditcheat Church
66. Wrax Hill (view)
67. West Pennard Church
68. West Pennard Court Barn (C15) (NT)
69. Glastonbury Tor (view) (NT) St. Michael's Tower (C14, restored)
70. *Glastonbury Abbey* (C12–14) Abbot's Barn (C13) Abbot's Tribunal (C15–16) George Inn (C15 pilgrims' hostelry) Glastonbury Thorn St. John's Church
71. Windmill Hill (Hood Column, views), Polden Hills
72. Ivythorne & Walton Hills (views) (NT)
73. North Petherton Church
74. Weston Zoyland Church
75. St. Mary's Church, Bridgwater Castle Street (C18) Market Hall (1834) *Admiral Blake Museum*
76. *Coleridge Cottage* (museum) (NT), Nether Stowey
77. Stogursey Church Stogursey Castle (C13 ruin)
78. Pawlett Church
79. Longstone Hill (views) (NT) Quantock Hills Willoughby Cleeve (moor & woodland) (NT)
81. Shervage Wood (views) (NT), Quantock Hills

Dowsborough Camp (hillfort)
82. Trendle Ring (hillfort), Bicknoller
83. Heddon Oak
84. Crowcombe Church Churchyard & Village Crosses (mediaeval) Church House (mediaeval)
85. St. Pancras' Church, West Bagborough
86. Bishop's Lydeard Church Churchyard Cross (C14)
87. *Cothelstone Manor* (C16)
88. Kingston Church
89. St. Mary Magdalene's Church, Taunton *Taunton Castle* (Norman & later; County Museum) Priory Barn (mediaeval) Gray's Almshouses (1635) Ramshorn Packhorse Bridge
90. Trull Church
91. Blackdown Hills (view to Welsh mountains) Wellington Monument (obelisk, 1818) (NT)
92. Churchstanton Church
93. Castle Neroche (hillfort)
94. Every's Almshouses (C16), Broadway
95. *Barrington Court* (NT)
96. *East Lambrook Manor, House & Garden*
97. Martock Church *Treasurer's House* (mediaeval) (NT)
98. Tintinhull Church & Village *Tintinhull House & Gardens* (NT)
99. Kingsbury Episcopi Church
100. Isle Abbots Church
101. Swell Church
102. Muchelney Abbey (C12–16 remains) Priest's House (C14) (NT)
103. Curry Rivel Church
104. North Curry Church
105. Red Hill (views) (NT), Sedgemoor
106. Huish Episcopi Church
107. Long Sutton Church
108. *Lytes Cary, Manor House & Garden* (NT)
109. Queen Camel Church Packhorse Bridge
110. Cadbury Castle (hillfort) King Arthur's Palace (earthwork)
111. North Cadbury Church
112. Somerton Church Market Cross (1673)
113. Heronry, Somerton Hill
114. Burrow Mump (ruined chapel, views) (NT)
115. Turn Hill (view over Sedgemoor battlefield) (NT)
116. High Ham Church High Ham Mill (thatched windmill 1820) (NT)
117. Dundon Beacon (views)
118. Abbot's Fish House (c. 1325), Meare *Manor Farm* (C14)
119. Sutton Mallet Church
120. Pilton Church Tithe Barn (C14)
121. Shepton Mallet Church (nave roof) Market Cross (c. 1500) The Shambles (mediaeval market) *Shepton Mallet Museum*
122. Manor Farm Tithe Barn (C15) Doulting
123. Witham Friary Church
124. *Longleat House & Park*
125. Nonconformist Chapel (1566), Horningsham Twelve Apostles (lime trees)
126. Heytesbury Church St. John's Hospital (C15 almshouses, rebuilt 1770)

127. *The Manor House*, Sandford Orcas
128. Trent Church
129. Bradford Abbas Church
130. St. John Baptist's Church, Yeovil
    Wyndham Museum
131. East Coker (village)
    Helyar Almshouses (1640)
132. Abbey Barn (C15), Preston Plucknett
133. Brympton D'Evercy Church &
    Manor House (C15–18)
134. Montacute (village)
    Priory Gatehouse (C15)
    Montacute House & Garden (NT)
135. Stoke-sub-Hamdon Church
    Priory Farm (C15 Chantry House)
    Ham Hill (stone quarries, fortified
    settlement, view)
136. Norton-sub-Hamdon Church &
    Village
137. Haselbury Bridge (C15)
138. Petherton Bridge (C15)
139. Crewkerne Church
140. Hinton St. George Church & Village
    Market Cross (C14)
141. Windwhistle (ridge, beech avenue)
142. *Whitelackington House* (C16)
143. Ilminster Church
    Grammar School (1586)
144. Dunster's Almshouses (1624)
    Donyatt
145. Court House (C16), Chard
    Grammar School (C16 & C17)
146. Ottery St. Mary Church
147. Hembury Fort (hillfort, view)
148. Sidmouth (Regency watering-place)
    Esplanade & Fortfield Terrace
    (c. 1805)
    Sid Meadows (river walk) (NT)
    Woolcombe House (mediaeval hall;
    museum)
149. Gittisham Church
150. Dumpdon Hill (view)
151. Blackbury Castle (hillfort)
152. Branscombe Church
153. Beer Head (views)
154. *Shute Barton* (C13–16 manor house)
    (NT)
155. Hawksdown Hill (hillfort, views)
156. *Bindon House* (C15–17), Axmouth
157. Dowlands Cliffs & Landslip
158. St. Michael's Church, Lyme Regis
    The Cobb (old quay, rebuilt 1825)
159. *Forde Abbey & Gardens*
160. Lamberts Castle Hill (hillfort, views)
    (NT)
161. Stonebarrow Hill (NT) to Golden
    Cap (cliffland, views) (NT)
162. Whitchurch Canonicorum Church
163. *Bettiscombe Manor* (C16–18)
164. Lewesdon Hill (views) (NT),
    Stoke Abbot
165. Pilsdon Pen (earthwork, views)
166. Loughwood Meeting House (C17)
    (NT)
167. *Parnham House*
168. Dodington Hall
169. Loders Church
170. Eggardon Camp (hillfort)
171. *Mapperton*, gardens
172. Rampisham Village &
    Preaching Cross
173. Yetminster Church
174. Melbury Bubb Church
175. Cattistock Church
176. Abbotsbury Abbey (C12–15 remains)
    Great Barn (c. 1400) & Dovecote
    St. Catherine's Chapel (C14)
    St. Nicholas' Church
    Swannery
177. Kingston Russell Stone Circle
178. Hell Stone (cromlech), Portisham
179. The Nine Stones (stone circle),
    Winterborne Abbas
180. Hardy Monument (1846) (NT)

Black Down (views)
181. Winterborne Steepleton Church
182. Maiden Castle (large neolithic &
    Iron Age earthwork)
183. Sydling St. Nicholas Church &
    Village
184. Castle Hill (earthwork, views),
    East Chelborough
185. Burton Cliff (NT)
186. Cerne Giant (Romano-British
    hill-figure) (NT)
187. Cerne Abbas Church
    Church Street (late mediaeval
    houses)
    Abbey Gatehouse (C15)
188. Piddletrenthide Church
189. *Minterne*, gardens
190. Charminster Church
    Wolfeton Gate House (Tudor)
191. Poundbury Camp (hillfort),
    Dorchester
    Maumbury Rings
    (Roman amphitheatre)
    Napper's Mite (C17 almshouse;
    restaurant)
    Dorset County Museum
    Dorset Military Museum, The Keep
192. *Hardy's Cottage* (NT),
    Higher Bockhampton
193. West Stafford Church
194. Whitcombe Church
195. White Horse (turf-cut figure of
    George III?), Osmington
196. Chalbury Camp (hillfort), Preston
197. Jordan Hill Roman Temple
198. Weymouth (Georgian
    watering-place)
    3, Trinity Street (Tudor)
    Sandsfoot Castle (remains
    Henry VIII blockhouse)
199. *Portland Castle* (C16–18)
200. St. George's Church, Portland
201. Portland Bill Bird Observatory
    (BTO)
202. Southdown Farm (cliffland) (NT),
    Ringstead Bay
203. *Moignes Court* (part mediaeval)
204. Durdle Door (natural rock arch)
205. Lulworth Cove
206. Moreton Church
207. Wool Bridge (transportation tablet)
208. *Royal Armoured Corps Tank
    Museum*, Bovington
209. Clouds Hill (T. E. Lawrence's
    cottage) (NT)
210. Affpuddle Church
211. Martyrs' Tree (NT), Tolpuddle
212. *Athelhampton, House & Garden*
213. Puddletown Church
214. Bere Regis Church
215. Winterborne Tomson Church
216. *Winterborne Clenston Manor* (Tudor)
217. Milton Abbas (C18 model village)
    Tregonwell Almshouses
    Manor House (c. 1773)
218. Milton Abbey Church
    Milton Abbey (Georgian Gothic
    house)
219. Bingham's Melcombe Church &
    Manor House (Tudor)
220. Hilton Church
221. Bulbarrow Hill (views)
    Rawlsbury Camp (hillfort)
222. Ibberton Church
223. Hazelbury Bryan Church
224. Mediaeval Bridge, Sturminster
    Newton
225. Shillingstone Church
226. Hambledon Hill Camp (hillfort)
227. Hod Hill Camp (hillfort)
228. Blandford Forum (Georgian town)
    St. Peter & St. Paul's Church
    Town Hall (1734)
    Legion House (Georgian)

Ryves Almshouses (1682)
The Old House (C17)
Mediaeval Bridge
229. High Stoy Hill (view)
230. Charlton Marshall Church
231. Crawford Bridge (mediaeval)
    Spettisbury Rings (hillfort)
232. Bindon Abbey (C12 remains)
233. *Creech Grange*
    Grange Arch (C18 folly) (NT)
234. Creech Barrow (view)
235. *Smedmore, House & Garden*
236. St. Aldhelm's Head (Norman chapel,
    views)
237. Worth Matravers Church
238. St. James's Church, Kingston
239. Corfe Castle (C11–16 remains)
240. Lady St. Mary's Church, Wareham
    St. Martin's Church (Saxon)
    Town Ramparts (earthworks)
    Streche's Almshouses (rebuilt 1741)
    Frome Bridge (mediaeval)
    Trent Bridge (C20)
241. *Brownsea Island* (heath, woodland
    & lakes; nature reserve) (NT)
242. Poole Quay (old warehouses) &
    Harbour
    Scaplen's Court (mediaeval
    guildhall)
    Town Cellars (C15 storehouse)
    Guildhall (1761)
    Poole Museum
243. *Dewlish House*
244. Wimborne Minster Church
    Chained Library
    Priest's House
245. Mediaeval Bridge,
    Sturminster Marshall
246. *Waterston Manor Gardens*
247. Tarrant Crawford Church
248. Badbury Rings (hillfort)
249. Witchampton (village)
250. Chalbury Church
251. Tarrant Rushton Church
252. *Pitt-Rivers Museum* (Evolution of
    Culture), Farnham
253. British Village, Woodcutts
254. St. Mary's Church, Cranborne
255. Castle Hill (view), Cranborne
256. Wimborne St. Giles Church
    Ashley's Almshouses (C17)
    St. Giles House & Grounds
257. Knowlton (ruined Norman church in
    earthwork)
258. Ellingham Church
259. *Moyles Court*
260. Hightown Common (view) (NT),
    Ringwood
261. Ridley Wood (beech), New Forest
262. Castle Hill (views), Burley
263. Sopley Church
264. St. Catherine's Hill (hillfort, view)
265. Iford Bridge (C14)
266. Christchurch Priory Church
    Christchurch Castle (Norman remains)
    Old Bridges
    Red House (Georgian; museum)
267. Double Dykes (Iron Age),
    Hengistbury Head
268. St. Stephen's Church, Bournemouth
    Russell-Cotes Art Gallery & Museum
269. Branksome Church
270. *Compton Acres, Gardens*, Parkstone
271. Branksome Dene Chine
    (ravine, park)
272. Agglestone & Puckstone
    (ancient sandstone blocks)
273. Studland Church
274. Old Harry Rocks, Studland
275. Bridport (Georgian houses &
    Town Hall)
    Gundry's Ropemaking Works
    (Georgian)
    PYMORE MILL (C 18 watermill)

Map 10

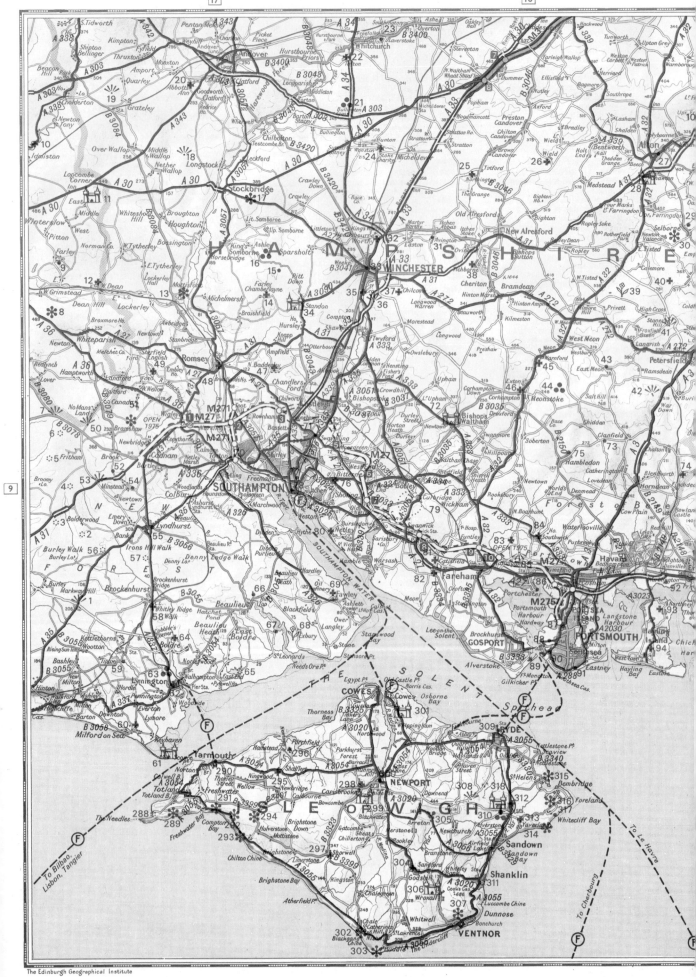

Map 11

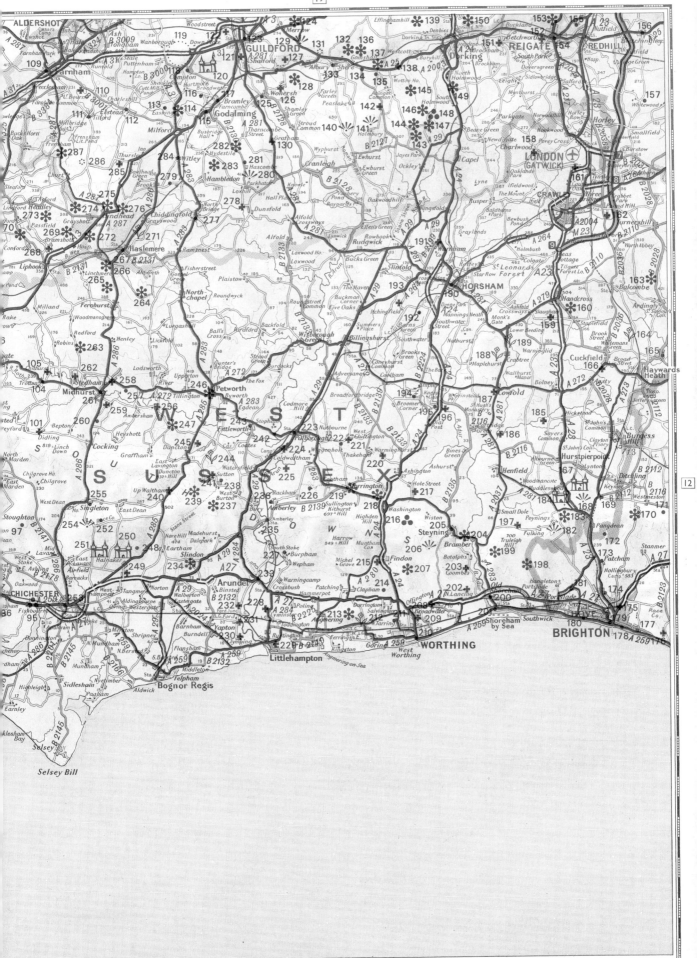

1 2 3 4 5 Miles

© — John Bartholomew & Son Ltd.

Gazetteer to Maps 10·11

1. Wilverley Post
   (New Forest viewpoint)
2. Mark Ash Wood (beech),
   Bolderwood
3. Bushey Bratley (beech wood),
   Bolderwood
4. Ocknell Inclosure & Dewpond
5. Sloden Inclosure (yew)
6. Eyeworth Wood (beech)
7. Bramshaw Telegraph
   (New Forest viewpoint)
8. Pepperbox Hill (views, C17 folly) (NT)
   Grimstead Beeches (NT)
9. Farley Church
   Fox's Hospital (almshouses, 1682)
10. Boscombe Church
11. *Roche Old Court* (c. 1650 & earlier)
12. Evelyn Chapel (C17 monuments),
    West Dean
13. *Mottisfont Abbey & Grounds* (NT)
14. Farley Chamberlayne Church
15. Farley Monument (C18), Pitt Down
16. Roman Camp, Ashley
17. Woolbury Ring (hillfort)
    Stockbridge Down (NT)
18. Danebury Hill (hillfort, view)
19. Quarley Hill (hillfort, views)
20. Abbotts Ann Church
    (maidens' garlands)
21. Tidbury Ring (hillfort, view)
22. Tufton Church
23. Old Paper Mill (paper for bank
    notes since 1724), Laverstoke
24. Stoke Charity Church
25. Northington Church
26. Wield Church
27. *Curtis Museum*, Alton
28. *Jane Austen's Home*, Chawton
29. Selborne Church
    Oates & Gilbert White Museum
30. Selborne Hill (Gilbert White
    associations) (NT)
31. Avington Church
    Avington Park (house)
32. Headbourne Worthy Church
    (Saxon rood)
33. Winchester Cathedral
    St. John's Church
    Great Hall (C11–13), Castle Hill
    Wolvesey Castle (C12 remains)
    King's Gate (C13)
    West Gate (C13–14; *museum*)
    The Pilgrims' Hall (C14),
    The Deanery
    Winchester College (C14)
    City Mill (1744) (NT) &
    Bridge (C18)
    City Museum
34. Merdon Castle (Norman ruin),
    Hursley
35. Church & Hospital of St. Cross
    (C12–15 almshouse)
36. St. Catherine's Hill (hillfort,
    miz maze, view), Winchester
37. Chilcomb Church
38. Tichborne Church
39. *Coles, Gardens*, Privett
40. Priors Dean Church, Hawkley
41. Stoner Hill (views)
42. Butser Hill (hillfort, view)
43. East Meon Church
    Court House (C14–15)
44. Old Winchester Hill (hillfort, view)
45. Warnford Church
46. Corhampton Church (Saxon)
47. North Baddesley Church
48. Romsey Abbey Church
49. East Wellow Church
50. Pipers Wait (viewpoint), New Forest
51. Bramshaw, Cadnam, Furzley, Penn
    & Plaitford Commons (NT)
52. Rufus Stone, New Forest
53. Stoney Cross (viewpoint), New
    Forest
54. Minstead Church & Village

55. Queen's House (early C18),
    Lyndhurst
    Verderers' Hall (Court of
    Swainmote)
56. Knightwood Inclosure (oaks),
    New Forest
57. Whitley Wood (oaks), New Forest
58. St. Nicholas Church, Brockenhurst
59. Peterson's Tower (C18 concrete),
    Sway
60. Milford-on-Sea Church
61. Hurst Castle (Henry VIII
    blockhouse)
62. St. Thomas's Church, Lymington
63. Buckland Rings (hillfort)
64. St. John's Church, Boldre
65. Sowley Pond
66. Beaulieu Church & Abbey
    (C13 remains)
    Palace House & Gardens
    Montagu Motor Museum
67. Bucklers Hard (C18 shipyard)
    Maritime Museum
68. *Exbury Gardens*
69. Fawley Church
70. Redbridge (C17 bridge)
71. St. Alban's Church, Swaythling
    Mediaeval Bridge
72. Bishop's Waltham Palace (C12–14
    remains)
73. Broadhalfpenny Down, Hambledon
    Bat & Ball Inn & Cricket Club
    Monument
74. Idsworth Church
75. Hambledon Church
    Manor Farm House (part C13)
76. Bitterne Church
77. *Southampton Art Gallery*
78. Bargate (C14; *Guildhall Museum*),
    Southampton
    West Gate (C14) & Town Walls
    God's House Tower (C15 fort;
    museum)
    Tudor House Museum
    Docks & Ocean Terminal
79. Hamble River (scenery)
    Riverside Land (NT) at Curbridge
80. Netley Abbey (C13 remains)
81. Titchfield Abbey (C13 & C16
    remains)
82. St. Peter's Church, Titchfield
83. Boarhunt Church (Saxon)
84. Southwick Church
85. Nelson Monument (view), Portsdown
86. Portchester Castle (Roman, Norman
    & mediaeval)
    St. Mary's Church (Norman)
87. *Dickens' Birthplace*, 393
    Commercial Road, Portsmouth
88. Naval Dockyards (C18 storehouses),
    Portsmouth
    H.M.S. Victory
    Nelson Museum
89. Haslar Hospital (C18), Alverstoke
90. St. Thomas's Cathedral, Portsmouth
    Garrison Church (C13 hospital
    chapel)
    King James's Gate (1687)
    Landport Gate (1698)
91. *Cumberland House Museum*,
    Southsea
92. Warblington Church & Castle
    (C15 ruin)
93. North Hayling Church
94. South Hayling Church
95. *The Roman Palace*, Fishbourne
96. Bosham Church & Village
    Quay Meadow (Canute & Harold
    associations) (NT)
97. Bow Hill (earthworks), Stoughton
    Kingley Vale (ancient yews)
98. Stoughton Church
99. Upmarden Church
100. North Marden Church
101. Didling Church

102. *Uppark* (NT)
103. South Harting Church
104. Trotton Church
     Mediaeval Bridge
105. Chithurst Church
106. Darford Heath (NT)
107. Froyle Church
108. Crondall Church
109. St. Andrew's Church, Farnham
     Farnham Castle (Norman keep &
     Bishop's residence)
     The Grange (c. 1710), Odiham Road
     Castle Street (Georgian houses)
     Vernon House (C16, restored),
     West Street
     Willmer House (1718; museum)
     The Ranger's House
110. Waverley Abbey (C13 remains)
111. Tilford (village, oak tree &
     old bridges)
112. Elstead Bridge (C16), Water-Mill
     (C17–18) & *The Mill House*
113. Peper Harow Church & Farm
     (C17 & C18 buildings)
114. Eashing Bridges (C13) (NT)
115. St. Peter & St. Paul's Church,
     Godalming
     Church House (C15–17)
     Old Town Hall (1814; museum)
116. *Charterhouse School Museum*
117. Wyatt's Almshouses (1622),
     Farncombe
118. Compton Church
     G. F. Watts Gallery &
     Mortuary Chapel (1897)
119. Hogs Back (six mile ridge, views)
120. *Loseley House*
121. St. Catherine's Chapel (C14 ruin,
     view), Guildford
122. Guildford Cathedral
123. Holy Trinity Church, Guildford
     St. Mary's Church
     Guildhall (1683), High Street
     Grammar School (C16)
     Guildford Castle (Norman keep)
     Trinity Hospital (almshouses, 1619)
     Museum & Muniment Room,
     Castle Arch
124. *Clandon Park, House & Garden* (NT)
125. Wonersh Church & Village
     The Sharp Collection (bygones),
     Green Place
126. Blackheath Church
127. St. Martha's Chapel, Chilworth
128. Blackheath (heathland) (NT)
129. Newlands Corner (view)
130. Grafham Church
131. The Silent Pool, Albury
132. Netley Park (woodlands) (NT)
133. Shere Church & Village
134. Hammer Clock, Abinger Hammer
135. *Crossways Farm* (C17)
136. Hackhurst Down (views) (NT)
     Gomshall
137. Abinger Roughs (wooded ridge) (NT)
138. Wotton Church
139. Ranmore Common (views) (NT),
     Dorking
140. Coneyhurst Hill (views), Ewhurst
141. Holmbury Hill (hillfort, views)
142. Holmbury St. Mary Church
143. Leith Hill Place Woods
     (flowering shrubs) (NT)
144. Leith Hill Summit (tower, 1029 ft)
     (NT)
145. Severell's Copse (lakeside) (NT),
     Friday Street
146. Duke's Warren (heath & woodland)
     (NT), Coldharbour
147. Mosses Wood (bluebells) (NT)
     Leith Hill
148. Anstiebury Camp (hillfort)
149. Holmwood Common (NT), Dorking
150. Box Hill (down & woodland, flora
     & fauna, views) (NT)

151. Betchworth Church
152. Windmill Church (1765), Reigate Heath
153. Reigate Hill & Colley Hill (views) (NT)
154. St. Mary's Church, Reigate
    Old Town Hall (1728)
    Reigate Priory (C18; school)
155. Wray Common Windmill (1824), Reigate
156. Bletchingley Church & Village
157. Outwood Post Mill (1665)
158. Charlwood Church
159. Slaugham Church
160. *Nymans Gardens & woodland* (NT)
161. Lowfield Heath Church
162. Worth Church (Saxon)
163. *Wakehurst Place* (gardens & woodlands administered by Royal Botanic Gardens, Kew) (NT)
164. *Borde Hill Gardens*
165. Lindfield House (C18) & Village
    Old Place (C16)
166. Cuckfield Church
167. *Danny, House & Garden*
168. Wolstonbury Hill (hillfort, view)
169. Clayton Church & Windmills
170. Ditchling Beacon (hillfort, view) (NT)
171. V-Plantation (Queen Victoria's jubilee, 1887), Streat Hill
172. The Chattri (Indian War Memorial)
173. Patcham Tithe Barn & Dovecote (C17)
174. St. Peter's Church, Preston
    Preston Manor (1739; museum)
175. St. Martin's Church, Lewes Road, Brighton
176—180 Refer to Gazetteer 12/13
181. Windmill (1831), West Blatchington
182. Devil's Dyke (earthwork, views)
183. Newtimber Hill (views) (NT), Poynings
    Beggars Lane (beeches) (NT)
184. *Newtimber Place*
185. Twineham Church
186. Shermanbury Church
187. Cowfold Church
188. *South Lodge, Gardens*, Crabtree
189. *Leonardslee, Gardens*, Lower Beeding
190. St. Mary's Church, Horsham
    The Causeway (old houses)
    Causeway House (Tudor; museum)
191. Warnham Church
192. *Christ's Hospital* (painting by Verrio)
193. Itchingfield Church
194. Shipley Church
195. Kneppmill Pond & Old Castle (Norman ruin)
196. West Grinstead Church
197. Edburton Church
198. Southwick Hill (NT)
199. Bushey Bottom & The Warren (NT), Shoreham Gap (downs)
200. St. Nicholas' Church, Old Shoreham
    Old Timber Bridge (rebuilt 1916)
201. St. Mary De Haura's Church, New Shoreham
    Marlipins (mediaeval house; museum)
202. Lancing College Chapel (begun 1868)
203. Coombes Church
204. Bramber Castle (Norman ruin, view) (NT) & Village
    St. Mary's (C15 house)
205. Steyning Church & Town
    Old Grammar School (mediaeval brotherhood hall)
    Chantry Green House
206. Steyning Round Hill (views)
207. Cissbury Ring (hillfort, views) (NT)
208. Sompting Church
209. St. Mary's Church, Broadwater
210. *Worthing Museum*

211. West Tarring Church
    Parish Hall (mediaeval)
    Parsonage Row (C15 cottages)
    Fig Garden (mainly 1745)
212. *Highdown, Gardens*, Goring-by-Sea
213. Highdown Hill (hillfort) NT), Ferring
214. Salvington Post Mill
215. Findon Church
216. Chanctonbury Ring (hillfort, views)
217. Norman Chapel, Buncton
218. Washington Common (views) (NT)
219. Sullington Warren (views) (NT)
220. Warminghurst Church
221. West Chiltington Church
222. West Chiltington Windmill
223. Pulborough Church
    Swan Bridge (mediaeval), St. Clement's
224. Hardham Church
225. Greatham Church
226. *Parham, House & Gardens*
    St. Peter's Church
227. Burpham Church
    Saxon Defensive Earthwork
228. Lyminster Church
229. St. Mary's Church, Littlehampton
230. Climping Church
231. Ford Church
232. Tortington Church
233. *Arundel Castle* & Park
    St. Nicholas' Church & Fitzalan Chapel (RC)
    St. Philip's Church (RC)
234. Slindon Park (NT)
235. Houghton Bridge (1875; view)
236. Amberley Church & Village
    Amberley Castle (C14 remains)
237. Bignor Hill (views) (NT)
238. Bignor Church
    Old Village Shop (C15)
    Roman Villa
239. Coldharbour Hill (views) (NT)
    Glatting Beacon (NT)
240. Upwaltham Church
241. Sutton Church & Rectory (mediaeval)
242. Stopham Bridge (C14)
243. Fittleworth (village)
244. *Sutton End, Gardens*
245. Burton Church
246. *Petworth House* & Park (NT)
    Somerset Lodge
    Lombard Street & Saddler's Row (old houses)
247. Lavington Common (NT)
248. Halnaker Hill (old windmill, view)
249. Boxgrove Priory Church
250. Halnaker House (Tudor ruin)
251. *Goodwood House*
252. Goodwood Park & Race Course
253. Chichester Cathedral
    Vicar's Close (C14 buildings)
    St. John's Church
    City Walls (mediaeval)
    Market Cross (c. 1500)
    Greyfriars Chapel (C13), Priory Park
    St. Mary's Hospital (C13 almshouse)
    County Library (C17)
    St. Martin's Square & The Pallants (Georgian houses)
    Dodo House (1712), North Pallant
254. St. Roche Hill (views) & The Trundle (hillfort)
255. Singleton Church
    Weald & Downland Museum
256. Selham Church
257. Cowdray Park
258. Easebourne Church
259. West Lavington Church
260. *Richard Cobden Collection*, Dunford House
261. Market Hall (1552), Midhurst

Spread Eagle Hotel (C15 & C17)
    Rother Bridge & North Mill
    Cowdray House (C16 ruin)
262. Woolbeding Church
263. Woolbeding Common (NT)
264. Black Down Hill (918 ft; woods, views) (NT)
265. Marley Heights (viewpoint) (NT)
266. Shottermill Hammer Ponds (NT)
    Marley Common & Wood (NT)
267. *Haslemere Educational Museum*
268. Bramshott Church
269. Waggoners' Wells (hammer ponds, woods) (NT)
270. Passfield Common (NT)
    Conford Moor (NT)
271. *Grayswood Hill, Gardens*
272. Nutcombe Valley (NT), Hindhead
273. Ludshott Common (NT)
274. Whitmoor & Golden Valleys (NT)
275. Devil's Punchbowl (canyon) (NT)
276. Gibbet Hill (views) & Hindhead Common (NT)
277. Chiddingfold (village)
    Crown Inn (C14)
278. Dunsfold Church
279. Sandhills (hamlet) & Common (NT)
280. Hascombe Hill (hillfort, view)
281. Hascombe Church
    Hascombe Court, Gardens
282. Winkworth Arboretum (NT)
283. Hydon Heath & Hydon's Ball (hill, view) (NT)
284. Witley Church & Village
285. Thursley Church
286. The Devil's Jumps (heather hills) (part NT), Churt
287. Frensham Ponds & Common (NT)
288. Alum Bay (sands near The Needles)
289. Tennyson Down (cliffland) (NT)
290. St. James's Church, Yarmouth
    Yarmouth Castle Henry VIII coastal
291. Afton Down (views) (NT)
292. Compton Bay (beaches) & Compton Down (views) (NT)
293. Brook Bay & Hanover Point (coastland & beaches) (NT)
294. Brook Down (views) (NT)
    Five Barrows (tumuli, viewpoint)
295. Shalfleet Church
296. Old Town Hall (C18) (NT), Newtown
    Noah's Ark (old inn c. 1700) (NT)
    Town Copse (estuary woodland) (NT)
297. Shorwell Church
298. Carisbrooke Church
299. *Carisbrooke Castle* (C12–16)
300. Guildhall (Nash, 1814), Newport
    Grammar School (C17)
301. *Osborne House*
302. St. Catherine's Oratory (C14) (NT)
    St. Catherine's Down (views) (NT)
303. St. Catherine's Point (geology & migrant birds) (NT)
304. Godshill Church
305. Arreton Church & *Manor*
306. Appuldurcombe House (ruin, 1710)
307. St. Boniface Down (views) (NT), Ventnor
308. Ashey Down (viewpoint)
309. Ryde Pier (view of Spithead)
    St. Mary's Church (RC)
310. *Roman Villa* (remains), Morton
311. Shanklin Chine (ravine)
312. Brading Church
313. Yaverland Church
314. Culver Cliff (old fort, view) (NT)
315. St. Helen's Common & The Duver (overlooking harbour) (NT)
316. *Bembridge Windmill* (c. 1700) (NT)
317. *Ruskin Gallery*, Bembridge School
318. *Nunwell House*

Map 12

The Edinburgh Geographical Institute

Map 13

1   2   3   4   5 Miles

Gazetteer to Maps 12·13

1. Broadstairs Jetty (1809)
   Bleak House (Dickens associations)
2. Ramsgate Harbour (completed 1776)
   St. George's Church
   St. Lawrence's Church
   St. Augustine's Abbey (Pugin)
   Wellington Crescent (Regency)
3. Deal (C18 houses)
   St. Leonard's Church
   St. George's Church
   Deal Castle (Henry VIII coastal fort)
   Town Hall (*Deal Museum*)
4. Walmer Castle (Henry VIII coastal fort) & *Gardens*
5. Margate Harbour (pier by Rennie, 1815)
   The Grotto (discovered 1837)
6. *Salmestone Grange* (part mediaeval)
7. Sandwich Bay (BTO Bird Observatory & plants)
8. St. Augustine Monument, Ebbsfleet
9. Sandwich (mediaeval port)
   St. Clement's Church
   St. Peter's Church
   Fisher Gate (C14–16)
   Barbican (Tudor) & Tollbridge
   Guildhall (C16; *museum*)
   Manwood Court (C16)
   Strand Street (C16 houses)
   Town Walls (promenade)
10. St. Bartholomew's Hospital (C13 almshouses), Sandwich
11. Northbourne Church
12. Eastry Church
13. *Richborough Castle* (Roman remains)
    Roman Amphitheatre
14. Minster-in-Thanet Church
    Minster Abbey (C11 remains)
15. *Powell-Cotton Museum* (zoological), Quex Park
16. Ash-by-Sandwich Church
17. St. Nicholas-at-Wade Church
18. Chillenden Post Mill
19. Barfreston Church
20. Goodnestone Church
21. Wingham Church & Village
22. Roman Fort, Reculver
    Reculver Towers (Norman church remains)
23. Wickhambreaux (village)
24. Old Smock Mill, Barham Downs
25. Broome Park (C17; hotel)
26. Denton (village)
27 to 65 Refer to Gazetteer 20/21
66. St. Margaret's-at-Cliffe Church
67. Northfall Meadows (views), Dover
68. Dover Castle (C12) & Grounds
    St. Mary-in-Castro Church
    Roman Lighthouse
69. *St. Martin's Priory* (C12 remains), Dover College
    Maison Dieu Hall (C14)
    Maison Dieu House (1665; public library)
    Admiralty Pier (¾ mile long; views)
70. Shakespeare Cliff (views), Dover
71. St. Radigund's Abbey (C12 Remains)
72. Capel-le-Ferne Church
73. *Acrise Place, House & Gardens*
74. Elham Church
75. Saltwood Castle (C12–14 remains)
76. St. Leonard's Church, Hythe
    St. Leonard's Church Undercroft (mediaeval human bones)
    Town Hall (1794)
    Royal Military Canal (1804–06)
    Romney, Hythe & Dymchurch Railway (one third normal scale)
    Oaklands Museum (Cinque Ports charters)
77. *Sandling Park, Gardens*
78. Monks Horton Church
79. Lympne Church & *Castle*
    Stutfall Castle (Roman fort remains)

80. Dymchurch Church
    Roman Sea Wall (4 miles long)
    New Hall (old Court House, 1580)
81. Aldington Knoll (viewof Romney Marsh)
82. Aldington Church
83. *Mersham-le-Hatch* (Robert Adam house)
84. Brook Church
    Agricultural Museum, Wye College
85. Mersham Church
86. Newchurch Church
87. St. Mary-in-the-Marsh Church
88. New Romney Church
89. Dungeness Point (BTO Bird Observatory & *RSPB Bird Sanctuary*; plants & insects)
90. Lydd Church
91. Old Romney Church
92. Ivychurch Church
93. St. Mary's Church, Ashford
    Fogge's House (C15)
    Old Grammar School (C18)
94. *Godington Park, House & Garden*
95. Shadoxhurst Church (funeral armour)
96. Warehorne Church
97. Brookland Church
98. Fairfield Church
99. Appledore Church & Village
    Royal Military Canal (Appledore to Warehorne NT)
100. Woodchurch Church & Windmill
101. Stone-in-Oxney Church
102. Playden Church
103. Rye (mediaeval port)
     St. Mary's Church & Clock (C16)
     Ypres Tower (C13; *Rye Museum*)
     Land Gate (C14)
     Augustinian Friary (C14 remains)
     Old Flushing Inn (mediaeval)
     Watchbell Street (C14 & C15 houses)
     Mermaid Street (C17 houses)
     Old Grammar School (1636)
     Town Hall (1744)
     Lamb House (Henry James's home) (NT)
104. Camber Castle (Henry VIII coastal fort)
105. Winchelsea (mediaeval port)
     St. Thomas's Church
     Court Hall (C14, restored; museum)
     Strand Gate (C13)
     Land Gate (C15)
106. New Gate (C13–15), Winchelsea
107. Cliffland (NT) near Fairlight
108. Hog Hill Windmill (C18), Icklesham
109. Icklesham Church
110. *Smallythe Place* (Ellen Terry Museum) (NT)
111. Tenterden Church & Town
     Unitarian Meeting House (C18)
112. High Halden Church
113. Horne's Place Chapel (C14)
114. Biddenden Church & Village
115. Smarden Church & Village
116. Hollingbourne Church
117. View of Leeds Castle (C13, restored)
118. Leeds Church
119. Thurnham Castle (ruin, view)
120. *Stoneacre* (C15 house) (NT), Otham
121. Headcorn (village)
122. All Saints Church, Maidstone
     College of Secular Canons (C14 remains)
     Archbishop's Manor House (C14–16)
     Archbishop's Stables (Carriage Museum)
     Chillington House (C16; museum)
     Sir John Bank's Almshouses (1700)
123. *Boughton Monchelsea Place*
     View of Weald
124. Linton Church
125. *Allington Castle* (C13)
126. Kit's Coty House (chamber of long barrow)

127. Aylesford Bridge (C14)
     St. Peter's Church
     Holy Trinity Almshouses (1610)
     The Friars (C13–14 remains)
128. East Farleigh Bridge (C15)
129. Hunton Church
130. Barming Church
     Barming Place (1768)
131. *Starkey Castle*
132. Teston Bridge (Tudor)
133. Yalding Church & Village
     C15 Bridge
134. C15 Bridge, Yalding
135. Nettlestead Church
     Nettlestead Place Gateway (C14) & Barn
136. *St. Mary's Abbey* (C11 & C15 remains), West Malling
137. St. Leonard's Tower (Norman)
138. *Mereworth Castle*
139. Coldrum Long Barrow (NT)
140. Trottiscliffe Church
141. Mereworth Church
142. West Peckham Church
143. Gover Hill (view over Weald) (NT)
144. Meopham Green (Windmill & Cricket Ground)
145. *Great Comp Garden*
146. *Old Soar Manor* (NT)
147. Wrotham Church
148. Wrotham Hill (view)
149. Ightham Church
150. Plaxtol Church
151. Somerhill Park
152. Tonbridge Castle (C12–14 remains)
     Portreeve's House (Tudor)
     Chequers Inn (Tudor)
     Rose & Crown Hotel (Georgian fronted Tudor)
153. *Ightham Mote* (mediaeval moated house)
154. Oldbury Hill (hillfort, views) (NT)
     Styants Wood (NT)
155. Wray Common Windmill (1824), Reigate
156. Bletchingley Church & Village
157. Outwood Post Mill (1665)
158. Godstone Green
159. Gatton (down & woodland) (NT)
160. Gatton Church
     Old Town Hall (temple, 1765)
161. Lowfield Heath Church
162. Worth Church (Saxon)
163. *Wakehurst Place* (gardens & woodlands administered by Royal Botanic Gardens, Kew) (NT)
164. *Borde Hill Gardens*
165. Lindfield House (C18) & Village
     Old Place (C16)
166. Cuckfield Church
167. *Danny, House & Garden*
168. Wolstonbury Hill (hillfort, view)
169. Clayton Church & Windmills
170. Ditchling Beacon (hillfort, view) (NT)
171. V-Plantation (Queen Victoria's jubilee, 1887), Street Hill
172. The Chattri (Indian War Memorial)
173. Patcham Tithe Barn & Dovecote (C17)
174. St. Peter's Church, Preston
     Preston Manor (1739; museum)
175. St. Martin's Church, Lewes Road, Brighton
176. Ovingdean Church
177. Kemp Town (Regency development)
     Lewes Crescent & Sussex Square (1823–28)
178. Royal Crescent (1798–1807), Brighton
179. Royal Pavilion (1787–1822), Brighton
     The Dome (old stables, 1803–1935; *Art Gallery & Museum*)
     Regency Square (1818–28)
     St. Bartholomew's Church

St. Mary's Church
Volk's Electric Railway
(first in England, 1883)
Booth Museum of British Birds
180. All Saints Church, Hove
St. Andrew's Church,
Waterloo Street
Adelaide Crescent (1830–60)
Brunswick Square & Terrace
(1825–28)
Hove Museum of Art
181. Rainham Church
182. Naval Dockyard (C18 & C19
buildings), Chatham
St. Bartholomew's Hospital Chapel
(Norman)
Hawkins' Almshouses (C19)
Royal Engineers Museum
Gordon Monument
183. Watts' Charity (C16 almshouse),
Rochester
Restoration House (1587)
Eastgate House (1591; museum)
Guildhall (1687)
Bull Hotel (Dickens associations)
184. Frindsbury Church
185. Rochester Cathedral
Rochester Castle (C12)
Minor Canons Row (C18)
186. *Temple Manor*, Strood
187. *Cobham Hall, House & Gardens*
188. *Luddesdown Court* (part mediaeval)
189. Cobham Church & Village
Cobham College (C14–16
almshouses)
190. *Owletts, House & Gardens* (NT)
191. *Nurstead Court* (C14 hall)
192. Ash-by-Wrotham Church
193. Water Mill (Georgian), Farningham
194. Eynsford Church
Eynsford Castle (C12 ruin)
Packhorse Bridge (C15)
Little Mote (Tudor House)
195. *Lullingstone Roman Villa*
196. *Lullingstone Castle, Gardens &
Church*
197. Shoreham Church
198. Otford Church
Archbishop's Manor House
(Tudor ruin)
199. Kemsing Church
200. One Tree Hill (Roman cemetery,
views) (NT)
201. *Knole* (house) (NT)
202. Knole Park, Sevenoaks
203. *Penshurst Place*
Penshurst Church
Leicester Square (C15 cottages)
204. Chiddingstone Church & Village
(part NT)
Chiddingstone Castle
205. Hever Church
Hever Castle & Gardens
206. Toys Hill (woodland, views) (NT),
Brasted Chart
Parson's Marsh (woodland) (NT)
Scord's Wood (NT)
Emmetts (shrub gardens) (NT)
207. Old Meeting House (1716; Unitarian
Church), Bessels Green
208. *Chartwell* (NT)
209. Mariner's Hill (views) (NT)
210. Westerham Church
Quebec House (NT)
211. *Squerryes Court, House & Garden*
212. Chevening Church & Park
213. *Down House* (Darwin's home),
Downe
214. St. John's Church, West Wickham
Wickham Court (C15, restored)
215. Addiscombe Church
216. *The Old Palace*, Croydon
St. Michael & All Angels Church
Whitgift Hospital (almshouses, 1596)
217. St. Mary's Church, Beddington

218. All Saints Church, Carshalton
Carshalton House & Garden
219. Chipstead Church
220. Chaldon Church
221. Hanging Wood (views) (NT),
Tandridge
222. *Puttenden Manor* (early Tudor)
223. Lingfield Church
College Guest House (C15)
Butcher's Shop (C16)
Village Lock-up (1763)
224. St. Swithun's Church,
East Grinstead
Sackville College (almshouse, 1609)
225. Cowden Church
226. Groombridge Church
227. Speldhurst Church & Village
228. King Charles the Martyr's Church,
Tunbridge Wells
The Pantiles (C17 parade)
Calverley Crescent (Regency) &
Grounds
Mount Ephraim (common, rocks)
229. Pembury Old Church
230. Castle Hill (view), Brenchley
231. Brenchley Church & Village
232. Furnace Pond, Horsmonden
233. St. Margaret's Church, Horsmonden
234. *Sissinghurst Castle Gardens* (NT)
235. Goudhurst Church & Village
236. *Sissinghurst Place Gardens*
237. *Nap Wood* (Nature Reserve) (NT)
238. Cranbrook (town)
St. Dunstan's Church
George Hotel (staircase)
Union Windmill (1814)
239. Bedgebury Pinetum
240. *Scotney Castle, Gardens & ruins* (NT)
241. Lamberhurst Church & Village
242. *The Owl House, Gardens*,
Lamberhurst
243. Old Furnace Mill, Lamberhurst
244. Bayham Abbey (C13 ruins)
245. Eridge Park
246. Withyham Church
247. *Ashdown House*, Forest Row
248. Brambletye House (C17 ruin)
249. *Kidbrooke Park* (house)
250. Selsfield Common (views) (NT)
251. Gravetye Manor (1598; hotel)
Gardens
252. *The Priest House* (C15; museum),
West Hoathly
253. The Warren (woodland) (NT),
Ashdown Forest
254. Nutley Post Mill
255. Rotherfield Church
256. Wadhurst Church
257. Ticehurst Church
258. Benenden (village)
259. *Hole Park, Gardens*
260. Rolvenden Windmill
261. Rolvenden Church
262. Mayfield Church
Middle House Hotel (1575)
263. *Haremere Hall*
264. Etchingham Church
265. *Bateman's, House & Garden* (NT),
Burwash
266. *Sheffield Park Garden* (NT)
267. Chailey Windmill
268. *Beeches Farm, House & Gardens*,
Uckfield
269. Cross in Hand Windmill
Holy Cross Priory
270. Brightling Down
(Fuller's obelisk, view)
271. Sugar Loaf (Mad Jack Fuller's folly,
c. 1820)
272. Brightling Church
The Pyramid (Fuller's mausoleum,
1810)
273. *Bodiam Castle* (NT)
274. *Great Dixter, House & Garden*,
Northiam

275. Robertsbridge Abbey (C12 remains)
276. Isfield Church
277. Warbleton Church
278. Ashburnham Church
279. Penhurst Church
280. Standard Hill (viewpoint), Ninfield
281. St. Mary's Church, Battle
Battle Abbey (C11–14 remains)
Battle Museum
Lake Meadow (view) (NT)
282. Brede Church
283. *Brickwall*
284. North Seat (viewpoint), Fairlight
285. Fairlight Glen
286. Hastings Castle (C12–13 remains)
The Stade (fishermen's huts)
Old Town Hall (1823; museum)
Pelham Crescent (1824)
287. Wartling Church
288. Herstmonceux Castle (C15,
restored; Royal Observatory)
289. All Saints Church, Herstmonceux
290. Chiddingly Church
291. *Michelham Priory, House & Grounds*
292. Glynde Church
Glynde Place
293. *Glyndebourne* (Opera House,
gardens)
294. Mount Caburn (hillfort)
295. Hamsey Church
296. St. Michael's Church, Lewes
St. Thomas's Church
Lewes Castle (C11 & C14 remains)
Barbican House Museum
(archaeology)
Bull House (C15–16)
297. St. John Baptist's Church,
Southover, Lewes
St. Pancras Priory (C11–12 remains)
Anne of Cleves House (C16;
museum)
Southover Grange (1572)
298. Southease Church
299. Telscombe (Downland Village)
300. Rottingdean Church
The Grange Art Gallery & Museum
Old Smock Mill, Beacon Hill
301. St. Michael's Church, Newhaven
302. *Firle Place*
West Firle Church
303. Firle Beacon (view)
304. Bishopstone Church
305. Monastic Barn (C14), Alciston
306. Berwick Church
307. Alfriston Church & Village
Clergy House (c. 1350) (NT)
Star Inn (C15)
308. *Charleston Manor, House & Garden*
309. Exceat Saltings (NT)
310. Westdean Church, Rectory
(mediaeval) & Village
311. *Wilmington Priory* (mediaeval
remains & agricultural museum)
312. Long Man of Wilmington
(ancient turf-cut figure)
313. Crowlink Down (NT)
314. Friston Church
315. Folkington Church
316. Went Hill (NT), Birling Gap
Seven Sisters Cliff (part NT)
317. Eastdean Church
318. Wannock Mill
319. Willingdon Church
320. Pevensey Castle
(Roman & Norman remains)
St. Nicholas' Church
Mint House (mediaeval & C16)
Old Court House
Westham Church
321. St. Mary's Church, Eastbourne,
Towner Art Gallery
322. St. Saviour's Church, Eastbourne
*Royal National Lifeboat Institute
Museum*,
Wish Tower (restored Martello tower)
323. Beachy Head (cliffs 536 ft; views)

Map 14

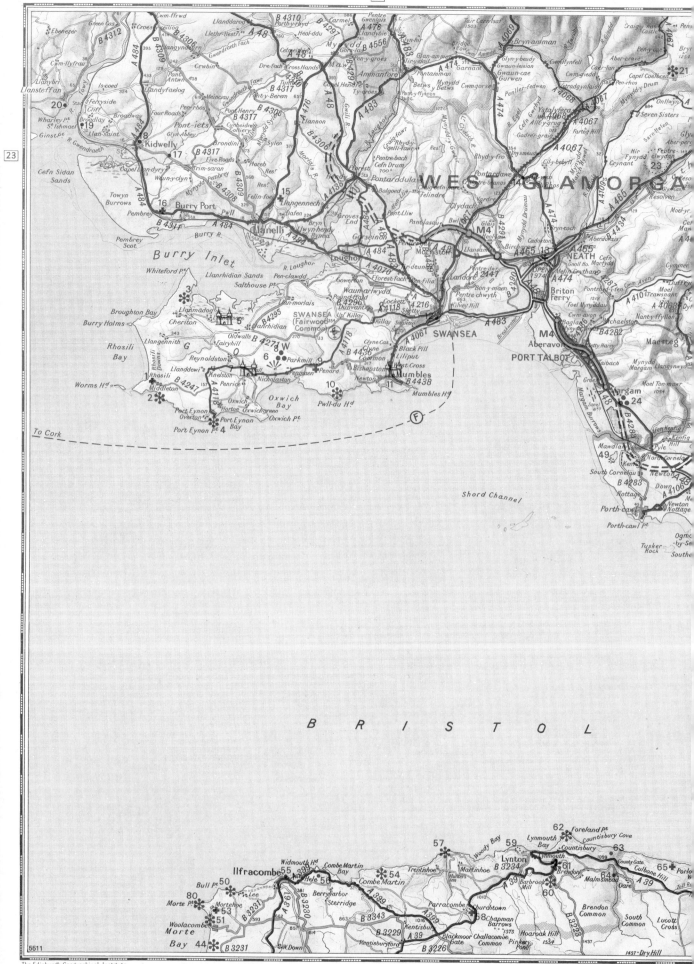

Map 15

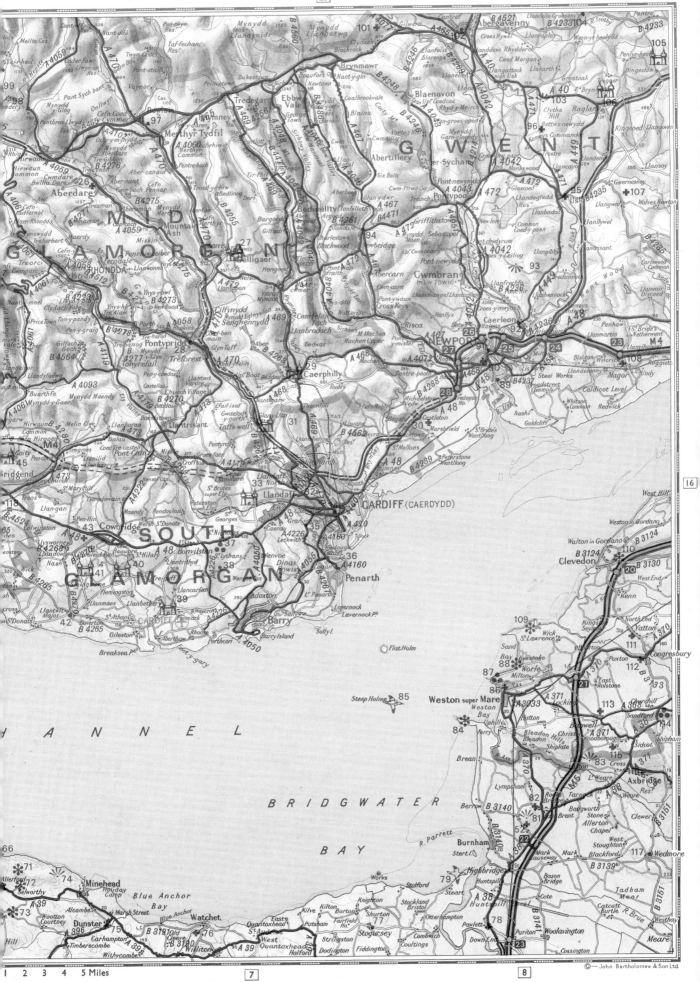

1 2 3 4 5 Miles

Gazetteer to Maps 14·15

1. St. Mary's Church, Rhossili
2. Thurba Head (cliff scenery) (NT), Gower
3. Whitford Burrows (birds and plants) (NT)
4. Port Eynon to Worms Head (geology, birds, plants) (NC & NT)
5. *Weobley Castle* (C13–14 remains)
6. Cefn Bryn (views)
7. *Penrice Castle* (C12 ruins & C18)
8. Parc Le Breos (long cairn)
9. Ilston (remains first Baptist church in Glamorgan)
10. Pennard & Bishopston Valley (headland & incised valley) (NT)
11. Oystermouth Castle (C13 remains)
12. *Royal Institution of South Wales* (c. 1835), Swansea
13. Neath Abbey (C12 remains)
14. Pontardawe Bridge (mid-C18)
15. Adulam Baptist Chapel (baptismal pool), Felin-foel
16. Pembrey Church
17. Pont Spwdwr (mediaeval bridge)
18. Kidwelly Church
    Kidwelly Castle (C13 & C14 remains)
19. St. Ishmael's Church
    Tregoning Hill (views) (NT)
20. Llanstephan Castle (C11–13 remains) & Village
21. Henrhyd Falls (NT), Coelbren
22. Scwdeinon Gam (waterfall), Pont-Nedd Fechan
23. Rheola Forest, Resolven
24. Margam Inscribed Stones & Celtic Crosses
25. Craig-y-Llen (views)
26. St. John's Church, Aberdare
27. *Llancaiach Fawr* (C16 house)
28. Pont-y-Pridd (pierced stone bridge, 1755)
29. Caerphilly Castle (C13)
30. Marshfield Church
31. Castell Coch (C13, restored)
32. Llandaff Cathedral
33. *St. Fagans Castle* (Welsh folk museum)
34. St. John's Church, Cardiff
    Cardiff Castle (Roman to C19)
    National Museum of Wales
35. Leckwith Bridge (mediaeval)
36. Penarth Head (alabaster in cliffs)
37. Tinkinswood Burial Chamber, St. Nicholas
38. St. Lythan's Burial Chamber
    Dyffryn House & Gardens
39. *Fonmon Castle* (Norman to C17)
40. Old Beaupre Castle (C16)
41. Llanmihangel Place (Tudor)
42. St. Illtyd's Church, Llantwit Major
    Town Hall (C16)
    The Great House (C16)
43. Llanfrynach Church

44. Woolacombe Warren (sand dunes; surf bathing) (NT)
45. Coity Castle (C12–15 remains)
46. Newcastle (C12 remains), Bridgend
47. Sheep-Dip Bridge, Merthyr Mawr
48. Ogmore Castle (C12–13 remains)
49. Kenfig Pool & Dunes
50. Damage Cliffs (NT)
51. Combegate Beach (NT), Woolacombe
    Potters Hill (views) (NT)
52. South Brent Church
53. Mortehoe Church
54. Great Hangman (1043 ft) (NT)
55. Ilfracombe, Torrs Walks (NT)
    Chambercombe Manor
56. *Watermouth Castle* (1825 Gothick) & Gardens
    Golden Cove (NT)
57. Heddon's Mouth (cove & cliffs) (NT)
    Trentishoe Down (views) (NT)
58. St. Petrock's Church, Parracombe
59. Valley of the Rocks, Lynton
60. Combe Park (Hoar Oak Water woods) (NT)
61. Watersmeet (East Lyn river gorge) (NT), Lynmouth
62. The Foreland & Countisbury Hill (NT)
63. Old Barrow Hill (views), Countisbury
    Roman Signal Station (C4 earthwork)
64. Malmsmead Bridge, Badgworthy Valley
65. Culbone Church, Porlock
66. Hurlstone Point (views)
67. Bossington (village) (NT)
68. Allerford (village & packhorse bridge) (NT)
69. Horner Water Valley (West Luccombe to Cloutsham) (NT)
    Horner & West Luccombe Packhorse Bridges
70. Dunkery Beacon (views) (NT)
71. Bossington Hill (NT)
    Selworthy Beacon (views) (NT)
72. Selworthy Church & Village (NT)
    Tithe Barn (C15)
    Bury Castle (earthwork)
73. Luccombe (village) (NT)
74. North Hill (views & ruined chapel), Minehead
75. Dunster (village)
    St. George's Church & Priory remains
    Butter Cross (mediaeval)
    Luttrell Arms Hotel (C16 & C17)
    Yarn Market (c. 1589, repaired 1647)
    Gallox Bridge (packhorse)
    Dunster Castle (C13–18) & Grounds
76. St. Decuman's Church, Watchet
77. Stogursey Church
    Stogursey Castle (C13 ruin)

78. Pawlett Church
79. Fenning Island (wildfowl & waders), (NC), Bridgater Bay
80. Morte Point (cliffland; views) (NT)
81. Brent Knoll (view)
82. East Brent Church
83. Crook Peak (view)
84. Brean Down (headland, bird sanctuary) (NT)
85. *Steep Holme* (Bird Reserve)
86. All Saints Church Weston-super-Mare
87. Worlebury Camp (hillfort)
88. Monk's Steps (viewpoint) (NT), Kewstoke
89. Transporter Bridge (1906), Newport
90. St. Woolos Church, Newport
91. *Newport Museum*
92. Isca (Roman legionary fortress remains), Caerleon
    The Legionary Museum
    The Bull (C16)
    The Hanbury Arms (C16)
93. Llandegveth Reservoir (view from dam)
94. Crumlin Viaduct (1857)
95. St. Mary's Church, Usk
96. Bettws-Newydd Church
97. Cyfarthfa Castle (1825; *museum*) & Park
98. Sewd-yr-Eira (waterfall), Penderyn
99. Clyn-Gwyn Falls, Mellte Gorge
100. Porth-yr-Ogof Cavern, Ystradfellte
101. Llanelly Church
102. Abergavenny Castle (C12 ruin)
     St. Mary's Church (tombs)
     Abergavenny & District Museum
103. Clytha Castle (C18 folly, views)
104. Llantilio Crossenny Church
     Hen Gwrt (moated mediaeval house site)
105. *Treowen* (C16 manor house)
106. Raglan Castle (C15–17 remains)
107. St. Hierom's Church, Llangwm
108. Magor Church
109. *Woodspring Priory* (C15) (NT)
110. *Clevedon Court & Gardens* (NT)
111. Yatton Church & Rectory (C15)
112. Congresbury Church
     Mediaeval Stone Cross
     Vicarage (C15)
113. Banwell Church
114. Dolebury Camp (hillfort)
115. Winscombe Church
116. St. John Baptist's Church, Axbridge
     The Old Manor House
     Axbridge Caving & Archaeol. Soc. Museum
     King John's Hunting Lodge (c. 1500) (NT)
117. Wedmore Church
     Village Cross (C14)
118. Ewenny Priory Church

Map 16

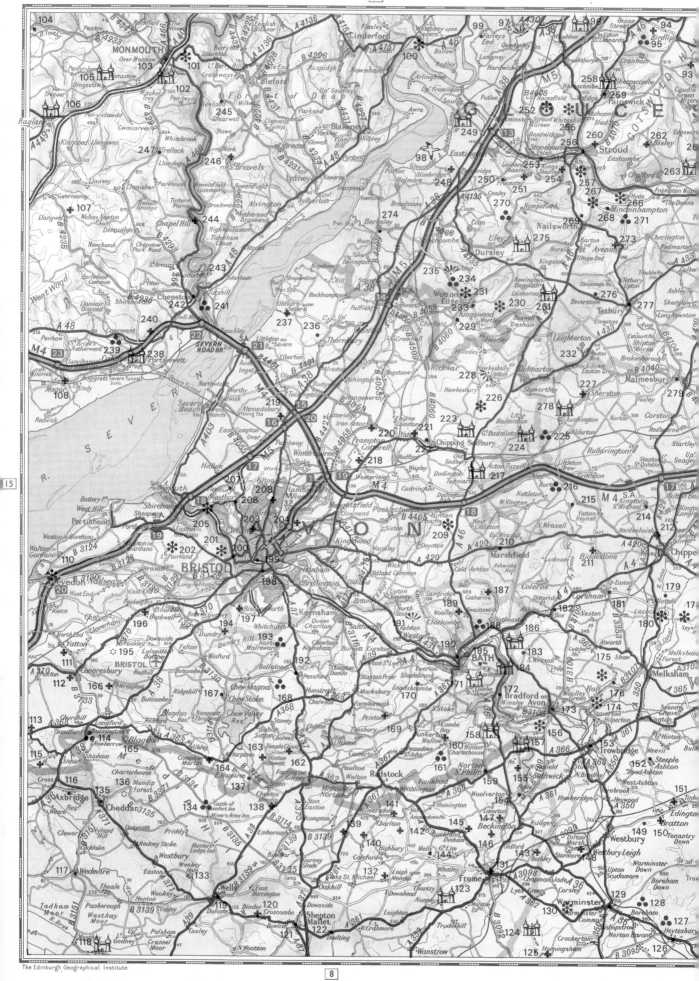

Map 17

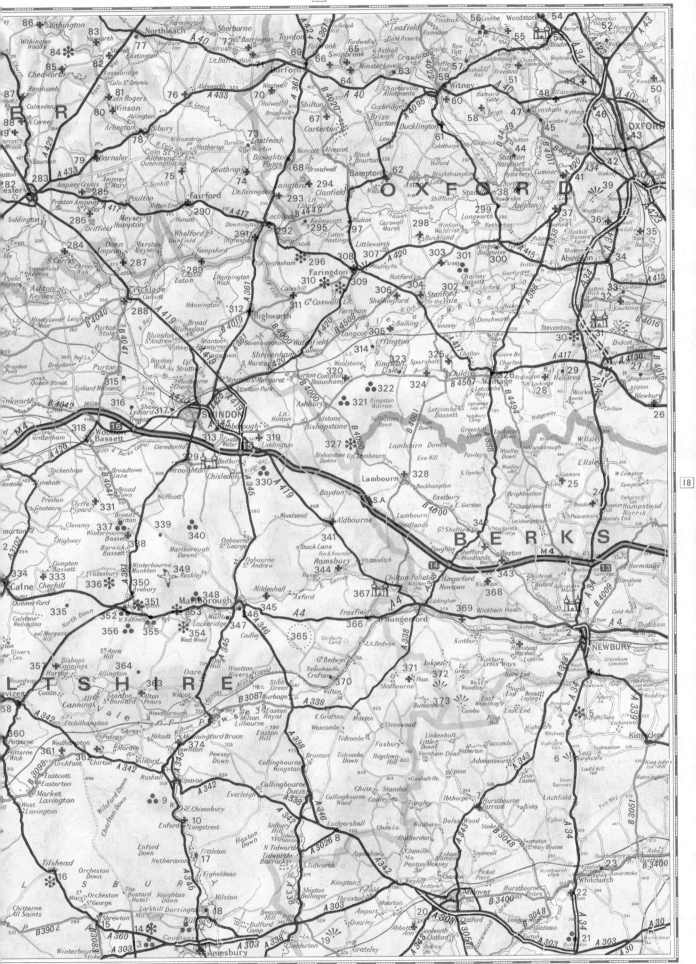

2   3   4   5 Miles

1. Donnington Castle (C14 remains)
2. St. Nicholas' Church, Newbury
   Old Cloth Hall (C17)
   Borough Museum
3. Hampstead Marshall Church
4. *Sandleford Priory* (Wyatt, 1781)
5. Sandham Memorial Chapel (NT)
6. Beacon Hill (hillfort, view),
   Burghclere
7. Hurstbourne Tarrant Church
8. Ludgershall Castle
   (Norman remains)
   Market Cross (mediaeval remains)
9. Casterley Camp (hillfort), Upavon
10. Enford Church
11. Amesbury Church
12. Woodhenge (Bronze Age ritual site)
13. Stonehenge (Bronze Age stone
    circle)
    The Avenue (Chalcolithic)
14. Stonehenge Down
    (Bronze Age barrows) (NT)
    The Cursus (neolithic ritual site)
    (NT)
15. Maddington Tithe Barn, Shrewton
16. White Barrow (neolithic long
    barrow) (NT), Tilshead
17. Netheravon Church
    Dovecote (C18), Netheravon House
18. Durrington Cross
    (mediaeval remains)
19. Quarley Hill (hillfort, views)
20. Abbotts Ann Church
    (maidens' garlands)
21 to 53 Refer to Gazetteer 18/19
54 to 103 Refer to Gazetteer 26/27
104 to 117 Refer to Gazetteer 14/15
118. Abbot's Fish House (c. 1325), Meare
     Manor Farm (C14)
119. Wells Cathedral
     Bishop's Palace (C13–14)
     Vicar's Close (C14)
     Deanery (C15)
     St. Cuthbert's Church
     Bishop Bubwith's Almshouses (1424)
     Bishop's Barn (C15)
     Wells Museum
     Tor Hill (view) (NT)
120. Croscombe Church
121. Shepton Mallet Church (nave roof)
     Market Cross (c. 1500)
     The Shambles (mediaeval market)
     Shepton Mallet Museum
122. Manor Farm Tithe Barn (C15),
     Doulting
123. Nunney Castle (C14)
124. *Longleat House & Park*
125. Nonconformist Chapel (1566),
     Horningsham
     Twelve Apostles (lime trees)
126. Heytesbury Church
     St. John's Hospital (C15 almshouses,
     rebuilt 1770)
127. Scratchbury Hill (hillfort, views)
128. Battlesbury Hill (hillfort, views)
129. Grammar School (1707),
     Warminster
130. Cley Hill (hillfort) (NT)
131. Rook Lane Congregational Chapel
     Frome
     Bluecoat School & Almshouses (1726)
132. Leigh-upon-Mendip Church
133. *Wookey Hole* (caves)
     Ebbor Gorge (nature reserve) (NT)
134. Priddy Circles & Barrows
135. St. Andrew's Church, Cheddar
     Market Cross (mediaeval)
     Cox's Cave
     Gough's Cave & Museum
136. Cheddar Cliffs (NT) & Gorge
137. *Eastwood Manor Farm* (model farm
     c. 1858)
138. Chewton Mendip Church
139. *Downside Abbey*, Stratton-on-the-
     Fosse
140. St. Andrew's Church, Holcombe

141. Kilmersdon Church
142. Babington Church
143. Berkley Church
144. Mells Church & Village
145. Buckland Denham Church
146. Orchardleigh Church
147. Lullington Church
148. Dilton Marsh Church
149. Westbury White Horse (C18 turfcut)
     Bratton Castle (hillfort)
150. St. James's Church, Bratton
151. Edington Church
152. Steeple Ashton Church & Village
153. Yerbury Almshouses (C17),
     Trowbridge
     Prade House (C18), Wicker Hill
154. Packhorse Bridge, Woolverton
155. Tellisford Church
156. Westwood Church & *Manor* (NT)
157. *Farleigh Castle* (C14; museum of
     arms & armour)
158. Hinton Priory (C13 remains)
159. George Inn (C15), Norton St. Philip
160. Wellow Church
161. Stoney Littleton Long Barrow
162. Cameley Church
163. Hinton Blewett Church
164. Compton Martin Church
165. Burrington Combe (gorge)
166. Wrington Church
167. Packhorse Bridge, Chew Stoke
168. Stanton Drew Stone Circles &
     Avenues
     The Cove (burial chamber)
     Hautville's Quoit (large boulder)
169. Priston Church
170. Wansdyke (section of), Englishcombe
     Tithe Barn
171. *Prior Park, House & Grounds*,
     Widcombe
172. Monkton Bridge (packhorse)
173. Bradford-on-Avon (town)
     Holy Trinity Church
     St. Laurence's Church (Saxon)
     The Hermitage (restored mediaeval
     hospitium)
     Town Bridge (C14) & Oratory
     Church House (C15)
     Old Priory (C15)
     Chantry House (C16)
     The Hall (C16 & C17)
     Hall's Old Men's Almshouses (1700)
     Barton Farm Tithe Barn (C14)
174. *The Courts, Gardens* (NT), Holt
175. *Great Chalfield Manor* (NT)
176. Packhorse Bridge, Broughton Gifford
177. Bromham Church
     Baynton Almshouses (1612)
178. Bewley Common (NT)
179. *Lackham School of Agriculture
     Museum*
180. Lacock (village) (NT)
     St. Cyriac's Church
     *Lacock Abbey, House, Garden &
     Conventual Remains* (NT)
181. Hungerford Almshouses (1663),
     Corsham
     Corsham Court, House & Gardens
182. Box Railway Tunnels (Brunel)
183. Monks Conduit (C13),
     Monkton Farleigh
184. *Claverton Manor* (American
     Museum) & *Gardens*
185. Sham Castle (Ralph Allen's folly,
     1762), Bath
186. *Whitehaven* ('Titan Barrow', elder
     Wood, 1748), Bathford
187. St. Catherine Church
188. Little Solsbury Hill (hillfort, views)
     (NT)
189. Woolley Church
190. Bath Abbey Church
     Roman Baths & Museum
     Many notable C18 Buildings,
     including:
     Queen Square (elder Wood, c. 1735)

     Ralph Allen's House (elder Wood,
     c. 1735)
     The Circus (younger Wood, 1764)
     Pulteney Bridge (Adam, c. 1770)
     Assembly Rooms (younger Wood,
     1771; restored) (NT)
     Royal Crescent (younger Wood,
     1775)
     Guildhall (Baldwin, 1775)
     Grand Pump Room (1796) & King's
     Bath
     Holburne of Menstrie Museum of Art
     Victoria Art Gallery
     Partis College (almshouses, 1825–7)
     St. Swithun's Church, Walcot
     Methodist Chapel (1815), Walcot
     Beechen Cliff (viewpoint)
     Beckford's Tower (1827, viewpoint),
     Lansdown
191. Prospect Stile (view of Bath &
     Bristol)
192. Pensford Viaduct & View of Publow
     Church Tower
193. Maesknoll Camp (earthwork),
     Norton Malreward
194. Dundry Church Tower (views)
195. Goblin Combe, Cleeve
196. Backwell Church
197. Bishopsworth Church
198. St. Mary Redcliffe Church, Bristol
     Chatterton's Birthplace, Redcliffe Way
199. Bristol Cathedral
     All Saints Church
     Christ Church
     St. Stephen's Church
     St. John's Church & Gate
     St. Mark's Church (Lord Mayor's
     Chapel)
     St. Mary's-on-the-Quay Church (RC)
     St. Nicholas' Church
     St. Paul's Church, Portland Square
     Temple Church
     The New Room (Wesleyan Chapel,
     1748)
     Colston's Almshouses (C17)
     Merchant Seamen's Almshouses (C17)
     St. Nicholas' Almshouses (C17)
     Red Lodge (C17 furniture)
     Llandoger Trow Inn (C17)
     Christmas Steps (C17 street)
     Corn Exchange (1743) &
     The 'Nails' (market tables)
     Cooper's Hall (1744 facade)
     Theatre Royal (1766)
     Georgian House (1789), 7, Great
     George Street
     Cabot Tower (1898)
     University Tower (1925 Gothic)
     City Museum & Art Gallery
200. Avon Gorge, Clifton
     Clifton Suspension Bridge (Brunel)
     Royal York Crescent (Regency)
     The Paragon (Regency crescent)
201. Leigh Woods & Nightingale Valley
     (NT)
     Stokeleigh Camp (hillfort) (NT)
202. Failand (views over Severn) (NT)
203. Redland Chapel, Bristol
204. Holy Trinity Church, Stapleton
205. Shirehampton Park (NT)
206. Holy Trinity Church,
     Westbury-on-Trym
     Westbury College Gatehouse (C15)
     (NT)
207. Hembury Church
     Blaise Hamlet (estate cottages,
     John Nash, 1809) (NT)
     Blaise Castle (C18 folly)
     Blaise Castle House (Folk museum)
208. St. Gregory's Church, Horfield
209. *Dyrham Park, House & Garden* (NT)
     Dyrham Church
210. Crispe's Almshouses (C17),
     Marshfield
211. Biddestone Church
212. Hardenhuish Church

213. Maud Heath's Causeway (C15),
     Langley Burrell
214. Lyte's Almshouses (1672),
     Kington St. Michael
215. Castle Combe (village)
     Market Cross (C13)
216. Lugbury Long Barrow, Nettleton
217. Dodington Park & *House* (Regency)
218. Coalpit Heath Church
219. Almondsbury Church
220. Iron Acton Church & Churchyard
     Cross (C15)
221. Yate Church
222. Chipping Sodbury Church
     Tudor House
223. *Little Sodbury Manor*
224. Great Badminton Church
     Badminton House
     Hunt Kennels
225. Giant's Cave (chambered long
     barrow), Luckington
226. *Horton Court* (Norman hall,
     ambulatory) (NT)
227. Sherston Church
228. Somerset Monument (view),
     Hawkesbury
229. Kingswood Abbey Gatehouse (C14)
230. Newark Park (views) (NT)
231. Westridge Woods (NT)
232. Weston Birt Arboretum
233. Wotton-under-Edge Church
     Perry & Dawes Hospital
     (almshouses, 1632)
234. Brackenbury Ditches (hillfort, view),
     North Nibley
235. Tyndale Monument, Nibley Knoll
     (view)
236. Thornbury Church & Castle (Tudor)
237. Oldbury-on-Severn Church (view)
238. Caldicot Castle (part C14)
239. Venta Silurium (Roman town
     remains), Caerwent
240. Runston Chapel (C12 ruin), Crick
241. Bulwarks Camp (hillfort), Chepstow
242. Chepstow Castle (C11–13)
     St. Mary's Church
     Town Walls (C13 remains)
     Town Gate (C16; *museum*)
     Montagu Almshouses (C17)
     Iron Lattice Road Bridge (1815)
243. Piercefield Park (cliff walks, views)
244. Tintern Abbey (C13–14 remains)
245. Newland Church
     Almshouses (C17)
     Great Oak
246. St. Briavels Church
247. Trelleck Church & Village
248. Slimbridge Church
249. *Frampton Court,*
     Frampton-on-Severn
250. Tithe Barn (C13), Frocester
251. Leonard Stanley Church & Priory
     remains (Norman)
252. Haresfield Beacon (hillfort, views)
     (NT)
253. Stanley Mill (textile, 1813),
     Stonehouse
254. Selsey Church (view)
255. Stockend & Maitland Woods (NT),
     Scottsquar Hill
256. Town Hall (C16 façade), Stroud
     Subscription Rooms (1836)
     Stroud Museum
257. Rodborough Common (NT)
258. *Painswick House*
259. Painswick (town)
     St. Mary's Churchyard
     (yew plantation)
     Little Fleece (C17; bookshop) (NT)
     Court House
260. All Saints Church, Uplands, Stroud
261. *Lasborough Manor*
262. Bisley Church
263. *Daneway House* (C14–17), Sapperton
264. Edgeworth Church
     Scriven's Conduit (C17)

265. Sapperton Church
266. Hyde & Besbury Commons
     (above Golden Valley) (NT)
267. Littleworth Common (NT)
     Amberley Camp (earthwork) (NT)
     St. Chloe's Green (NT)
268. Holy Trinity Church,
     Minchinhampton
     Market House (C17)
     Minchinhampton Commons (NT)
269. Early Textile Mills, Nailsworth
     Watledge Hill (NT)
270. Hetty Pegler's Tump
     (long barrow, view), Uley
271. Long Stone (megalithic), Avening
272. Thames Head (source of r. Thames)
273. Avening Church
274. Berkeley Church, *Castle & Gardens*
275. *Owlpen Manor*
276. Beverstone Church & Castle
     (mediaeval remains)
277. St. Mary's Church, Tetbury
     Town Hall (C17)
278. *Luckington Court*
279. Malmesbury Abbey
     St. John's Hospital (C13 almshouse)
     Market Cross (C16)
280. Dauntsey Church
281. Oaksey Church
282. Cirencester Park
283. St. John Baptist's Church, Cirencester
     Corinium Museum
284. South Cerney Church
285. Ampney Crucia Church &
     Churchyard Cross (C15)
286. Harnhill Church
287. Down Ampney Church
288. St. Sampson's Church, Cricklade
     Churchyard Crosses
289. Kempsford Church
290. Fairford Church
291. Inglesham Church
292. Lechlade Church
293. Little Faringdon Church
294. Langford Church
295. Kelmscott Church & Village
     Kelmscott Manor (C16–17) (asstd.
     with William Morris: Socy. of
     Antiquaries of London)
296. *Buscot Park, House & Garden* (NT)
     Buscott Village (NT)
     The Old Parsonage (NT)
297. Radcot Bridge (C14)
298. Buckland Church
299. New Bridge (C14)
300. *Kingston House, Gardens*
     Kingston Bagpuize Church
301. Cherbury Camp (earthwork)
302. Charney Bassett Church & Manor
     (C13; hotel)
303. Pusey Church
304. Stanford-in-the-Vale Church
305. Balking Church
306. Shellingford Church
307. Folly Hill (view), Faringdon
308. Faringdon Church
309. Court House Tithe Barn (C13) (NT),
     Great Coxwell
310. Badbury hill (hillfort, views) (NT)
311. All Saints Church, Coleshill
312. Highworth Church
313. *Richard Jefferies Museum*, Coate
314. Uffington Church
     School House (C17)
315. Purton Church
     Manor House (c. 1600) & Tithe Barn
316. Lydiard Tregoze Church
     Lydiard Mansion
317. *Great Western Railway Museum*,
     Swindon
318. Old Town Hall (c. 1700),
     Wootton Bassett
319. Wanborough Church
320. Compton Beauchamp Church
321. Wayland's Smithy (long barrow),
     Ashbury

322. Uffington White Horse (Iron Age,
     turf-cut)
     Uffington Castle (hillfort)
     Dragon Hill (mound)
323. Kingston Lisle Church
     Blowing Stone (perforated sarson
     stone)
324. Sparsholt Church
325. West Challow Church
326. Wantage Church
     Stile's Almshouses (1680)
327. *Ashdown House, Garden & Roof*
     (view) (NT)
328. Lambourn Church
329. *Burderop Park*
330. Liddington Castle (hillfort, views)
331. Cliffe Pypard Church
332. Market & Churchyard Crosses
     (mediaeval), Bremhill
333. Compton Bassett Church
334. St. Mary's Church, Calne
335. Cherhill White Horse (C18, turf-cut)
336. Windmill Hill (neolithic causewayed
     enclosure) (NT), Avebury
337. Stone Circle, Winterbourne Bassett
338. Winterbourne Bassett Church
339. Hackpen Hill (turf-cut White Horse,
     views)
     The Ridge Way (prehistoric track)
340. Barbury Castle (hillfort)
341. Aldbourne Church
342. East Shefford Church
343. Welford Church
344. Ramsbury Church
345. Mildenhall Church
346. *Minal School* (1824 Grecian),
     Marlborough
347. Marlborough White Horse
     (C19 turf-cut)
348. Devil's Den (barrow), Fyfield
349. *Fyfield Down* (Nature Reserve,
     sarsen stones)
350. Avebury Circle (megalithic
     monument) (NT)
     Avebury Museum
     St. James's Church
     Avebury Manor, House & Garden
351. West Kennett Avenue
     (megalithic) (NT), Avebury
352. Silbury Hill (pre-Roman mound;
     largest in Europe)
353. Grey Wethers (sarsen stones) (NT),
     Fyfield
354. Grey Wethers (sarsen stones) (NT),
     Lockeridge Dene
355. The Sanctuary (site of stone circles),
     Overton Hill
356. West Kennett Long Barrow
357. Bishops Cannings Church
358. Devizes (Georgian town houses)
     St. John's Church
     St. Mary's Church
     Town Hall (Georgian)
     Devizes Museum
359. Flight of 29 Locks (Rennie, 1807),
     Kennet & Avon Canal
360. Potterne Church & Village
     The Porch House & Gardens
361. Urchfont Church
362. Chirton Church
363. Alton Priors Church
     Alton Barnes Church
364. White Horse (turf-cut 1812),
     Alton Barnes
365. Savernake Forest (rides, views)
366. Somerset Almshouses (C17), Froxfield
367. *Littlecote House*, Chilton Foliat
368. Wickham Church
369. Avington Church
370. Canal Engine House
     (Beam engines, 1801–3), Crofton
371. Ham Church
372. Inkpen Beacon (views)
373. Walbury Beacon (975 ft; hillfort,
     views), Combe
374. Manningford Bruce Church (Saxon)

Map 18

OXFORD

OXFORDSHIRE

BERKSHIRE

AYLESBURY

HIGH WYCOMBE

Princes Risborough

Thame

Amersham

Marlow

Henley on Thames

Maidenhead

WINDSOR

READING

Wallingford

Abingdon

NEWBURY

Kingsclere

BASINGSTOKE

ALDERSHOT

Farnborough

Bracknell

Whitchurch

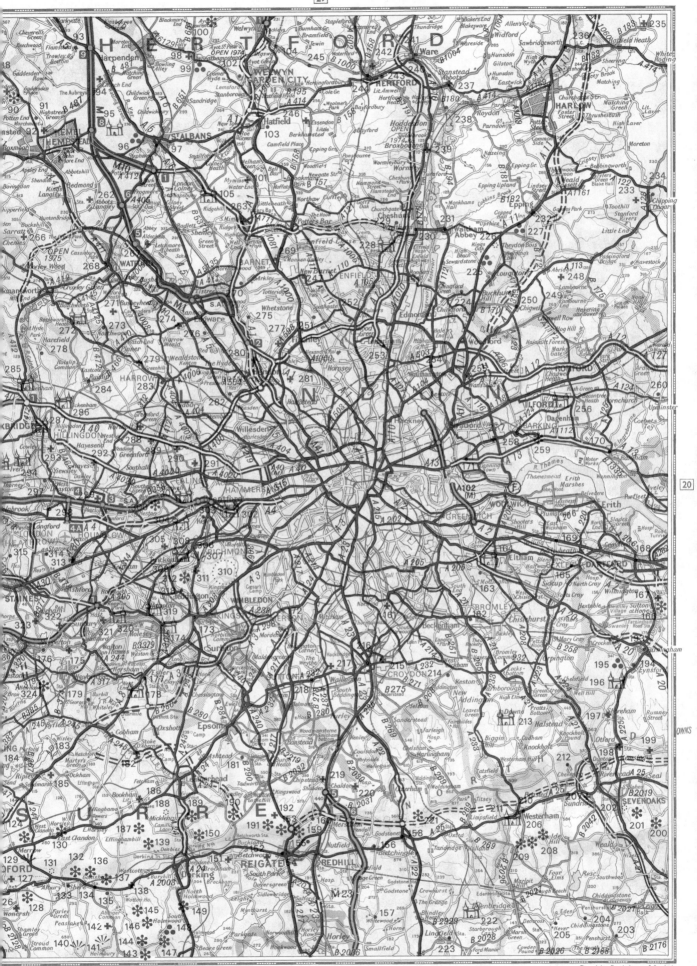

Map 19

Gazetteer to Maps 18·19

1. Donnington Castle (C14 remains)
2. St. Nicholas' Church, Newbury
   Old Cloth Hall (C17)
   Borough Museum
3. Hampstead Marshall Church
4. *Sandleford Priory* (Wyatt, 1781)
5. Sandham Memorial Chapel (NT)
6. Beacon Hill (hillfort, view),
   Burghclere
7. Wasing Church
8. Aldermaston Church
9. Padworth Church
10. Wolverton Church
11. Pamber Priory Church
12. St. Peter's Church, Tadley
13. *Calleva Museum*
14. Silchester Church
    Calleva Atrebatum (site of
    Roman city)
15. Bramley Church
16. Hartley Wespall Church
17. *The Vyne, House & Gardens* (NT)
18. Nateley Scures Church
19. Basing Church
    Basing House (C16 ruin; *museum*)
20. St. Michael's Church, Basingstoke
    Deane Almshouses (C17)
    Willis Museum
21. Tidbury Ring (hillfort, view)
22. Tufton Church
23. Old Paper Mill (paper for bank
    notes since 1724), Laverstoke
24. Beedon Church
25. Catmore Church
26. Blewbury Church
27. East Hagbourne Church & Village
    Market Cross (mediaeval)
28. West Hendred Church
29. East Hendred (village)
30. *Priory Cottages* (NT), Steventon
    39/43 The Causeway (C14)
31. *Milton Manor House*
32. Sutton Courtenay Church
33. Culham Bridge (C15)
34. St. Helen s Church, Abingdon
    Abingdon Abbey (C13–16 remains)
    Guidhall (C13–19 ; Art *Gallery*)
    Long Alley Almshouses (C15)
    Brick Alley Almshouses (C18)
    County Hall (c. 1680 ; *museum*)
    Twickenham House
    Burford Bridge (part C15)
35. Radley Church
36. Sunningwell Church
37. Besselsleigh Church
38. Northmoor Church
39. Jarn Mound (view), Boars Hill
40. Iffley Church
41. Cumnor Church
42. Oxford University Colleges (thirty
    dating from 1249. Halls, Chapels
    & Gardens)
    Christ Church Cathedral
    Christ Church Library
    Sheldonian Theatre (Wren, 1669)
    Clarendon Building (Hawksmoor
    1713)
    Bodleian Library & Radcliffe
    Camera (Gibbs, 1749)
    Magdalen Bridge (Gwynne, 1782)
    All Saints Church
    St. Mary the Virgin Church
    St. Peter's-in-the-East Church
    Stone's Almshouses (C17)
    Ashmolean Museum
    Old Ashmolean (1682; History of
    Science Museum)
    Botanic Garden (founded 1621)
    Christ Church Meadow
43. University Parks, Oxford
    University Museum
    Pitt Rivers Museum (prehistory)
44. Stanton Harcourt Church, Village
    & Manor House (Tudor remains)
45. Swinford Bridge (1777)
46. Godstow Nunnery (C15 remains)

47. Market Cross (C14), Eynsham
48. Cassington Church
49. Yarnton Church
50. Woodeaton Church
51. Church Hanborough Church
52. Kidlington Church
    Morton Almshouses (C17)
53. *Blenheim Palace & Park*
54. Garsington Village & Manor
    House (C16)
55. Cuddesdon Church
    Bishop's Palace (1679)
56 to 100. Refer to Gazetteer 28-29
101. North Mimms Church
102. Brocket Park
     Lemsford Mill
103. Hatfield Park, *House, Gardens
     & Bishop's Palace*
     St. Etheldreda's Church
     Fore Street (Georgian houses)
104. Digswell Viaduct (Cubitt, 1850)
105. *Salisbury Hall*, London Colney
106. Odiham Church & Almshouses (C17)
107. Froyle Church
108. Crondall Church
109. St. Andrew's Church, Farnham
     Farnham Castle (Norman keep
     & *Bishop's residence*)
     The Grange (c. 1710), Odiham Road
     Castle Street (Georgian houses)
     Vernon House (C16, restored),
     West Street
     Willmer House (1718; museum)
     The Ranger's House
110. Waverley Abbey (C13 remains)
111. Tilford (village, oak tree & old
     bridges)
112. Elstead Bridge (C16) Water-Mill
     (C17-18) & *The Mill House*
113. Peper Harow Church & Farm
     (C17 & C18 buildings)
114. Eashing Bridges (C13) (NT)
115. St. Peter and St. Paul's Church
     Godalming
     Church House (C15–17)
     Old Town Hall (1814; museum)
116. *Charterhouse School Museum*
117. Wyatt's Almshouses (1622),
     Farncombe
118. Compton Church
     G. F. Watts Gallery & Mortuary
     Chapel (1898)
119. Hogs Back (six-mile ridge, views)
120. *Loseley House*
121. St. Catherine's Chapel (C14 ruin,
     view), Guildford
122. Guildford Cathedral
123. Holy Trinity Church, Guildford
     St. Mary's Church
     Guildhall (1683), High Street
     Grammar School (C16)
     Guildford Castle (Norman keep)
     Trinity Hospital (almshouses, 1619)
     Museum & Muniment Room,
     Castle Arch
124. *Clandon Park, House & Garden* (NT)
125. Wonersh Church & Village
     The Sharp Collection (bygones)
     Green Place
126. Blackheath Church
127. St. Martha's Chapel, Chilworth
128. Blackheath (heathland) (NT)
129. Newlands Corner (view)
130. *Hatchlands* (NT), East Clandon
131 to 151. Refer to Gazetteer 10-11
152. Windmill Church (1765), Reigate
     Heath
153. Reigate Hill & Colley Hill
     (views) (NT)
154. St. Mary's Church, Reigate
     Old Town Hall (1728)
     Reigate Priory (C18; school)
155. Wray Common Windmill (1824)
     Reigate
156. Bletchingley Church & Village
157. Outwood Post Mill (1665)

158. Godstone Green
159. Gatton (down & woodland) (NT)
160. Gatton Church
     Old Town Hall (temple 1765)
161 to 171. Refer to Gazetteer 20-21
172. Morden Hall (deer park, river walks)
173. All Saints Church, Kingston-
     upon-Thames
     Cleave's Almshouses (1668)
     Coronation Stone (Saxon)
     Clattern Bridge (part C12)
     Kingston Bridge (1828 & later)
     Borough Museum
     (zoopraxiscope, 1881)
174. Hampton Court Palace & Gardens
175. Shepperton Church & Rectory
     (c. 1700 front)
176. Chertsey Bridge (James Paine, 1785)
177. St. George's Church, Esher
     Esher Place Gatehouse (C15 & C18)
178. *Claremont* (1772 ; school)
179. Whiteley Village (William Whiteley's
     almshouses, 1907)
     St. Mark's Church
180. St. Peter's Church, Woking
     Shah Jehan Mosque (1889)
181. Racecourse, Epsom Downs
182. Stoke d'Abernon Church
183. Royal Horticultural Society Gardens
     Wisley
184. Pyrford Church
     Newark Priory (C13 ruin)
     Newark Mill (early C19)
185. Ockham Church
186. Great Bookham Church
187. *Polesden Lacey, House & Gardens*
     (NT)
188. Druids' Grove (yews), Norbury Park
189. White Hill & Mickleham Downs
     (NT)
     Juniper Hall (Talleyrand house ;
     Field Studies Centre (NT)
190. Headley Heath (NT)
191. Juniper Hill (views), (NT), Reigate
192. Wisdom of God Church, Lower
     Kingswood
193 to 260. Refer to Gazetteer 20-21
261. St. Mary's Church, Amersham
     Drake's Almshouses (1657)
     Market Hall (C17)
262. Abbot's Langley Church
263. South Mimms Church
264. Flaunden Old Church (C13 ruin)
265. Bedford Chapel (C14–20 monuments)
     Chenies
266. Sarratt Church
267. Aldenham Church
268. St. Mary's Church, Watford
     Church of the Holy Rood (RC)
     Bedford Almshouses (C16)
     Elizabeth Fuller's Free School (1704)
     Watford Art Collection
269. St. John's Church, Barnet
     Queen Elizabeth Grammar School
     (C16)
     Wilbraham Almshouses (1612),
     Hadley Green
270. Tower Windmill (early C19), Arkley
271. Oxhey Chapel (1612)
272. *Moor Park* (c. 1720 house),
     Richmansworth
273. *Pinto Collection of Wooden
     Bygones*, Northwood
274. St. John's Church (C17 ruin),
     Stanmore
275. The Ridgeway (Georgian houses,
     view), Mill Hill
     John Keble Church (1936),
     Dean's Lane
276. St. Lawrence's Church, Canons Park
     Lake's Almshouses (1693), Little
     Stanmore
277. St. Mary's Church, Church End,
     Finchley
278. Harefield Church
     Derby Almshouses (c. 1610)

279. St. Alban's Church, The Ridgeway, North Harrow
280. St. Mary's Church, Hendon
281. St. Jude-on-the-Hill Church, Hampstead Garden Suburb
282. St. Andrew's Church, Kingsbury
    Brent Reservoir (birds & plants)
283. St. Mary's Church, Harrow-on-the-Hill
    Harrow School (Old School 1611 & 1820)
    Butler Museum (Natural History)
284. St. Martin's Church, Ruislip
    Manor Farm (C16–18 buildings)
285. *Denham Place*
286. *Swakeleys*, Ickenham
287. Market House (1789), Uxbridge
    Crown & Treaty House (C16 & C17)
288. St. Mary's Church, Northolt
289. All Hallows Old Church, Greenford
290. St. Mary's Church, Perivale
291. St. Peter's Church, Mount Park Road, Ealing
292. St. Mary's Church, Hayes
293. Cowley Church
294. *Bridgefoot* (early C18 house), Iver
295. *Iver Grove* (Vanbrugh, 1724), Shredding Green
296. Langley Marish Church
    Kederminster Almshouses (1617)
    Seymour Almshouses (c. 1675)
297. West Drayton Church
    Manor House Gateway (Tudor)
298. Harmondsworth Church
    Manor Farm Tithe Barn (c. 1400)
299. Cranford Church
300. *Osterley Park* (house) & Park (NT)
301. *Boston Manor House & Gardens*, Brentford
302. Chiswick Park & *House*
    Hogarth's House
303. Royal Botanic Gardens, Kew
    Kew Palace (1631)
    St. Anne's Church, Kew Green
304. *Syon House & Gardens*
305. All Hallows Church, Twickenham
306. Richmond Green (C17 & C18 houses, Tudor palace remains)
    Maids of Honour Row (c. 1720)
    St. Mary's Church
    Richmond Bridge (James Paine, 1777)
307. Richmond Hill (view)
    The Terrace (C18 houses)
308. Marble Hill (c. 1720 house & grounds), Twickenham
    Orleans House Octagon (Gibbs, 1730)
    Montpelier Row (1720 terrace)
309. St. Mary's Church, Twickenham
    York House (c. 1700) & Gardens
    Sion Road (1721 houses)
310. Richmond Park
311. St. Peter's Church, Petersham
312. *Ham House* & Gardens (NT)
313. East Bedfont Church
314. Stanwell Church
    Lord Knyvett's Free School (1624)
315. *Staines Moor & Reservoirs* (aquatic birds)
316. Runnymede (riverside meadows) (NT)
317. Royal Holloway College (1886 ; *Picture Gallery*), Egham
318. Teddington Lock
    St. Mary's Church
    St. Alban's Church
319. Hampton House & Garrick's Temple (C18)
320. *Sunbury Court* (C18 wall paintings)
321. Sunbury Church
322. Littleton Church
323. Laleham Church
324. Wey Navigation (19½ miles Godalming to Weybridge) (NT)
325. Monks Risborough Church

326. Whiteleaf Cross (C17? turf-cut)
327. St. Mary's Church, Princes Risborough
    Manor House (C17) (NT)
328. Little Hampden Church
329. Bledlow Church
330. Great Hampden Church
331. Wain Hill (views)
    Bledlow Cross (C17? turf-cut)
332. Smock Mill (1650), Lacey Green
333. Little Missenden Church
334. Market Hall (C17), Watlington
335. Radnage Church
336. Lewknor Church
337. Wheatfield Church & Stables (C18)
338. Chislehampton Church
    Mediaeval Bridge
339. All Saints Church, Nuneham Courtney
340. Newington Church
341. Hampden Monument (1643), Chalgrove
342. Chalgrove Church
343. Aston Wood (beeches, views) (NT)
344. *Hughenden Manor* (Disraeli Museum) (NT)
345. St. Lawrence's Church & Dashwood Mausoleum (1764), West Wycombe
    Iron Age Hillfort (view)
    Caves (Dashwood, c. 1750)
346. West Wycombe (village) (NT)
    West Wycombe Park, House & Grounds (NT)
347. All Saints Church, High Wycombe
    Guildhall (1757)
    Little Market House (1761)
    Art Gallery & Museum
348. Penn Church
349. Chalfont St. Giles Church
    Milton's Cottage (museum)
350. Friends' Meeting House (1688), Jordans
351. St. Mary's Church, Beaconsfield
    Bekonscot Model Village
352. Fingest Church
353. Watlington Hill (downland, views) (NT)
354. *Nuneham Park* (C18), University of Oxford
355. Brightwell Baldwin Church
356. Clifton Bridge (C19), Long Wittenham
    Barley Mow Inn
357. Long Wittenham Church
358. Abbey Church, Dorchester
359. Dyke Hills (earthworks), Dorchester
360. Wittenham Clumps (hillfort, views)
361. Warborough Church
362. Shillingford Bridge (C18)
363. Ewelme Church & Village
    Almshouses & School House (C15, restored)
364. Swyncombe Church
365. *Stonor Park, House, Grounds & Chapel* (RC, C14)
366. St. Leonard's Church, Wallingford
    St. Peter's Church
    Town Hall (C17)
    Wallingford Bridge (1809 & C13)
367. North Moreton Church
368. Cholsey Church
369. Hambleden Church
370. Little Marlow Church
371. Hedgerley Church
372. Cock Marsh (bowl-barrows) (NT), Cookham
373. Winter Hill (view) (NT), Cookham
374. Marlow Bridge (suspension, 1832) & Weir
    Marlow Place (Archer, c. 1720)
    West Street (Georgian houses)
375. *Stanley Spencer Gallery*, Cookham
376. *Cliveden, House & Grounds* (NT)
    Cliveden Reach (r. Thames)
377. Burnham Beeches

378. Bisham Church
    Bisham Abbey (mediaeval & Tudor)
379. Hurley Church & Priory Remains
380. Stoke Poges Church
    Gray's Monument (1799) (NT)
381. Hitcham Church
382. Boulter's Lock (r. Thames)
383. Maidenhead Bridge (1772)
    Railway Bridge (Brunel; world's flattest elliptical-arched span)
    James Smith's Almshouses (1659)
    Henry Reitlinger Bequest (oriental art)
384. All Saints Church, Boyne Hill
385. Maidenhead Thicket (NT)
386. Henley-on-Thames Regatta Course
    Henley Bridge (1786)
    Churchyard Almshouses (rebuilt C19)
387. *Grey's Court* (NT)
388. Checkendon Church
389. Rotherfield Greys Church
390. Lardon Chase (downland, views) (NT), Streatley
391. Aldworth Church
392. Allnatt's Almshouses (1726), Goring Heath
393. Shiplake Church
394. Jesus Hospital (almshouses, 1627), Bray
395. Upton Church, Slough
396. Dorney Church
397. Boveney Church
398. Eton College (C15 & later)
    College Chapel (C15)
    College Natural History Museum
399. Windsor Castle (Norman to C19)
    State Apartments & Round Tower
    St. George's Chapel (C15)
    Guildhall (1689; *museum*)
    Park Street (C18 houses)
400. Shottesbrooke Church
401. Waltham St. Lawrence Church
402. Twyford Almshouses (C17)
403. Sonning Village, Bridge (c. 1730) & Lock (r. Thames)
404. Mapledurham Lock (r. Thames), Mill & Manor House (Tudor)
405. Pangbourne Weir (r. Thames) & Meadow (NT)
406. Ashampstead Church
407. Bucklebury Church
408. Bradfield Church
409. Caversham Bridge (C20)
410. St. Lawrence's Church, Reading
    Reading Abbey (C12 remains)
    Museum and Art Gallery
411. *English Rural Life Museum*, Reading University
412. Hurst Church
    Barker Almshouses (C17)
413. Warfield Church
414. The Long Walk, Windsor Great Park
    Queen Anne's Ride
415. *Savill Gardens*, Windsor Great Park
416. Ascot Heath & Race Course
417. Virginia Water (lake, woodland rides)
418. Henry Lucas Hospital (almshouses, 1665), Wokingham
419. Finchampstead Church
420. Finchampstead Ridges (heath & woodland, views) (NT)
    Heath Pool (NT)
421. *National Army Museum*, R.M.A., Sandhurst
422. Yateley Church
423. Mattingley Church
424. *West Green House* (NT), Hartley Wintney
425. Hartley Wintney Old Church
426. *Napoleon III's Tomb*, Farnborough
427. Winchfield Church
428. Odiham Castle (C13 remains), North Warnborough
429. Wellington Monument (1846; from Hyde Park Corner), Aldershot

Map 20

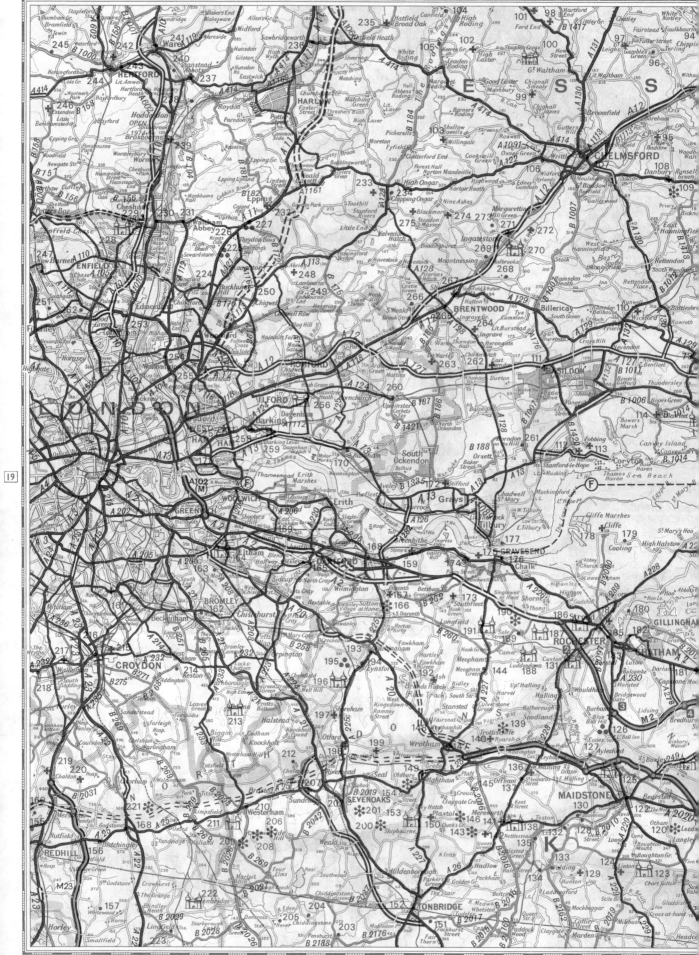

Map 21

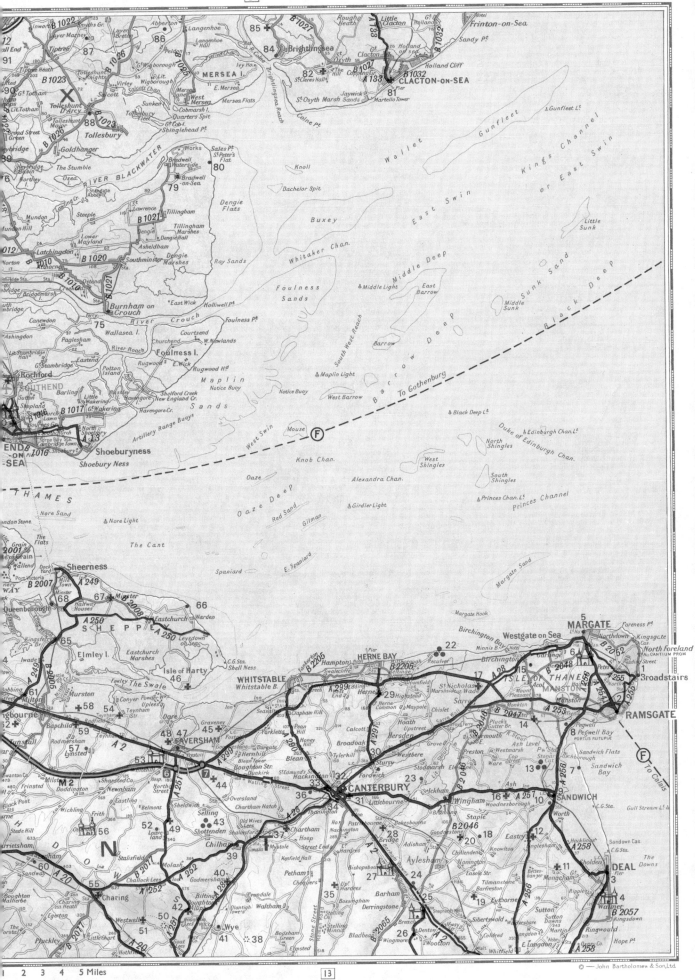

1 2 3 4 5 Miles

© — John Bartholomew & Son, Ltd.

Gazetteer to Maps 20·21

1. Broadstairs Jetty (1809)
   Bleak House (Dickens associations)
2. Ramsgate Harbour (completed 1776)
   St. George's Church
   St. Lawrence's Church
   St. Augustine's Abbey (Pugin)
   Wellington Crescent (Regency)
3. Deal (C18 houses)
   St. Leonard's Church
   St. George's Church
   Deal Castle (Henry VIII coastal fort)
   Town Hall (*Deal Museum*)
4. Walmer Castle (Henry VIII coastal fort) & *Gardens*
5. Margate Harbour (pier by Rennie, 1815)
   The Grotto (discovered 1837)
6. *Salmestone Grange* (part mediaeval)
7. Sandwich Bay (BTO Bird Observatory & plants)
8. St. Augustine Monument, Ebbsfleet
9. Sandwich (mediaeval port)
   St. Clement's Church
   St. Peter's Church
   Fisher Gate (C14–16)
   Barbican (Tudor) & Tollbridge
   Guildhall (C16; *museum*)
   Manwood Court (C16)
   Strand Street (C16 houses)
   Town Walls (promenade)
10. St. Bartholomew's Hospital (C13 almshouses), Sandwich
11. Northbourne Church
12. Eastry Church
13. *Richborough Castle* (Roman remains)
    Roman Amphitheatre
14. Minster-in-Thanet Church
    Minster Abbey (C11 remains)
15. *Powell-Cotton Museum* (zoological), Quex Park
16. Ash-by-Sandwich Church
17. St. Nicholas-at-Wade Church
18. Chillenden Post Mill
19. Barfreston Church
20. Goodnestone Church
21. Wingham Church & Village
22. Roman Fort, Reculver
    Reculver Towers (Norman church remains)
23. Wickhambreaux (village)
24. Old Smock Mill, Barham Downs
25. Broome Park (C17 ; hotel)
26. Denton (village)
27. *Charlton Park*, Bishopsbourne
28. Patrixbourne Church
29. Herne Church
30. Fordwich Church
    Town Hall (C15; ducking-stool crane)
31. St. Martin's Church, Canterbury
32. Canterbury Cathedral
    St. Augustine's Abbey & St. Pancras Church (C11–16 remains)
    St. Augustine's Abbey Museum
    Grey Friars (C13 remains)
    Black Friars (C13 remains)
    St. Thomas's Hospital (C12–14 almshouses)
    St. John's Hospital (Chapel & Tudor Hall)
    Poor Priests' Hospital (Buffs regimental museum)
    City Walls (Roman & mediaeval)
    West Gate (C14; *museum of arms*)
    Christ Church Gate (C16)
    Weavers' Houses (Tudor)
    Canterbury Royal Museum
    Roman Pavement, Butchery Lane
33. St. Dunstan's Church (head of Sir Thomas More), Canterbury

34. Dane John (mound, view), Canterbury
    Canterbury Castle (C12 keep)
    St. Mildred's Church
    Invicta (G. Stephenson's Locomotive, 1830)
35. Upper Hardres Church
36. Harbledown Church
    St. Nicholas Hospital (almshouses, c. 1840)
    View of Canterbury
37. Chartham Church
38. Wye Downs (chalk plants)
39. Chilham Church & Village
    Chilham Castle, Gardens
40. Godmersham Church (C12 Becket bas-relief)
41. Wye Church & Town
    Stour Bridge (1638)
42. Boughton Aluph Church
43. The Pulpit (earthwork, view)
    Perry Wood, Selling
44. Boughton-under-Blean Church
    Hawkins monument)
45. Graveney Church
46. Harty Church
47. Our Lady of Charity Church, Faversham
    Arden's House (C15)
    Freemasons' Hall (C16)
    Ship Hotel (part C16)
    Town Hall (1814, over earlier arcade)
    Boyle Tomb (C17), Preston Church
48. Davington Church & Monastic remains (C12)
49. Badlesmere Church
50. Eastwell Park (lake, walks, views)
51. Westwell Church
52. Leaveland Church & Court (C15)
53. Maison Dieu (C15 house), Ospringe
54. Teynham Church
55. Charing Church
    Archbishop's Manor House (C14 remains)
56. *Otterden Place* & Church
57. Lynsted Church & Village
58. Tonge Church
59. Bapchild Church
60. Lenham Church & Market Place
61. Milton Regis Church
    The Court Hall (museum)
62. Borden Church
63. Newington Church
64. Lower Halstow Church
65. Kingsferry Bridge (concrete liftbridge 1961)
66. Warden Point (view)
    Warden Manor
67. Minster-in-Sheppey Church & Priory Gatehouse
68. Queenborough Church & High Street
69. *Leecroft Art Gallery*, Westcliff-on-Sea
70. St. Mary's Church, Prittlewell
71. *Prittlewell Priory* (C12 : museum)
72. Hadleigh Church
73. Rayleigh Church
    Rayleigh Mount (Norman castle site) (NT)
74. Rochford Church
75. Burnham-on-Crouch Quay
76. All Saints Church, Maldon
    St. Peter's Library
    Moot Hall (C15)
77. Woodham Walter Church
    Bell Inn (C16)
78. *Beeleigh Abbey* (C12)
79. *Bradwell Lodge*
    Bradwell Bird Observatory
80. Site of Othona (Roman Fort) Bradwell
    St. Peter-on-the-Wall Church (C7)
81. St. James's Church, Clacton-on-Sea

82. St. Osyth Church
    St Osyth Priory & Gardens
84. Brightlingsea Quay
    Jacobe's Hall (C15)
85. All Saints Church, Brightlingsea
86. *Abberton Reservoir* (birds)
87. Layer Marney Gatehouse (C16) & Church
88. Tolleshunt D'Arcy Church & Hall (c. 1500)
89. Heybirdge Mill (Georgian)
90. Beacon Hill (view), Great Totham
91. Great Braxted Church, Braxted Park
92. Langford Church
93. Rivenhall Church
94. Faulkbourne Church
95. Little Baddow Church
96. Terling Smock Mill
97. Great Leighs Church
98. Ford End Church
99. Chignal Smealey Church
100. Pleshey Castle (motte & bailey, C15 bridge)
101. Black Chapel & Priest House (C15), North End
102. High Easter Church
103. Willingale Doe Church
     Willingale Spain Church
104. Great Canfield Church & Castle Mound
105. Post Mill, Aythorpe Roding
106. Writtle (village green)
107. St. Mary's Cathedral, Chelmsford
     Shire Hall (1792)
     Springfield, Barnes & Moulsham Mills (Georgian)
     Can Bridge (1788)
108. Danbury Church
109. Danbury Common (NT)
110. Runwell Church
111. St. Nicholas' Church & Priest's House (C15), Laindon
112. Corringham Church
113. Fobbing Church
114. South Benfleet Church
115. Hadleigh Castle (C14 remains)
116. Hollingbourne Church
117. View of Leeds Castle (C13, restored)
118. Leeds Church
119. Thurnham Castle (ruin, view)
120. *Stoneacre* (C15 house) (NT), Otham
121. Headcorn (village)
122. All Saints Church, Maidstone
     College of Secular Canons (C14 remains)
     Archbishop's Manor House (C14–16)
     Archbishop's Stables (Carriage Museum)
     Chillington House (C16: museum)
     Sir John Bank's Almshouses (1700)
123. *Boughton Monchelsea Place*
     View of Weald
124. Linton Church
125. *Allington Castle* (C13)
126. Kit's Coty House (chamber of long barrow)
127. Aylesford Bridge (C14)
     St. Peter's Church
     Holy Trinity Almshouses (1610)
     The Friars (C13–14 remains)
128. East Farleigh Bridge (C15)
129. Hunton Church
130. Barming Church
     Barming Place (1768)
131. *Starkey Castle*
132. Teston Bridge (Tudor)
133. Yalding Church & Village
     C15 Bridge
134. C15 Bridge, Yalding
135. Nettlestead Church
     Nettlestead Place Gateway (C14) & Barn

136. *St. Mary's Abbey* (C11 & C15 remains), West Malling
137. St. Leonard's Tower (Norman)
138. *Mereworth Castle*
139. Coldrum Long Barrow (NT)
140. Trottiscliffe Church
141. Mereworth Church
142. West Peckham Church
143. Gover Hill (view over Weald) (NT)
144. Meopham Green (Windmill & Cricket Ground)
145. *Great Comp Garden*
146. *Old Soar Manor* (NT)
147. Wrotham Church
148. Wrotham Hill (view)
149. Ightham Church
150. Plaxtol Church
151. Somerhill Park
152. Tonbridge Castle (C12–14 remains)
    Portreeve's House (Tudor)
    Chequers Inn (Tudor)
    Rose & Crown Hotel (Georgian fronted Tudor)
153. *Ightham Mote* (mediaeval moated house)
154. Oldbury Hill (hillfort, views) (NT)
    Styants Wood (NT)
155. Wray Common Windmill (1824), Reigate
156. Bletchingley Church & Village
157. Outwood Post Mill (1665)
158. Godstone Green
159. Stone Church
160. Gatton Church
    Old Town Hall (temple, 1765)
161. St. John's Church, Upper Norwood
162. St. Peter & St. Paul's Church, Bromley
    Bromley College (almshouses, 1666)
163. Geffery's Almshouses (1912), Mottingham
164. *Eltham Palace* (Banqueting Hall, 1479)
165. St. Mary's Church, Bexley
    Hall Place (C16 & C17) & Park
166. *St. John's Jerusalem, Garden & Chapel* (NT)
167. Darenth Church
168. Holy Trinity Church, Dartford
    Borough Museum
169. Christ Church, Bexleyheath
    Danson Park & *Mansion*
    The Red House (William Morris, 1859), Upton
170. Rainham Church & *Hall* (NT)
171. All Saints Church, West Ham
    Passmore Edwards Museum, Ranford Road
172. Stifford Church
173. Southfleet Church
174. St. Botolph's Church, Northfleet
175. All Saints Church, Perry Street
176. St. George's Church, Gravesend
    Gordon Promenade (view of shipping)
177. Tilbury Fort (1682)
178. Cliffe-at-Hoo Church
179. Cooling Church & Castle Gatehouse (C15)
180. Upnor Castle (C16 fort)
181. Rainham Church
182. Naval Dockyard (C18 & C19 buildings), Chatham
    St. Bartholomew's Hospital Chapel (Norman)
    Hawkins' Almshouses (C19)
    Royal Engineers Museum
    Gordon Monument
183. Watts' Charity (C16 almshouse), Rochester
    Restoration House (1587)
    Eastgate House (1591; museum)

Guildhall (1687)
    Bull Hotel (Dickens associations)
184. Frindsbury Church
185. Rochester Cathedral
    Rochester Castle (C12)
    Minor Canons Row (C18)
186. *Temple Manor*, Strood
187. *Cobham Hall, House & Gardens*
188. *Luddesdown Court* (part mediaeval)
189. Cobham Church & Village
    Cobham College (C14–16 almshouses)
190. *Owletts, House & Garden* (NT)
191. *Nurstead Court* (C14 hall)
192. Ash-by-Wrotham Church
193. Water Mill (Georgian), Farningham
194. Eynsford Church
    Eynsford Castle (C12 ruin)
    Packhorse Bridge (C15)
    Little Mote (Tudor House)
195. *Lullingstone Roman Villa*
196. *Lullingstone Castle, Gardens & Church*
197. Shoreham Church
198. Otford Church
    Archbishop's Manor House (Tudor ruin)
199. Kemsing Church
200. One Tree Hill (Roman cemetery, views) (NT)
201. *Knole* (house) (NT)
202. Knole Park, Sevenoaks
203. *Penshurst Place*
    Penshurst Church
    Leicester Square (C15 cottages)
204. Chiddingstone Church & Village (part NT)
    Chiddingstone Castle
205. Hever Church
    Hever Castle & Gardens
206. Toys Hill (woodland, views) (NT)
    Brasted Chart
    Parson's Marsh (woodland) (NT)
    Scord's Wood (NT)
    Emmetts, shrub gardens (NT)
207. Old Meeting House (1716; Unitarian Church), Bessels Green
208. *Chartwell* (NT)
209. Mariner's Hill (views) (NT)
210. Westerham Church
    Quebec House (NT)
211. *Squerryes Court, House & Garden*
212. Chevening Church & Park
213. *Down House* (Darwin's home), Downe
214. St. John's Church, West Wickham
    Wickham Court (C15, restored)
215. Addiscombe Church
216. *The Old Palace*, Croydon
    St. Michael & All Angels Church
    Whitgift Hospital (almshouses, 1596)
217. St. Mary's Church, Beddington
218. All Saints Church, Carshalton
    Carshalton House & Garden
219. Chipstead Church
220. Chaldon Church
221. Hanging Wood (views) (NT), Tandridge
222. *Puttenden Manor* (early Tudor)
223. Lingfield Church
    College Guest House (C15)
    Butcher's Shop (C16)
    Village Lock-up (1763)
224. *Queen Elizabeth's Hunting Lodge* (Epping Forest Museum), Chingford
225. Loughton Camp (earthwork)
226. Monk Wood, Epping Forest
227. Ambersbury Banks (earthwork)
228. *Forty Hall* (C17; museum), Enfield
229. Temple Bar (Wren, 1672), Theobald's Park, Cheshunt

230. Eleanor Cross (C13), Waltham Cross
231. Waltham Abbey Church & Gatehouse (C14)
    Harold's Bridge (C14)
232. St. John Baptist's Church, Epping
233. Greensted Church (Saxon)
234. St. Martin's Church, Chipping Ongar
    Saxon Castle Mound
235. Hatfield Broad Oak Church
236. Sawbridgeworth Church
    Burton's Flour Mill (Georgian)
237. St. James's Church, Stanstead Abbots
238. Rye House Gateway (c. 1443), Hoddesdon
239. Broxbourne Church
240. Great Amwell Church
    New River Source & Myddleton Monument (1800)
241. St. Mary's Church, Ware
    Bluecoat House (C15–17)
    The Priory (C15–19)
    Canons Maltings (c. 1600)
    Corn Storehouses in Star Street (C17)
    Riverside Gazebos (C18 & C19)
242. St. Leonard's Church, Bengeo
243. Christ's Hospital School (part C17)
244. All Saints Church, Hertford
    St. Andrew's Street (C16–18 houses)
    Friends' Meeting House (1670)
    Lombard House (C17)
    Shire Hall (James Adam, 1769)
    Hertford Castle (Norman to C19)
    Hertford Museum
245. Tewin Mill (C18)
246. Essendon Church (Wedgwood font)
247. *Abbey Art Centre & Museum*, New Barnet
248. Lambourne Church
249. Hainault Forest
250. King's Head Inn (C17), Chigwell
251. St. John's Church, Friern Barnet
    Campe Almshouses (1612)
252. *Broomfield House* (C17; Southgate Museum)
    Grovelands Hospital (Nash, 1797)
253. All Hallows Church, Tottenham
    All Hallows Vicarage (1620 & Georgian)
    Bruce Castle (Elizabethan; Post Office Museum)
254. Monoux Almshouses (c. 1760), Walthamstow
    Vestry House (C18; museum)
255. St. Mary's Church, Wanstead
256. *Valence House* (C17; museum), Dagenham
257. St. Mary's Church, East Ham
258. St. Margaret's Church & Abbey Gate Tower (C12), Barking
259. Eastbury House (C16 manor house) (NT), Barking
260. Upminster Smock Mill
261. Horndon-on-the-Hill Church (view)
    Old Market Hall (C16)
262. East Horndon Church
263. Great Warley Church
264. Ingrave Church
265. White Hart Hotel (Tudor courtyard), Brentwood
266. South Weald Church Tower (c. 1500)
    Browne's Almshouses (1858)
267. Shenfield Church
268. Mountnessing Church & Hall (Georgian & earlier)
269. Mountnessing Post Mill (C17)
270. *Ingatestone Hall*
271. Ingatestone Church
272. Margaretting Church
273. Post Mill (C18), Fryerning
274. Blackmore Church
275. Stondon Massey Church

Map 22

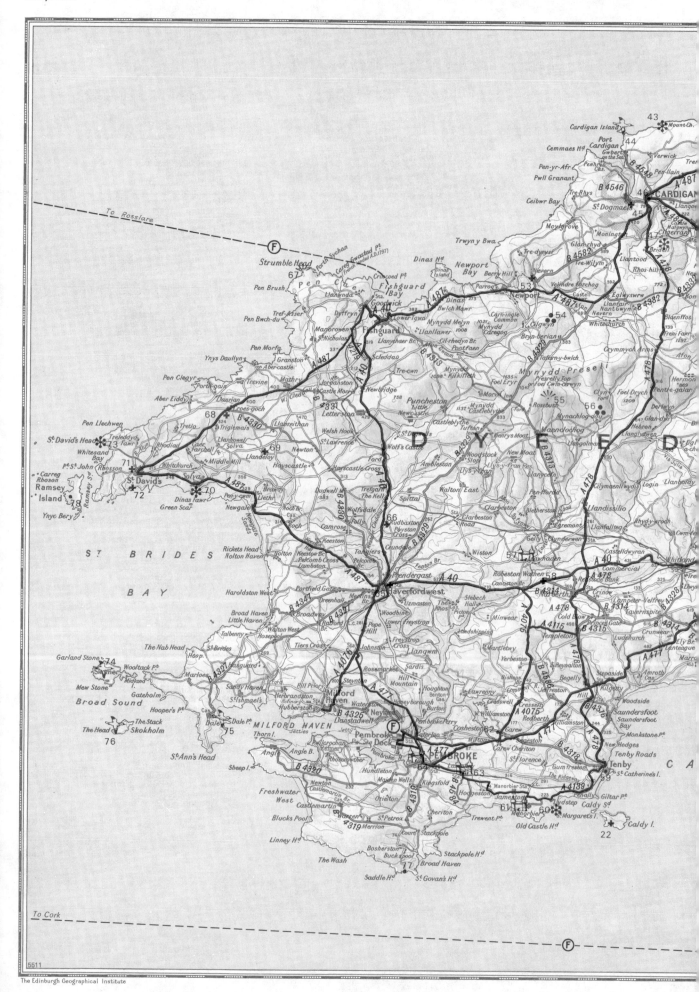

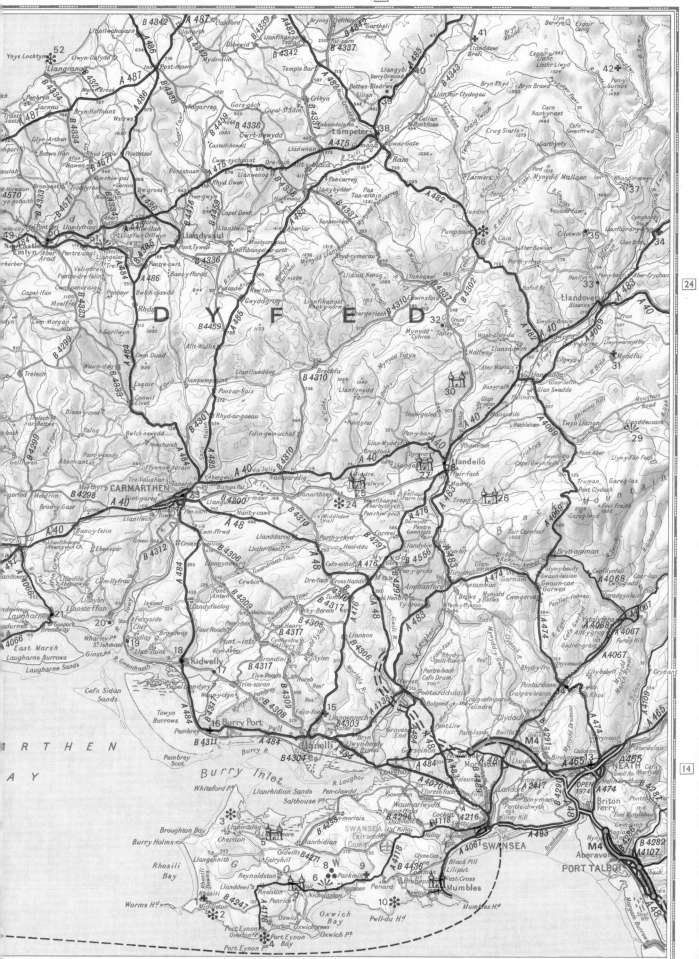

Map 23

© — John Bartholomew & Son.Ltd.

Gazetteer to Maps 22·23

1. St. Mary's Church, Rhossili
2. Thurba Head (cliff scenery) (NT), Gower
3. Whitford Burrows (birds and plants) (NT)
4. Port Eynon to Worms Head (geology, birds, plants) (NC & NT)
5. *Weobley Castle* (C13–14 remains)
6. Cefn Bryn (views)
7. *Penrice Castle* (C12 ruins & C18)
8. Parc Le Breos (long cairn)
9. Ilston (remains first Baptist church in Glamorgan)
10. Pennard & Bishopston Valley (headland & incised valley) (NT)
11. Oystermouth Castle (C13 remains)
12. *Royal Institution of South Wales* (c. 1835), Swansea
13. Neath Abbey (C12 remains)
14. Pontardawe Bridge (mid-C18)
15. Adulam Baptist Chapel (baptismal pool), Felin-foel
16. Pembrey Church
17. Pont Spwdwr (mediaeval bridge)
18. Kidwelly Church
    Kidwelly Castle (C13 & C14 remains)
19. St. Ishmael's Church
    Tregoning Hill (views) (NT)
20. Llansteffan Castle (C11–13 remains) & Village
21. Laugharne Castle (C13 remains) & Town
    St. Martin's Church
22. *Caldy Abbey*
23. St. Peter's Church, Carmarthen
    Castle Gatehouse (C14)
    Carmarthen Bridge (ancient, rebuilt 1938)
    County Museum

24. Paxton's Tower (1807), Llanarthney (NT)
25. Dryslwyn Castle (ruin)
26. Carreg Cennen Castle (C13 remains, view)
27. Old Dynevor Castle (C13 remains)
28. Llandeilo Bridge (Williams, c. 1845)
29. Llanddeusant (views)
30. *Taliaris Park* (C17 house)
31. Myddfai Church
32. Talley Abbey (C12 remains) & Lakes
33. Dolau-Hirion Bridge (1773)
34. Llanfair-ar-y-bryn Church
35. Cilycwm Church & Village
36. Dolaucothi (Goldmines & scenery) (NT)
37. Rhandir-Mwyn, Vale of Towy (scenery)
38. *St. David's College* (1822), Lampeter
39. Derry Ormond Tower (c. 1780)
40. Llangybi (village & holy well)
41. Llanddewi Brefi Church
42. Soar-y-Mynydd Chapel
43. Mwnt (views) (NT)
44. Cardigan Island (birds)
45. St. Dogmael's Abbey (C13–15 remains)
46. Cardigan Castle (C12 remains)
    Cardigan Bridge (view)
47. Cilgerran Castle (C13 ruin) (NT)
48. Llechryd Bridge (C17)
49. Cenarth Bridge & Falls
50. Old Pierced Bridge, Newcastle Emlyn
51. Henllan Bridge (views)
52. Lochtyn (views) (NT), Llangranog
53. Nevern Church

54. Pentre Ifan Burial Chamber
55. Prescelly Hills (views)
56. Gors Fawr Stone Circle, Mynachlogddu
57. Llawhaden Castle (C14 remains)
58. Robeston Wathen Church
59. Tenby Harbour
    St. Mary's Church
    Tenby Castle (C13 remains)
    Five Arches (C14 town gateway)
    Plantagenet House
    Tudor Merchant's House (NT)
    Tenby Museum
60. Lydstep Caves (NT)
61. *Manorbier Castle* (C12–16)
62. *Carew Castle* (C13–16)
    Carew Cross (Celtic)
63. Bishop's Palace (C13–14), Lamphey
64. Pembroke Castle (C12–13)
65. St. Mary's Church, Haverfordwest
    County Museum
66. Rudbaxton Church
67. Strumble Head (views)
68. Croes-goch Chapel
69. Llandeloy Church
70. Solva Harbour (NT)
71. St. David's Cathedral
    Bishop's Palace (C13–14)
72. St. Non's Chapel & Holy Well
73. St. David's Head (NT)
74. *Skomer Island* (seabirds) (NC)
75. Dale Fort (Field Studies Centre)
76. *Skokholm Island* (BTO seabird colony, bird observatory, Field Studies Centre)
77. St. Govan's Head (cliff scenery)
    St. Govan's Chapel (mediaeval)
78. *Ramsey Island* (seal colony)

Map 24

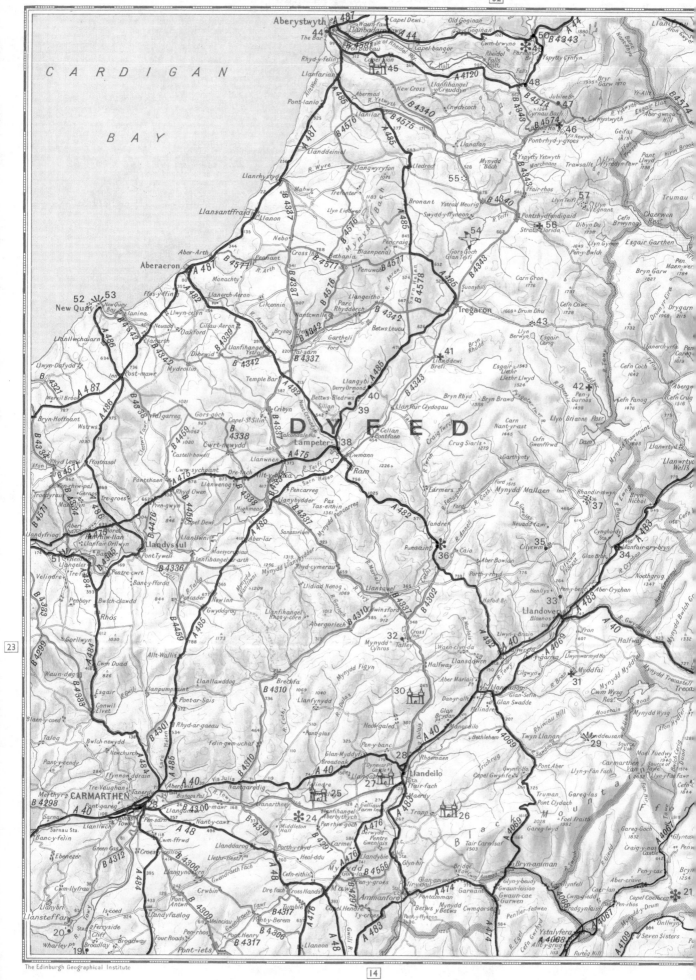

CARDIGAN

BAY

DYFED

Aberystwyth

Aberaeron

New Quay

Tregaron

Lampeter

Llandyssul

CARMARTHEN

Llandeilo

Llandovery

Ammanford

The Edinburgh Geographical Institute

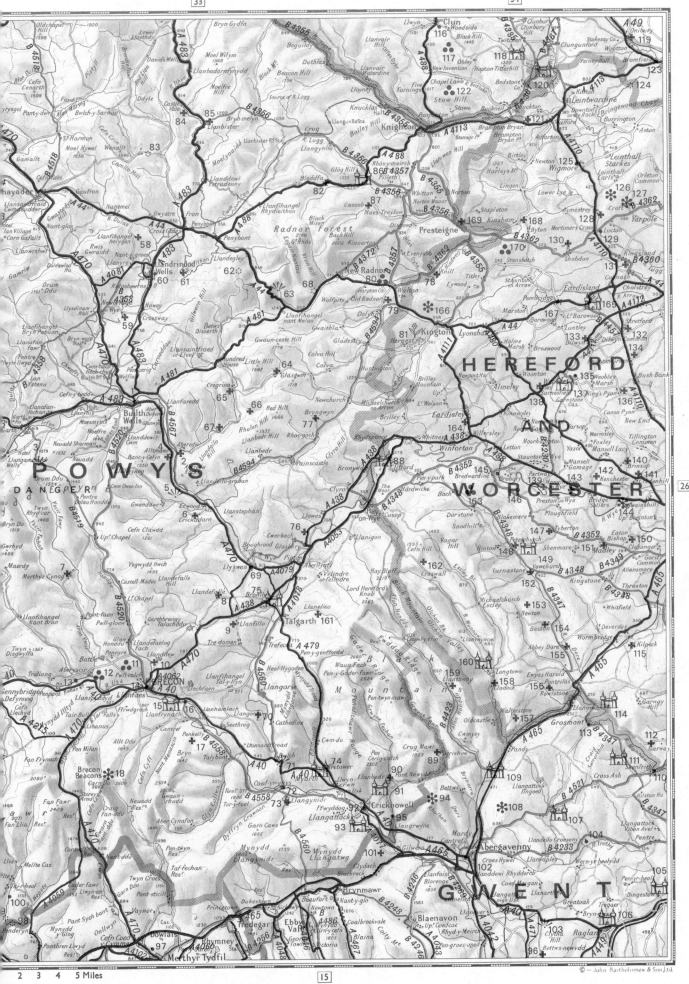

Map 25

© — John Bartholomew & Son Ltd.

Gazetteer to Maps 24·25

1. Builth Bridge (C18)
2. Aberedw Church
3. Eppynt Mountain View
4. Alltmawr Church
5. Twmpath Hill (view of Wye Valley)
6. Crickadarn Church
7. Merthyr-Cynog Church
8. Llandefalle Church
9. Llanfillo Church
10. Llanddew Church
11. Pen-y-Crug (hillfort)
12. Brecon Gaer (Roman fort), Aberyscir
13. Aber-Bran Bridge (C17)
14. Brecon Cathedral
    Calvinistic Methodist Chapel
    Brecon Castle (C12–13 remains)
    Usk Bridge (1563)
    Brecknock Museum
15. *Abercynrig* (c. 1650 manor house)
16. Usk Bridge & Aqueduct, Llanfrynach
17. Llanfigan Church
18. Pen-y-Fan (2906 ft), Brecon Beacons (NT)
19. St. Ishmael's Church
    Tregoning Hill (views) (NT)
20. Llansteffan Castle (C11–13 remains) & Village
21. Henrhyd Falls (NT), Coelbren
22. Scwdeinon Gam (waterfall), Pont-Nedd Fechan
23. St. Peter's Church, Carmarthen
    Castle Gatehouse (C14)
    Carmarthen Bridge (ancient, rebuilt 1938)
    County Museum
24. Paxton's Tower (1807), Llanarthney (NT)
25. Dryslwyn Castle (ruin)
26. Carreg Cennen Castle (C13 remains, view)
27. Old Dynevor Castle (C13 remains)
28. Llandello Bridge (Williams, c. 1845)
29. Llanddeusant (views)
30. *Taliaris Park* (C17 house)
31. Myddfai Church
32. Talley Abbey (C12 remains) & Lakes
33. Dolau-Hirion Bridge (1773)
34. Llanfair-ar-y-bryn Church
35. Cilycwm Church & Village
36. Dolaucothi (Goldmines & scenery) (NT)
37. Rhandir-Mwyn, Vale of Towy (scenery)
38. *St. David's College* (1822), Lampeter
39. Derry Ormond Tower (c. 1780)
40. Llangybi (village & holy well)
41. Llanddewi Brefi Church
42. Soar-y-Mynydd Chapel
43. Mountain Road from Tregaron to Llanwrtyd Wells
44. Aberystwyth Castle (C13 remains)
    Old Town Hall (1770)
    National Library of Wales
    University College of Wales Museums
    Pendinas (hillfort, Wellington Monument, view)
    Light Railway to Devil's Bridge via Rheidol Valley
45. *Nanteos* (C18 house & stables)
46. Hafod Church, Ystwyth Valley
47. Johnes' Arch (1810)
48. Devil's Bridge (triple bridge: mediaeval, 1753 & 1901)
    Hafod Arms Hotel (view)
    Mynach, Gyfarllwyd & Nant Llettys Falls, Rheidol Gorge
49. Bryn Bras (sheep farm above Rheidol Gorge) (NT)

50. Ponterwyd Old Bridge
51. Henllan Bridge (views)
52. Craig-yr-Adar (Birds Rock)
53. New Quay Head (300 ft; view)
54. Tregaron Bog (nature reserve)
55. Caradog Falls, Ystrad Meurig
56. Strata Florida Abbey (C12 remains)
57. Teifi Pools
58. Llanfihangel-helygen Church
59. Disserth Church
60. *Radnorshire County Museum*, Llandrindod Wells
61. Cefallys Church
62. Llandegley Rocks (escarpment)
63. Tomen (castle site, view), Llanfihangel-nant-Melan
64. Glascwm Church
65. Cregrina Church
66. Rhulen Church
67. Llanbadarn-y-garreg Church
68. Water-Break-Its-Neck (waterfall)
69. Llyswen (village)
70. Llangasty-Tal-y-Llyn Church
71. Bwlch (view of Usk Valley)
72. Llangynidr Bridge (mediaeval)
73. Llangynidr Church
74. Tretower Castle (C13 keep)
    Tretower Court (mediaeval fortified manor)
75. Bronllys Castle (C12–13)
76. Maes-yr-onen Chapel (C17)
77. Bryngwyn Church (view)
78. Knill Church
    Churchyard Cross (C14)
79. Old Radnor Church
80. The Four Stones (Bronze Age standing stones), Walton
81. *Hergest Croft Garden*, Kington
82. Bleddfa Church
83. Abbey Cwmhir (valley)
84. Llananno Church, Ithon Valley
85. Llanbister Church
86. *Monaughty* (Tudor manor house)
87. Cascob Church
88. Clifford Castle (C13 remains)
89. Partrishow Church
90. Llanbedr Church
91. *Moor Park* (c. 1750 house), Llanbedr
92. Crickhowell Bridge (C17) & Town
    Porth-Mawr (C14 gatehouse)
    Crickhowell Castle (Norman remains, view)
93. *Plas Llangattock* (Regency)
94. Sugar Loaf (1955 ft; views) (NT)
95. Llangenny Church
    Old Bridge, Grwyne Valley
96. Bettws-Newydd Church
97. Cyfarthfa Castle (1825; *museum*) & Park
98. Scwd-yr-Eira (waterfall), Penderyn
99. Clyn-Gwyn Falls, Mellte Gorge
100. Porth-yr-Ogof Cavern, Ystradfellte
101. Llanelly Church
102. Abergavenny Castle (C12 ruin)
     St. Mary's Church (tombs)
     Abergavenny & District Museum
103. Clytha Castle (C18 folly, views)
104. Llantilio Crossenny Church
     Hen Gwrt (moated mediaeval house site)
105. *Treowen* (C16 manor house)
106. Raglan Castle (C15–17 remains)
107. White Castle (C12–13 remains), Llanvetherine
108. Skirrid Fawr (1596 ft; views) (NT)
109. *Llanvihangel Court*
110. Skenfrith Church
     Skenfrith Castle (C11–13 remains) (NT)
111. *Blackbrook House* (Georgian)

112. Garway Church
     Dovecote (of the Knights Templar, C14)
113. Grosmont Church
     Grosmont Castle (C13 & C14 remains)
114. *Kentchurch Court* (C14 & John Nash, 1824)
115. Kilpeck Church
116. Clun Church
     Trinity Hospital (almshouses, 1614)
     Clun Castle (Norman ruin)
     Clun Town Trust Museum
117. Pen-y-Wern Stone Circle
118. Hopton Castle (ruined keep)
119. Onibury Church
120. *Heath House* (C17), Leintwardine
121. Brampton Bryan Church
122. Caer Caradoc Camp
123. St. Mary's Church, Bromfield
     Priory Gatehouse (mediaeval)
124. Bringewood Forge Bridge (C18)
     Teme Gorge
125. Wigmore Church & Castle (Norman ruin)
126. Croft Ambrey (hillfort, view) (NT)
     Fishpool Valley (NT)
127. *Croft Castle* (NT) & *Church*
128. Aymestrey Church
129. Mortimer's Cross Watermill (C18)
130. Shobdon Church
     Norman Arches from old church
131. Kingsland Church
132. Stretford Church
133. Dilwyn Church
134. Birley Church
135. Weobley Church & Village
136. King's Pyon Church
137. *The Ley* (1589), Weobley
138. Sarnesfield Church
139. Monnington-On-Wye Church
140. Brinsop Church
141. Credenhill Church
142. Bishopstone Church
143. Byford Church
144. *The Weir*, *Gardens* (NT), Swainshill
145. Bredwardine Church
     Wye Bridge (1769)
146. Moccas Church, *Moccas Court*
147. Tyberton Church
     Churchyard Cross (C14)
148. Peterchurch Church
149. *Wellbrook Manor* (C14 hall), Peterchurch
150. Eaton Bishop Church
151. Madley Church
152. Vowchurch Church
153. St. Margaret's Church
154. Bacton Church
155. Abbey Dore Church
156. Rowlstone Church
157. Walterstone Church
     Churchyard Cross (C15) & View
158. Clodock Church
159. Llanthony Priory (C13 remains)
160. Longtown Castle (Norman ruin)
161. Llanelieu Church
162. Craswall Priory (C13 remains)
163. Arthur's Stone (megalithic burial chamber), Dorstone
164. Eardisley Church
165. *Burton Court* (C14 hall)
166. Bradnor Hill (NT)
167. Pembridge (village)
     St. Mary's Church & Belfry (C14)
     Market Hall (C15)
168. Kinsham Church
169. Presteigne Church
170. Wapley Hill (hillfort, views)

Map 26

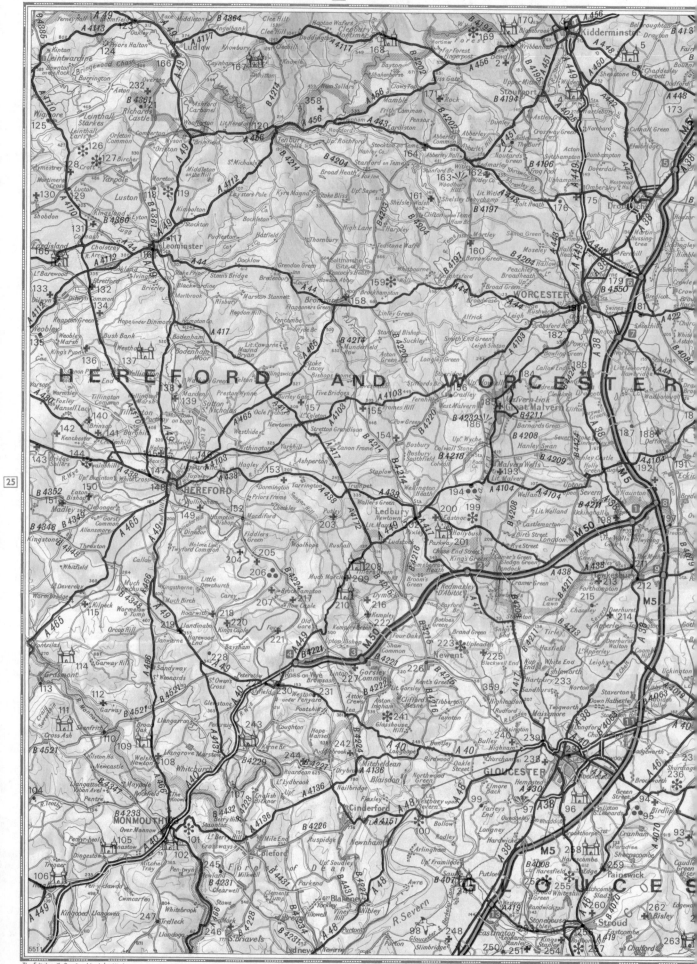

Map 27

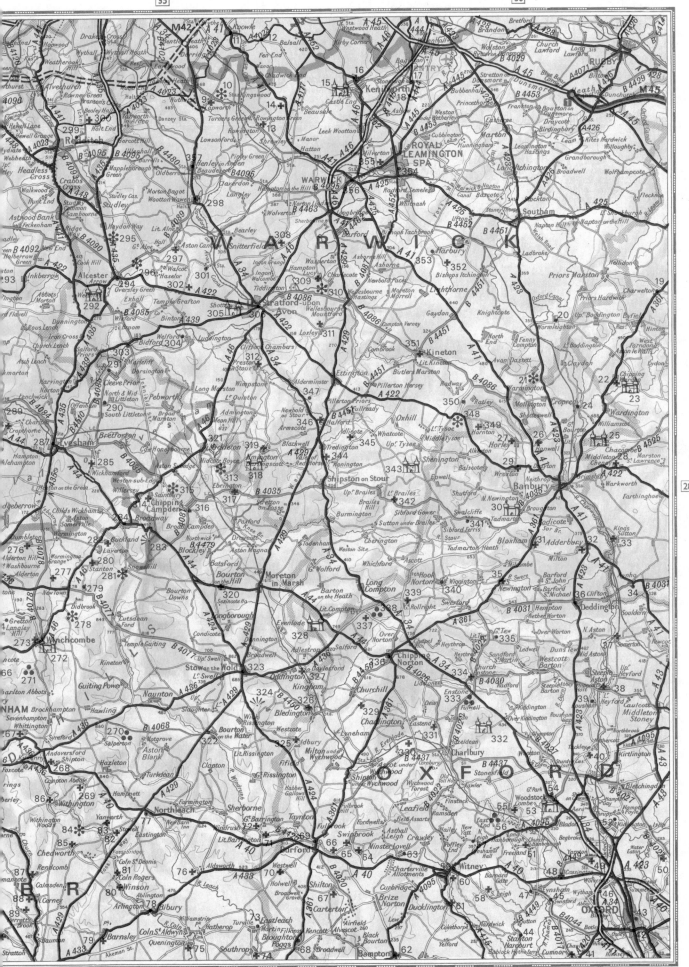

1 2 3 4 5 Miles

© — John Bartholomew & Son, Ltd.

1. St. Anne's Church, Bewdley
   Recorder's House (1610)
   Severn Bridge (Telford, 1800)
2. Ribbesford Church
3. St. Mary's Church, Kidderminster
   Museum & Art Gallery
4. *Hartlebury Castle*
5. *Harvington Hall*
6. Chaddesley Corbett Church
   Delabere Almshouses (1637)
   Talbot Inn (1600)
7. Sling Pool (wooded valley) (NT),
   Clent Hills
8. St. John Baptist's Church,
   Bromsgrove
9. Lapworth Church
10. *Packwood House & Gardens* (NT)
11. Knowle Church
    Guild House (C15)
12. Temple Balsall Church
    Leveson Hospital (almshouses, 1677)
13. Rowington Church
14. Wroxall Abbey Church
    Priory Remains (C14)
15. *Kenilworth Castle* (C12–16)
16. Kenilworth Abbey (C14 remains)
17. Stoneleigh Church
    Alice Leigh's Almshouses (C17)
18. Stare Bridge (C15), Stoneleigh Park
19 to 53 Refer to Gazetteer 28/29
54. Woodstock Town Hall
    (Chambers, 1766)
    Chaucer's House (rebuilt C18)
    Hope House (early C18)
55. Combe Church
56. North Leigh Roman Villa (remains)
57. North Leigh Church & Windmill
58. South Leigh Church
59. Witney Church
    Butter Cross (C17)
    Town Hall (C18)
60. Cogges Church
61. Ducklington Church
62. Bampton Church
63. Minster Lovell Church
    Minster Lovell Hall (C15 remains)
64. Asthall Church
65. Swinbrook Church
66. Widford Church
67. Shilton Church
68. Filkins Church
    Filkins & Broughton Poggs Museum
69. Burford (town)
    St. John Baptist's Church
    Grammar School (C15–16)
    Old Tolsey (C16; *museum*)
    Old Vicarage (1672)
    Great House (1690), Witney Street
70. Westwell Church
71. Little Barrington Church
72. Great Barrington Church
73. Eastleach Turville Church
    Eastleach Martin Church
    Keble's Bridge (clapper)
74. Southrop Church
75. Quenington Church
76. Aldsworth Church
77. Northleach Church
    Dutton's Almshouses (C17)
78. Bibury (village)
    St. Mary's Church
    Arlington Row & Rack Isle (C17
    wool factory & drying field) (NT)
    Arlington Mill (C17)
79. Barnsley Church
80. Winson Church
81. Coln Rogers Church
82. Stowell Church
83. Yanworth Church
84. *Chedworth Roman Villa* (NT)
85. Chedworth Church
86. Withington Church
87. Rendcomb Church
88. North Cerney Church
    Churchyard Cross (C14)

89. Bagendon Church
90. Daglingworth Church
91. Duntisbourne Rouse Church
    Churchyard Cross (C14)
92. Elkstone Church
93. Brimpsfield Church
94. Great Witcombe Church
95. Witcombe Roman Villa (remains)
96. *Matson House* (C16)
97. Stone Bench (viewpoint for Severn
    Bore), Elmore
98. *Wildfowl Trust Grounds*, Slimbridge
99. Guise Mausoleum (C18), Elmore
100. Westbury-on-Severn Church
     Westbury Court Garden
     (early water-garden) (NT)
101. The Kymin (hill, views) (NT)
     Naval Temple (1802) (NT)
     The Round House (C18 tower) (NT)
102. *Troy House* (C15–17), Monmouth
103. Monmouth Castle (C12 remains)
     Great Castle House (1673)
     Monnow Bridge (C13)
     Shire Hall (1724)
     Nelson Museum
104. Llantilio Crossenny Church
     Hen Gwrt (moated mediaeval
     house site)
105. *Treowen* (C16 manor house)
106. Raglan Castle (C15–17 remains)
107. Symonds Yat (r. Wye gorge)
108. Welsh Newton Church
109. *Pembridge Castle* (C13)
110 to 115 Refer to Gazetteer 24/25
116. Leominster Priory Church
     Grange Court (re-erected old Town
     Hall of 1633)
117. Eaton Hall Bridge (C16), Leominster
118. Eye Manor & Church
119. *Berrington Hall* (NT)
120. Burford Church
     Burford House Gardens
121. Richard's Castle (Norman castle
     site, views)
     St. Bartholomew's Church
123 to 136 Refer to Gazetteer 24/25
137. *Dinmore Manor*
138. Laystone Bridge (C17)
139. Marden Church
140. Brinsop Church
141. Credenhill Church
142. Bishopstone Church
143. Byford Church
144. *The Weir, Gardens* (NT), Swainshill
145. Holmer Church
146. Lugg Bridges (C14 & C17),
     Lugwardine
147. Plague Cross (C14), Hereford
148. Hereford Cathedral
     Cathedral Chained Library
     All Saints Church & Chained
     Library
     Coningsby Hospital (1614) &
     Blackfriars Preaching Cross (C14)
     Aubrey Almshouses (C17)
     The Old House (1621; museum)
     Wye Bridge (part C15)
     City Museum & Art Gallery
149. Rotherwas Chapel (C16)
150. Eaton Bishop Church
151. Madley Church
152. Mordiford Bridge (part mediaeval)
153. Stoke Edith Church
154. Bosbury Church
     Churchyard Cross (mediaeval)
155. Castle Frome Church
156. Cradley Parish Hall (C15)
157. Much Cowarne Church
158. Bromyard Church
159. *Lower Brockhampton House* (NT)
160. Martley Church
161. Shelsley Walsh Church
162. Great Witley Church, Witley Park
163. Woodbury Hill (hillfort, views)
164. Stockton-on-Teme Church

165. *Burton Court* (C14 hall)
166. *Ludlow Castle* (C11–16)
     St. Laurence's Church
     Hosyer's Almshouses (rebuilt 1758)
     Broad Gate (mediaeval)
     The Reader's House (mediaeval &
     C17)
     Feathers Hotel (1603)
     Butter Cross (1744; *Ludlow Museum*)
     Ludford Bridge (mediaeval)
     Dinham Bridge (1823)
167. *Whitton Court*
168. *Mawley Hall*
169. Knowles Mill (NT), Wyre Forest
170. *Dowles Manor* (C16), Bewdley
171. Rock Church
172. Astley Church
     Old Watermill
173. *Grafton Manor* (part C16),
     Bromsgrove
174. Stoke Prior Church
175. Ombersley Church
176. Holt Church
     Holt Castle (Norman tower & hall)
     Holt Fleet Bridge (Telford, 1828)
177. Himbleton Church
178. Huddington Church
179. Warndon Church
180. Worcester Cathedral
     All Saints Church
     St. Swithun's Church
     Berkeley Hospital (almshouses, 1702)
     Edgar Tower (C14)
     The Commandery
     (mediaeval hospital)
     The Grey Friars (C15 house) (NT)
     Guildhall (1723)
     Royal Porcelain Works
     The Dyson Perrins Museum (porcelain)
     City Museum & Art Gallery
     Severn Bridge (Gwynne, 1771,
     restored)
     Fort Royal (view)
181. Spetchley Church
     Spetchley Park, Gardens
182. Powick Bridge (mediaeval)
183. Kempsey Church
184. Newland Church & Beauchamp
     Almshouses (1864)
185. Malvern Priory Church
186. Worcestershire Beacon (1395 ft;
     views), Malvern Hills
187. Croome D'Abitot Church
     Croome Court (mid-C18)
188. Besford Church
189. Pershore Abbey Church
190. Pershore Bridge (C17)
191. Eckington Bridge (1728)
192. Strensham Church
193. Little Malvern Church
194. Herefordshire Beacon (hillfort, views)
195. Bredon Hill (hillfort, views)
196. Overbury Church
197. Bredon Church, Rectory & Village
     Tithe Barn (C14) (NT)
198. Ripple Church
199. Midsummer Hill (hillfort, view) (NT)
200. Eastnor Church
201. *Eastnor Castle* (1808)
202. Ledbury (town)
     St. Michael's Church
     St. Katherine's Hospital
     (C14 almshouses)
     Market Hall (C17)
203. Putley Church
     Churchyard Cross (C14)
204. Holme Lacy Church
205. Fownhope Church
206. Capler Camp (hillfort, view)
207. Brockhampton-by-Ross Church
208. *Hellens*, Much Marcle
209. Much Marcle Church
210. *Homme House* (C16 & C18),
     Much Marcle
211. Mythe Bridge (Telford)

212. Tewkesbury Abbey Church
     Old Baptist Chapel (C17)
     Avon Bridge (part C13)
213. Forthampton Church
214. Deerhurst Church (Saxon)
     Odda's Chapel (Saxon)
215. Chaceley Church & *Hall*
     (part C15–16)
216. St. Mary's Church, Kempley
217. How Caple Church
218. Hoarwithy Church
219. Llandinabo Church
220. King's Caple Church
221. Foy Church
222. St. Edward's Church, Kempley
223. Eden's Hill (views) (NT), Upleadon
224. Bishop's Cleeve Church
225. Upleadon Church Tower
226. Newent Church
     Market Hall (C16)
227. Linton-by-Ross Church
228. Hentland Church & Churchyard
     Cross (C14)
     Pengethly Park (NT)
229. Wilton Bridge (1597), Ross-on-Wye
230. St. Mary's Church, Ross-on-Wye
     Market House (1670)
     The Prospect (view) & Kyrle's
     Gateways (1700)
231. Weston-under-Penyard Church
     Weston Hall (c. 1600)
232. All Saints Church, Richard's Castle
233. Ashleworth Church
     Ashleworth Court (C15) & Tithe
     Barn (C15) (NT)
     Ashleworth Manor (Tudor)
234. St. Paul's Church, Cheltenham
     The Promenade
     Pittville Pump Room (1825)
     Art Gallery & Museum
     Cheltenham College Museum
     Thirlestaine House (1823–50;
     Cheltenham College)
235. Devil's Chimney (rock pinnacle,
     view), Leckhampton
236. The Scrubbs (hillfort, views) (NT)
     Crickley Hill
237. Gloucester Cathedral
     St. Mary-de-Crypt Church
     St. John's Church
     St. Nicholas' Church, Westgate Street
     New Inn (C15 pilgrims' hostel)
     Robert Raikes' House (C16)
     Bishop Hooper's Lodging
     (C15; museum)
     City Museum
238. Llanthony Priory (C15 remains),
     Gloucester
239. Over Bridge (Telford, 1830)
240. Highnam Church
241. May Hill (view of ten counties) (NT)
242. Mitcheldean Church
243. *Goodrich Castle* (C12–14 remains)
244. Ruardean Church
245. Newland Church
     Almshouses (C17)
     Great Oak
246. St. Briavels Church
247. Trelleck Church & Village
248. Slimbridge Church
249. *Frampton Court*, Frampton-on-Severn
250. Tithe Barn (C13), Frocester
251. Leonard Stanley Church & Priory
     remains (Norman)
252. Haresfield Beacon (hillfort, views)
     (NT)
253. Stanley Mill (textile, 1813),
     Stonehouse
254. Selsley Church (view)
255. Stockend & Maitland Woods (NT),
     Scottsquar Hill
256. Town Hall (C16 facade), Stroud
     Subscription Rooms (1836)
     Stroud Museum
257. Rodborough Common (NT)

258. *Painswick House*
259. Painswick (town)
     St. Mary's Churchyard
     (yew plantation)
     Little Fleece (C17; bookshop) (NT)
     Court House
260. All Saints Church, Uplands, Stroud
262. Bisley Church
263. *Daneway House* (C14–17), Sapperton
264. Edgeworth Church
     Scriven's Conduit (C17)
265. Sapperton Church
266. Cleeve Hill (views, earthwork)
267. Whittington Church
268. Shipton Solers Church
269. Compton Abdale Church
270. Notgrove Long Barrow
271. Belas Knap (long barrow),
     Charlton Abbots
272. *Sudeley Castle*
273. Winchcombe Church & *Church Porch*
     Museum
274. *The Cottage*, Stanley Pontlarge
275. Great Washbourne Church
276. Dumbleton Church
277. Toddington Church
278. Hailes Church & *Abbey remains*
     (C13; museum) (NT)
279. Tithe Barn (mediaeval), Stanway
     Stanway House Gateway (C17)
280. Stanton Church
281. *Snowshill Manor* (Tudor House;
     museum) (NT)
282. Buckland Church & *Rectory*
283. Broadway Hill (tower, view)
284. Broadway (village)
     St. Eadburgh's Church
285. Wickhamford Church
286. Elmley Castle Church & Village
287. Evesham Abbey (Norman & C16
     gateway; Bell Tower, 1533)
     Almonry (C14; museum)
     All Saints Church
     Church House (Tudor)
288. Cropthorne Church
289. Fladbury Church
     Fladbury Mill (Avon watermill)
290. Middle Littleton Tithe Barn (C14)
291. Cleeve Prior Mill (part C17) &
     Village
292. *Ragley Hall*
293. Dormston Church
294. St. Nicholas' Church, Alcester
     Town Hall (early C17)
     Henley Street (C17 & C18 houses)
295. *Coughton Court* (NT) & Church
296. Kinwarton Dovecote (C14) (NT)
297. Aston Cantlow Church
298. Wootton Wawen Church
299. Old Forge Mill, Redditch
300. Beoley Church
301. Wilmcote Church
     Mary Arden's House (Tudor)
302. Billesley Church
303. Bidford Bridge (C15)
     Old Falcon Inn (Tudor)
304. Welford-on-Avon Church & Village
305. *Anne Hathaway's Cottage*, Shottery
306. Holy Trinity Church,
     Stratford-on-Avon
     Old Guildhall & Grammar School
     (C15)
     Clopton Bridge (C15)
     Shakespeare's Birthplace (Tudor)
     Hall's Croft (Tudor)
     Nash's House (C16) & *New Place* (site)
     Harvard House (1596)
     Town Hall (1767)
     Royal Shakespeare Theatre
     Picture Gallery
307. *Hanbury Hall* (NT)
308. Snitterfield Church
309. Hampton Lucy Church
310. *Charlecote Park, House & Garden* (NT)
     Charlecote Church (Lucy Chapel)

311. Loxley Church
312. Preston-on-Stour Church
313. *Hidcote Manor Garden* (NT)
314. Saintbury Church
315. Dover's Hill (views) (NT)
316. Chipping Camden (town)
     St. James's Church
     Grevel House (C14)
     Almshouses (1612)
     Market Hall (1627)
317. Ebrington Church
318. *Foxcote* (C18), Ilmington
319. Ilmington Church
320. Bourton-on-the-Hill Church
321. *Kiftsgate Court Gardens*
322. Bourton-on-the-Water (village)
323. Market Cross (C14),
     Stow-on-the-Wold
     St. Edward's Hall (1594; museum)
324. Icomb Hill (view, earthwork)
325. Idbury Church
326. Bledington Church
327. St. Nicholas' Church, Oddington
328. *Chastleton House*
329. Sarsden Church
330. Shorthampton Church
331. Spelsbury Church
332. *Ditchley Park* (house)
333. Hoar Stone (megalithic), Enstone
334. Enstone Church
335. Great Tew Church & Village
336. Chipping Norton Almshouses (1640)
     Guildhall (Repton, early C19)
337. Little Rollright Church
338. The King's Men (stone circle),
     Rollright
     The Whispering Knights
     (burial chamber)
339. Great Rollright Church
340. Hook Norton Church & Brewery
341. Swalcliffe Tithe Barn (C15)
342. Brailes Church
343. *Compton Wyngates, House, Gardens
     & Church*
344. Honington Church
345. Idlicote Church
346. Halford Church
347. Ettington Old Church
     (mediaeval remains) & Park
348. *Upton House & Gardens* (NT)
     Sunrising Hill (view)
349. Hornton Church
350. Edgehill Tower (1749; site of battle,
     view)
351. Kineton Church
352. Chesterton Church
353. Chesterton Windmill (1632)
354. All Saints Church, Leamington Spa
     Jephson Gardens
     Art Gallery & Museum
355. St. Mark's Church, New Milverton
356. *Warwick Castle & Grounds*
     St. Mary's Church & Beauchamp
     Chapel (C15)
     St. Nicholas' Church
     West Gate (C12 & C16) & Chapel
     (C14)
     Lord Leycester's Hospital
     (mediaeval & 1571)
     Oken's House (C16; Doll Museum)
     Old Market Hall (c. 1670;
     County Museum)
     St. John's House (C17; *museum*)
     Landor House (C17; school)
     Court House (c. 1725)
     Shire Hall (c. 1754)
     Mill Street & Old Bridge (C14 ruin)
     Castle Bridge (1790; 105 ft span, view)
357. Henley-in-Arden Church & Town
     Old Guildhall (C15)
     Beaudesert Church
     Norman Castle Mound
358. Knighton-on-Teme Church
359. Hartpury Tithe Barn (mediaeval)

Map 28

NO LEFT TURN FROM
M45 TO M1 (NORTH)
AT JUNCTION 17 36

NORTHAMPTON

OXFORD

BUCKINGHAM

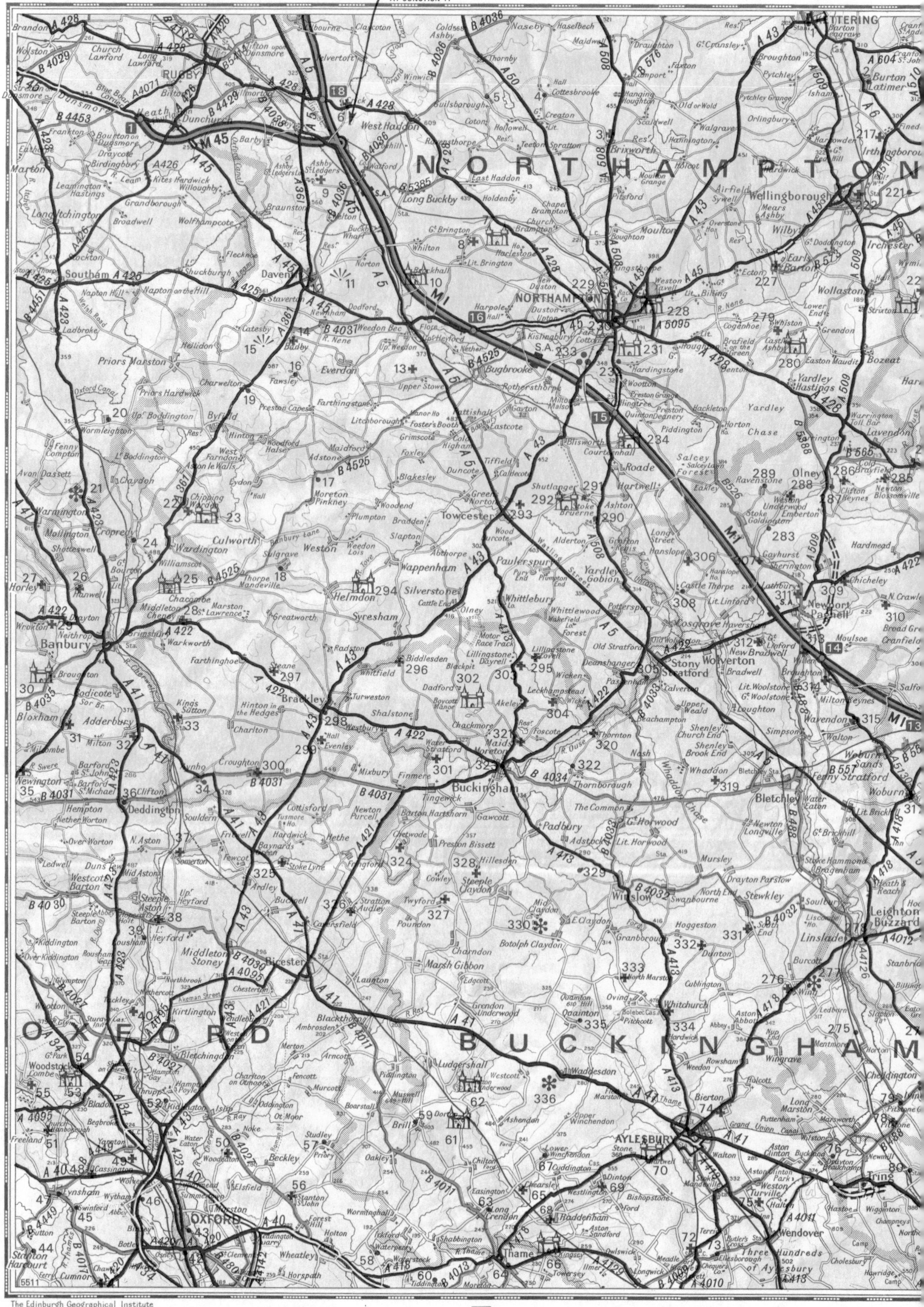

The Edinburgh Geographical Institute

27

Map 29

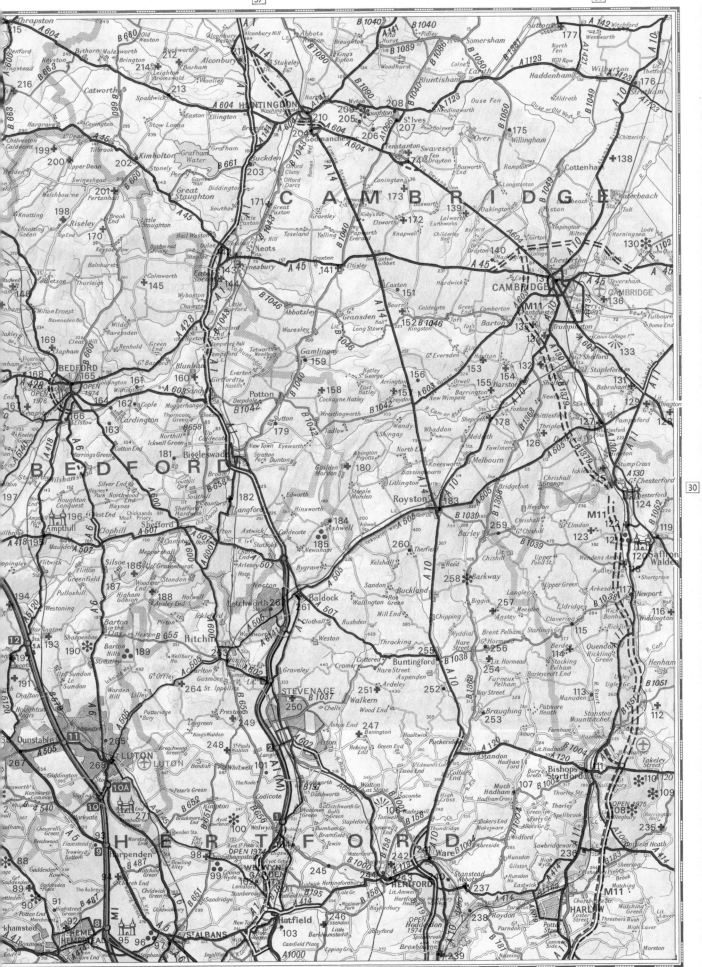

1 2 3 4 5 Miles

Gazetteer to Maps 28·29

1. St. Peter & St. Paul's Church, Kettering
   Alfred East Art Gallery
   Westfield Museum
2. Burton Latimer Church
   School House (1622)
3. Brixworth Church (Saxon)
4. Cottesbrooke Church
   View of Cottesbrooke Hall
   (Queen Anne)
5. Guilsborough Grammar School (1670)
6. Crick Church
7. *Althorp*
8. Great Brington Church
9. Ashby St. Ledgers Church
10. *Brockhall* (C16–18)
11. Borough Hill (hillfort, view), Daventry
12. Holy Cross Church, Daventry
    Moot Hall (1769)
13. Stowe Nine Churches Church
14. Badby Church
15. Arbury Hill (hillfort, view), Badby
16. Fawsley Church & Hall (C16)
17. Canons Ashby Church & Priory Remains (C13)
    Canons Ashby House
18. Sulgrave Church & *Manor*
19. Packhorse Bridge (C13), Charwelton
20. Wormleighton Church
    Manor Gatehouse (1613)
21. *Farnborough Hall & Grounds* (NT)
22. Chipping Warden Church
23. *Edgcote*, Chipping Warden
24. Cropredy Church
    Oxford Canal (hand-operated drawbridges)
25. *Chacombe Priory*
26. Hanwell Church
27. Horley Church
28. Middleton Cheney Church
29. Wroxton Church
30. *Broughton Castle & Church*
31. Bloxham Church
32. Adderbury Church
33. King's Sutton Church
34. Aynho Church & Village
    Aynhoe Park (house)
35. South Newington Church
36. Deddington Church & Castle (C12 remains)
37. Somerton Church
38. Lower Heyford Church
39. *Rousham House, Gardens* & Church
    Old Stone Bridge in village
40. Tackley Church
41. Cumnor Church
42. Oxford University Colleges (thirty dating from 1249. Halls, Chapels & Gardens)
    Christ Church Cathedral
    Christ Church Library
    Sheldonian Theatre (Wren, 1669)
    Clarendon Building (Hawksmoor, 1713)
    Bodleian Library & Radcliffe Camera (Gibbs, 1749)
    Magdalen Bridge (Gwynne, 1782)
    All Saints Church
    St. Mary the Virgin Church
    St. Peter's-in-the-East Church
    Stone's Almshouses (C17)
    Ashmolean Museum
    Old Ashmolean (1682; History of Science Museum)
    Botanic Garden (founded 1621)
    Christ Church Meadow (avenues, walks)
43. University Parks, Oxford
    University Museum
    Pitt Rivers Museum (prehistory)
44. Stanton Harcourt Church, Village & Manor House (Tudor remains)
45. Swinford Bridge (1777)
46. Godstow Nunnery (C15 remains)
47. Market Cross (C14), Eynsham

48. Cassington Church
49. Yarnton Church
50. Woodeaton Church
51. Church Hanborough Church
52. Kidlington Church
    Morton Almshouses (C17)
53. *Blenheim Palace & Park*
54. Woodstock Town Hall (Chambers, 1766)
    Chaucer's House (rebuilt C18)
    Hope House (early C18)
55. Combe Church
56. Stanton St. John Church
57. Croke's Almshouses (1636), Studley
58. Waterperry Church
    Horticultural School Grounds
59. Brill Post Mill (1668)
60. Rycote Park & Chapel (C15)
61. *Dorton House*
62. *Wotton House*
63. Long Crendon Church
    Court House (C14) (NT)
64. Thame Church & High Street
    Old Grammar School (1575)
65. Chearsley Church
66. *Tythrop Park*
67. Lower Winchendon Church
    Nether Winchendon House & Gardens
68. Haddenham Church
69. Dinton Church
70. *Hartwell House & Garden*
71. St. Mary's Church, Aylesbury
    King's Head Hotel (C15) (NT)
    Bucks County Museum
72. Little Kimble Church
73. Ellesborough Church
    Lady Dodd's Almshouses (1746)
74. Bierton Church
75. Weston Turville Church
76. *Tring Reservoir* (birds)
77. St. Peter & St. Paul's Church, Tring
    Tring Park
    Zoological Museum
78. Pitstone Church
79. Ivinghoe Church
    Post Mill (1627) (NT) Pitstone Green
80. Tring Railway Station (1837)
81. Ivinghoe Beacon (views) (NT)
82. Aldbury Church & Village
83. Bridgewater Monument (NT)
84. Church Almshouses (C16), Northchurch
85. Ashridge Estate (3937 acres wood, heath & down) (NT)
    Ashridge House & Gardens
86. Berkhamstead Castle (C11 remains)
    St. Peter's Church
    Old Grammar School (C16)
    Court House (C16)
    Incent's House (C16)
    Sayer Almshouses (1684)
87. Little Gaddesden Church
    The Manor House
88. Hudnall Common (NT)
89. Great Gaddesden Church
90. Waterend Moor (NT)
91. *138, Piccotts End* (mediaeval murals), Hemel Hempstead
92. St. Mary's Church, Hemel Hempstead
93. Flamstead Church
    Saunders Almshouses (1669)
94. Redbourne Church
95. *Gorhambury House*
96. *Verulamium* (Roman city remains)
97. St. Albans Cathedral
    St. Michael's Church
    St. Stephen's Church
    Great Gate (C14)
    Clock Tower (C15)
    Marlborough Almshouses (1736)
    City Museum
98. Wheathampstead Church
99. Devil's Dyke & The Slad (earthworks), Wheathampstead

100. Ayot St. Lawrence Church
     Shaw's Corner (NT)
101. *Knebworth House & Gardens*
     St. Mary & St. Thomas's Church
102. Brocket Park
     Lemsford Mill
103. Hatfield Park, *House, Gardens & Bishop's Palace*
     St. Etheldreda's Church
     Fore Street (Georgian houses)
104. Digswell Viaduct (Cubitt, 1850)
106. View of Woodhall Park (Leverton, 1777)
107. Much Hadham Church & Village
108. Woodside Green (NT), Hatfield Forest
     Wall Wood (NT)
109. Hatfield Forest Lake (boating, fishing) (NT)
110. Portingbury Hills (earthwork, woods) (NT), Hatfield Forest
111. St. Michael's Church, Bishop's Stortford
     Rhodes Memorial Museum
112. Elsenham Church
113. Manuden Church & Village
114. Berden Church
115. Clavering Church, Village & Castle Mound
116 to 137. Refer to Gazetteer 30-31
138. Denny Abbey (C12–14 remains)
139. Lolworth Church
140. Madingley Church
     Post Mill
141. Eltisley Church
142. St. Mary's Church, St. Neots
     Market Square
     Ouse Bridge (restored mediaeval)
143. Eynesbury Church
144. Eaton Socon Church
145. Colmworth Church
146. Felmersham Church
147. Radwell Bridge (1766)
148. Pavenham Church
149. Stevington Church
     Stevington Post Mill (1770, restored)
150. *Stagsden Bird Gardens*
151. Bourn Post Mill (c. 1633, oldest in country)
152. Bourn Church
153. Harlton Church
154. Haslingfield Church
155. Barrington Church
156. Wimpole Church
     View of Wimpole Hall (1632) & Avenue
157. Croydon Church
158. Cockayne Hatley Church
159. Gamlingay Church
     Jacob's Almshouses (1665)
160. Blunham Church
161. Willington Church
     Dovecote & Stables (C16) (NT)
162. Cople Church & Village
163. Airship Sheds (for R 100 & R 101, 1917), Cardington
164. Cardington Bridge (Smeaton, C18)
165. St. Paul's Church, Bedford
     St. Mary's Church
     Swan Hotel (C17 staircase)
     Bunyan Meeting Library & Museum
     The Bunyan Collection, Public Library
     Cecil Higgins Art Gallery
166. Elstow Church
     Moot Hall (mediaeval; *Bunyan Collection*)
167. Kempston Church
168. Bromham Bridge (restored mediaeval) & Mill
169. Clapham Church Tower (Saxon look-out)
170. Keysoe Church
171. Great Paxton Church
172. Elsworth Church
173. Conington Church

174. Fenstanton Church
175. Willingham Church
    Cattell's Mill (Smock mill, 1828)
176. Preaching Cross (C15), Stretham
    Tower Windmill (C19)
    Engine House (1830 Beam Engine)
177. Sutton Church
178. Shepreth Church
179. Packhorse Bridge (mediaeval),
    Sutton
180. Guilden Morden Church
181. Old Warden Church
    Shuttleworth Collection (*transport*)
182. Langford Church
183. St. John's Church, Royston
    The Cave (mediaeval? carved
    reliefs)
    18, Melbourne Street
184. Ashwell Church & Village
    St. John's Guildhall (C15?)
    Chantry House (C15)
    Town House (C15–16: museum)
    Ashwell Springs
185. Arbury Banks (earthwork), Ashwell
186. Lower Gravenhurst Church
187. *Wrest Park* (canal garden &
    pavilion (Archer, c. 1711)
188. Shillington Church
189. Ravensburgh Castle (hillfort, view)
190. The Clappers (down & woodland,
    views) (NT), Sharpenhoe
191. Chalgrave Church
192. Toddington Church & Priest's
    House (C15)
193. Harlington Church
194. Tingrith Church
195. Ampthill Church
    Oxford Hospital (almshouses, 1697)
196. Houghton House (C17 ruin)
197. Marston Moretaine Church
198. Riseley Church
199. Shelton Church
200. Upper Dean Church
201. Pertenhall Church
202. Kimbolton Church & *Castle*
203. Buckden Church
    Buckden Palace
    Lion Hotel (C15)
    George Hotel (c. 1730 & earlier)
204. St. Mary's Church, Godmanchester
    Port Holme (water meadow,
    willow-pattern bridge)
205. Hemingford Abbots (village)
206. Hemingford Grey (village)
207. All Saints Church, St. Ives
    Ouse Bridge & Chapel (1426)
    Norris Library & Museum
208. Oliver Cromwell's Barn (C14),
    St. Ives
209. Houghton Church
    Houghton Mill (C17 watermill) (NT)
210. Huntingdon Bridge (C14)
    St. Mary's Church
    Old Grammar School (C12 remains
    St. John's Hospital)
    George Hotel (galleried courtyard)
    The Cromwell Museum
211. Alconbury Church
    C15 Bridge
212. Barham Church
213. Spaldwick Bridge (C15 & later)
214. Leighton Bromswold Church
215. Thrapston Bridge (mediaeval &
    later)
216. Raunds Church
217. Finedon Church
218. Irthlingborough Church
    Market Cross (mediaeval)
219. Mediaeval Bridge, Irthlingborough
220. Higham Ferrers Church
    Churchyard Cross (C14)
    Chichele College (1422)
    Bede House (1428)
    Market Cross (C14)
221. Ditchford Bridge (C14)
222. St. Mary's Church, Wellingborough

223. St. Mary's Church, Rushden
224. Wymington Church
225. Podington Church
226. *Hinwick House*
227. Earls Barton Church
228. Abington Park & *Museum*
    (C15–18 manor house)
229. Raynsford's Almshouses (1673),
    Dallington
230. All Saints Church, Northampton
    Holy Sepulchre Church
    St. Peter's Church
    St. John's Hospital & Chapel
    (RC, C14)
    Hazelrigg Mansion (1662)
    Sessions House (1678)
    Central Museum & Art Gallery
231. *Delapré Abbey*
232. Eleanor Cross (C13), Hardingstone
233. Hunsbury Hill (hillfort)
234. *Courteenhall Hall* (C18)
235. Hatfield Broad Oak Church
236. Sawbridgeworth Church
    Burton's Flour Mill (Georgian)
237. St. James's Church, Stanstead
    Abbots
238. Rye House Gateway (c. 1443)
    Hoddesdon
239. Broxbourne Church
240. Great Amwell Church
    New River Source & Myddleton
    Monument (1800)
241. St. Mary's Church, Ware
    Bluecoat House (C15–17)
    The Priory (C15–19)
    Canons Maltings (c. 1600)
    Corn Storehouses in Star Street
    (C17)
    Riverside Gazebos (C18 & C19)
242. St. Leonard's Church, Bengeo
243. Christ's Hospital School (part C17)
244. All Saints Church, Hertford
    St. Andrew's Street (C16–18 houses)
    Friends' Meeting House (1670)
    Lombard House (C17)
    Shire Hall (James Adam, 1769)
    Hertford Castle (Norman to C19)
    Hertford Museum
245. Tewin Mill (C18)
246. Essendon Church (Wedgwood font)
247. Benington Church
248. St. Paul's Walden Church
249. Minsden Chapel (C14 ruin)
250. St. Nicholas' Church, Stevenage
251. Ardeley Church
252. Westmill (village)
253. Braughing (village)
254. Little Hormead Church
255. St. Peter's Church, Buntingford
    Bishop Seth Ward's Hospital
    (almshouses, 1684)
    High Street (C16–18 houses)
256. Great Hormead (village)
    The Brick House (C16)
257. Anstey Church
258. Berg Cottage (1687) (NT), Barkway
    Milestone (c. 1725)
259. Great Chishill Post Mill
    (rebuilt 1819)
260. *Therfield Rectory* (C15 & C18)
261. St. Mary's Church, Baldock
262. *Letchworth Museum & Art Gallery*
263. St. Mary's Church, Hitchin
    Biggin Almshouses (C17)
    Tilehouse Street (C15–18 houses)
264. Offley Church
265. *Luton Museum & Art Gallery*,
    Wardown Park
266. Maiden Bower (hillfort)
267. Dunstable Priory Church
    Jane Cart's Almshouses (1728)
268. St. Mary's Church, Luton
269. Totternhoe Church
270. Dunstable Downs (views) (NT)
271. *Luton Hoo, House & Gardens*
272. *Whipsnade Park* (Zoo)

273. Edlesborough Church
274. Eaton Bray Church
275. Bridego Bridge (site of Great Train
    Robbery, 1963), Cheddington
276. All Saints Church, Wing
277. *Ascott, House & Grounds* (NT)
278. Leighton Buzzard Church & Town
    Market Cross (C15)
279. Whiston Church
280. *Castle Ashby, House & Gardens*
281. Odell Church
282. Harrold Market House (C18)
    & Lock-up
    Ouse Bridge (part mediaeval)
283. Tyringham Bridge
284. Turvey Church
    C16 Bridge
285. Newton Blossomville Church
286. Clifton Reynes Church
287. Olney Church & Town
    Ouse Bridge (1832) & Mill (Georgian)
    Cowper Memorial Museum
288. Weston Underwood Church
289. Ravenstone Church & Almshouses
    (C17)
290. *Stoke Park Pavilions*
291. *Waterways Museum*, Stoke Bruerne
    Blisworth Tunnel (Grand Union
    canal)
292. *The Monastery* (C14 hall-house),
    Shutlanger
293. Easton Neston Church
294. *Astwell Castle* (part C15)
295. Lillingstone Lovell Church
296. Biddlesden Church
297. *Steane Church* (1620 chapel)
298. Town Hall (1706), Brackley
299. Evenley Church
300. Croughton Church
301. Water Stratford Church
302. *Stowe, Grounds & Garden Buildings*
    Church of the Assumption
303. Lillingstone Dayrell Church
304. Leckhampstead Church
305. Passenham Church
    Manor Barns (C16 & C17)
306. Hanslope Church
307. Gayhurst Church & House (c. 1600)
308. Castlethorpe Church
    Castle Motte & Bailey
309. Chicheley Church
310. North Crawley Church
311. Lathbury Church
312. Great Linford Church
313. Willen Church
314. Broughton Church
315. Wavendon Church
316. Husborne Crawley Church
317. Woburn Church
318. *Woburn Abbey, House, Park & Zoo*
319. Tattenhoe Church
320. Thornton Church
321. Maids Moreton Church
322. Thornbotough Bridge (mediaeval)
323. St. Peter & St. Paul's Church,
    Buckingham
    Chantry Chapel (Norman & 1475)
    (NT), Market Hill
    Old Gaol (1748 & 1839)
324. Chetwode Church
325. Stoke Lyne Church
326. Stratton Audley Church
327. Twyford Church
328. Hillesden Church
329. Addington Tithe Barn (C16), Winslow
330. *Claydon House* (Florence
    Nightingale Museum) (NT)
331. Stewkley Church
332. Dunton Church
333. North Marston Church
334. Whitchurch Church
335. Quainton Church & Village
    Winwood Almshouses (1687)
    Brudenell House (C16–18)
336. *Waddesdon Manor, House &*
    Grounds (NT)

Map 30

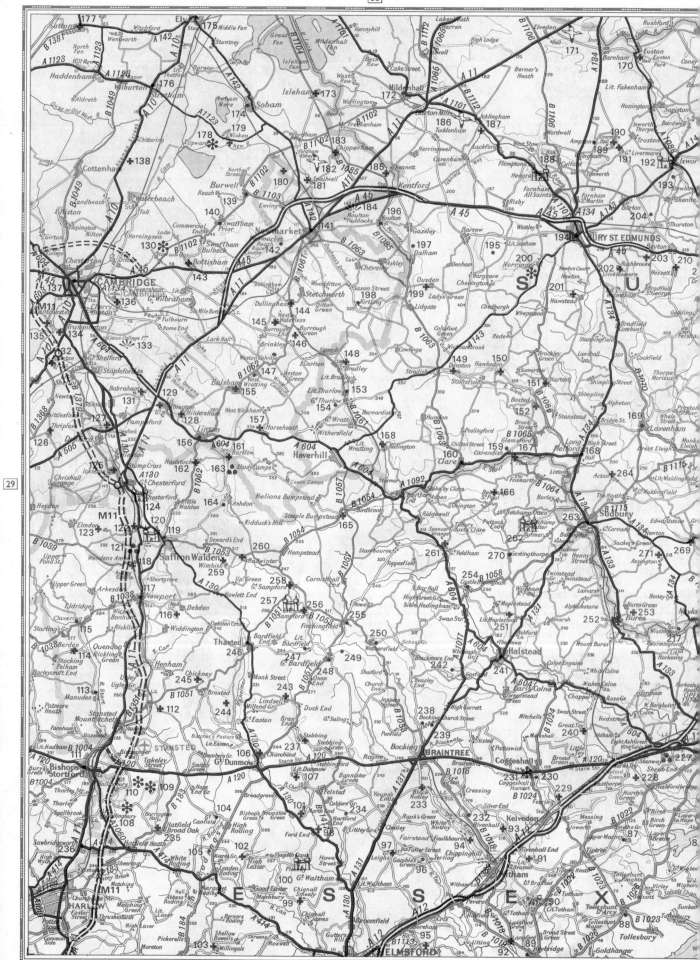

Map 31

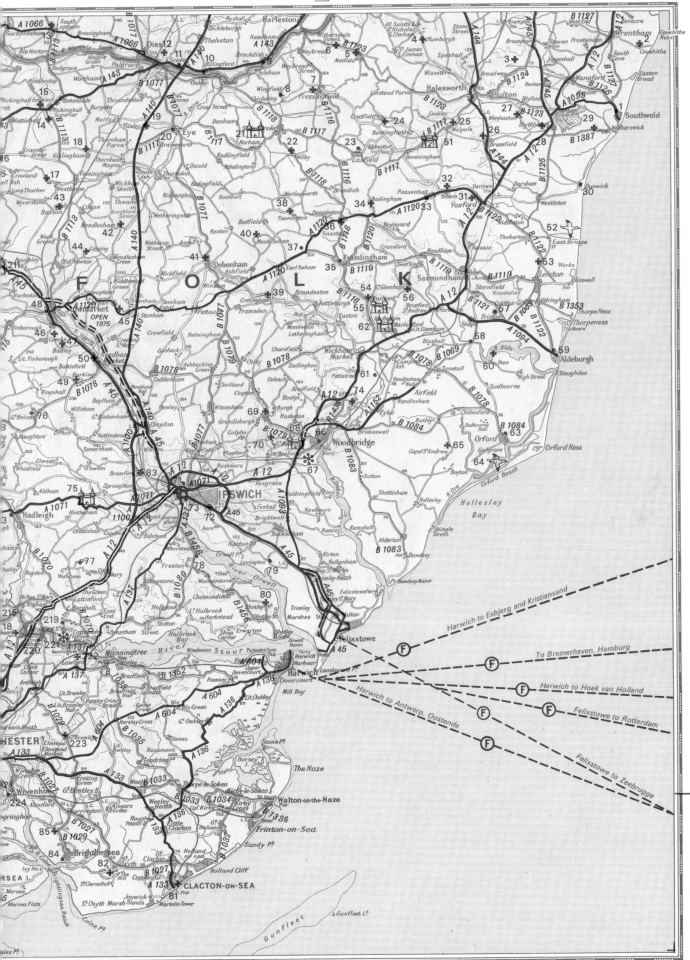

1 2 3 4 5 Miles

Gazetteer to Maps 30·31

1. St. Edmund's Church, Southwold
   Southwold Museum
2. Covehithe Church
3. Westhall Church
4. Rumburgh Church
5. Metfield Church
6. Withersdale Church, Mendham
7. Fressingfield Church
8. Wingfield Church
   College Farm (c. 1760)
   Wingfield Castle (C14 & C16)
9. Old Post Mill, Syleham
10. *Billingford Mill* (tower windmill, c. 1800)
11. White Hart Hotel (1655), Scole
12. Frenze Church, Diss
13. South Lopham Church Tower (Norman)
14. Rickinghall Superior Church
15. Rickinghall Inferior Church
16. Walsham-le-Willows Church
17. Westhorpe Church
18. Gislingham Church
19. Yaxley Church
20. Eye Church
    Eye Castle (Norman motte & bailey)
    Linden House (c. 1750)
21. *Thorpe Hall* (C16)
22. Wilby Church
23. Laxfield Church & Guildhall (C15)
24. Cratfield Church
25. Walpole Congregational Chapel (1647)
26. Bramfield Church
27. Wenhaston Church
28. Blythburgh Church
29. Walberswick Church
30. Dunwich Museum & Muniment Room (old city records)
    Priory Ruins (C13)
31. Yoxford Church
32. Sibton Abbey (C12 remains)
33. Smock Mill & Drill Mill (1805), Peasenhall
34. Badingham Church
35. Framlington Castle (C12–16) & Town
    St. Michael's Church
    Hitcham's Almshouses (1654)
    Mills' Almshouses (1709)
36. Dennington Church
37. Post Mill (C18–19), Saxtead Green
38. Tannington Church
39. Cretlingham Church
40. Monk Soham Church
41. Debenham Church
42. Mendlesham Church
43. Bacton Church
44. Gipping Church
45. Earl Stonham Church
46. Combs Church
47. Badley Church
48. *Abbot's Hall Museum of Rural Life of East Anglia*, Stowmarket
49. Barking Church
50. Needham Market Church
51. *Hevingham Hall* (Georgian mansion and park)
52. *Minsmere Level* (RSPB, marsh birds)
53. Leiston Abbey (C14 remains)
54. Parham Church
55. *Moat Hall* (C16), Parham
56. Great Glemham Church
57. Friston Post Mill
58. The Maltings (C19), Snape
59. St. Peter & St. Paul's Church, Aldeburgh
    Moot Hall (C16)
60. Iken Church (view)
61. Ash Priory Site & Old Watermill

62. *Glemham Hall* (C17–18)
63. Orford Church & Town
    Orford Castle (C12 keep)
64. *Havergate Island* (RSPB, breeding avocets & other birds)
65. Butley Abbey Gatehouse (C14)
66. Woodbridge (town)
    St. Mary's Church
    Shire Hall (C16–19)
    Cumberland Street (Georgian houses)
    Seckford Hospital (1840) & Almshouses (1869)
    Steelyard (C17?), New Street
    The Quay (C16 houses) & Tide Mill
    Buttrum's Mill (windmill 1817)
67. Kyson Hill (riverside parkland) (NT), Woodbridge
68. Seckford Hall (C16; hotel), Great Bealings
69. Grundisburgh Church
70. Great Bealings Church
71. St. Margaret's Church, Ipswich
    St. Mary-le-Tower Church
    St. Nicholas' Church
    Unitarian Meeting House (1700), Friars Street
    Ancient House (C16–17) *& Chapel*
    Christchurch Mansion (C16; museum)
    Ipswich Museum
72. St. Augustine's Church (1927) Ipswich
73. St. Mary Quay Church, Ipswich
    Fore Street (C16 & C17 houses)
    Custom House (1844)
74. Uford Church
75. *Hintlesham Hall*
76. Great Bricett Church
    The Hall (c. 1250)
77. Little Wrenham Hall (C13 & C16)
    Tithe Barn (C16)
78. Freston Tower (C16)
79. Hitcham's Almshouses (1636) Levington
80. Shotley Church
81. St. James's Church, Clacton-on-Sea
82. St. Osyth Church
    St. Osyth's Priory & Gardens
83. Bramford Church
84. Brightlingsea Quay
    Jacobe's Hall (C15)
85. All Saints Church, Brightlingsea
86. *Abberton Reservoir* (birds)
87. Layer Marney Gatehouse (C16) & Church
88. Tolleshunt D'Arcy Church & Hall (c. 1500)
89. Heybridge Mill (Georgian)
90. Beacon Hill (view), Great Totham
91. Great Braxted Church, Braxted Park
92. Langford Church
93. Rivenhall Church
94. Faulkbourne Church
95. Little Baddow Church
96. Terling Smock Mill
97. Great Leighs Church
98. Ford End Church
99. Chignal Smealey Church
100. Pleshey Castle (motte & bailey, C15 bridge)
101. Black Chapel & Priest House (C15), North End
102. High Easter Church
103. Willingale Doe Church
     Willingale Spain Church
104. Great Canfield Church & Castle Mound
105. Post Mill, Aythorpe Roding
106. Great Dunmow Church
107. Little Dunmow Church

108. Woodside Green (NT), Hatfield Forest
     Wall Wood (NT)
109. Hatfield Forest Lake (boating, fishing) (NT)
110. Portingbury Hills (earthwork, woods) (NT), Hatfield Forest
111. St. Michael's Church, Bishop's Stortford
     Rhodes Memorial Museum
112. Elsenham Church
113. Maunden Church & Village
114. Berden Church
115. Clavering Church, Village & Castle Mound
116. Debden Church
117. Newport Church & Village
     Monks Barn (C15 house)
     Crown House (C17)
118. Wendens Ambo Church
119. Saffron Walden (town)
     St. Mary's Church
     Norman Castle Remains
     Old Sun Inn (C15–17) (NT), Church Street
     1 Myddylton Place (c. 1500), Bridge Street
     Rose & Crown Hotel (C16–18)
     Saffron Walden Museum
120. *Audley End, House & Grounds*
121. Ring Hill Camp (hillfort), Littlebury
122. Littlebury Church
123. Strethall Church (Saxon)
124. *Manor House* (C13), Little Chesterford
125. Ickleton Church
126. Thriplow Church
127. Duxford Chapel (C14 ruin) Whittlesford
128. Hildersham Church
129. Little Abington Church
130. *Anglesey Abbey* (about 1600 and gardens) (NT)
131. Babraham Church
132. Hauxton Church
133. Gog Magog Hills (views)
     Via Devana (Roman road)
134. Trumpington Church
135. Granchester Church
136. Cherry Hinton Church
137. Cambridge University Colleges (seventeen dating from 1284 to 1800. Halls, Chapels & Gardens)
     King's College Chapel (1446–1515)
     Trinity College Library (Wren, 1695)
     The Old Schools (C14–18; University Archives)
     Senate House (Gibbs, 1730)
     St. Michael's Church
     Great St. Mary's Church
     St. Mary The Less Church
     Holy Sepulchre Church (circular)
     St. Benet's Church Tower (Saxon)
     Hobson's Conduit (1614)
     Fitzwilliam Museum
     University Museum of Geology
     University Museum of Zoology
     Whipple Museum of the History of Science
     Scott Polar Research Institute
     Cambridge & County Folk Museum
     Castle Mound (view of city)
     The Backs (stretch of r. Cam)
     University Botanic Garden
138. Denny Abbey (C12–14 remains)
139. Burwell Church & Village
     Steven's Mill (tower windmill)
140. St. Mary's Church, Swaffham Prior
     St. Cyriac's Church
     Tower Windmill (c. 1875)
141. Jockey Club Rooms (1933), Newmarket
     Old Railway Station (1848)

142. Newmarket Heath (racecourses)
     Devil's Ditch (earthworks)
143. Bottisham Church
144. Dullingham Church
145. Westley Waterless Church
146. Burrough Green Church
147. Smock Mill (1726), West Wratting
148. Great Bradley Church
149. Denston Church
150. Hawkedon Church
151. Hartest Church
152. Boxted Church
153. Little Thurlow Church
     Soame's Almshouses & School
     (1614–18)
154. Great Thurlow Smock Mill
155. Balsham Church
156. Linton Church
     Trinity Guildhall (Tudor)
157. Horseheath Church
158. Kedington Church
159. Cavendish Church & Green
     Hyde Park Corner Cottages
     (almshouse)
160. Clare Church & Town
     Castle Mound (remains C13 keep)
     Clare Priory (C14 Friary remains)
     The Ancient House (C15 & earlier)
161. Bartlow Church
162. Hadstock Church
163. Bartlow Hills (Romano-British
     burial grounds)
164. Ashdon Church
     Old Guildhall (c. 1500)
165. Steeple Bumpstead Church
166. Belchamp St. Paul's Church
167. Pentlow Church
168. Long Melford Church & Green
     Trinity Hospital (almshouses, 1573,
     restored)
     Melford Hall (NT)
     Mill Bridge (1764)
169. Lavenham (mediaeval town)
     St. Peter & St. Paul's Church
     Wool Hall (C15)
     De Vere House (C15)
     Guildhall (C16) (NT)
170. Euston Church
171. Thetford Heath (NC, health plants
     & birds)
172. Mildenhall Church
     Market Cross (C16?)
173. St. Andrew's Church, Isleham
     Priory Remains (Norman chapel)
174. Soham Church
     Steelyard (1740)
     Downfield Tower Windmill
     (rebuilt 1890)
175. Ely Cathedral
     Prior Cranden's Chapel (C14)
     King's School (monastic buildings)
     Bishop's Palace (C15–18)
     The Chantry (C17–18 house)
176. Preaching Cross (C15), Stretham
     Tower Windmill (C19)
     Engine House (1830 Beam Engine)
177. Sutton Church
178. *Wicken Fen Nature Reserve*
     (NT, insects, birds & plants)
     Smock Mill
179. Wicken Church
180. Landwade Church
181. Snailwell Church
182. *Chippenham Fen Nature Reserve*
     (NC, insects, birds & plants)
183. Chippenham Church
184. Bury Hills (view of gallops & Ely),
     Newmarket
185. Kennett Church
186. Cavenham Heath (NC, heath
     plants & birds)

187. All Saints Church, Icklingham
188. *Hengrave Hall* (c. 1525)
189. Ampton Church & Village
     Calthorpe Almshouses (1693)
     Bluecoat School (1705)
190. Little Livermere Church
191. Great Livermere Church
192. *Ixworth Abbey*
193. Ixworth Mill (tower windmill)
194. Bury St. Edmunds Abbey
     (Norman & C14 Gateways)
     St. James's Cathedral
     St. Mary's Church
     St. John's Church
     Unitarian Chapel (1711)
     Moyse's Hall (restored C12; *museum*)
     Guildhall (C13 doorway)
     Cupola House (1693)
     Provost's House (Clopton Asylum,
     1730)
     Town Hall (Robert Adam, c. 1775)
     Angel Corner (C18; *Clock Museum*)
     (NT), Angel Hill
     Theatre Royal (1819)
195. Great Saxham Church
     Saxham Hall (c. 1797)
196. Packhorse Bridge (C15), Moulton
197. Dalham Church, Hall (1705),
     Village & Smock Mill
198. All Saints Church, Kirtling
     Kirtling Tower (1530 gatehouse)
199. Ousden Church Tower (Norman)
200. *Ickworth House* (NT)
201. Hawstead Church
     (Drury monument)
202. Ruchbrooke Church
203. Rougham Church
204. Tower Windmill (c. 1820), Pakenham
205. Stowlangtoft Church
206. *The Wurlie* (C15 hall-house),
     Badwell Ash
207. Elmswell Church
     Gardiner's Almshouses (1614)
208. Woolpit Church
209. Drinkstone Post Mill (1689)
210. Hessett Church
211. *Haughley Park*
212. Shelland Church
213. Rattlesden Church
214. Stoke-by-Nayland Church
     Old Guildhall (C16)
     The Maltings (C16)
215. *Thorington Hall* (NT)
216. Nayland Church
     Alston Court (C15–16)
217. Wissington Church
     Old Watermill (r. Stour)
218. Langham Church (view)
219. East Bergholt Church & Bell House
     (C16)
220. Dedham Church & Town
     Southfields (c. 1500 clothier's house)
     Marlborough Head Inn (c. 1500)
     Sun Inn (C16)
     Old Grammar School
     (early Georgian)
     Shermans (c. 1735 house)
     Castle House (Munnings' studios)
221. Flatford Mill (C18) (NT)
     Valley Farm (C15; Field Studies
     Centre) (NT)
     Willy Lott's Cottage (c. 1600)
     Thatched Cottage
222. Lawford Church
223. Great Bromley Church
224. Wivenhoe Quay
225. *Bourne Mill* (1591) (NT), Colchester
226. *Colchester Castle* (C11; museum)
     Balkerne Gate & City Walls
     (Roman & mediaeval)
     St. Botolph's Priory (C11–12
     remains)

Holy Trinity Church (Saxon tower)
St. John's Abbey Gate (C15)
Kendall Almshouses (1791 & 1803)
West Stockwell Street (C15–18
houses)
East Street (Tudor houses)
North Hill (Tudor & Georgian
houses)
Holly Trees Mansion
(1718; museum)
The Minories (museum)
227. Lexden Dykes (C1 earthworks)
228. Copford Church
229. Feering Church
230. Abbey Remains (C12),
     Little Coggeshall
     Old Watermill (from C17)
231. *Paycocke's* (NT), Coggeshall
232. Cressing Temple Barns
     (c. 1450 & 1530)
233. Black Notley Church
234. Leez Priory Gatehouse (C16)
235. Hatfield Broad Oak Church
236. Sawbridgeworth Church
     Burton's Flour Mill (Georgian)
237. Stebbing Church
238. St. Mary's Church, Bocking
     Bocking Mill (Georgian watermill)
239. Bocking Post Mill (c. 1680)
240. Great Tey Church
241. St. Andrew's Church, Halstead
     Holy Trinity Church
     Halstead Mill (C18 watermill,
     Courtauld's)
     Blue Bridge House (1710–14)
242. Gosfield Church
     Gosfield Hall & Park
243. Lindsell Church
244. Tilty Church & Abbey Remains (C12)
245. Chickney Church
246. Thaxted Church & Town
     Guildhall (C16)
     Clarance House (1718)
247. Little Bardfield Church & Hall
248. Great Bardfield Church & Village
249. Tower Windmill, Great Bardfield
250. Wethersfield Church & Village
251. Little Maplestead Church (circular)
252. Bures Church
253. St. Stephen's Chapel (C13), Bures
254. Castle Hedingham Church
     Hedingham Castle (C12 keep)
255. Finchingfield Church & Village
     Post Mill
256. Little Sampford Church
257. *Tewes*, Little Sampford
258. Great Sampford Church
259. Wimbish Church
260. Radwinter Church
261. Great Yeldham Church
262. *Belchamp Hall* (1720)
263. St. Peter's Church, Sudbury
     St. Gregory's Church
     All Saints Church
     Salter's Hall (c. 1450), Stour Street
     The Chantry (C15)
     Gainsborough's House (c. 1725 front)
264. Acton Church (de Bures brass 1302)
265. Bildeston Church
266. Chelsworth Church
267. St. James's Chapel (C13), Lindsey
268. Kersey Church & Village
     Priory Remains (C13)
269. Boxford Church
270. Gestingthorpe Church & Hall (1735)
271. Assington Church
272. Polstead Church
273. Hadleigh Church & Town
     The Deanery (Tudor gatehouse)
     Guildhall (C15)
     Toppesfield Bridge (mediaeval)

Map 32

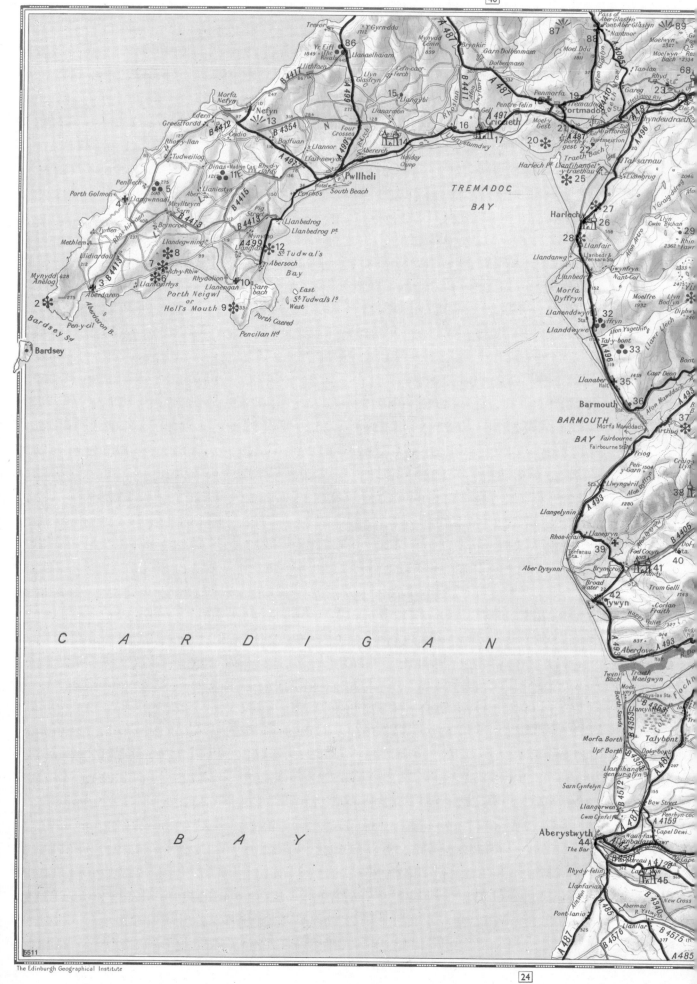

5511

The Edinburgh Geographical Institute

Map 33

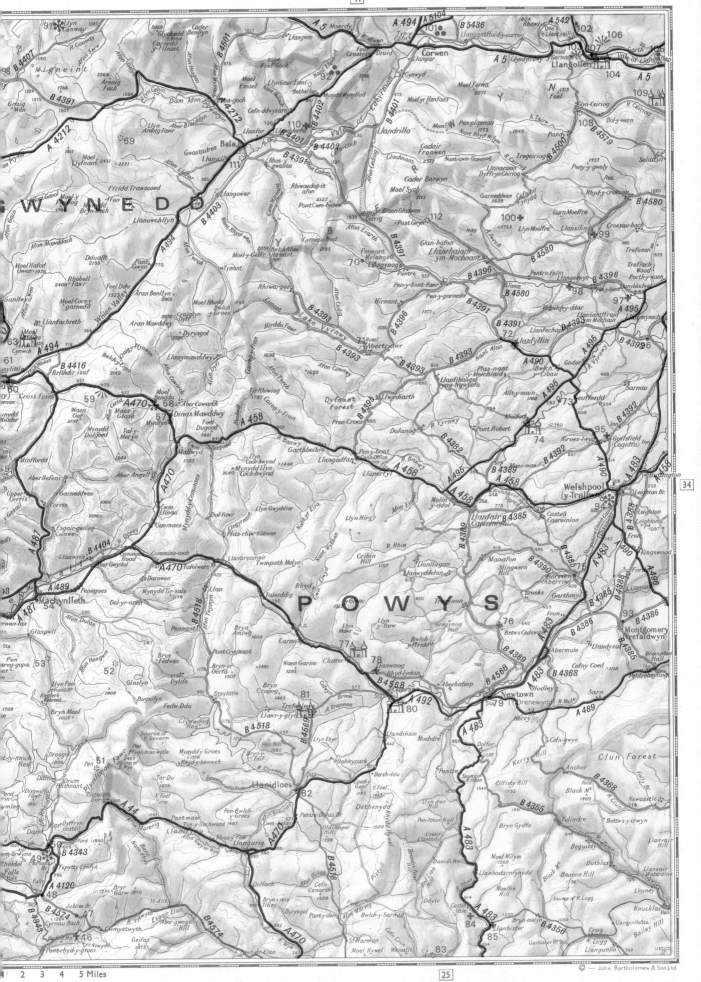

© — John Bartholomew & Son Ltd.

Gazetteer to Maps 32·33

1. *Bardsey Island* (BTO Bird Observatory)
   Abbey remains (C13) & *ancient crosses*
   Lighthouse (1821)
2. Braich-y-Pwll
   Holy Well & St. Mary's Chapel (remains)
3. Aberdaron Church
4. Llangwadl Church
5. Mynydd Cefnamwich Burial Chamber, Penllech
6. Mynydd-y-Graig (headland) (NT), Porth Neigwl
   Gwynedd Rocks (views to Ireland & Snowdon) (NT)
   Syntir (traditional Welsh cottage) (NT)
   Tan-y-Muriau Long Cairn, Rhiw
7. *Plas-yn-Rhiw* (views to Cader Idris) (NT)
8. Mynydd Rhiw (views) (NT)
   Tan-yr-Ardd (traditional Welsh cottage) (NT)
9. Mynydd Cilan (views) (NT)
10. Llanengan Church
11. Carn Fadryn (hillfort)
12. Sandburrows (NT), Abersoch
13. Garn Bodfean (hillfort, views)
14. Penarth Fawr House (C15)
15. St. Cybi's Well (C5–6), Llangybi
    Almshouses (1760)
16. Lloyd George's Grave & Museum, Llanystumdwy
    Ynysgain (coastland) (NT)
17. Criccieth Castle (C13)
18. Penmorfa Church & Lychgate (1698)
19. Tremadoc (village)
    Market Hall (c. 1810)
20. Morfa Bychan (sand dunes & seashore) (NT), Portmadoc
21. *Ffestiniog Railway Museum*, Portmadoc
    Ynys Towyn (views over Glaslyn Estuary) (NT)
22. *Portmeirion* (gardens, follies, Italian village)
    C12 Castle Vallum
23. Tan-y-Bwlch Station, Rhyd— Ffestiniog Railway (1836–69)
    Views of Vale of Ffestiniog
24. Maentwrog (village)
    Maentwrog Bridge (c. 1780)
    Oakley Arms Hotel
25. *Morfa Harlech* (nature reserve: flora)
26. Harlech Castle (1283–90)
    Colleg Harlech
27. Llechwedd Wood (views over Tremadoc Bay) (NT)
28. Harlech Cliff (NT)
29. 'Roman Steps' (mediaeval paved packhorse route), Cwm Bychan
30. Llyn Hywel & Rhinog Fach (mountain lakes, views)
31. Diffwys-y-Llethr Ridge (2475 ft) (NT)
32. Dyffryn Chambered Cairns (neolithic)
33. Carneddau Hengwm (chambered long cairns)

Ancient Ardudwy (rich prehistoric centre)
34. Mawddach Estuary
35. Llanaber Church
36. Barmouth Church
    Dinas Oleu (views; NT's first acquisition)
    Ty Crwn (lock-up c. 1822)
37. Cregennan (views, lakes, ascent of Cader Idris) (NT)
38. *Castell-y-Bere* (C13 castle remains)
39. Llanegryn Church
40. Dolgoch Viaduct, Tal-y-Llyn Railway (1866)
41. *Dolaugwyn* (house c. 1620)
42. St. Cadfan's Stone (c. 650, inscribed), Towyn Church
    Tal-y-Llyn Railway (1866)
    Narrow Gauge Railway Museum
43. Eglwysfach Church
44. Aberystwyth Castle (C13 remains)
    Old Town Hall (1770)
    National Library of Wales
    University College of Wales
    Museums
    Pendinas (hillfort, Wellington Monument, view)
    Light Railway to Devil's Bridge via Rheidol Valley
45. *Nanteos* (C18 house & stables)
46. Hafod Church, Ystwyth Valley
47. Johnes' Arch (1810)
48. Devil's Bridge (triple bridge: mediaeval, 1753 & 1901)
    Hafod Arms Hotel (view)
    Mynach, Gyfarllwyd & Nant Llettys Falls, Rheidol Gorge
49. Bryn Bras (sheep farm above Rheidol Gorge) (NT)
50. Ponterwyd Old Bridge
51. Plynlimon Fawr (2469 ft)
52. Rhosygarreg Rocks, Plynlimon
53. Cwmrhaiadr Falls, Llyfnant Valley
    Gelli Cascades
54. Old Parliament House (C14), Machynlleth
    Court House (1628)
    Plas Machynlleth (Regency house & park; *museum*)
55. Tal-y-Llyn (an ascent of Cader Idris)
56. Cader Idris (2927 ft; mountain lakes, flora & geology) (NC)
57. Dinas Mawddwy Packhorse Bridge
58. Dolobran & Braich-Melyn (early Welsh mountain farms) (NT)
59. Bwlch Oerddrws (mountain pass, views)
60. Dolgellau Bridge (C17) & Turnpike House
    Court House (1825)
61. Cymmer Abbey (C13–14 remains)
    Llanelltyd Bridge
    Precipice Walk (views)
62. Llanelltyd Church
    Inscribed Stone (C12)
63. *Nannau* (C18 house, views)
64. Dolmelynllyn (hotels, *fishing*) (NT), Ganllwyd
65. Rhaiadr Ddu (waterfall) (NT), Ganllwyd

66. Derlwyn (moorland & lake) (NT), Ganllwyd Glen
67. Tomen-y-Mur (Roman fort & Norman motte)
68. *Dduallt* (c. 1600)
69. Arenig Fawr (2800 ft)
70. Pennant-Melangell Church (C12 shrine)
    Pennant Valley
71. Lake Vyrnwy
72. Llanfyllin Church
73. Cil Bridge (C19)
74. *Pen-y-Lan Hall* (C18), Meifod
75. Berriew (village)
76. Bettws Cedewain Church
77. *Plasau Duon* (c. 1600), Clatter
78. Llanwnog Church
79. Newtown Hall (C16 Town Hall)
    Robert Owen Memorial Museum
80. *Maesmawr Hall* ('black & white' house), Caersws
81. *Rhydycarw* ('black & white' house), Trefeglwys
82. Llanidloes Church
    Market Hall (C16; *museum*)
83. Abbey Cwmhir (valley)
84. Llananno Church, Ithon Valley
85. Llanbister Church
86. Tre'r Ceiri (Iron Age hillfort)
87. Moel Hebog (2566 ft; views)
88. Aberglaslyn Pass (view from bridge) (NT)
89. Culcht (view of Glaslyn Estuary. Ascent via Garreg & Croesor)
90. Slate Quarries, Blaenau Ffestiniog
    Pumped Water Power Station
    Nonconformist Chapels
91. Llyn Conwy (mountain lake, 1488 ft) (NT)
92. Caer Euni (hillfort)
93. Montgomery Church
    Montgomery Castle (C13 remains)
    Guildhall (1790)
    Iron Age Hillfort (view)
94. *Powis Castle & Gardens* (NT), Welshpool
95. Guilsfield Church
96. Pentreheylin Bridge (C18), Llandysilio
97. Llan-y-Blodwell Church
98. Llangedwyn Church
99. Llansilin Church
100. Cymdu Chapel (1905)
101. Caer Drewyn (Iron Age hillfort), Corwen
102. Valle Crucis Abbey (C13–14 remains)
     Eliseg's Pillar (C9 cross)
103. Barber's Hill (view of Vale of Llangollen)
104. *Plas Newydd* (house of Ladies of Llangollen)
105. Pontcysyllte Aqueduct (Telford, 1805)
106. Castell Dinas Bran (castle ruin, view)
107. Llangollen Bridge (mediaeval) & Old Canal
108. Vale of Ceirog
109. *Chirk Castle & Gardens*
110. Llandderfel Church
111. Bala Lake
112. Pistyll Rhaiadr (waterfall)

Map 34

SHREWSBURY

S A L O P

Llangollen · Oswestry · Welshpool · Montgomery · Whitchurch · Market Drayton · Telford · Bridgnorth · Ludlow · Knighton · Clun · Church Stretton · Much Wenlock · Bishop's Castle

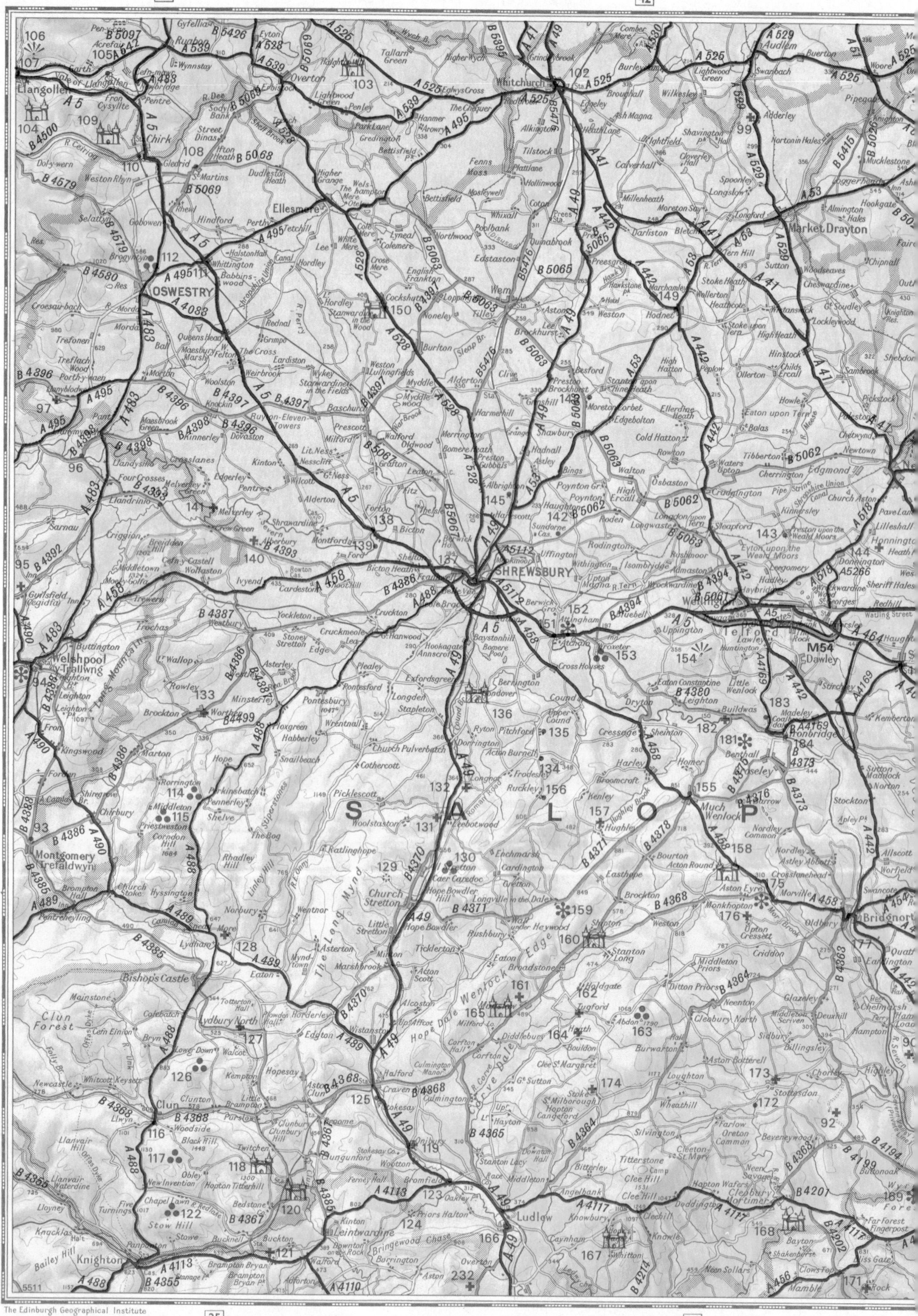

Map 35

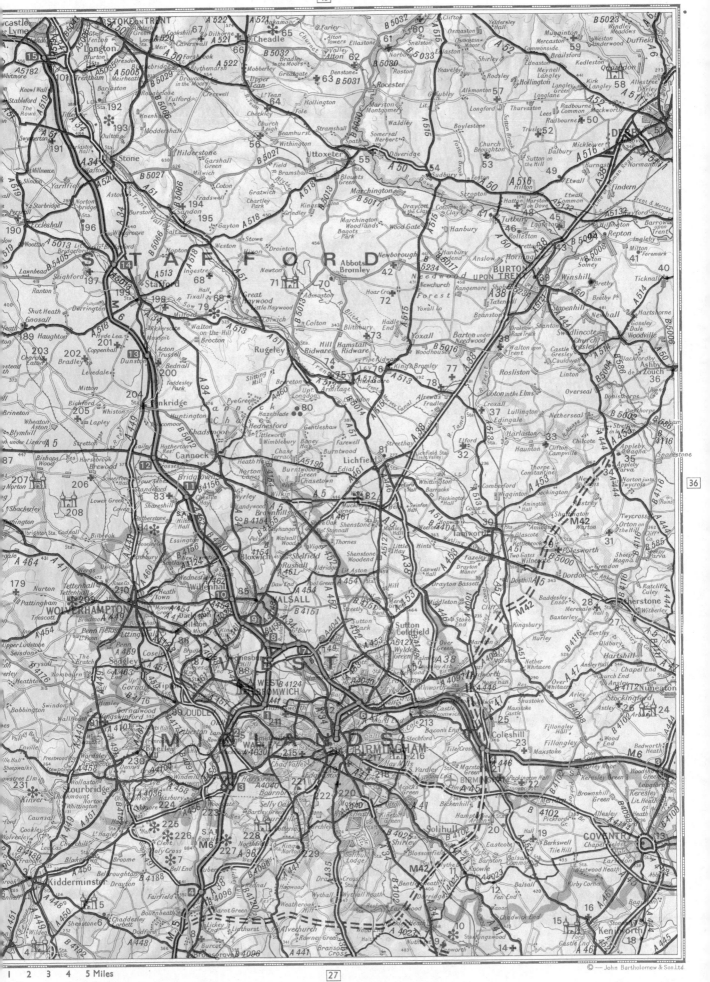

1 2 3 4 5 Miles

Gazetteer to Maps 34·35

1. St. Anne's Church, Bewdley
   Recorder's House (1610)
   Severn Bridge (Telford, 1800)
2. Ribbesford Church
3. St. Mary's Church, Kidderminster
   Museum & Art Gallery
4. *Hartlebury Castle*
5. *Harvington Hall*
6. Chaddesley Corbett Church
   Delabere Almshouses (1637)
   Talbot Inn (1600)
7. Sling Pool (wooded valley) (NT)
   Clent Hills
8. St. John Baptist's Church, Bromsgrove
9. Lapworth Church
10. *Packwood House & Gardens* (NT)
11. Knowle Church
    Guild House (C15)
12. Temple Balsall Church
    Leveson Hospital (almshouses, 1677)
13. Coventry Cathedral
    St. Mary's Hall (C14)
    Holy Trinity Church
    St. John Baptist's Church
    Ford's Hospital (C16 almshouses)
    Bond's Hospital (C16 almshouses)
    Herbert Art Gallery & Museum
14. Wroxall Abbey Church
    Priory Remains (C14)
15. *Kenilworth Castle* (C12–16)
16. Kenilworth Abbey (C14 remains)
17. Stoneleigh Church
    Alice Leigh's Almshouses (C17)
18. Stare Bridge (C15), Stoneleigh Park
19. Berkswell Church
20. Packhorse Bridge (C15),
    Hampton-in-Arden
21. Little Packington Church
22. Great Packington Church
23. Maxstoke Priory (C14 remains)
24. *Arbury Hall & Gardens*
25. Coleshill Church
    Pillory
26. Astley Church
27. Mancetter Church
    Gramer's Almshouses (c. 1728)
28. Merevale Church
29. Polesworth Church
30. St. Editha's Church, Tamworth
    Tamworth Castle (C10–17; *museum*)
    Town Hall (1701)
31. Orton-on-the-Hill Church
32. Elford Church
33. Clifton Campville Church
34. Grammar School (1697),
    Appleby Parva
35. Appleby Magna Church
    The Moat House (C15–16)
36. Ashby-de-la-Zouch Castle
    (mediaeval remains)
    St. Helen's Church
37. Croxall Church
38. Walton-on-Trent Church
39. St. Chad's Church, Burton-on-Trent
    St. Paul's Church
    Museum & Art Gallery

40. Ticknall Hospital (almshouses, 1772)
41. Foremark Church & *Hall*
42. Newborough Church
43. Monks' Bridge (mediaeval), Egginton
44. Repton Church (Saxon crypt)
    Priory Gateway (C12)
    Market Cross (restored mediaeval)
    Prior Overton's Tower (C15)
    Repton School Museum
    (Norman undercroft)
45. Egginton Church
46. Rolleston Church
    Almshouses (C18)
47. St. Mary's Priory Church, Tutbury
    Tutbury Castle (C14 remains)
48. Marston-on-Dove Church
49. Etwall Church
    Etwall Hospital (almshouses, 1550 &
    1681)
50. Radbourne Church
51. All Saints Cathedral, Derby
    St. Alkmund's Church
    St. Mary's Church (RC, Pugin)
    St. Mary's Bridge (1788) & Chapel
    (C14)
    County Hall (1660)
    Old Assembly Rooms (c. 1764)
    Friargate (Georgian houses)
    Derby Museum & Art Gallery
    Royal Crown Derby Porcelain Works
52. Trusley Church
53. Church Broughton Church
54. Sudbury (village)
    Sudbury Hall (C17) (NT)
55. Doveridge Church
56. Church Leigh Church
57. Longford Church
58. *Kedleston Hall & Gardens*
59. Mugginton Church
60. Mayfield Church
61. Norbury Church
62. Denstone Church
63. Croxden Abbey (C12–14 remains)
64. Checkley Church
65. Hawksmoor (nature reserve) (NT)
66. St. Giles' Church (RC, Pugin),
    Cheadle
67. Dilhorne Church
68. Ingestre Church
69. Essex Bridge (C16), Great Haywood
70. Abbots Bromley Hospital
    Market Cross (restored mediaeval)
71. *Blithfield Hall, House, Gardens &
    Church*
72. Hoar Cross Church
73. Hamstall Ridware Church
74. Mavesyn Ridware Church
    The Old Gatehouse (C15)
75. Armitage Church Font (Norman)
    Churchyard Cross (Norman)
76. Kings Bromley Church
77. Wychnor Church
78. Alrewas Church
79. *Shugborough* (NT)
80. Castle Ring (hillfort, view),
    Gentleshaw

81. Lichfield Cathedral
    St. Chad's Church
    St. Chad's Well (C7)
    St. John's Hospital (C15 almshouses)
    Dr. Johnson's Birthplace (museum)
    Lichfield Art Gallery & Museum
82. Letocetum (Roman baths &
    museum) (NT), Wall
83. Shareshill Church
84. *Moseley Old Hall* (NT)
85. St. Matthew's Church, Walsall
    E. M. Flint Art Gallery
86. St. Leonard's Church, Bilston
87. Watt's Pumping Engine (1777),
    Ocker Hill Canal Works
88. *Oak House* (C15; museum),
    West Bromwich
89. St. Thomas's Church, Dudley
    Dudley Castle (C14 remains; zoo)
    Art Gallery & Museum
90. Alveley Church
91. Kingswinford Church (tympanum)
92. Kinlet Church
93. Montgomery Church
    Montgomery Castle (C13 remains)
    Guildhall (1790)
    Iron Age Hillfort (view)
94. *Powis Castle & Gardens* (NT),
    Welshpool
95. Guilsfield Church
96. Pentreheylin Bridge (C18),
    Llandysilio
97. Llan-y-Blodwel Church
98. Broughton Church, Wetwood
99. Adderley Church
100. Ashley Church
101. Trentham Park
102. St. Alkmund's Church, Whitchurch
103. *Halghton Hall* (c. 1662)
104. *Plas Newydd* (house of Ladies of
     Llangollen)
105. Pontcysylie Aqueduct
     (Telford, 1805)
106. Castell Dinas Bran (castle ruin,
     view)
107. Llangollen Bridge (mediaeval) &
     Old Canal
108. St. Martin's Church
     Almshouses (1698 & 1810)
109. *Chirk Castle & Gardens*
110. Chirk Aqueduct (Telford, 1801)
111. Whittington Church
     Whittington Castle (C13 remains)
112. Old Oswestry (hillfort)
113. Llandrinio Bridge (1775)
114. Marsh Pool Stone Circle, Middleton
115. Mitchell's Fold Stone Circle,
     Middleton
116. Clun Church
     Trinity Hospital (almshouses, 1614)
     Clun Castle (Norman ruin)
     Clun Town Trust Museum
117. Pen-y-Wern Stone Circle
118. Hopton Castle (ruined keep)
119. Onibury Church
120. *Heath House* (C17), Leintwardine

121. Brampton Bryan Church
122. Caer Caradoc Camp
123. St. Mary's Church, Bromfield
     Priory Gatehouse (mediaeval)
124. Bringewood Forge Bridge (C18)
     Teme Gorge
125. *Stokesay Castle*
     Stokesay Church
126. Bury Ditches (earthwork), Clun
127. Lydbury North Church
128. More Church
129. Cardingmill Valley, Long Mynd Hills
130. Caer Caradoc (1500 ft; hillfort)
131. Leebotwood Church
132. Longnor Church
133. Worthen Church
134. Acton Burnell Church
     Acton Burnell Castle (C13 remains)
135. Pitchford Church & Hall (c. 1560)
136. *Condover Hall*
137. Shrewsbury Abbey Church
     St. Chad's Church
     St. Mary's Church
     Millington's Hospital (almshouses,
     1748)
     Town Walls Tower (C14) (NT)
     The Council House (C15–17)
     Ireland's Mansion (c. 1575)
     Owen's House (1592)
     Old Market Hall (1596)
     Butcher Row (C16 shops)
     Rowley's House (C17; Roman
     museum)
     Old School (C17; *Museum &
     Art Gallery*)
     Guildhall (1696)
     Assembly Room (c. 1775), Lion Hotel
     English & Welsh Bridges
     (C18, restored)
     Jones' Maltings (1796 flax mill),
     Spring Gardens
138. Montford Bridge (Telford, 1790)
139. Preston Montford Field Studies
     Centre
140. Alberbury Church
141. Melverley Church
142. Haughmond Abbey (C12–14
     remains)
     Mediaeval Well House
143. Preston Trust Homes
     (almshouses, c. 1725)
144. Lilleshall Abbey (C12 remains)
145. Battlefield Church
     Site of Battle of Shrewsbury (1403)
146. Forton Church
147. Norbury Church
148. Moreton Corbet Castle (c. 1200 &
     C16 remains)
     St. Bartholomew's Church
149. *Hodnet Hall & Gardens*
     Home Farm Tithe Barn (1619)
150. *Standwardine Hall* (C16)
151. Severn Bridge (Gwynne, 1769),
     Atcham
     Tern Bridge (Mylne, 1774)
152. *Attingham Park, State Rooms* (NT)

153. Viroconium (Roman city remains)
     Viroconium Museum
     Wroxeter Church
154. The Wrekin (hillfort, view)
155. *Wenlock Priory* (C11 & later
     remains), Much Wenlock
     Old Guildhall (C16)
     Raynald's Mansion (C17)
156. Langley Chapel (1601)
     C16 Gatehouse
157. Hughley Church
158. *Acton Round Hall*
159. *Wilderhope Manor* (NT),
     Wenlock Edge
160. *Shipton Hall*
161. Munslow Church
162. Tugford Church
163. Abdon Burf (hillfort, view),
     Brown Clee Hill
164. Heath Chapel (Norman)
165. *White House (The)*, Aston Munslow
166. *Ludlow Castle* (C11–16)
     St. Laurence's Church
     Hosyer's Almshouses (rebuilt 1758)
     Broad Gate (mediaeval)
     The Reader's House (mediaeval &
     C17)
     Feathers Hotel (1603)
     Butter Cross (1744; *Ludlow Museum*)
     Ludford Bridge (mediaeval)
     Dinham Bridge (1823)
167. *Whitton Court*
168. *Mawley Hall*
169. Knowles Mill (NT), Wyre Forest
170. *Dowles Manor* (C16), Bewdley
171. Rock Church
172. Ancient Stone Bridge, Stottesdon
173. Stottesdon Church
174. Stoke St. Milborough Church
175. *Morville Hall* (NT)
176. Upton Cresset Church
177. Bridgnorth Castle (C12 remains)
     & Town
     St. Mary's Church (Telford)
     Bishop Percy's House (1580)
     Town Hall (c. 1650)
178. Claverley Church
179. Pattingham Church
180. Patshull Church
181. *Benthall Hall* (NT)
182. Buildwas Abbey (C12 remains)
183. *Allied Ironfounders' Museum*,
     Coalbrookdale
184. Iron Bridge (1779), & Gorge
     Industrial Museum, Ironbridge
185. St. Andrew's Church, Shifnal
186. Tong Church
187. Weston-under-Lizard Church
     Weston Park, House & Gardens
188. Blymhill Church
189. Gnosall Church
190. Eccleshall Church
191. Swynnerton Church
192. *Wedgwood Museum*, Barlaston
193. Downs Banks (moorland) (NT)
194. Sandon Church

195. *Sandon Hall Gardens*
196. *Isaak Walton Cottage & Museum*,
     Shallowford
197. Seighford Church
198. Baswich Church
199. St. Mary's Church, Stafford
     St. Chad's Church
     High House (1555)
     Noel's Almshouses (c. 1645)
     Stafford Museum & Art Gallery
200. Acton Trussell Church
201. Coppenhall Church
202. Bradley Church
203. Church Eaton Church
204. Penkridge Church
205. Lapley Church
206. Brewood Church
207. *Boscobel House*
208. *Chillington Hall*
209. *Wightwick Manor* (NT)
210. St. Peter's Church, Wolverhampton
     Churchyard Cross (Saxon)
     St. John s Church
     Municipal Art Gallery & Museum
     Bantock House (museum)
211. St. James's Church, Handsworth
     St. Mary's Church
212. St. Peter & St. Paul's Church, Aston
     Aston Hall (C17)
213. Castle Bromwich Church
214. St. Philip's Cathedral, Birmingham
     St. Chad's Cathedral (RC, Pugin)
     St. George's Church
     St. Martin's Church
     St. Paul s Church
     Town Hall (Hansom & Welch, 1850)
     City Museum & Art Gallery
215. St. John's Church, Ladywood
216. *Blakesley Hall* (C16; museum),
     Yardley
217. St. Alban's Church, Bordesley
     Holy Trinity Church
     St. Patrick's Church
218. St. Aidan's Church, Small Heath
219. St. Agatha's Church, Sparkbrook
220. St. Paul's Church, Balsall Heath
221. *Barber Institute of Fine Arts*,
     Birmingham University
222. *Cannon Hill Museum*
     (Natural History), Selly Oak
223. Halesowen Abbey (C13 remains)
224. Wychbury Hill (hillfort, views)
225. Clent Hill (views) (NT)
226. Walton Hill (views) (NT), Clent Hills
227. Frankley Beeches (view) (NT),
     Lickey Hills
228. *Weoley Castle* (mediaeval remains)
229. Old Grammar School (C14),
     King's Norton
230. St. Michael s Church, Brierley Hill
     Brierley Hill Museum (glass)
231. Kinver Edge (hillfort, heath &
     woodland) (NT)
     Holy Austin & Nanny's Rocks
     (rock dwellings) (NT)
232. All Saints' Church, Richard's Castle

Map 36

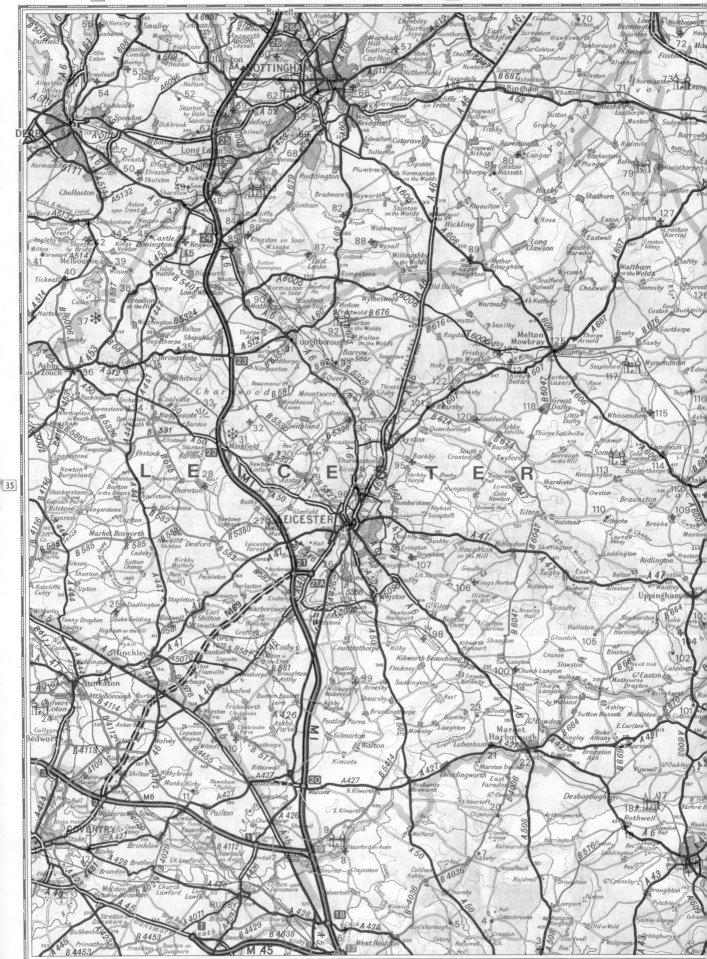

Map 37

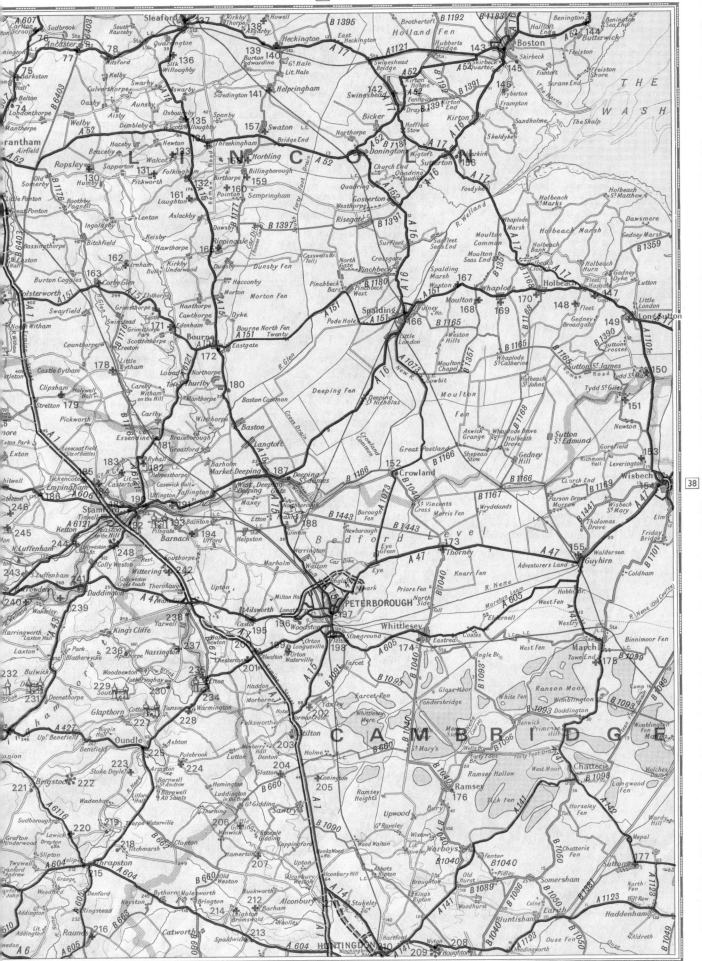

© — John Bartholomew & Son.Ltd.

Gazetteer to Maps 36·37

1. St. Peter & St. Paul's Church, Kettering
    Alfred East Art Gallery
    Westfield Museum
2. Burton Latimer Church
    School House (1622)
3. Brixworth Church (Saxon)
4. Cottesbrooke Church
    View of Cottesbrooke Hall (Queen Anne)
5. Guilsborough Grammar School (1670)
6. Crick Church
7. Battle of Naseby Memorial
8. Stanford-on-Avon Church
9. *Stanford Hall & Park*
10. Claybrooke Church
11. Monks Kirby Church
    Newnham Paddox Gates (c. 1720)
12. Binley Church
13. Coventry Cathedral
    St. Mary's Hall (C14)
    Holy Trinity Church
    St. John Baptist's Church
    Ford's Hospital (C16 almshouses)
    Bond's Hospital (C16 almshouses)
    Herbert Art Gallery & Museum
14. Warkton Church
15. Geddington Church
    Eleanor Cross (C13)
    Geddington Bridge (C13 & C18)
16. Newton Dovecote (C16)
17. *Rushton Hall*
18. The Triangular Lodge (C16), Rushton
19. Rothwell Church
    Jesus Hospital (C16 almshouses)
    Market House (C16)
20. Clipston Old School & Hospital (1668)
21. Lubenham Church
22. St. Dionysius' Church, Market Harborough
    Old Grammar School (1614)
23. Foxton Locks (C19 tank transporters)
24. *Arbury Hall & Gardens*
25. Stoke Golding Church
26. Aylestone Church
    Mediaeval Bridge
27. *Kirby Muxloe Castle* (C15 ruin)
28. Thornton Church
29. Packhorse Bridge (C17?), Anstey
30. Bradgate Park & House (Tudor ruin)
31. Rocky Plantation (NT), Ulverscroft
32. Ulverscroft Priory (C13–14 remains)
33. Bardon Hill (view), Charnwood Forest
34. Ravenstone Almshouses (C18)
35. Grace Dieu Priory (C13 remains), Belton
36. Ashby-de-la-Zouch Castle (mediaeval remains)
    St. Helen's Church
37. *Staunton Harold Hall* (C17 & C18)
    Staunton Harold Church (C17 private chapel) (NT)
38. Breedon-on-the-Hill Church
    Village Lock-up (C18)
    The Bulwarks (hillfort)

39. St. Michael's Church, Melbourne
    Melbourne Pool
    Melbourne Hall & Gardens
40. Ticknall Hospital (almshouses, 1772)
41. Foremark Church & *Hall*
42. Stanton-by-Bridge Church
43. Swarkeston Bridge (mediaeval, ¾ mile long)
    Swarkeston Church (Harpur chapel)
44. Weston-on-Trent Church
45. King's Mills (old paper mills on r. Trent)
46. Castle Donington Church
47. Cavendish Bridge (1771), Shardlow
48. Sawley Church
49. Wilne Church
    St. Chad's Well (C7)
50. Elvaston Church
51. All Saints Cathedral, Derby
    St. Alkmund's Church
    St. Mary's Church (RC, Pugin)
    St. Mary's Bridge (1788) & Chapel (C14)
    County Hall (1660)
    Old Assembly Rooms (c. 1764)
    Friargate (Georgian houses)
    Derby Museum & Art Gallery
    Royal Crown Derby Porcelain Works
52. Dale Abbey (C13 remains)
    All Saints Church
    Rock Hermitage (c. 1130)
    C18 Cave (view)
    Cat & Fiddle Windmill (1788)
53. Morley Church
54. Breadsall Church
55. Horsley Church
56. Basford Pumping Station
57. Gedling Church
58. Sandiacre Church
59. Stapleford Cross (Saxon), St. Helen's Churchyard
60. Strelley Church
61. Wollaton Church
62. Wollaton Hall (C16; *Natural History Museum*) & Park
63. *Nottingham University* (1928) *& Park*
64. Holy Trinity Church (Norman font), Lenton
65. Nottingham Castle (C17, restored; *City Museum & Art Gallery*)
    St. Mary's Church
    St. Nicholas' Church
    St. Peter's Church
    Collins' Almshouses (1709)
    Newdigate House (C17), Castle Gate
    Bromley House (1752)
    Salutation Inn (C15 rock cellars)
    Trip to Jerusalem Inn (rock cellars)
66. St. Stephen's Church, Sneinton
67. Risley Church
    Old Schools & Rectory (C18)
68. Clifton Church
    C18 Almshouses & Dovecote
69. Clifton Grove (C18 plantation)
70. Sibthorpe Church
    Dovecote (C14)
71. Bottesford Church
    Fleming's Bridge (c. 1600)

72. Westborough Church
73. *Old Manor House* (C17), Allington
74. *Belton House*
    Belton Church
    Brownlow Almshouses (C17)
75. Barkston Church
76. Carlton Scroop Church
77. Ancaster Church
78. Wilsford Church
79. *Belvoir Castle*
80. Langar Church
81. Colston Bassett Church
    Market Cross (C18 & mediaeval) (NT)
82. Bunny Church
83. *Thrumpton Hall* (Jacobean)
84. Ratcliffe-on-Soar Church
85. Kegworth Church
86. Kingston-on-Soar Church
87. East Leake Church
88. Wysall Church
89. Upper Broughton Church
90. Normanton-on-Soar Church
91. All Saints Church, Loughborough
    Grand Carillon (1923)
92. *Prestwold Hall & Gardens*
93. Babington's Almshouses (1694), Barrow-on-Soar
94. Rothley Church
    Churchyard Cross (Saxon)
95. Barkby Church
96. Belgrave Hall (1709; *museum*), Leicester
97. St. Martin's Cathedral, Leicester
    St. Margaret's Church
    St. Mary-De-Castro Church
    All Souls Church
    The Jewry Wall (Roman Forum remains)
    The Newarke (castle remains; *museum*)
    Guildhall (mediaeval)
    Arch of Remembrance (Lutyens, 1923), Victoria Park
    Leicester Museum & Art Gallery
98. Wistow Church
99. Peatling Magna Church
100. Church Langton Church
101. Rockingham (village)
    St. Leonard's Church
    Rockingham Castle
102. Eye Brook Reservoir (migrant & interesting birds)
103. Lyddington Church & Village
    Bede House (C15–17)
104. Stoke Dry Church
105. Hallaton Church & Village
    Market Cross & Conduit (C17?)
106. King's Norton Church
107. Churchyard Cross (C14), Stoughton
108. Ancient Turf Maze, Wing
109. Brooke Church
110. Withcote Church (Tudor) & Hall (C18)
111. Egleton Church
112. All Saints Church, Oakham
    Oakham Castle (Norman hall)
    Old Grammar School (1584)
    Butter Cross
    Oakham School Museum

113. *Cold Overton Hall* (C17)
114. Langham Church
115. Whissendine Church
116. Teigh Church
117. *Stapleford Park*, House & Gardens
     Stapleford Church
118. Great Dalby Church
119. Exton Church & Village
120. Gaddesby Church
121. Packhorse Bridge (C14), Rearsby
122. Brooksby Church
123. Asfordby Church
124. Kirby Bellars Church
125. St. Mary's Church, Melton Mowbray
     Hudson's Bede House (1640)
126. Buckminster Church
127. Croxton Kerrial Church
128. Great Ponton Church
129. St. Wulfram's Church, Grantham
     Angel and Royal Hotel (part C15)
     King's School Old Hall (C15)
     Conduit (1597), Market Place
     Grantham Museum
     Grantham House (C14–18) (NT)
130. Ropsley Church
131. Pickworth Church
132. Folkingham Church
     Market Place
133. Walcot Church
134. Threckingham Church
135. Osbournby Church
136. Silk Willoughby Church
137. Sleaford Church
     Vicarage (1568)
138. Howell Church
139. Tower Windmill (1813, eight sails),
     Heckington
140. Heckington Church
141. Helpringham Church
142. Swineshead Church
143. St. Botolph's Church, Boston
     Pescod House (C14)
     Guildhall (C15; *Boston Museum*)
     Grammar School Hall (1567)
     Fydell House (1726)
     Old Warehouses & Iron Bridge
144. Benington Church
145. St. Nicholas' Church, Skirbeck
     Maud Foster Windmill (1819)
146. Wyberton Church
     Wyberton Park (C17)
147. Gedney Church
148. Fleet Church
149. Long Sutton Church
150. Tydd St. Mary Church
151. Tydd St. Giles Church Tower
152. Crowland Abbey Church
     Trinity Bridge (C14)
153. Leverington Church
154. Wisbech (town)
     North & South Brinks (C18 houses)
     St. Peter & St. Paul's Church
     Peckover House (NT), North Brink
155. St. Mary's Church, Guyhirne
156. Algarkirk Church
157. Swaton Church
158. Horbling Church
159. Billingborough Church
160. Sempringham Abbey (C12 remains)

161. Laughton Church
162. Irnham Church
163. St. John's Church, Corby
164. *Woolsthorpe Manor* (NT)
165. Rippingale Church
166. St. Mary's Church, Spalding
     Ayscoughfee Hall (Bird museum)
     Spalding Museum
167. Weston Church
168. Moulton Church
169. Whaplode Church
170. Holbeach Church
171. Edenham Church
172. Bourne Abbey Church
     Car Dyke (Roman canal)
173. Thorney Abbey Church
174. St. Mary's Church, Whittlesey
     Market House (C17)
175. St. Wendreda's Church, March
176. Ramsey Church
     Ramsey Abbey Gatehouse (C15)
     (NT)
177. Sutton Church
178. Little Bytham Church
179. Clipsham Church
180. Thurlby-by-Bourne Church
     Car Dyke (Roman canal)
181. Essendine Church
     Norman Castle Mound
     Glen Bridge (C17)
182. Ryhall Church
183. Little Casterton Church
184. Great Casterton Church
185. Tickencote Church
186. Empingham Church
     Gwash Bridge (C17)
187. Deeping St. James Church
     Deeping Gate Bridge (C17)
188. Wildfowl Trust Gardens, Peakirk
189. Stamford (town)
     All Saints Church
     St. George's Church
     St. John's Church
     St. Mary's Church
     Browne's Hospital (C15 almshouses)
     Town Hall (C18)
190. St. Leonard's Priory (Norman
     remains), Stamford
191. Uffington Church
192. St. Martin's Without Church,
     Stamford
     George Inn (C13 crypt)
     Burghley Park
193. *Burghley House*
194. Barnack Church
195. Castor Church
196. Longthorpe Tower (c. 1300 house
     remains)
197. Peterborough Cathedral
     Old Guildhall (1671)
     Museum & Art Gallery
198. Fletton Church
199. Orton Longueville Church
200. Alwalton Church
201. Chesterton Church
202. Yaxley Church
203. Bell Inn (C17), Stilton
204. Glatton Church
205. Conington Church

206. Little Gidding Church
207. Hamerton Church
208. Oliver Cromwell's Barn (C14),
     St. Ives
209. Houghton Church
     Houghton Mill (C17 watermill) (NT)
210. Huntingdon Bridge (C14)
     St. Mary's Church
     Old Grammar School (C12 remains
     St. John's Hospital)
     George Hotel (galleried courtyard)
     The Cromwell Museum
211. Alconbury Church
     C15 Bridge
212. Barham Church
213. Spaldwick Bridge (C15 & later)
214. Leighton Bromswold Church
215. Thrapston Bridge (mediaeval &
     later)
216. Raunds Church
217. Finedon Church
218. Titchmarsh Church
     Pickering Almshouses (1756)
219. Aldwinkle All Saints Church &
     Village
220. Lowick Church
221. Brigstock Church
     Market Cross (C16)
222. Lyveden New Bield (c. 1600 house
     shell) (NT)
223. Stoke Doyle Church
224. Polebrook Church
225. St. Peter's Church, Oundle
     Parson Latham's Hospital
     (C17 almshouses)
     Talbot Inn (1626)
     White Lion Inn (1661)
     Paine's Cottages, West Street
226. Weldon Church
227. *Cotterstock Hall*
228. Warmington Church
229. *Southwick Hall*
230. Fotheringhay Church
     Castle Mound (C12)
231. *Deene Park* (C16 Great Hall)
     Deene Church
232. *Kirby Hall* (C16 ruin, gardens)
233. Gretton Church
234. *Elton Hall*
235. Elton Church
236. Apethorpe Church
     Apethorpe Hall (C16–18; school)
237. Nassington Church
238. Wansford Bridge (C16–18)
     Haycock Inn (early C18)
239. Tixover Church
240. Barrowden Church
241. Duddington Mill (watermill, 1664)
242. Wittering Church
243. North Luffenham Church
     North Luffenham Hall (part C17)
244. Ketton Church
245. Edith Weston Church
246. Normanton Church
247. Hambleton Church
248. *Priest's House*, Easton-on-the-Hill
     (NT)
249. Cottesmore Church

Map 38

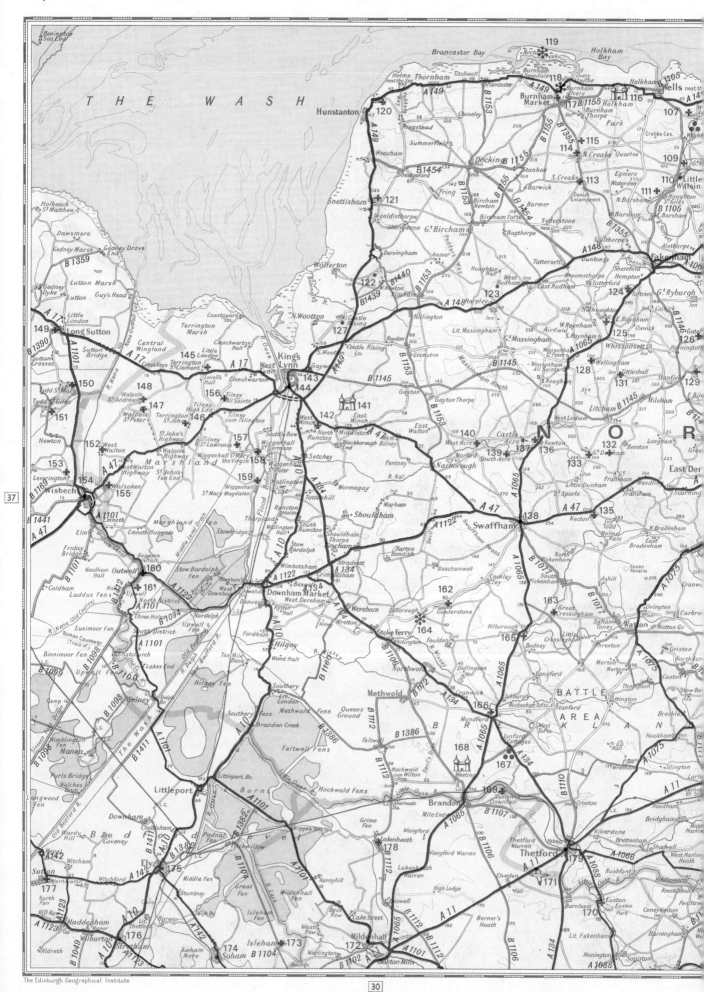

Map 39

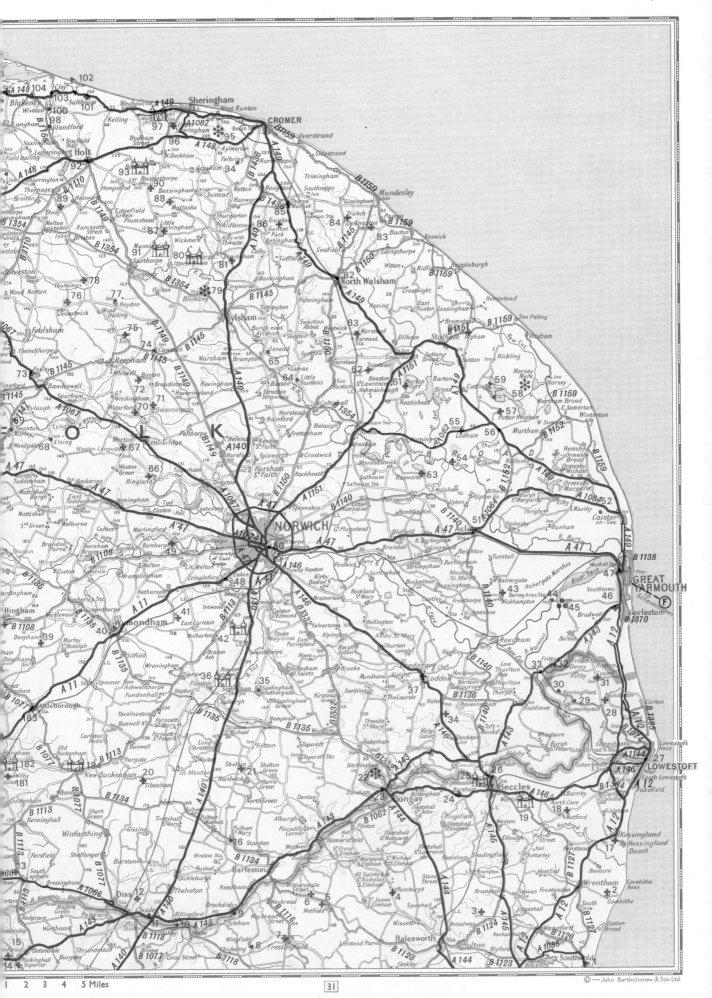

1 2 3 4 5 Miles

© —John Bartholomew & Son Ltd.

1. St. Edmund's Church, Southwold
   Southwold Museum
2. Covehithe Church
3. Westhall Church
4. Rumburgh Church
5. Metfield Church
6. Withersdale Church, Mendham
7. Fressingfield Church
8. Wingfield Church
   College Farm (c. 1760)
   Wingfield Castle (C14 & C16)
9. Old Post Mill, Syleham
10. *Billingford Mill*
    (tower windmill c. 1800)
11. White Hart Hotel (1655), Scole
12. Frenze Church, Diss
13. South Lopham Church Tower
    (Norman)
14. Rickinghall Superior Church
15. Rickinghall Inferior Church
16. Pulham St. Mary the Virgin Church
    Pennoyer's School
    (C15 chapel/classroom)
17. Kessingland Church
18. Mutford Church
19. *Worlingham Hall* (c. 1800)
20. Tibenham Church
21. Shelton Church
22. Outney Common (NT), Bungay
23. St. Mary's Church, Bungay
    Holy Trinity Church
    Butter Cross (1689)
    Bungay Castle (Norman remains)
24. Barsham Church
25. *Roos Hall* (1583)
26. St. Michael's Church, Beccles
    Leman House (1631 & later),
    Ballygate Street
    Northgate (C18 houses)
27. St. Margaret's Church, Lowestoft
    The Scores (narrow lanes in
    Old Town)
    North Lighthouse
28. Blundeston Church
29. *Somerleyton Hall & Gardens*
    St. Mary's Church
30. Herringfleet Church
    Smock Mill (c. 1830)
31. Lound Church
32. Fritton Church
    Fritton Decoy (wildfowl)
33. St. Olave's Priory (C13 remains)
    Priory Mill (water scoop, 1910)
34. Hales Church (Norman)
35. Saxlingham Nethergate Rectory
    (Soane, 1784)
36. *Rainthorpe Hall* (1579)

37. Loddon Church
38. Hingham Church
39. Deopham Church
40. Wymondham Church (Abbey)
    & Town
    Chapel of St. Thomas Becket
    (C14; county library)
    Green Dragon Inn (mediaeval)
    Market Cross (1616)
    Cavick House (early C18)
41. Ketteringham Church
42. *Gowthorpe Manor* (C16), Swardeston
43. Wickhampton Church
44. Berney Arms Mill (water scoop,
    c. 1864)
45. Burgh Castle (Roman fort)
46. Gorleston Church
47. St. Nicholas Church,
    Great Yarmouth
    Old St. George's Church (1714)
    4, South Quay (mediaeval; museum)
    (NT)
    The Tolhouse (mediaeval; museum)
    The Rows (C17 alley houses)
    The Merchant's House (c. 1600),
    Row 117
    Fishermen's Hospital (almshouses,
    1702)
    Nelson Tower (1817)
48. Cringleford Bridge (C18) & Mill
49. Bawburgh Church
50. Norwich Cathedral
    St. Peter's Mancroft Church
    St. Andrew's Church
    St. Catherine's-in-Mile Cross Church
    St. George's-in-Colegate Church
    St. George's-in-Tombland Church
    St. John's-on-Timberhill Church
    St. Gregory's Church
    St. Michael's-at-Coslany Church
    Great Hospital & St. Helen's Chapel
    (C13 & C16)
    Octagon Chapel (Unitarian, 1756)
    Norwich Castle (Norman keep;
    museum)
    Bishop's Bridge (C14)
    Cow Tower (C14)
    Guildhall (1407)
    Elm Hill (C15 houses)
    Bethel Street (C18 houses)
    Assembly Rooms (restored C18)
    City Hall (1938)
    Strangers' Hall (mediaeval; museum)
    Bridewell Museum (crafts)
    St. Peter's Hungate Church Museum
    Pull's Ferry (view, C15 bridge)

Mousehold Heath (view of Norwich
City)
51. Acle Church
52. Caister Castle (C15 remains)
    Caister Hall (Gardens & C15 tower)
53. Ranworth Church
54. St. Benet's Abbey
    (mediaeval remains), Horning
    Monks' Causeway
55. Ludham Church
56. Heigham Bridge (C13)
57. Potter Heigham Church
58. Stubb Windmill (drainage, 1912),
    Horsey Mere (NT)
59. *Hickling Broad* (NC, marsh birds,
    insects & flora)
60. Ingham Church
61. Barton Turf Church
62. Tunstead Church
63. Worstead Church
64. *Little Hautbois Hall* (C16–17)
    Mayton Bridge (Tudor)
65. Oxnead Church & Hall (C17
    remains)
66. Ringland Church
67. Weston Longville Church
68. Elsing Church & Hall (C15)
69. Swanton Morley Church
    Angel Inn (remains Lincoln
    ancestral home)
70. Alderford Church
71. Swanington Church
72. Booton Church
73. Foxley Church
74. Cawston Church & Duelling Stone
75. Sall Church
76. Nonconformist Chapel (1652),
    Guestwick
77. Heydon Church & Village
78. Thurning Church
79. *Blickling Hall* & Park (NT)
    St. Andrew's Church
80. *Wolterton Hall*, Itteringham
81. Erpingham Church
82. Market Cross (1550),
    North Walsham
83. Knapton Church
84. Trunch Church
85. Thorpe Market Church
86. Gunton Church
87. Little Barningham Church
88. North Barningham Church
89. Stody Church
90. Baconsthorpe Church
91. *Mannington Hall* (C15)
92. Letheringsett Church, Holt
93. Baconsthorpe Castle (C15 remains)

94. Felbrigg Church & Hall (1620)
95. Beacon Hill ('The Roman Camp', views) (NT), West Runton
96. Upper Sheringham Church
97. *Sheringham Hall* (1812–17) *& Park* (Repton)
98. Glandford Church
    Museum of Shells
99. Binham Church
    Binham Priory (C12 remains)
100. Wiveton Church
     C14 Bridge
101. Salthouse Church
102. Arnold's Marsh (nature reserve) (NT)
     Cley Bird Observatory
103. Cley Church & Town
     Old Custom House (C18) & Quay
     Tower Windmill
104. Blakeney Church & Town
     Old Guildhall (C14 remains)
     Tower Windmill
105. Morston Church
106. *Blakeney Point* (nature reserve: birds & plants) (NT)
107. Warham St. Mary Church
108. 'Danish Camp' (Iron Age), Warham
109. St. Peter's Church, Great Walsingham
110. Little Walsingham Parish Church (font) & Town
     Walsingham Abbey (Priory remains)
     Grey Friars (C14 Friary remains)
111. Slipper Chapel (RC, C14), Houghton St. Giles
112. Bale Church
     Bale Oaks (ilexes) (NT)
113. South Creake Church
114. North Creake Church
115. Creake Abbey (C13 remains)
116. *Holkham Hall*
117. Burnham Norton Church
     C13 Friary remains
118. Burnham Overy Water Mill (c. 1795) (NT)
     Tower Windmill (1816) (NT)
119. *Scolt Head Island* (nature reserve: birds & plants) (NT)
120. Old Hunstanton Church (Le Strange monuments)
121. Snettisham Church
122. *Sandringham Grounds*
123. Houghton (village)
     View of Houghton Hall (c. 1730) & Park
124. Toftrees Church (font)
125. East Raynham Church (C17)
126. Gateley Church

127. Castle Rising Castle (Norman remains)
     Trinity Hospital (almshouses, 1614)
128. Wellington Church (screen)
129. Brisley Church
130. North Elmham Church
     Saxon Cathedral Site
131. Tittleshall Church
132. Beeston Church
133. Great Dunham Church
134. East Dereham Church
     Bonner's Cottages (1502)
135. Necton Church (roof)
136. Newton Church
137. Castle Acre Church
     Bailey Gate (C13) & Norman Castle remains
     Castle Acre Priory (C12–15 remains)
138. Swaffham (C18 town)
     St. Peter & St. Paul's Church
     Market Cross (C18)
139. South Acre Church
140. West Acre Church & Priory remains
141. *Middleton Tower*
142. North Runcton Church
143. St. Mary's Hospital (almshouses, 1649), Gaywood
144. King's Lynn (town)
     St. Margaret's Church
     St. Nicholas' Church
     Our Lady of the Mount Chapel (C15), The Walks
     Greyfriars Lantern Tower (C13)
     St. George's Guildhall (C15) (NT)
     Mediaeval Warehouses, King Street
     Town Hall (C15), Saturday Market Place
     Hampton Court (C15), Nelson Street
     South Gate (1520)
     Thoresby College (C15–17), Queen Street
     Clifton House (C17), Queen Street
     Custom House (1683)
     Duke's Head Hotel (1689), Tuesday Market Place
     Museum & Art Gallery
145. Terrington St. Clement Church
146. Terrington St. John Church
147. Walpole St. Peter Church
148. Walpole St. Andrew's Church
149. Long Sutton Church
150. Tydd St. Mary Church
151. Tydd St. Giles Church Tower
152. West Walton Church
153. Leverington Church

154. Wisbech (town)
     North & South Brinks (C18 houses)
     St. Peter & St. Paul's Church
     Peckover House (NT), North Brink
155. Walsoken Church
156. Tilney All Saints Church
157. Wiggenhall St. Mary the Virgin Church
158. Wiggenhall St. German Church
159. Wiggenhall St. Mary Magdalene Church
160. Outwell Church
161. Upwell Church
162. Gooderstone Church
163. Great Cressingham Church
164. *Oxburgh Hall, Gatehouse & Gardens* (NT)
     Oxborough Church
165. Hilborough Church
166. Mundford Church
167. Grimes Graves (neolithic flint mines)
168. *Weeting Castle* (Norman ruin)
169. Santon Downham Church
170. Euston Church
171. Thetford Heath (NC, heath plants & birds)
172. Mildenhall Church
     Market Cross (C16?)
173. St. Andrew's Church, Isleham
     Priory Remains (Norman chapel)
174. Soham Church
     Steelyard (1740)
     Downfield Tower Windmill (rebuilt 1890)
175. Ely Cathedral
     Prior Crauden's Chapel (C14)
     King's School (monastic buildings)
     Bishop's Place (C15–18)
     The Chantry (C17–18 house)
176. Preaching Cross (C15), Stretham
     Tower Windmill (C19)
     Engine House (1830 beam engine)
177. Sutton Church
178. Lakenheath Church
179. Thetford (mediaeval town plan & Georgian houses)
     Thetford Castle (80 ft high mound)
     Cluniac Priory (C12–14 remains)
     Grammar School (Saxon foundation)
     The Ancient House (C15; museum)
     Duleep Singh Collection, Guildhall
180. East Harling Church
181. Wilby Church
182. *Wilby Hall* (C17)
183. Attleborough Church
184. Market House (C17), New Buckenham

Map 40

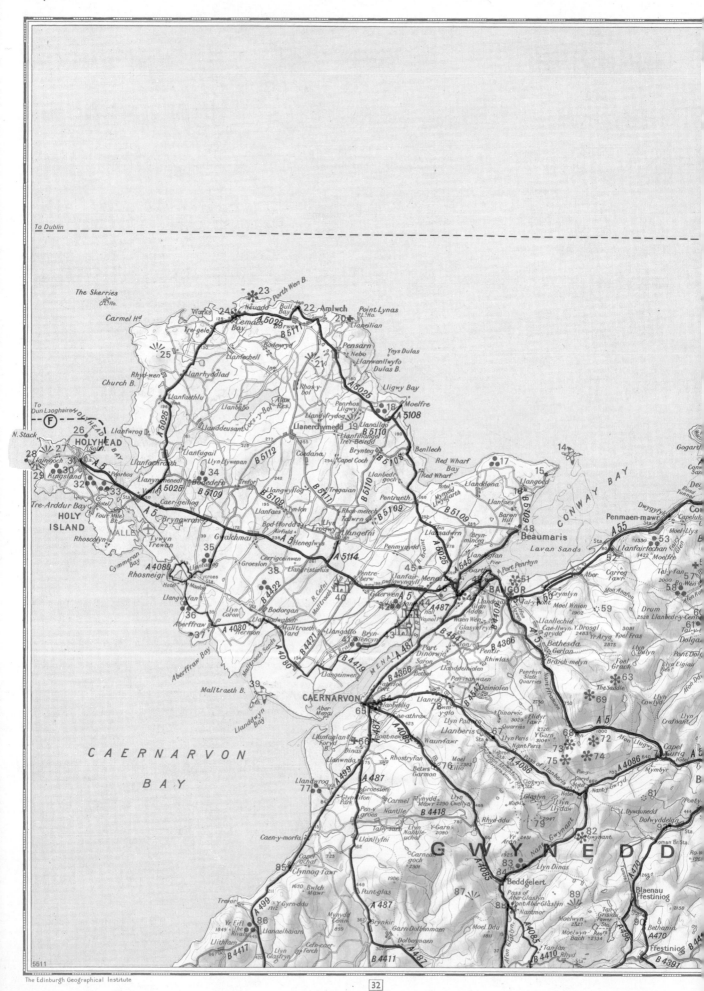

Map 41

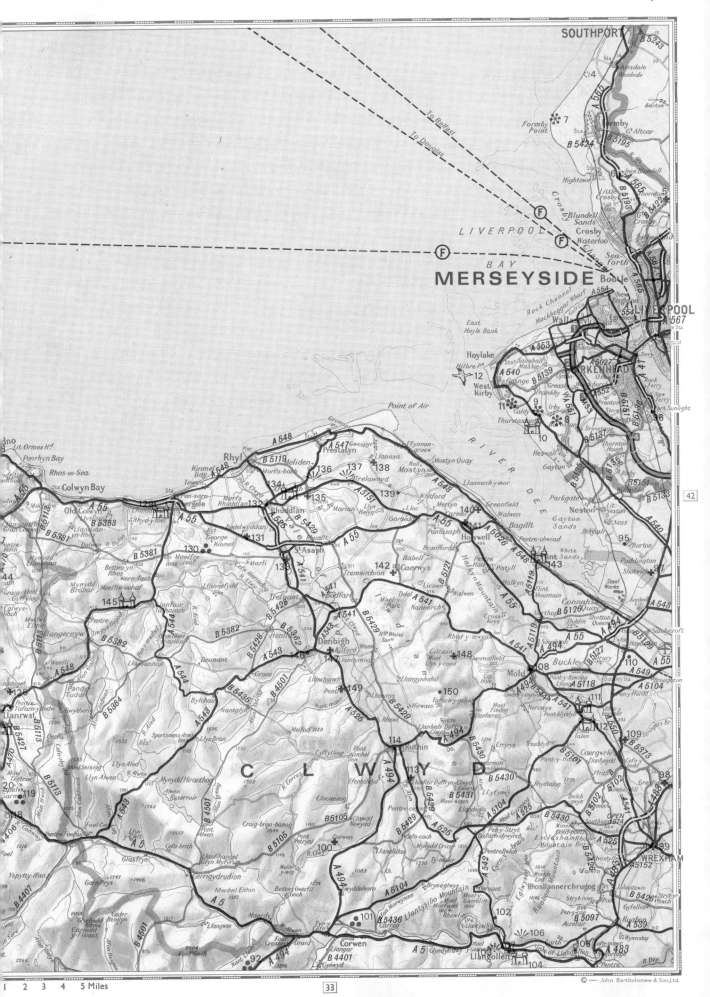

1 2 3 4 5 Miles

© — John Bartholomew & Son, Ltd.

Gazetteer to Maps 40·41

1. Liverpool Cathedral
   St. James's Church
   St. Luke's Church (ruin)
   St. George's Church, Everton
   Bluecoat Chambers (1714)
   Town Hall (Wood of Bath, 1754;
   reception rooms c. 1795)
   Rodney Street (C18 houses)
   Huskinson Monument (1836),
   St. James's Cemetery
   St. George's Hall (1838–54)
   Albert Dock (1845)
   William Brown Street
   (Public Buildings)
   Bank of England (1848)
   Oriel Chambers (1865)
   White Star Building (1900)
   Liver Building (1910)
   Cunard Building (1916)
   Walker Art Gallery
   City Museums & Hornby Library
2. Birkenhead Park (Paxton, 1847)
   Hamilton Square (civic buildings)
   Williamson Art Gallery & Museum
3. *Bootle Museum & Art Gallery*
4. Ainsdale Sand Dunes (plants &
   birds)
5. Sefton Church
   Rectory (Georgian)
6. Ince Blundell Church (RC, 1858)
7. Formby Links (NT)
8. Harrock Wood (NT), Irby
9. Irby Heath (views of Dee) (NT)
   Thurstaston Common (NT)
10. *Thurstaston Hall*
11. Caldy Hill (views of Dee) (NT)
12. *Hilbre Island* (resting place for
    shorebirds)
13. Great Orme's Head (view)
    St. Tudno's Church
14. *Puffin Island* (seabirds, monastic
    remains)
15. Penmon Church (C12) & Cross (C11)
    Priory Remains (C13 & C16)
    Dovecote (c. 1600)
    Cross (c. 1000), Penmon Deer Park
    St. Seiriol's Well (C6)
16. Castell Aber Llienawg
    (castle mound c. 1090)
17. Bwrdd Arthur (hillfort, view)

18. Lligwy Burial Chamber (neolithic)
    Din Lligwy (C4 fortified village)
    Capel Lligwy (C12)
19. Bodafon Mountain (hut circles, view)
20. Llaneilian Church (part C5 & C12)
21. Pary's Mountain (old copper mines,
    view)
22. 'Roman Baths' (folly), Bull Bay
23. Dinas Gynfor (cliffs, hillfort) (NT)
24. Cemaes Bay (cliffland & beaches)
    (NT)
25. Mynydd-y-Garn (view),
    Llanfairynghornwy
26. Breakwater (1½ miles long)
27. Caer-y-Twr (hillfort, views of
    Ireland & Snowdon)
28. South Stack Lighthouse
    (view, birds & geology)
29. Holyhead Mountain (hut circles,
    views)
30. Penrhos-Feilw Standing Stones
    (Bronze Age)
31. Holyhead Church
    Caer Gybi (Roman fort)
    Memorial Arch (1824),
    Holyhead harbour
32. Ty Mawr Standing Stone
    (Bronze Age)
33. Trefignath Burial Chamber
    (neolithic)
34. Presaddfed Burial Chamber
    (neolithic), Bodedern
35. Ty Newydd Burial Chamber
    (neolithic), Llanfaelog
36. Barclodiad-y-Gawres Burial
    Chamber (neolithic)
37. Llangwyfan Church & Bay
38. Din Dryfol Burial Chamber
    (neolithic)
39. *Newborough Warren* (geology, plants
    & birds) (NC)
    Llanddwyn Island (nature reserve,
    church ruins)
40. *Plas Berw* (C15 & C17), Holland
    Arms
41. Bodowyr Burial Chamber
    (neolithic), Bryn-Siencyn
    Castell Bryn-Gwyn
    (Bronze Age ritual enclosure)
    Caerleb (C3 fortified settlement)

42. Bryn-celli-ddu Burial Chamber
    (c. 1500 BC)
43. *Plas Coch* (Tudor), Llanedwen
44. *Plas Newydd* (C18)
45. Penmynydd Bridge (Tudor?)
46. Tubular Railway Bridge
    (R. Stephenson, 1850)
    Anglesey Column (1816),
    Llanfairpwllgwyngyll
47. Menai Suspension Bridge
    (Telford, 1826) (NT)
    Cae Glan-y-Mor (views of Straits
    & Snowdon range) (NT)
48. Beaumaris Castle (1295–1323)
    Beaumaris Church
    Court House (1614)
    Gaol (1829, treadmill)
49. Bangor Cathedral
    RC Church
    Town Hall (C16–18;
    old Bishop's palace)
    University College of North Wales
    (1910)
    Museum of Welsh Antiquities
50. Llandegai Church
51. *Penrhyn Castle & Grounds* (NT)
52. The Close (estate, school & church,
    1910), Llanfairfechan
53. Graig-Lwyd (neolithic axe factory),
    Penmaenmawr
    Stone Circle (Bronze Age)
    Arrow Stones
54. Conwy Town Walls (C13)
    Conwy Church
    Aberconwy (c. 1500 house) (NT)
    Plas Mawr (C16; Royal Cambrian
    Academy of Art)
55. Conwy Castle (C13)
    Suspension Bridge (Telford, 1826)
    Railway Bridge
    (R. Stephenson, 1848)
56. Llangelynin Old Church (900 ft)
57. *Gilfach Garden*, Roewen
58. Maen-y-Bardd Cromlech & Roman
    Road
59. Aber Falls
60. Llanbedr-y-Cennin Church
61. Pen-y-Gaer (Iron Age hillfort)
62. Caerhun Church
    Canovium (Roman fort)

63. Carnedd Llewelyn (3485 ft) (NT)
64. Segontium (Roman fort & museum)
    (NT)
65. Caernarvon Castle (1283–1323)
    Town Walls (C13)
    Chapel of St. Mary
    Royal Welsh Yacht Club House (C13)
66. Llanfaglan Old Church
67. Dolbadarn Castle (C13 remains)
    Dolbadarn Church
    St. Peri's Well
    Snowdon Mountain Railway
68. Llyn Ogwen (climbing centre)
    Nant Ffrancon Pass (NT)
    Penrhyn Slate Quarries
69. Carnedd Dafydd (3427 ft) (NT)
70. Swallow Falls
71. Capel Curig Old Church
72. Tryfan (3010 ft) (NT)
73. Llyn Idwal (mountain lake, 1223 ft)
    (NT)
74. Glyder Fach (3262 ft) (NT)
75. Glyder Fawr (3279 ft) (NT)
76. Hafodty (water gardens),
    Betws Garmon
77. Dinas Dinlle (hillfort)
78. *Bryn Bras Castle*, gardens & views
79. Snowdon (3560 ft; views, flora &
    geology) (NC)
80. Pen-y-Pass (easy ascent of Snowdon
    via Llyn Llydaw)
81. Moel Siabod (2860 ft)
82. Hafod Lwyfog (NT)
    overlooking Llyn Gwynant
83. Dinas Emrys (Iron Age hillfort)
84. Beddgelert Church
    Gelert's Grave
85. Clynnog-Fawr Church
    Church of the Grave
    St. Beuno's Well
    Bachwen & Penarth (megaliths)
86. Tre'r Ceiri (Iron Age hillfort)
87. Moel Hebog (2566 ft; views)
88. Aberglaslyn Pass (view from bridge)
    (NT)
89. Cnicht (view of Glaslyn Estuary.
    Ascent via Garreg & Croesor)
90. Slate Quarries, Blaenau Ffestiniog
    Pumped Water Power Station
    Nonconformist Chapels

91. Llyn Conwy (mountain lake, 1488 ft)
    (NT)
92. Caer Euni (hillfort)
93. Dolwyddelan Castle (C12–13)
    Dolwyddelan Church
94. Rhiw Goch (view) (NT), Pont-y-pant
95. Burton Church
    Burton Wood (NT)
96. *Lady Lever Art Gallery*, Port Sunlight
97. Shotwick Church
98. Gresford Church
99. St. Giles' Church, Wrexham
100. Derwen Churchyard Cross (C14–15)
101. Caer Drewyn (Iron Age hillfort),
     Corwen
102. Valle Crucis Abbey (C13–14 remains)
     Eliseg's Pillar (C9 cross)
103. Barber's Hill (view of Vale of
     Llangollen)
104. *Plas Newydd* (house of Ladies of
     Llangollen)
105. Pontcysyllte Aqueduct
     (Telford, 1805)
106. Castell Dinas Bran (castle ruin, view)
107. Llangollen Bridge (mediaeval) &
     Old Canal
108. Mold Church
109. Hope Church
110. *Hawarden Castle* (park &
     Norman castle ruins)
111. *Fferm* (C16 house), Pontblyddyn
112. *Plas Teg* (C17)
113. Llanfair-Dyffryn-Clwyd Church
114. St. Peter's Church, Ruthin
     Castle Street (C16 houses)
     Old Myddleton Arms (C16),
     Castle Hotel
115. *Ty Mawr* (birthplace of Bishop
     William Morgan) (NT)
116. Penmachno Bridge (part Roman?)
     Early Christian Monuments (C5–6)
117. Fedw Deg Old House (C16),
     Penmachno
118. Conwy Falls
119. Capel Garmon Burial Chamber
     (neolithic)
120. Waterloo Bridge (Telford, 1815),
     Betws-y-Coed
121. Bridge of the Cauldron (C15),
     Pont-y-Pair

122. *Gwydir Castle*, Llanrwst
     Gwydir Uchaf Chapel (1673)
123. St. Gwrst's Church, Llanrwst
     Gwydir Chapel (1634)
     Jesus Hospital (almshouses, 1610)
     Tu Hwnt i'r Bont (C15 court house)
     (NT)
     Llanrwst Bridge (1636)
124. Llanrhychwyn Church, Trefriw
125. Llanddoget Church
126. Cadair Ifan Goch (views) (NT)
127. *Cymryd Isaf* (C16 & C17), Conway
128. *Rapallo House Museum & Art
     Gallery*, Llandudno
129. Gwrych Castle (1815), Abergele
130. Dinorben (hillfort with 60 ft
     ramparts)
131. Bodelwyddan Church
132. Rhuddlan Castle (C13)
     Rhuddlan Church
     Twt Hill (Norman earthwork)
     Old Parliament House (C16)
     Rhuddlan Bridge (C16)
133. St. Asaph Cathedral
     St. Asaph Church
134. *Bodrhyddan Hall*
135. Dyserth Church Cross (C11)
136. Dyserth Castle Site (view)
137. Gop Hill (tumulus, view),
     Newmarket Trelawnyd
138. Llanasa Church
139. Maen Achwyfan (C11 wheel cross)
140. Basingwerk Abbey (C13 remains),
     Greenfield
141. St. Winefride's Church (RC),
     Holywell
     St. Winefride's Well & Chapel (C15)
142. Caerwys Church
143. Flint Castle (C13 remains)
144. *Bodnant Gardens* (NT), Talycafn
145. *Garthewin*, Llanfair Talhaiarn
146. Denbigh Castle & Town Walls (C13)
     Carmelite Friary (C14 remains)
     Hawk & Buckle Inn (C17 cockpit)
147. St. Marcella's Church, Denbigh
148. Cilcain Church
149. Llanrhaiadr Church
150. Moel Fammau (George III Jubilee
     tower, views)

Map 42

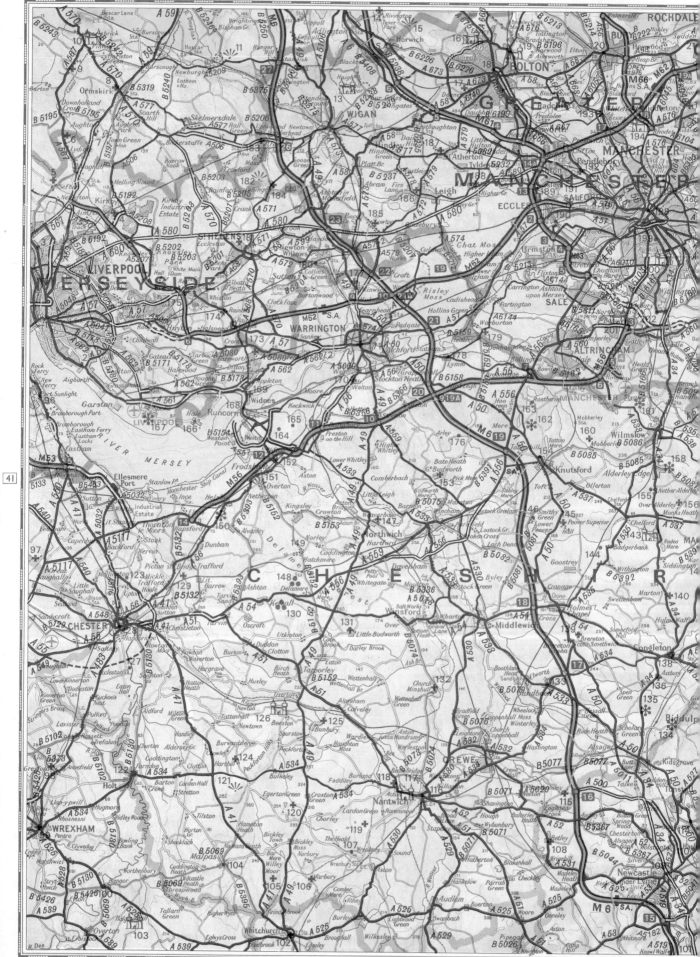

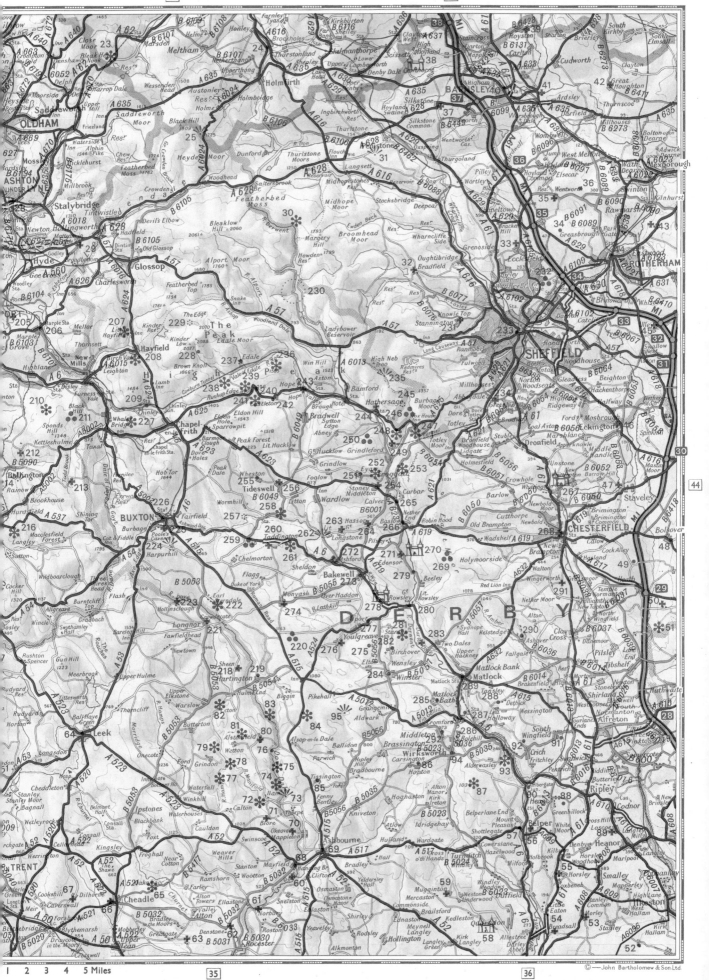

Map 43

1 2 3 4 5 Miles

© —John Bartholomew & Son Ltd.

Gazetteer to Maps 42·43

1. Liverpool Cathedral
   St. James's Church
   St. Luke's Church (ruin)
   St. George's Church, Everton
   Bluecoat Chambers (1714)
   Town Hall (Wood of Bath, 1754;
      reception rooms c. 1795)
   Rodney Street (C18 houses)
   Huskinson Monument (1836),
      St. James's Cemetery
   St. George's Hall (1838–54)
   Albert Dock (1845)
   William Brown Street
      (Public Buildings)
   Bank of England (1848)
   Oriel Chambers (1865)
   White Star Building (1900)
   Liver Building (1910)
   Cunard Building (1916)
   Walker Art Gallery
   City Museums & Hornby Library
2. St. Anne's Church, Aigburth
   All Hallows Church, Allerton
   All Saints Church, Childwall
   St. Mary's Church (view), Edge Hill
   St. Agnes' Church & Sefton Park
   St. Michael's-in-the-Hamlet Church,
      Toxteth
   Toxteth Chapel (C17)
   Holy Trinity Church, Wavertree
   Sudley Art Gallery & Museum
   Prince's Park (Decimus Burton)
   Calderstone Ridge
3. *Bootle Museum & Art Gallery*
4. Kirkby Church
5. Sefton Church & Rectory (Georgian)
6. Lydiate Hall & Chapel (C15 ruins)
   RC Church (1854)
7. St. Michael's Church, Aughton
   Cranford Garden
8. Ormskirk Church
9. Halsall Church
10. Scarisbrick Hall (1814–1870)
11. Parbold Hill (view)
12. Standish Church
13. *Haigh Hall* (c. 1840; *museum*)
14. Rivington Church
    Unitarian Chapel (1703)
15. Rivington Pike (1191 ft; tower 1733,
       view)
16. *Smithills Hall*
17. Deane Church
18 to 24 Refer to Gazetteer 48/49
25. Holme Moss (views), Longdendale
26. Oldham Church
    Municipal Art Gallery & Museum
    Oldham Edge (view)
27. Medlock Vale (NT)
28. St. Michael's Church,
       Ashton-under-Lyne
29. Mottram-in-Longendale Church
       (view)
30. Howden Moors (NT)
    Pike Low & Bole Low (cairns) (NT)
31. Hartcliff Tower (1851, view),
       Penistone
32. Bradfield Church
33. Ecclesfield Church
34. Keppel's Pillar (1782)
35. Wentworth Old Church
36. Hoober Stand (folly, 1748),
       Wentworth
37. Silkstone Church
38. *Cannon Hall & Park*, Cawthorne
39. Royston Church
40. *Cooper Art Gallery*, Barnsley
41. Monk Bretton Priory (C14 remains)
42 to 52 Refer to Gazetteer 44/45
53. Morley Church
54. Breadsall Church
55. Horsley Church
56. St. John's Church (old Foresters'
       Chapel), Belper
57. Strutt's Mills (from 1797), Belper
58 to 63 Refer to Gazetteer 34/35
64. All Saints Church, Leek

St. Edward's Church
Leek Art Gallery
65 to 67 Refer to Gazetteer 34/35
68. Hanging Bridge (mediaeval)
69. St. Oswald's Church, Ashbourne
    Old Grammar School (C16),
       Church Street
    Owlfield & Pegg Almshouses (C17)
70. Okeover Church
71. Blore Church
72. Ilam Hall Estate (r. Manifold valley)
       (NT)
    Ilam Church Font (C11)
73. Thorpe Cloud (view of Dovedale)
74. Jacob's Ladder & Twelve Apostles
       (rock formations) (NT)
    Tissington Spires (rock formation)
75. Dove Holes & The Nabbs
       (rock formations, views) (NT)
76. Viator's Bridge (packhorse),
       Mill Dale
77. Soles Hill (r. Hamps valley) (NT)
78. Beeston Tor (NT)
    Oldpark Hill (NT)
79. Ossum's Hill (NT), Grindon
    Thor's Cave
80. Alstonfield Church
81. Wetton Hill (NT)
82. Apes Tor (NT), Ecton Hill
83. Wolfscote Dale (glen r. Dove) (NT)
    Wolfscote Hill 1272 ft) (NT)
    Biggin Dale (NT)
84. Alsop Moor Plantation (NT)
85. Tissington (village)
    St. Mary's Church
    Five Wells (dressed at Ascension)
86. Gell's Almshouses (c. 1720), Hopton
87. Alport Height (views) (NT)
88. Iron Furnaces (C18), Morley Park
       Farm, Heage
89. Loscoe Church (1937)
90. Bullbridge Aqueduct & Limekilns
91. Wingfield Manor (C15 ruin)
92. Crich Church
    Crich Stand (955 ft, views)
    Tramway Museum
93. Shining Cliff Wood (NT)
94. Wirksworth Church & Town
95. Minninglow Hill (barrows, view)
96. *Lady Lever Art Gallery*, Port Sunlight
97. Shotwick Church
98. Gresford Church
99. St. Giles' Church, Wrexham
100. Bangor Bridge (C17)
101. Trentham Park
102. St. Alkmund's Church, Whitchurch
103. *Halghton Hall* (c. 1662)
104. Malpas Church
     Cholmondeley Almshouses (1721)
105. St. Chad's Church, Tushingham
106. Marbury Church
107. Wrenbury Church
     Canal Drawbridges
108. Betley Church
109. St. Giles' Church,
        Newcastle-under-Lyme
     Borough Museum & Art Gallery
110. Wedgwood Works, Etruria
111. All Saints Church, Hanley,
        Stoke-on-Trent
     City Museum & Art Gallery
     Spode-Copeland Museum
112. *Arnold Bennett Museum*, Cobridge
113. *Ford Green Hall* (C16; *museum*),
        Smallthorne
114. *Wedgewood Institute*, Burslem
115. Barthomley Church
116. Nantwich Church & Town
     Churche's Mansion (C16)
     Thomas Cleese's House (1584)
     Sweet Briar Hall (C16)
     Wright's Almshouses (1638)
     Crown Hotel (C16; *C18 ballroom*)
117. *Dorfold Hall*, Acton
118. Acton Church
119. Baddiley Church
120. Cholmondeley Castle Chapel

121. Maiden Castle (hillfort, view)
122. Farndon Church
     Dee Bridge (C14)
     Holt Church
123. *Upton Zoological Gardens*
124. Harthill Church
125. Bunbury Church
126. *Beeston Castle* (C13 remains)
127. Eccleston Church & Village
128. Chester Cathedral
     St. John Baptist's Church
     Town Walls (part Roman)
     Water Tower (C14; *museum*)
     King Charles's Tower (museum)
     The Rows (mediaeval arcaded shops)
     Leche House (1570)
     Bishop Lloyd's House (1615)
     Old King's Head Hotel (1621)
     Bear & Billet Inn (1664)
     God's Providence House (C17,
        rebuilt 1862)
     Chester Castle (Regimental museum
        & C12 chapel)
     Grosvenor Museum (Roman
        antiquities)
     Old Dee Bridge (part C13)
     Grosvenor Bridge (1827)
     Roman Amphitheatre
129. Plemstall Church
130. Kelsborrow Castle (hillfort), Kelsall
131. Little Budworth Church
132. Church Minshull Church
133. Sandbach Crosses (C9)
134. Mow Cop (views, C18 folly) (NT)
135. *Little Moreton Hall* (NT)
136. Astbury Church
137. The Cloud (hill, views) (NT)
     Bridestones (megalithic tomb)
138. St. Peter's Church, Congleton
139. Brereton Church
140. Marton Church
141. Gawsworth Church & *Hall*
142. Maggoty's Wood (Maggoty
        Johnson's grave, 1773) (NT)
143. *Capesthorne Hall*, Chelford
     Holy Trinity Chapel (1722)
144. Jodrell Bank Radio Telescope
145. Over Peover Church
146. Lower Peover Church
     Schoolhouse (1710)
147. Weaverham Church
148. Eddisbury Hill (hillfort), Delamere
149. Hatch Mere, Delamere Forest
150. Helsby Hill (hillfort, views) (NT)
151. Overton Hill (viewpoint)
152. Weaver Railway Viaduct, Frodsham
153. Great Budworth Church
154. St. John Baptist's Church, Knutsford
     Unitarian Chapel (1688)
     Sessions House (1818)
155. St. Mary's Church, Nether Alderley
     Alderley Old Mill (C15) (NT)
156. Birtles Church, Over Alderley
157. Prestbury Church & Village
     Norman Chapel
     District Bank (C14 Priest's House)
     Old Water Mill (r. Bollin)
158. Alderley Beacon (views) (NT),
        Alderley Edge
     Dickens Wood (NT)
159. *Adlington Hall*
160. Mobberley Church
161. Styal (C18 village) (NT)
     Bollin Valley (woodlands) & Quarry
        Bank Cotton Mill (1784) (NT)
162. *Tatton Hall, Gardens & Park* (NT)
163. Rostherne Church
     Rostherne Mere (NC, *birds & plants*)
164. Halton Church
     Norman Castle Ruin (view)
     Castle Hotel (old Court House)
     Sir John Chessbyre's Library (1733)
165. Norton Water Tower (1892)
166. Hale (village & C17 manor house)
167. *Speke Hall* (NT)
168. New Road Suspension Bridge,
        Runcorn

Railway Bridge (1868)
Bridgewater House & Flight of
Locks
Bethesda Congregational Church
(1835)
169. St. Mary's Church (1910), Widnes
170. Walton Superior Church
171. Holy Trinity Church, Warrington
St. Elphin's Church
Unitarian Chapel (1745), Cairo Street
Methodist Chapel (1850), Bold Street
Town Hall (Gibbs, 1750)
172. Great Sankey Church
173. Farnworth Church
174. Rainhill RC Church
175. Prescot Church
Old Court House (1755)
176. Arley Green
Arley Hall Garden
177. Winwick Church
178. Market Cross (C17), Lymm
179. Warburton Old Church
180. Sankey Viaduct (Stephenson, 1826)
181. Windleshaw Abbey (C15 ruin),
St. Helens
Quaker Meeting House (C17)
182. Billinge Hill (view)
183. Upholland Church & Priory
remains
184. Billinge Church
185. Lowton Church
186. Leigh Church
187. Atherton Church
188. Astley Church
189. Bridgewater Canal (begun 1759),
Worsley Delph
190. Barton Swing Aqueduct (1893)
191. Eccles Church
192. St. Augustine's Church, Pendlebury
193. Stand Church
194. *Heaton Hall, Park & Museum*
195. Middleton Church
196. *Queen's Park Art Gallery*, Harpurhey
Boggart Hole Clough (dell)
197. Salford Parish Church
St. Philip's Church
Museum & Art Gallery, Peel Park
Ordsall Hall (C15–17) (*museum*)
198. St. Mary's Cathedral, Manchester
St. Ann's Church
St. George's Church
St. Thomas's Church, Ardwick Green
St. Luke's Church, Cheetham
St. Matthew's Church, Crumpsall
Portico Library (1806)
Town Hall (1877)
Manchester & Liverpool Railway
Terminus (1830)
Warehouses, Bridgewater Canal
Terminus
Cheetham's Hospital & Library
(C15–17)
Rylands Library (1899)
City Art Gallery
Athenaeum Annexe Museum
199. *Whitworth Art Gallery*, Manchester
University
Manchester Museum
200. *Platt Hall* (Gallery of English
Costume), Rusholme
201. *Wythenshawe Hall* (C16 & later;
museum)
202. Didsbury Church
Fletcher Moss Museum,
The Old Parsonage
203. St. Peter's Church, Stockport
St. Mary's Church
Railway Viaduct
Municipal Museum, Vernon Park
War Memorial Art Gallery
204. *Bramall Hall*
205. Chadkirk Church, Romiley
206. All Saints Church, Marple
Canal Aqueduct & Chain of Sixteen
Locks
Railway Viaduct
207. Lantern Pike (views) (NT)

208. Ridge Top (views) (NT), Hayfield
209. Unitarian Chapel (c. 1662), Chinley
Railway Viaducts (C19)
210. *Lyme Hall* & Park (NT)
211. Bow Stones (ancient stone pillars),
Lyme Moor
212. Pott Shrigley Church
213. Jenkin Chapel (1733), Saltersford
214. White Nancy (1820 tower, view),
Bollington
215. St. Michael's Church, Macclesfield
Christ Church
Silk Mills (C18)
West Park Museum & Art Gallery
216. Eddisbury Park Field (view) (NT)
217. Rushton Church
218. Sheen Church
219. Hartington Church & Hall (1611)
220. Arbor Low Stone Circle (Bronze Age)
Gib Hill (Bronze Age round
barrow)
221. Longnor Church
222. High Wheeldon Hill (NT)
223. Hollingsclough Church
224. Solomon's Temple, Grin Low
(tower, view)
225. St. Anne's Well Chapel (1625)
226. St. John's Church, Buxton
The Crescent (Carr, 1784)
Buxton Museum
227. Eccles Pike (views) (NT)
228. Edale Head (moorland, views)
Packhorse Bridge
Edale Cross (mediaeval)
229. The Downfall (waterfall),
Kinder Scout
Mermaid's Pool
230. Derwent Dale Reservoirs &
Moorlands
231. Underbank Chapel (1742),
Stannington
232. Wincobank Hill (hillfort)
233. St. Peter's Cathedral, Sheffield
St. George's Church
St. Mary's Church, Bramall Lane
Cutlers' Hall (1832)
Town Hall (1897)
City Hall (1932)
The Mount (terraced houses c. 1830)
King Edward VII Grammar School
(1840)
Graves Art Gallery
City Museum, Weston Park
Mappin Art Gallery
Botanic Gardens (1836)
234. Beauchief Abbey (C12–14 remains)
235. Stanage Edge (escarpment, view)
236. Lose Hill (barrow, views) (NT)
Edale
237. Peak District Information Centre,
Fieldhead
238. Lord's Seat (barrow, views) (NT)
Edale
239. Mam Tor (hillfort, views) (NT)
240. Blue John Mine, Castleton
Treak Cliff Cavern (Blue John spar)
241. Winnats Pass (ravine) (NT),
Castleton
Speedwell Mine (water tunnel &
cavern)
242. Castleton Church
Peveril Castle (C11–13 remains)
Peak Cavern
243. Hope Church
Churchyard Cross (Saxon shaft)
244. St. Michael's Church, Hathersage
245. Higger Tor (gritstone bastion)
246. Carl Wark (hillfort)
247. Longshaw Moor (NT)
Padley Woods (NT)
248. Bole Hill (moor & woodland) (NT),
Upper Padley
Surprise View
249. Padley Chapel (RC, C15)
250. Wet Withens (Bronze Age stone
circle), Eyam Moor

251. Eyam Church & Village
Churchyard Cross (Saxon)
252. Riley Graves (victims of 1665
Plague) (NT), Eyam
253. Froggatt Edge (escarpment) & Wood
(NT)
254. Stoney Middleton Church
255. Village Cross (C15), Wheston
256. Tideswell Church
257. Chee Dale (gorge)
Chee Tor (rock bastion)
258. Miller's Dale (wooded cliffs) (NT)
Cressbrook Mill (cotton, 1815)
259. Five Wells (Bronze Age round
barrow)
260. Taddington Church
261. Taddington Wood (NT)
262. Headstone Head (view), Monsal
Dale
263. Longstone Church
264. Hassop Church (RC 1816)
265. Calver Mill (cotton, 1785)
266. Baslow Bridge (C14)
267. *Revolution House* (Stuart museum)
Old Whittington
268. All Saints Church, Chesterfield
269. Hob Hurst's House (barrow),
Bunker's Hill
270. *Chatsworth, House & Gardens*
Chatsworth Park
Hunting Tower (C16)
Queen Mary's Bower (C16)
Aqueduct (1694)
Derwent Bridge (Paine, 1762)
271. Edensor Church
272. Ashford-In-The-Water Church
(maidens' garlands)
Sheepwash Bridge (C16)
273. All Saints Church, Bakewell
Churchyard Cross (Saxon)
Wye Bridge (C14)
Old Grammar School (1636)
St. John's Hospital (C17 almshouses)
Bath House (1697)
Old House & Museum
274. Monyash Church
275. Harthill Stones & Castle Ring
276. Youlgreave Church
277. Alport (village), Lathkill Dale
Packhorse Bridge (1718)
278. *Haddon Hall*
279. Edensor Bridge (C17), Beeley
280. Peacock Hotel (1652), Great Rowsley
281. Stanton Moor Edge (rock
formations, views) (NT)
Nine Ladies (Bronze Age stone circle)
282. *Heathcote Museum* (Bronze Age
finds), Birchover
283. Darley Dale Church
Churchyard Yew Tree
284. Winster Church
Market House (C17) (NT)
285. Bonsall Church
Village Cross (mediaeval)
286. Black Rocks (cliff, view), Cromford
287. Cromford Bridge & Chapel (C15)
Fishing Pavilion (early C18)
Old Mill (cotton 1771–77,
R. Arkwright)
Masson Mills (cotton 1783,
R. Arkwright)
Canal Pumping Engine (1793)
Willersley Castle (C18)
288. Dethick Old Church
Thithe Barn (C16)
289. Matlock Bridge (C15)
Riber Castle (C19 folly & fauna
reserve)
High Tor, Matlock Dale
290. Ashover Church
Crispin Inn (1416)
School House (C15)
291. Wingerworth Church
292. Middleton Incline & Winching Engine
Hopton Wood Quarries
(rock scenery)

Map 44

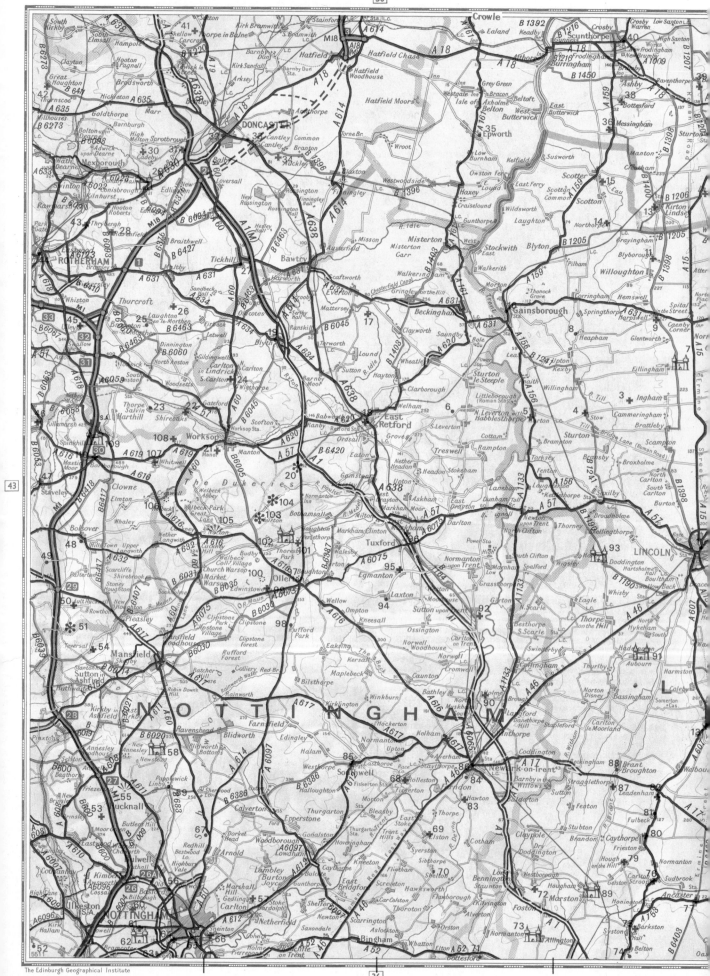

Map 45

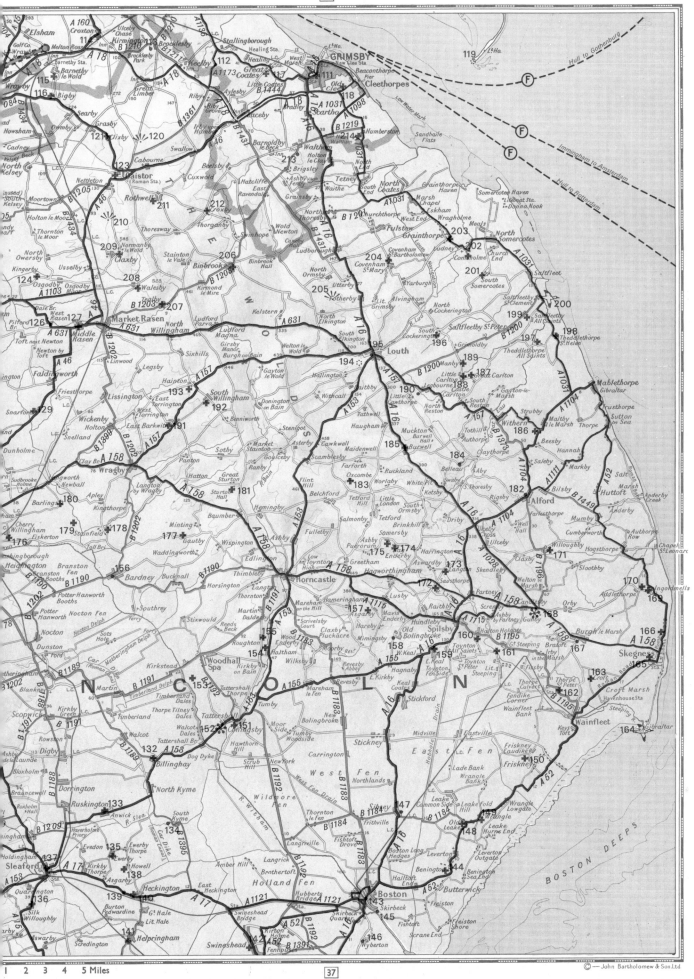

Gazetteer to Maps 44·45

1. Lincoln Cathedral
   St. Mary's-le-Wigford Church
   St. Benedict's Church
   Newport Arch (Roman gateway)
   Lincoln Castle (Norman remains)
   St. Mary's Guildhall (C12)
   The Jew's House (C12)
   Vicar's Court (mediaeval houses)
   Stonebow (mediaeval gateway)
   High Bridge (mediaeval)
   Brayford Pool (harbour)
   Lincoln City & County Museum
   Usher Art Gallery
2. Hackthorn Church
3. Coates-by-Stow Church
4. Stow Church
5. Marton Church
6. Tower Windmill (1812 & later),
   North Leverton
7. *Fillingham Castle* (c. 1760)
8. Tower Windmill (1875), Heapham
9. Harpswell Church
10. Caenby Church
11. Blyborough Church
12. Redbourne Church
13. Kirton-in-Lindsey Church
14. Northorpe Church
15. Scotter Church
16. All Saints Church, Gainsborough
    Gainsborough Old Hall (C15;
    folk museum)
17. Mattersey Priory (C12 remains)
18. West Retford Church
19. Blyth Church
    St. John's Hospital
    (C18 almshouses)
20. Apley Head Lodge, Clumber Park
    (NT) (end of Duke's Drive, 3 mile
    lime avenue)
21. Worksop Priory Church
    Priory Gatehouse (C14)
22. Shireoaks Church
23. Thorpe Salvin Church
    Ruined Manor House (C16)
24. Carlton-in-Lindrick Church
25. Laughton-en-le-Morthen Church
    Castle Mound (view)
26. Roche Abbey (C12 remains)
27. Tickhill Church
    Tickhill Castle (Norman remains)
    Austin Friary (C13 remains)
    St. Leonard's Hospital (1470)
    Market Cross (1777)
28. Ravenfield Church

29. Conisbrough Castle (C12 keep)
30. High Melton Church
31. Sprotborough Church
32. Christ Church, Doncaster
    St. George's Church
    Mansion House (1748)
33. Doncaster Racecourse Grandstand
    (part 1776)
34. Cantley Church
35. *Old Rectory* (Wesley's home),
    Epworth
36. Messingham Church
37. Scawby Church
38. Bottesford Church
39. Broughton Church
40. *Borough Museum & Art Gallery*,
    Scunthorpe
41. Owston Church
42. Great Houghton Chapel (c. 1650)
43. Thrybergh Church
44. All Saints Church, Rotherham
    Independent Chapel &
    Walker Mausoleum (C18)
    Rotherham Bridge & Chapel (C15)
    Museum & Art Gallery, Clifton Park
45. Ulley Church
46. Eckington Church
47. St. John's Church, Staveley
48. Bolsover Castle (C17)
    St. Mary's Church
    (Cavendish Chapel, 1618)
49. Sutton Scarsdale Hall (1724, ruin)
50. Ault Hucknall Church
51. *Hardwick Hall & Gardens* (NT)
52. Dale Abbey (C13 remains)
    All Saints Church
    Rock Hermitage (c. 1130)
    C18 Cave (view)
    Cat & Fiddle Windmill (1788)
53. Beauvale Priory (C14 remains)
54. Teversal Church
55. View of Annesley Park
56. Basford Pumping Station
57. Gedling Church
58. *Newstead Abbey, House & Grounds*
59. Papplewick Church
    Castle Mill (C18 watermill), Linby
60. Strelley Church
61. Wollaton Church
62. Wollaton Hall (C16; *Natural
    History Museum*) & Park
63. *Nottingham University* (1928) *& Park*
64. Holy Trinity Church (Norman font),
    Lenton

65. Nottingham Castle (C17, restored;
    City Museum & Art Gallery)
    St. Mary's Church
    St. Nicholas' Church
    St. Peter's Church
    Collins' Almshouses (1709)
    Newdigate House (C17), Castle Gate
    Bromley House (1752)
    Salutation Inn (C15 rock cellars)
    Trip to Jerusalem Inn (rock cellars)
66. St. Stephen's Church, Sneinton
67. Bestwood Pumping Station (1871)
68. Rolleston Church
69. Elston Chapel (unrestored early C19
    interior)
70. Sibthorpe Church
    Dovecote (C14)
71. Bottesford Church
    Fleming's Bridge (c. 1600)
72. Westborough Church
73. *Old Manor House* (C17), Allington
74. *Belton House*
    Belton Church
    Brownlow Almshouses (C17)
75. Barkston Church
76. Carlton Scroop Church
77. Ancaster Church
78. Wilsford Church
79. Hough-on-the-Hill Church
80. Caythorpe Church
81. Fulbeck Church & Village
82. Leadenham Church
83. Hawton Church
84. Queen's Sconce (C17 fort), Newark
85. Southwell Minster
86. Newark Castle (C12)
    St. Mary's Church
    Beaumond Cross (C15, restored)
    Old White Hart Inn (C14)
    Tudor Hall (old Grammar School.
    1529)
    Town Hall (Carr. 1773)
    Castle Gate (Georgian houses)
    Market Place
    Museum & Art Gallery
87. Stragglethorpe Church
88. Brant Broughton Church
    Friend's House (1701)
89. *Marston Hall* (C16 manor house)
90. Holme Church
91. *Aubourn Hall*
92. Sutton-on-Trent Church
93. *Doddington Hall*

Map 46

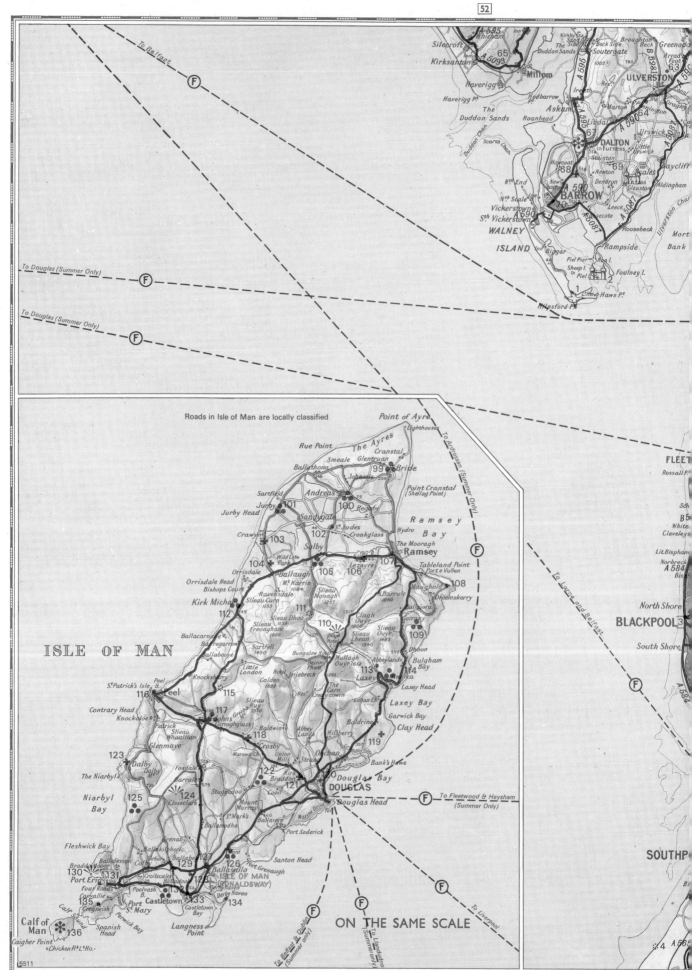

52

Roads in Isle of Man are locally classified

ISLE OF MAN

ON THE SAME SCALE

5511

The Edinburgh Geographical Institute

Map 47

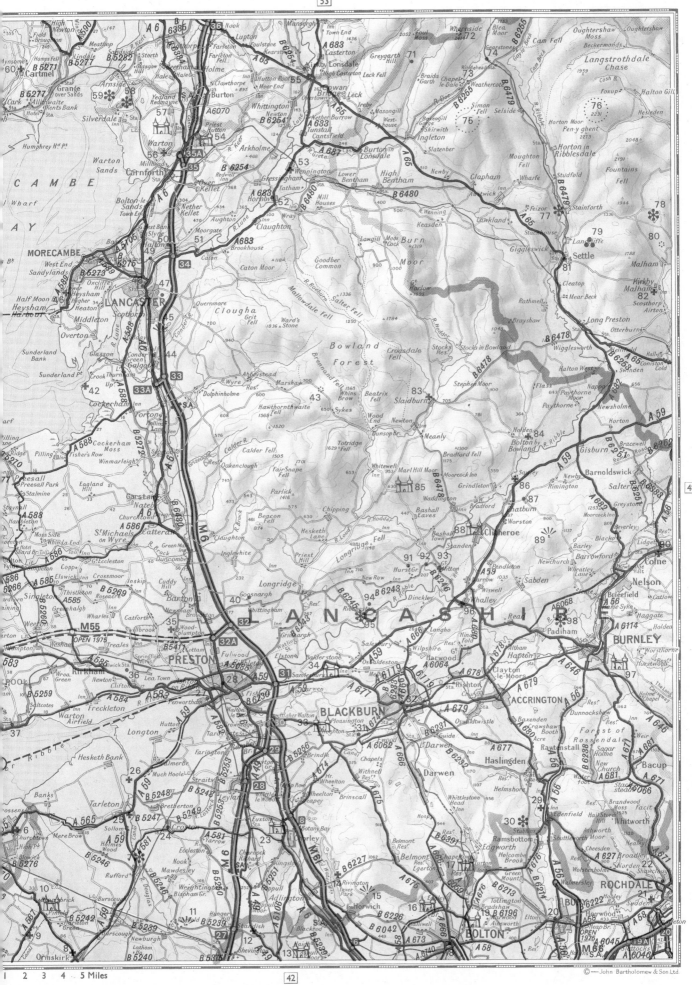

Gazetteer to Maps 46·47

1. Walney Island (sand dunes & birds)
2. Piel Castle (C14 ruin)
3. Blackpool Tower (Eiffel, 1891)
4. Ainsdale Sand Dunes (plants & birds)
5. Hesketh Park, Southport
   Atkinson Art Gallery
6. North Meols Church
7. *Rufford Old Hall* (NT)
8. Ormskirk Church
9. Halsall Church
10. Scarisbrick Hall (1814–1870)
11. Parbold Hill (view)
12. Standish Church
13. *Haigh Hall* (c. 1840; *museum*)
14. Rivington Church
    Unitarian Chapel (1703)
15. Rivington Pike (1191 ft; tower 1733, view)
16. *Smithills Hall*
17. *Turton Tower, garden & museum*
18. Bolton Town Hall (1873)
    Museum & Art Gallery
    Tonge Moor Textile Machinery Museum
19. Hall-i-th'-Wood (C16; museum)
20. Bury Art Gallery (Wrigley Collection)
21. Sudden Church
22. St. Chad's Church, Rochdale
    Town Hall (1871)
    Art Gallery & Museum
    Co-operative Museum, Toad Lane
    St. Mary's Church, Wardleworth
23. *Astley Hall & Museum*
24. Croston Church & Village
    Royal Umpire Museum
25. Tarleton Old Church
26. Hoole Church
27. Penwortham Church
    Castle Hill (Norman earthwork)
28. St. Peter's Church, Preston
    St. Walburgh's Church (RC)
    St. George's Church
    Swanson & Birley's Mills (c. 1830)
    Railway Viaduct (1838)
    Harris Museum & Art Gallery
29. Edenfield Church
30. Stubbins (view, Peel Monument) (NT), Holcombe Manor
31. Pleasington Church (RC)
32. St. Mary's Cathedral, Blackburn
    St. John's Church
    Museum & Art Gallery
    Lewis Textile Museum
    Witton Park
33. *Hoghton Tower & Garden*
34. *Samlesbury Old Hall* (museum)
35. Woodplumpton Church
36. Salwick Windmill
37. Lytham (Georgian watering place)
38. Poulton-le-Fylde Church
39. Thornton Windmill (1790)
40. Bushell's Hospital (almshouses, 1735), Goosnargh
41. Lighthouses (Decimus Burton, c. 1840), Fleetwood
42. Cockersand Abbey (C13 remains)
43. Trough of Bowland (moorland pass, views)
44. Galgate Silk Mill (c. 1790–1820)
45. Lancaster By-Pass (views)
46. Heysham Church
47. Ashton Memorial (1907–9) & Park, Lancaster
48. *Lancaster Castle*
    St. Mary's Church
    St. John's Church
    Penny's Hospital (almshouses, 1715)

Old Custom House & Warehouses, (1764)
Old Town Hall (1783; *museum*)
Skerton Bridge (1788)
Houses in Castle Park & Church Street
49. Lancaster Canal Aqueduct (Rennie, 1796)
50. Churchyard Cross (C11), Halton
    Castle Hill (earthwork)
51. Crook o' Lune Bridge, Lonsdale
52. Hornby Church
    Churchyard Cross (Saxon)
    Castle Stede (Norman earthwork)
    Loyn Bridge
53. Melling Church
54. *Borwick* (C16 manor house)
55. Kirkby Lonsdale Church (view)
    Devil's Bridge (C15)
56. Warton Church
57. *Leighton Hall & Garden*
58. Castlebarrow (view) (NT), Silverdale
    Eaves & Waterslack Woods (NT)
59. Arnside Knott (view) (NT)
60. Cartmel Priory Church
    Priory Gatehouse (c. 1330) (NT)
61. *Holker Hall & Garden*
62. Furness Railway (across the sea)
63. Barrow Monument (1850), Hoad Hill, Ulverston
64. Quakers' Meeting House (1688), Swarthmoor
65. Millom Castle (C13 remains)
    Millom Old Church
66. Chapel Island (ruined chapel), Morecambe Bay
67. Dalton Tower (C14) (NT)
68. *Furness Abbey* (C12–13 remains)
69. Gleaston Castle (C13 remains)
70. *Barrow-in-Furness Museum*
71. Yordas Cave, Kingsdale
72. Whernside (2414 ft)
73. Weathercote & Gatekirk Caves
74. Ribblehead Viaduct (1875)
75. Ingleborough (2373 ft; hillfort, geology & plants)
    Alum Pot
    Gaping Ghyll Hole
    White Scar Cavern
76. Pen-y-Ghent (2273 ft)
    Hunt Pot & Hell Pot
    Douk Gill Scar
77. Stainforth Bridge (C17) (NT)
78. Malham Tarn (field studies centre, geology & plants) (NT)
79. Victoria Cave (prehistoric site)
80. Malham Cove (natural amphitheatre)
81. *Settle Museum* (Craven cave finds)
    Folly Hall (C17)
82. Kirkby Malham Church
83. Slaidburn Church
84. Bolton-by-Bowland Church
85. *Browsholme Hall*
86. *Sawley Abbey* (C12 remains)
87. Downham (village)
88. Clitheroe Castle (Norman ruin)
89. Pendle Hill (1831 ft; views)
90. St. Bartholomew's Church, Colne
91. *Stonyhurst College* (c. 1594)
    Shireburn Almshouses (c. 1730)
92. Packhorse Bridge (1563), river Hodder
    New Bridge (1826)
93. Great Mitton Church
94. Stidd Chapel (Norman)
    Stidd Almshouses (1728)
95. *Roman Fort & Museum* (NT), Ribchester

St. Wilfred's Church
Ribble Bridge (1774)
96. Whalley Abbey (C13 remains)
    St. Mary's Church
97. *Towneley Hall, Art Gallery & Museum*
98. Gawthorpe Hall (NT)
99. Thor Cross (Norse), Kirk Bride
100. Odin Cross & Thorwald Cross (Norse), Kirk Andreas
101. Norse Crosses, Jurby
     Viking Burial Mounds
102. Ballachurry Fort (C17 earthwork)
103. Ballaugh Old Church
104. Ballaugh New Church
105. Cronk Sumark (Iron Age hillfort)
106. Lezayre Church
107. St. Paul's Church, Ramsey
     St. Maughold's Church (RC)
     Court House (C18)
108. Kirk Maughold Crosses (Celtic, Norse & mediaeval)
     Ruins of 3 Keeills
     St. Maughold's Well
     Maughold Head (views)
109. Cashtal Yn Ard (neolithic chambered cairn)
110. Snaefell (2034 ft; view, Edwardian electric railway)
111. Sulby Glen
112. Norse Crosses, Kirk Michael
113. Laxey Waterwheel (1854)
114. King Orry's Grave (neolithic chambered cairn)
115. Glen Helen
116. Peel (town)
     Peel Castle (mediaeval remains, cathedral, church & round tower)
117. Tynwald Hill (Norse assembly field)
     The Giant's Grave (Bronze Age)
118. St. Trinian's Chapel (C14 ruin)
119. Lonan Old Church (runic crosses)
120. St. George's Church, Douglas
     St. Ninian's Church
     Castle Mona Hotel (C18)
     Manx Museum
     The Tower of Refuge (1832), Douglas Bay
121. Kirk Braddan Old Church (runic crosses)
     Kirk Braddan New Church
122. Braaid Site (Celtic & Norse homesteads)
123. Dalby Church
124. South Barrule (1585 ft; hillfort view)
125. Cronk Ny Irree Laa (1499 ft; Bronze Age cairn)
126. Arragon Mooar Stone Circles (Bronze Age)
127. *Rushen Abbey* (C12 remains)
     Monk's Bridge (C14)
128. Kirk Malew
129. Franciscan Chapel (C14), Arbory
130. Bradda Head (400 ft; view, Milner Tower 1871)
131. *Marine Biological Station*, Port Erin
132. Chapel Hill (hillfort, Keeill Vael & Viking ship burial) Balladoole
133. Castletown Church
     Castle Rushen (mainly C14)
     Old St. Mary's Chapel & Grammar School
     Nautical Museum
134. Derby Fort (c. 1540), St. Michael's Island
135. *Manx Village Folk Museum*, Cregneish
136. Calf of Man (360 ft; views, *Bird Observatory*) (NT)

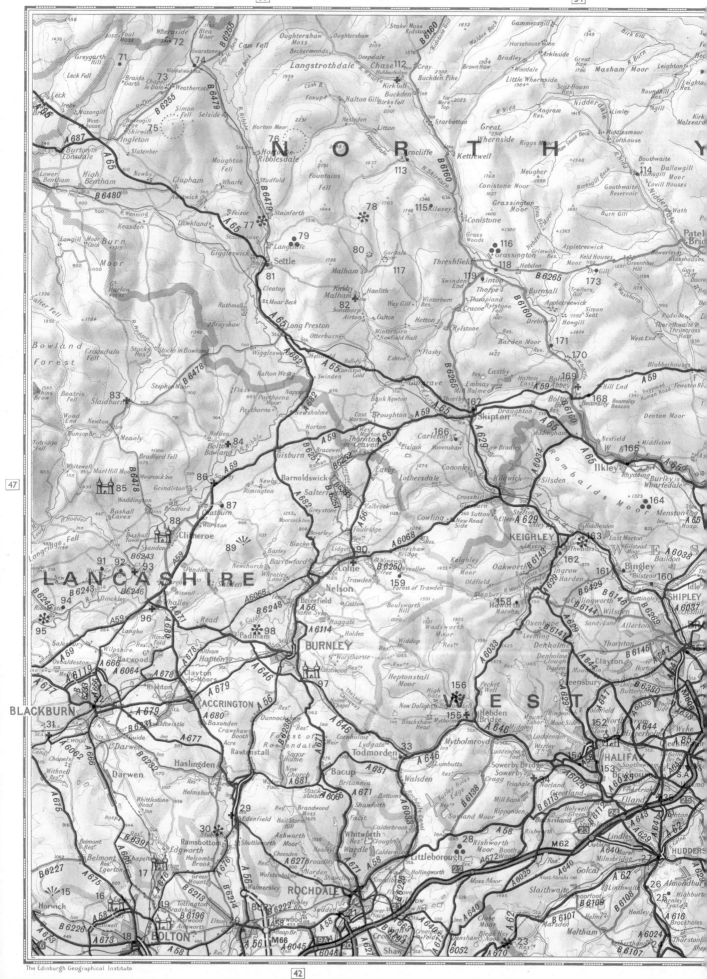

Map 48

Map 49

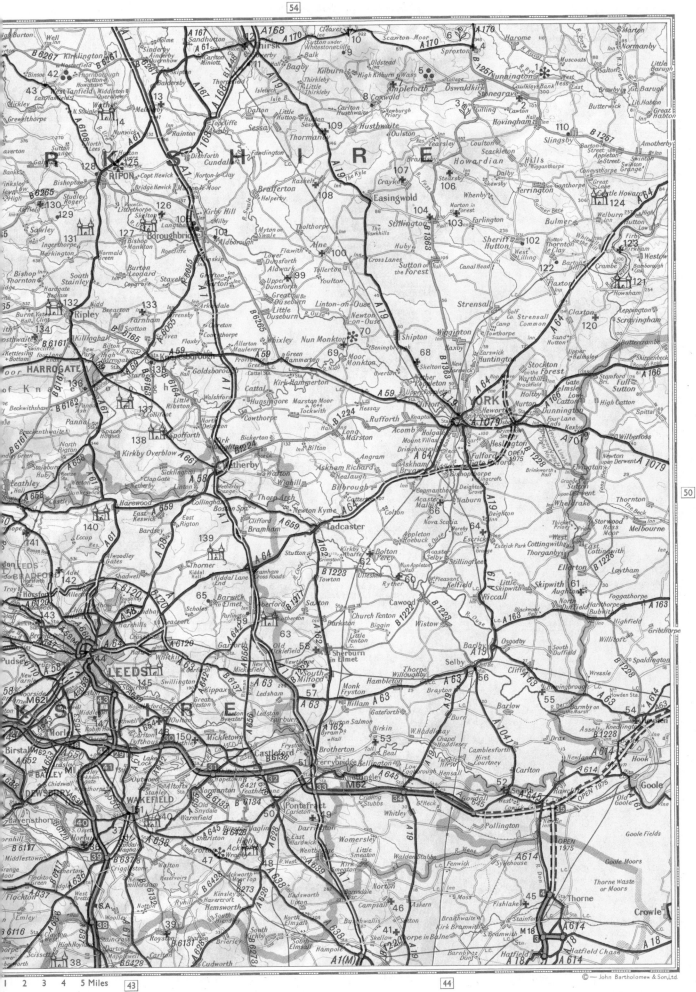

1 2 3 4 5 Miles

Gazetteer to Maps 48·49

1. *Nunnington Hall* (NT)
2. Stonegrave Church
3. *Gilling Castle Gardens*
4. Sproxton Church
5. Studfold Ring (hillfort), Ampleforth
6. *Duncombe Park Gardens*
   (C18 temples), Helmsley
7. Byland Abbey (C12–13 remains)
8. Coxwold (village)
   St. Michael's Church
   Fauconberg Almshouses (C17)
   Shandy Hall (Stern's home)
9. Kilburn White Horse (C19 turf-cut)
10. Sutton Bank (view)
11. Packhorse Bridge, Sowerby
12. Thirsk Church
13. Baldersby Church
14. *Norton Conyers* (C16–17)
15. Rivington Pike (1191 ft; tower
    1733, view)
16. *Smithills Hall*
17. *Turton Tower, garden & museum*
18. Bolton Town Hall (1873)
    Museum & Art Gallery
    *Tonge Moor Textile Machinery
    Museum*
19. *Hall-i'-th'-Wood* (C16; museum)
20. *Bury Art Gallery*
    (Wrigley Collection)
21. Sudden Church
22. St. Chad's Church, Rochdale
    Town Hall (1871)
    Art Gallery & Museum
    Cooperative Museum, Toad Lane
    St. Mary's Church, Wardleworth
23. Marsden Moor (NT)
24. Old Woollen Mills, Holme Valley
25. Almondbury Church
    Castle Hill (hillfort, tower, view)
26. Lockwood Viaduct (1848) & Mill
27. Huddersfield Railway Station (1848)
    Methodist Church (1819),
       Queen Street
    County Court (1825)
    Clock Tower (Lindley, 1902)
    Art Gallery
    *Tolson Memorial Museum,
    Ravensknowle Park*
28. Roman Road over Blackstone Edge
29. Edenfield Church
30. Stubbins (view, Peel Monument)
    (NT), Holcombe Moor
31. Pleasington Church (RC)
32. St. Mary's Cathedral, Blackburn
    St. John's Church
    Museum & Art Gallery
    Lewis Textile Museum
    Witlon Park
33. Todmorden Hall (C17; Port Office)
    Town Hall (1870)
34. Sowerby Church
35. St. Matthew's Church, Rastrick
36. Horbury Church
37. Sandal Castle (mediaeval
       earthwork, view)
38. *Cannon Hall & Park*, Cawthorne
39. Royston Church
40. Heath Hall, Heath
41. Owston Church
42. Thornborough Moor (stone circles)
43. West Tanfield Church
    Marmion Gatehouse (C15)
    Ure Bridge (view)
44. Masham Church
    Churchyard Cross (Saxon)
    Market Place & Cross
    Ure Bridge (C18)
45. Fishlake Church
46. Campsall Church
47. *Nostell Priory & Gardens* (NT)
    Wragby Church
48. *Ackworth School*
49. Darrington Church
50. All Saints Church, Pontefract
    New Hall (ruin, 1591)
    Butter Cross (1734)
    Castle Museum
51. Ferrybridge (1797)
52. Snaith Church
53. Birkin Church
54. Howden Minster
55. Hemingborough Church
56. Selby Abbey
    Selby Bridge (wooden, 1791)
57. Steeton Hall Gatehouse (C14)
58. Sherburn-in-Elmet Church
59. Aberford Almshouses (1844)
60. Ryther Church
61. Aughton Church
62. Bolton Percy Church
63. *Lotherton Hall* (Edwardian)
    (Gascoigne art collection)
64. Escrick Church
65. Barwick-in-Elmet earthworks
66. Acaster Malbis Church
67. York Minster
    All Saints Church, North Street
    All Saints Church, Pavement
    St. Denys's Church
    Holy Trinity Church, Goodramgate
    Holy Trinity Church, Micklegate
    St. Martin-cum-Gregory's Church
    St. Mary's Church, Bishophill Junior
    St. Mary's Church, Castlegate
    St. Michael's-le-Belfry Church
    City Walls & Bars (mediaeval,
       3 miles long)
    St. Mary's Abbey (C13 remains &
       Yorkshire Museum)
    St. Leonard's Hospital (C1 remains)
    Clifford's Tower (C13 catsle remains)
    Merchant Adventurers' Hall (C14)
    Merchant Taylor's Hall (C15)
    St. Anthony's Hall (C15)
    The Shambles (Tudor street of shops)
    St. William's College (C15–17)
    King's Manor (C16)
    Treasurer's House (C17) (NT)
    Herbert House (C17)
    Mansion House (1726)
    Assembly Rooms (Burlington, 1736)
    Old Debtors' Prison (1705; *museum*)
    Assize Courts (1777)
    Old Female Prison (Carr, 1780;
       Castle Museum)
    City of York Art Gallery
    Railway Museum
68. Skelton Church
69. Nun Monkton Church
70. *Beningbrough Hall* (NT)
71. Yordas Cave, Kingsdale
72. Whernside (2414 ft)
73. Weathercote & Gatekirk Caves
74. Ribblehead Viaduct (1875)
75. Ingleborough (2373 ft; hillfort,
       geology & plants)
    Alum Pot
    Gaping Ghyll Hole
    White Scar Cavern
76. Pen-y-Ghent (2273 ft)
    Hunt Pot & Hell Pot
    Douk Gill Scar
77. Stainforth Bridge (C17) (NT)
78. Malham Tarn (Field Studies Centre,
       geology & plants) (NT)
79. Victoria Cave (prehistoric site)
80. Malham Cove (natural
       amphitheatre)
81. *Settle Museum* (Craven cave finds)
    Folly Hall (C17)
82. Kirkby Malham Church
83. Slaidburn Church
84. Bolton-by-Bowland Church
85. *Browsholme Hall*
86. *Sawley Abbey* (C12 remains)
87. Downham (village)
88. Clitheroe Castle (Norman ruin)
89. Pendle Hill (1831 ft; views)
90. St. Bartholomew's Church, Colne
91. *Stonyhurst College* (c. 1594)
    Shireburn Almshouses (c. 1730)
92. Packhorse Bridge (1563), river
       Hodder
    New Bridge (1826)
93. Great Mitton Church
94. Stidd Chapel (Norman
    Stidd Almshouses (1728)
95. *Roman Fort & Museum* (NT),
       Ribchester
    St. Wilfred's Church
    Ribble Bridge
96. Whalley Abbey (C13 remains)
    St. Mary's Church

97. *Towneley Hall, Art Gallery & Museum*
98. *Gawthorpe Hall* (NT)
99. Aldwark Church
100. Alne Church
101. Aldborough Church
    Isurium (Roman town remains & museum)
102. Sheriff Hutton Castle (C14 ruin)
    St. Helen's Church
103. Marton-in-the-Forest Church
104. Stillington Church
105. Devil's Arrows (ancient? monoliths), Boroughbridge
106. Brandsby Church
107. Crayke Church
108. Raskelf Church
109. Thormanby Church
110. Slingsby Castle (C17 remains)
    Maypole (92 ft)
111. Druid's Temple (Regency folly)
112. Hubberholme Church, Langstrothdale
113. Arncliffe (village), Littondale
    Iron Age Enclosure System & Settlement
114. Ramsgill (village), Nidderdale
    Gouthwaite Reservoir
115. Dowkerbottom Cave
116. Grassington (prehistoric site), Wharfedale
117. Gordale Scar (ravine, waterfalls)
118. Linton Church
    Packhorse & Clapper Bridges
119. Fountaine's Hospital (almshouses, 1721), Linton
120. Bossall Church
121. *Howsham Hall*
122. *Foston Old Rectory*
123. Kirkham Priory (C13 remains)
124. *Castle Howard, House & Gardens*
125. Sharow Sanctuary Cross (NT)
126. Skelton Church
127. *Newby Hall & Garden*
128. Ripon Cathedral
    Maison Dieu (C15 ruined chapel)
    Hospital of St. Mary Magdalene (chapel)
    The Wakeman's House (C13; *museum*)
    Town Hall (Wyatt, 1799)
    The Old Hall (C18)
129. Fountains Abbey (C12–15)
    Studley Royal Park (C18 formal gardens)
    Fountains Hall
130. Studley Royal Church
    Aldfield Church
131. *Markenfield Hall*
132. *Ripley Castle & Garden*

133. Farnham Church
134. Hampsthwaite Church
135. Knaresborough Castle (C14 keep) & Town
    St. Robert's Chapel (C9 rock-hewn)
    Chapel of Our Lady of the Crag (1409)
    Dropping Well (petrifying spring)
    Viaduct (view)
136. St. Wilfred's Church, Harrogate
    Royal Pump Room (1842; *sulphur well, museum*)
    The Stray (200 acre town common)
    Valley Gardens
    Harlow Car Gardens
137. *Rudding Park, House & Garden*
138. Spofforth Castle (C14)
139. *Bramham Park, House & Gardens*
140. *Harewood House & Park*
    Harewood Church
141. Bramhope Chapel (1649)
142. Adel Church
143. Kirkstall Abbey (C12–15)
    Abbey House Museum
144. Holy Trinity Church, Leeds
    St. John's Church, Briggate
    St. Peter's Church
    St. Aidan's Church, Roundhay Road
    Town Hall (1858)
    Corn Exchange (1863)
    Gott's Park Mansion (1820)
    Roundhay Park Mansion (1826)
    Gott's Woollen Mill (1792), Bean Ing
    Calder Navigation Warehouse, Call Lane
    Marshall Mills (Bonomi, 1840 Egyptian)
    City Art Gallery
    City Museum
    Thoresby Society Library
145. *Temple Newsham, Museum & Garden*
146. Tong Church
147. Middleton Colliery Railway (1758)
148. Oulton Church
149. *Oakwell Hall, Garden & Museum, Birstall*
150. Methley Church
151. All Saints Cathedral, Wakefield
    Wakefield Bridge & Chapel (C14)
    Cathedral School (1598)
    Westgate Chapel (1752)
    Court House (1810)
    St. John's Square (Georgian houses & church)
    Town Hall (1880)
    City Art Gallery
    City Museum
152. Shibden Hall (C15–17; *West Yorkshire Folk Museum*) & Park
153. St. John Baptist's Church, Halifax
    Piece Hall (Clothmarket, 1775)

    Copley Mill (1847) & Workmen's Terraces (c. 1850)
    Haley Mills (1837) & Workmen's Terraces (c. 1860), Akroydon
    Bankfield Museum & Art Gallery
154. Wainhouse Tower (folly, 1875), Halifax
155. Heptonstall Old Church (mediaeval ruin)
156. Hardcastle Crags (NT), Hebden Dale
    Gibson's Wood (NT)
    High Green Wood & Black Dean (NT)
157. St. Peter's Cathedral, Bradford
    Bolling Hall (C14–18; *museum*)
    Court House (1843)
    Wool Exchange (1867)
    Town Hall (1873)
    City Art Gallery & Museum
158. *Bronte Parsonage Museum, Haworth*
159. Wycoller Hall (C16 ruin)
    Weavers' Bridge (C13 Packhorse)
    Clapper & Clam Bridges
160. Saltaire (Sir Titus Salt's model town for Alpaca manufactory, 1853)
161. Holy Trinity Church, Bingley
    Market House & Cross (1753), Prince of Wales Park
    Five Rise Locks, Leeds–Liverpool Canal
162. *Keighley Art Gallery & Museum, Cliffe Castle*
163. *East Riddlesden Hall* (NT)
164. Rombalds Moor (prehistoric sites)
165. Anglian Crosses in All Saint Churchyard, Ilkley
    Bronze Age Carvings, opp. St. Margaret's Church
    Manor House Museum (prehistory & Roman)
166. Spence's Hospital (almshouse, 1698), Carleton
167. Skipton Church
    Skipton Castle
    Craven Museum
168. Beamsley Hospital & Chapel (1593)
169. Bolton Priory Church
    Abbey Ruins and Grounds
170. The Strid (gorge, r. Wharfe)
171. Barden Tower (mediaeval ruin & chapel)
    Barden Bridge (C17)
172. Fewston Church
173. *Stump Cross Caverns*
174. All Saints Church, Otley
    Bramhope Tunnel Monument (c. 1850)
175. Brimham Rocks (millstone crags, views) (NT)

54

55

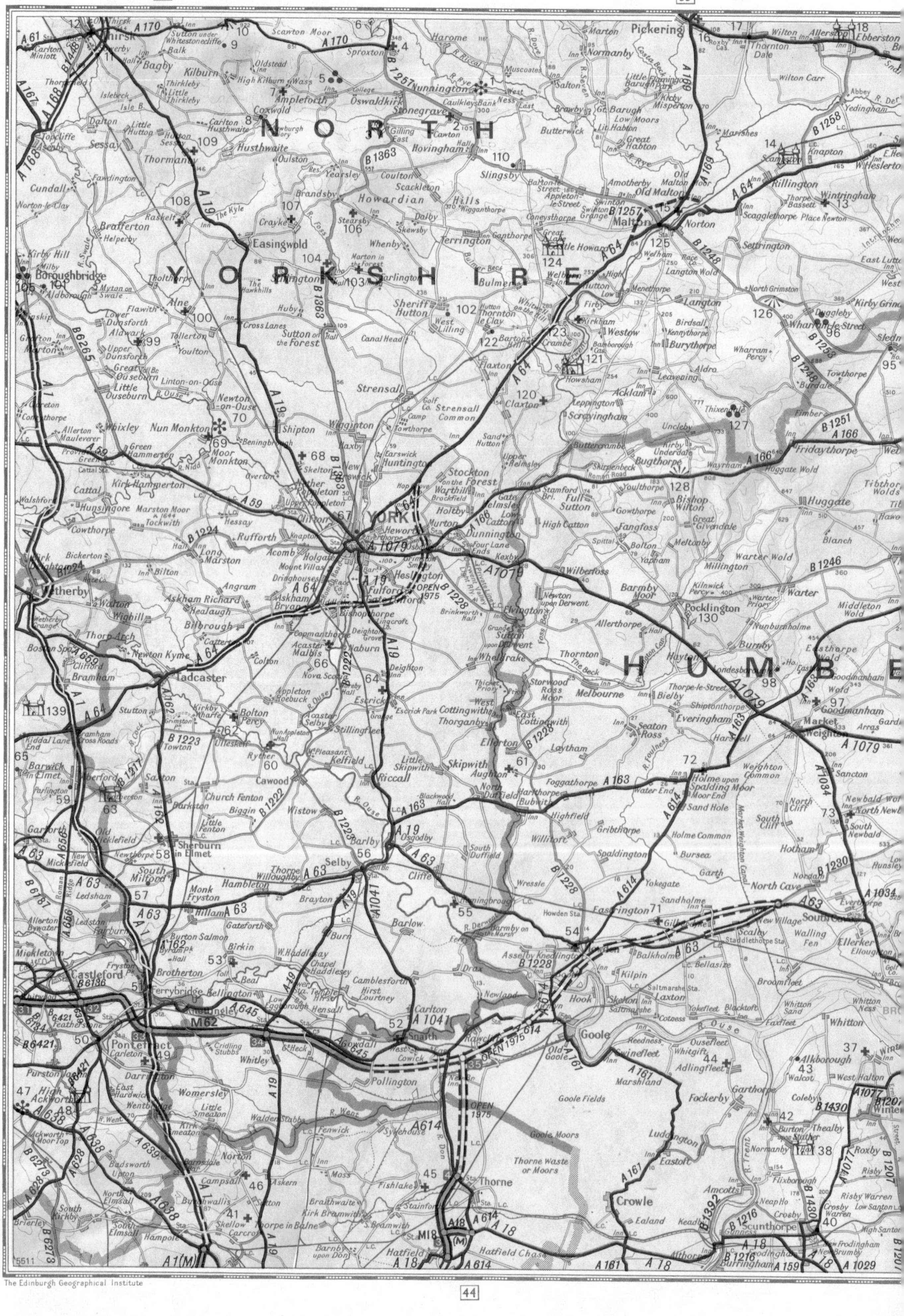
NORTH
YORKSHIRE
HUMBE
Thirsk
Pickering
Malton
Norton
Easingwold
Boroughbridge
York
Tadcaster
Selby
Castleford
Pontefract
Goole
Thorne
Crowle
Scunthorpe
Pocklington
Market Weighton
Howardian Hills
Wetherby
Ferrybridge
Snaith
Howden
Hatfield Chase
Thorne Waste or Moors
Goole Moors
Goole Fields
A 19
A 64
A 1079
A 166
A 163
A 63
A 614
A 1041
A 645
M62
M18
A 18
A1(M)
5511

49

44

Map 51

1   2   3   4   5 Miles

© — John Bartholomew & Son Ltd.

Gazetteer to Maps 50·51

1. *Nunnington Hall* (NT)
2. Stonegrave Church
3. *Gilling Castle Gardens*
4. Sproxton Church
5. Studfold Ring (hillfort), Ampleforth
6. *Duncombe Park Gardens* (C18 temples), Helmsley
7. Byland Abbey (C12–13 remains)
8. Coxwold (village)
   St. Michael's Church
   Fauconberg Almshouses (C17)
   Shandy Hall (Sterne's home)
9. Kilburn White Horse (C19 turf-cut)
10. Sutton Bank (view)
11. Packhorse Bridge, Sowerby
12. Thirsk Church
13. Wintringham Church
14. *Scampston Hall & Gardens*
15. Old Malton Priory Church
16. Pickering Church
17. Thornton-le-Dale (village)
    Lumley Almshouses (C17)
    Market Cross (mediaeval)
18. *Ebberston Hall*
19. Ganton Church
20. Star Carr (mesolithic settlement), Seamer
21. Flotmanby Wold (long barrow, view)
22. Grizthorpe Cliff
23. Hunmanby Gate (folly, 1809)
24. St. Oswald's Church, Filey
25. Filey Brigg (reef)
26. Bempton Cliffs
27. Willy Howe (round barrow)
28. Weaverthorpe Church
29. Monolith in churchyard, Rudston
30. Boynton Church
    Boynton Hall (Tudor & Georgian)
31. Sewerby Church
    Sewerby Hall (Art Gallery) & Park
32. Flamborough Church
    Danes Dike
33. Flamborough Head (cliffs, seabirds, tower)
34. St. Mary's Priory Church, Bridlington
    Bayle Gate (C14; *museum*)
35. Bessingby Church
36. Carnaby Temple (c. 1760)
37. Winteringham Church
38. *Normanby Hall* (Regency) & *Gardens*
39. Appleby Church
40. *Borough Museum & Art Gallery*, Scunthorpe
41. Owston Church
42. Burton-on-Stather Church (view)
43. Alkborough Church (view)
    Julian's Bower (turf maze)
44. Adlingfleet Church
45. Fishlake Church
46. Campsall Church
47. *Nostell Priory & Gardens* (NT)
    Wragby Church
48. Ackworth School
49. Darrington Church
50. All Saints Church, Pontefract
    New Hall (ruin, 1591)
    Butter Cross (1734)
    Castle Museum
51. Ferrybridge (1797)
52. Snaith Church
53. Birkin Church
54. Howden Minster

55. Hemingborough Church
56. Selby Abbey
    Selby Bridge (wooden, 1791)
57. Steeton Hall Gatehouse (C14)
58. Sherburn-in-Elmet Church
59. Aberford Almshouses (1844)
60. Ryther Church
61. Aughton Church
62. Bolton Percy Church
63. *Lotherton Hall* (Edwardian) (Gascoigne art collection)
64. Escrick Church
65. Barwick-in-Elmet Earthworks
66. Acaster Malbis Church
67. York Minster
    All Saints Church, North Street
    All Saints Church, Pavement
    St. Denys's Church
    Holy Trinity Church, Goodramgate
    Holy Trinity Church, Micklegate
    St. Martin-cum-Gregory's Church
    St. Mary's Church, Bishophill Junior
    St. Mary's Church, Castlegate
    St. Michael's-le-Belfry Church
    City Walls & Bars (mediaeval, 3 miles long)
    St. Mary's Abbey (C13 remains & *Yorkshire Museum*)
    St. Leonard's Hospital (C13 remains)
    Clifford's Tower (C13 castle remains)
    Merchant Adventurers' Hall (C14)
    Merchant Taylors' Hall (C15)
    St. Anthony's Hall (C15)
    The Shambles (Tudor street of shops)
    St. William's College (C15–17)
    King's Manor (C16)
    Treasurer's House (C17) (NT)
    Herbert House (C17)
    Mansion House (1726)
    Assembly Rooms (Burlington, 1736)
    Old Debtors' Prison (1705; *museum*)
    Assize Courts (1777)
    Old Female Prison (Carr, 1780; *Castle Museum*)
    City of York Art Gallery
    Railway Museum
68. Skelton Church
69. Nun Monkton Church
70. *Beningbrough Hall* (NT)
71. Eastrington Church
72. Holme-upon-Spaldingmoor Church
73. North Newbald Church
74. Beverley Minster
    St. Mary's Church
    Ann Routh's Hospital (1740 & 1809)
    Market Cross (1714) & C18 Town Houses
    Court House & Gaol (1804)
    Art Gallery and Museum
75. Skidby Windmill (1821)
76. Cottingham Church
77. Holy Trinity Church, Hull
    St. Mary's Church
    St. Mary's Church, Sculcoates
    Charterhouse (C18 almshouses)
    Wilberforce House (c. 1590; *museum*)
    Trinity House (1753)
    23 & 24 High Street (Georgian; *museum*)
    Wilberforce Monument (1834)
    Ferens Art Gallery
    Maritime Museum, Pickering Park
    Transport Museum
    Maister House (1744) (NT)

78. Swine Church
79. *Burton Constable*
80. Hedon Church
81. Ottringham Church
82. Winestead Church
83. Patrington Church
84. Welwick Church
85. Hilston Church
86. Hornsea Mere (birds)
87. Skipsea Church
    Skipsea Castle (Norman earthwork)
88. Barmston Church
89. Burton Agnes Church
    Burton Agnes Hall & Gardens
90. Harpham Church
91. Brandesburton Church
92. Lockington Church
93. Dalton Holme Church
94. Tatton Sykes Memorial (1865)
95. Sledmere Church
    Sledmere House
    Waggoners' Memorial (C20)
    Castle Farm
96. Duggleby Howe (round barrow)
97. Goodmanham Church
98. Londesborough Hospital (C17 almshouses)
99. Aldwark Church
100. Alne Church
101. Aldborough Church
     Isurium (Roman town remains & museum)
102. Sheriff Hutton Castle (C14 ruin)
     St. Helen's Church
103. Marton-in-the-Forest Church
104. Stillington Church
105. Devil's Arrows (ancient? monoliths), Boroughbridge
106. Brandsby Church
107. Crayke Church
108. Raskelf Church
109. Thormanby Church
110. Slingsby Castle (C17 remains)
     Maypole (92 ft)
111. St. James's Church, Grimsby
112. Tower Windmill (1875), Stallingborough
113. Brocklesby Church
     Mausoleum (Wyatt, 1787), Brocklesby Park
114. Croxton Church
115. Ulceby Church
116. Bonby Church
117. St. Mary's Church, Barton-upon-Humber
     St. Peter's Church
118. Thornton Abbey (C12–14 remains)
119. Spurn Head (BTO Bird Observatory)
120. Bossall Church
121. *Howsham Hall*
122. *Foston Old Rectory*
123. Kirkham Priory (C13 remains)
124. *Castle Howard, House & Gardens*
125. *Roman Malton Museum*, Malton
126. Grimston Hill (view)
127. Thixendale (numerous round barrows)
     Huggate Wold
128. Garrowby Hill (view)
129. Bainton Church
130. *Burnby Hall Gardens*
139. *Bramham Park, House & Gardens*

Map 52

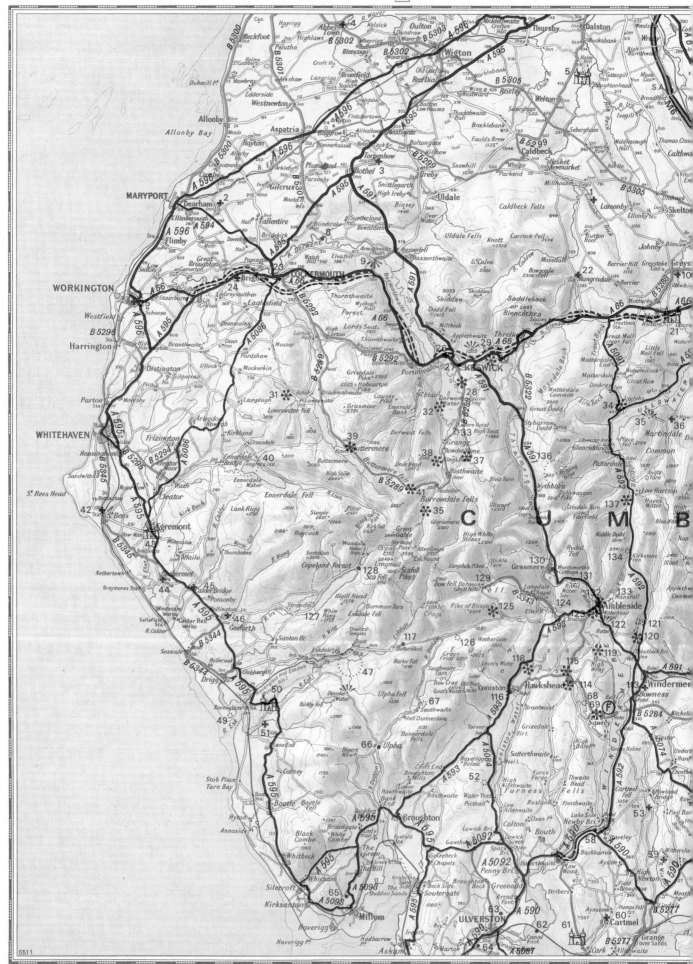

Map 53

60

61

DURHAM

NORTH YORKSHIRE

Edmondbyers

Alston
Nenthead
Nenthall
Coalcleugh
Allenheads
Carr Shield
Hartley Moor
Spartylea
Allergate Ho.
Cross Rigg
Muggleswick Common
Stanhope Common
Wolsingham Park Moor
Redburn Common
Hunstanworth
Middlehope Moor
Cornriggs
Cowshill
Wearhead
St. John's Chapel
Westgate
Stanhope
Frosterley
Brotherlee
Middleton Common
Harvey Hill
Bollihope Common

Cumrew
Newbiggin
Croglin Fell
Croglin
Ainstable
Renwick
Stafford
Kirkoswald
Lazonby
Glassonby
Gamblesby
Melmerby
Fiends Fell
Black Fell
Gilderdale Forest
Whitley Cas.
Kirkhaugh
Monope Moor
Egypt
Bayles
Nenthead
Garrigill
Windy Hall
Ashgill
Rotherhope Fell
Alston Moor
Killhope Moor
Burnhope Moor
Burnhope Seat
Harwood
Grasshill Common
Langdon Common
Cow Green Res.
Outberry Plain
Pawlaw Pike
Newbiggin
Carrs Hill
Eggleston Common
Monks Moor
Middleton-in-Teesdale
Eggleston
Romaldkirk
Mickleton
Hunderthwaite
Cotherstone
Cotherstone Moor
Startforth
Bowes
Gilmonby
Stainmore Forest
Bowes Moor
Barnard

Penrith
Edenhall
Langwathby
Skirwith
Milburn Forest
Cross Fell
Knock Fell
Dufton Fell
Milburn
Knock
Dufton
Murton
Kirkby Thore
Long Marton
Brampton
Keisley
Hilton Fell
Burton Fell
DANGER ZONE
Warcop Fell
Iron Band
Mickle Fell
Lune Forest
Lune Moor
Crossthwaite Common
Cronkley Fell
Holwick
Holwick Fell
Grassholme Res.
Hunderthwaite Moor
Mickleton Moor
Baldersdale

Appleby
Burrells
Ormside
Sandford
Warcop
Brough
Brough Sowerby
Musgrave
Little Musgrave
Soulby
Winton
Kaber
Hartley
Kirkby Stephen
Nateby
Kaber Fell
Taylor Rigg
Stainmore
Stainmore Common
A 66
Bowes Moor
Sleightholme Moor
Arkengarthdale Moor
Reeth

Shap
Crosby Ravensworth
Orton
Raisbeck
Kelleth
Crosby Garrett
Smardale
Waitby
Begin Hill
Ash Fell
Tebay
Newbiggin
Ravenstonedale
Artlegarth
Tarn House
Wild Boar Fell
Swarth Fell
Mallerstang
Birkdale Common
Birkdale
High Seat
Hoggarths
Angram
Stonesdale Moor
Water Crag
Great Pinseat
Melbecks Moor
Calver Hill
Healaugh
Gunnerside
Swaledale
Grinton
Harkerside Moor
Whitaside Moor

Firbank
Sedbergh
Howgill
The Calf
Baugh Fell
Yarlside
West Fell
Haygarth
Holmes Moss
Abbotside Common
Lovely Seat
Cotterdale
Oxnop Beck
Low Oxnop
Summer Lodge
Askrigg
Nappa Hall
Woodhall
Low Bolton
West Burton

New Hutton
Killington
Middleton
Barbon
Casterton
Kirkby Lonsdale
Leck Fell
Chapel-le-Dale
Weathercote
Whernside
Blea Moor
Cam Fell
Gearstones
Langstrothdale Chase
Cray
Buckden Pike
Kirk Gill
Buckden
Halton Gill
Foxup

Hawes
Gayle
Bainbridge
Semer Water
Stalling Busk
Marsett
Thoralby
Newbiggin
Redshaw Moss
Fleet Moss
Oughtershaw
Beckermonds
Cowgill
Dent Sta.
Deepdale
Gawthrop
Middleton
Barbon
Mansergh
Whittington

YORKSHIRE

1 2 3 4 5 Miles

© — John Bartholomew & Son Ltd.

48

54

1. Castle Sowerby Church
2. Dearham Church
3. Torpenhow Church
4. Holme Cultram Abbey Church
5. Rose Castle (C13–17)
6. Armathwaite Church
7. *Hutton-in-the-Forest Garden*
8. Isel Church
   Isel Hall (mediaeval & C16)
9. Ouse Bridge (viewpoint),
   Bassenthwaite Lake
10. Greystoke Church
11. St. Andrew's Church, Penrith
    Penrith Castle (C14)
12. St. Ninian's Church, Brougham
13. Brougham Castle (C12–13)
14. St. Wilfrid's Chapel, Brougham
    King Arthur's Round Table
    (earthwork)
    Eamont Bridge (mediaeval)
15. Kirkland (scenery)
16. Dufton (village)
17. Long Marton Church
18. Bolton Church
19. Lowther Church
20. Dacre Church
    Dacre Castle (C14)
21. *Hutton John* (C14 & later)
22. Mungrisdale Church
23. Cockermouth Castle (Norman ruin)
    Wordsworth House (NT)
24. Brigham Church
25. St. John's Church, Workington
26. Crosthwaite Church
27. Moot Hall (rebuilt 1813), Keswick
    Fitz Park Museum & Art Gallery
28. Castle Head (viewpoint) (NT),
    Derwentwater
    Friar's Crag (viewpoint)
29. Latrigg (viewpoint), Keswick
30. Castlerigg Stone Circle (NT)
31. Loweswater (NT)
32. Brandelhow Park (NT),
    Derwentwater
33. Lodore Falls
34. Gowbarrow Park (NT), Ullswater
    Aira Force (waterfall) (NT)
35. Sandwick (viewpoint), Ullswater
36. Martindale Old Church
37. Watendlath Tarn & Hamlet (NT)
    Packhorse Bridge
38. Castle Crag (viewpoint) (NT),
    Borrowdale
    Bowder Stone (balanced rock mass)
39. Buttermere (NT)
    Crummock Water (NT)
40. Ennerdale Water
41. Honister Hause (viewpoint)
    Honister Pass (NT)
42. St. Bees Church
43. Egremont Castle (C12 remains)
44. Beckermet Church
45. *Calder Abbey* (C12 remains)
46. Churchyard Cross (c. 1000), Gosforth
47. Eskdale (scenery, waterfalls)
48. Birker Fell (viewpoint)
49. Ravenglass Dunes (birds)
50. *Muncaster Castle, Gardens &
    Terrace* (view)
51. Waberthwaite Church
52. Blawith Fell (scenery)

53. Cartmel Fell Church
54. Holy Trinity Church, Kendal
    Kendal Castle (Norman remains)
    Abbot Hall Art Gallery & Museum
55. Kirkby Lonsdale Church (view)
    Devil's Bridge (C15)
56. *Levens Hall & Gardens*
57. *Sizergh Castle* (NT)
58. Newby Bridge (mediaeval)
59. Witherslack Church
60. Cartmel Priory Church
    Priory Gatehouse (c. 1330) (NT)
61. *Holker Hall & Garden*
62. Furness Railway (across the sea)
63. Barrow Monument (1850),
    Hoad Hill, Ulverston
64. Quakers' Meeting House (1688),
    Swarthmoor
65. Millom Old Church
    Millom Castle (C13 remains)
66. Ulpha Church
    Old Bridge
67. Dunnerdale (scenery)
68. Esthwaite Water
69. *Hill Top* (Beatrix Potter's home,
    C17) (NT), near Sawrey
70. Sedbergh Church
71. Yordas Cave, Kingsdale
72. Whernside (2414 ft)
73. Weathercote & Gatekirk Caves
74. Ribblehead Viaduct (1875)
75. Garsdale (scenery)
76. Dent (village)
77. Long Sleddale (scenery)
78. Tebay Fell (scenery)
79. Ravenstonedale Church
80. Cross Keys Inn (c. 1600, unlicensed)
    (NT), Cautley
81. Wharton Hall (C15–16 remains)
82. Kirkby Stephen Church
83. Viewpoint, Lune Forest
84. High Force (waterfall)
85. Upper Teesdale (geology, botany)
86. Blanchland (C18 planned village)
    St. Mary's Church
    Churchyard Cross
87. Hartside Height (view)
88. Kirkoswald (town)
    St. Oswald's Church
    Kirkoswald Castle (C13 remains)
89. Long Meg & Her Daughters
    (monolith & stone circle)
90. Melmerby (scenery)
91. Moor House Nature Reserve
    (NC. Geology & biology)
92. Upper Teesdale (limestone flora &
    fauna)
    Caldron Snout (waterfall)
93. Wear Dale (scenery)
94. Stanhope Church & Castle (1798)
95. Romaldkirk Church & Village
    Hutchinson's Almshouses
    (rebuilt 1829)
    Eggleston Bridge (C17)
96. Cotherstone, Teesdale (scenery)
97. Bowes Castle (Norman keep)
    Lavatrae (Roman fort)
    St. Giles's Church
98. God's Bridge (natural stone arch)
99. Rey Cross (ancient boundary mark)
    Roman Camp

100. Arkengarthdale (scenery)
101. Grinton Church
102. Bolton Castle (C14)
103. Redmire Force (waterfall)
104. Aysgarth Force (waterfalls)
     Aysgarth Bridge (1539)
105. Swaledale (scenery)
106. Tan Hill Inn (viewpoint)
107. Muker (village)
108. Buttertubs Pass
109. Mill Gill Force (waterfall), Askrigg
110. Hardraw Force (waterfall)
111. Addleborough (1564 ft; view of
     Wensleydale) (NT), Bainbridge
112. Hubberholme Church,
     Langstrothdale
113. Bowness-on-Windermere Church
114. Hawkshead (village) (NT)
115. Hawkshead Court House (Tudor)
     (NT)
116. Coniston (scenery)
     Ruskin Museum
117. Hard Knott Pass, Eskdale
     Hard Knott Castle (Roman fort)
118. Tarn Hows (viewpoint) (NT),
     Coniston
119. Wray Castle Grounds (NT),
     Lake Windermere
120. *Town End* (Yeoman's house, 1626)
     (NT), Troutbeck
121. Troutbeck (scenery)
122. Waterhead (view of Lake
     Windermere)
123. Galava (Roman fort) (NT),
     Ambleside
124. Skelwith Bridge (scenery)
     Skelwith Force (waterfall)
125. Blea Tarn (NT)
126. Wrynose Pass
127. Wast Water
     Nether Wasdale Church
128. Wasdale Head Church
     Packhorse Bridge
129. Langdale (scenery)
130. Grasmere Church
     *Dove Cottage & Wordsworth
     Museum*
131. Rydal (scenery)
132. Bridge House (C18 garden house)
     (NT), Ambleside
133. Stockghyll Force (waterfall)
134. Kirkstone Pass Summit
135. Seathwaite Farm (NT)
     Sty Head Pass
136. Helvellyn (Alpine plants)
137. Brothers Water (NT)
138. Hawes Water
139. Shap Summit (viewpoint)
140. Iron Age Villages (remains),
     Crosby Ravensworth
141. Keld Chapel (Tudor) (NT)
142. Shap Abbey (C13 remains)
143. Crosby Ravensworth Church
144. Ormside Church
145. St. Lawrence's Church, Appleby
     Appleby Castle (C12–17)
     Hospital of St. Anne (almshouses)
146. Warcop Bridge (mediaeval)
147. Brough Church
     Brough Castle (C12 remains)
148. Birkdale (scenery)

Map 54

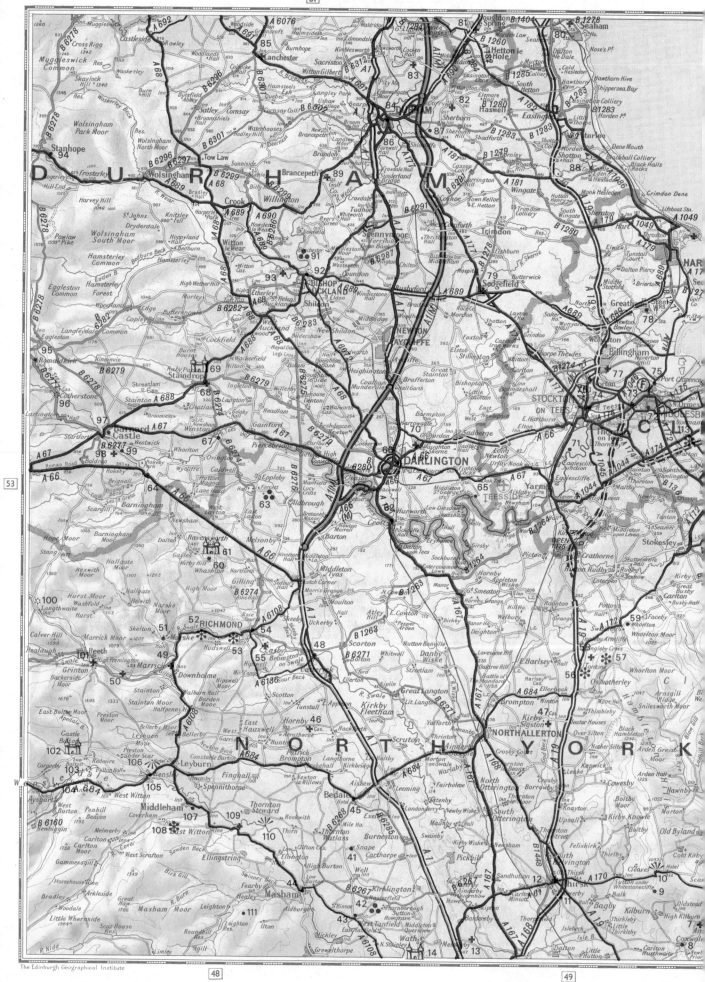

Map 55

1 2 3 4 5 Miles

© — John Bartholomew & Son,Ltd.

1. *Nunnington Hall* (NT)
2. Stonegrave Church
3. *Gilling Castle Gardens*
4. Sproxton Church
5. Studfold Ring (hill-fort), Ampleforth
6. *Duncombe Park Gardens*
   (C18 temples), Helmsley
7. Byland Abbey (C12–13 remains)
8. Coxwold (village)
   St. Michael's Church
   Fauconberg Almshouses (C17)
   Shandy Hall (Sterne's home)
9. Kilburn White Horse (C19 turf-cut)
10. Sutton Bank (view)
11. Packhorse Bridge, Sowerby
12. Thirsk Church
13. Baldersby Church
14. *Norton Conyers* (C16–17)
15. Helmsley Castle (C12 remains)
16. Pickering Church
17. Thornton-le-Dale (village)
    Lumley Almshouses (C17)
    Market Cross (mediaeval)
18. *Ebberston Hall*
19. Ganton Church
20. Star Carr (mesolithic settlement),
    Seamer
21. Flotmanby Wold (long barrow, view)
22. Grizthorpe Cliff
23. Hunmanby Gate (folly, 1809)
24. St. Oswald's Church, Filey
25. Filey Brigg (reef)
26. Oliver's Mount (viewpoint),
    Scarborough
27. Scarborough Castle (C12)
    St. Mary's Church
    Richard III House (C14)
    Wood End (Sitwell house, museum)
28. Scamridge Dikes (earthworks),
    Troutsdale
29. Pickering Castle (Norman remains)
30. Keld Head Springs, Pickering
31. Saxon Crosses, Middleton Church
32. Hackness Church
33. Bridestones Moor (rocks, barrows)
    (NT), Staindale
34. Hutton-le-Hole (village)
    Rydale Folk Museum
35. Appleton-le-Moors Church
36. Lastingham Church
37. Gillamoor (view)
38. Saxon Sundial, Kirkdale Church
    Kirkdale Cave
39. Ralph Cross (C18), Rosedale
40. Rievaulx Abbey (C12)
    Rievaulx Terrace (vistas, temples)
    (NT)
41. Snape Castle (Tudor remains)
    St. Mary's Chapel (C15)
42. Thornborough Moor (stone circles)
43. West Tanfield Church
    Marmion Gatehouse (C15)
    Ure Bridge (view)
44. Masham Church
    Churchyard Cross (Saxon)
    Market Place & Cross
    Ure Bridge (C18)
45. Bedale Church
    Market Cross (mediaeval)
    Bedale Hall
46. Hornby Church
47. Kirby Sigston Church
48. Catterick Bridge (mediaeval)

49. Downholme Church
50. Marrick Priory (C12 remains)
51. Marske Bridge (mediaeval)
52. Hag Wood (NT), Hudswell
53. Hudswell Woods (r. Swale) (NT),
    Richmond
54. Richmond Castle (Norman) & Town
    Greyfriars Tower (monastic remains)
    Theatre Royal (1788)
    The Green Howards Museum,
    Gallowgate
55. Easby Church
    Easby Abbey (C13 remains)
56. *Mount Grace Priory* (C14) (NT)
57. Scarth Wood Moor (views) (NT),
    Cleveland Hills
58. Ingleby Arncliffe Church
59. Whorlton Old Church
    Castle Remains (C15)
60. St. Peter's Church (view), Kirby Hill
    Kirby Hill Hospital (C15 school &
    almshouse)
61. Ravensworth Castle (mediaeval ruin)
62. Croft Church & Bridge
63. Stanwick Hillfort (Brigantian, C1),
    Aldbrough
64. Greta Bridge (C18)
    Morritt Arms Inn
65. Middleton-One-Row (village)
66. St. Cuthbert's Church, Darlington
    Locomotive No. 1 (G. Stephenson,
    1825), Bank Top Station
    Darlington Museum
67. Winston Bridge (1764)
68. Staindrop Church
69. *Raby Castle*
70. Haughton-le-Skerne Church
71. *Preston Hall Museum* (armour),
    Eaglescliffe
72. *Dorman Memorial Museum*,
    Middlesbrough
73. Newport Bridge (vertical lift),
    Middlesbrough
74. St. Thomas's Church,
    Stockton-on-Tees
    Church Road (c. 1730–40 houses)
    Town Hall (1736)
75. Transporter Bridge, Middlesbrough
76. Norton (village)
    St. Mary's Church
    St. Michael's Church
77. St. Cuthbert's Church, Billingham
78. Greatham Hospital (C18–19
    almshouses)
79. Sedgefield Church
80. St. Mary's Church, Seaham
81. Houghton-le-Spring Church
82. Pittington Church
83. Finchnale Priory (C13 remains)
84. Durham Cathedral
    St. Mary-le-Bow Church
    Durham Castle (Norman & later;
    university)
    Kepier Hospital (gatehouse, 1341)
    Bishop's Hospital (1666),
    Palace Green
    Bishop Cosin's Hall (C18)
    North & South Bailey (C18 houses)
    Elvet Bridge (C14)
    Framwellgate Bridge (C15)
    Prebends' Bridge (1777, view)
85. Lanchester Church

86. *Gulbenkian Museum of Oriental Art*,
    Elvet Hill
87. Sherburn Hospital (part C12)
88. Castle Eden Denes (nature reserve)
89. Brancepeth Church & View of Castle
90. St. Hilda's Church, Hartlepool
91. Vinovia (Roman station), Binchester
92. St. Helen's Church, Bishop Auckland
    Auckland Castle (Bishop's Palace,
    C16–18) & Park
    Newton Cap Bridge (from C14)
93. Escomb Church (Saxon)
94. Stanhope Church & Castle (1798)
95. Romaldkirk Church & Village
    Hutchinson's Almshouses
    (rebuilt 1829)
    Eggleston Bridge (C17)
96. Cotherstone, Teesdale (scenery)
97. Barnard Castle (C11–14 remains)
    Tees Bridge (from 1569)
    Blagroves House (Tudor), The Bank
    Town Hall (1747)
    Bowes Museum
98. Egglestone Abbey (C12–14 remains)
99. Abbey Bridge (1773), Egglestone
100. Arkengarthdale (scenery)
101. Grinton Church
102. Bolton Castle (C14)
103. Redmire Force (waterfall)
104. Aysgarth Force (waterfalls)
     Aysgarth Bridge (1539)
105. Wensley Church
     Mediaeval Bridge
106. Leyburn Shawl (natural terrace,
     views)
107. Middleham Castle (C12–13 remains)
     & Town
108. Braithwaite Hall (C17) (NT)
109. *Jervaulx Abbey* (C12–15 remains)
110. Kilgram Bridge (view), Thornton
     Steward
111. Druid's Temple (Regency folly)
112. All Saints Church, Great Ayton
113. *Ormesby Hall* (NT)
114. Kirkleatham Church
     Turner's Hospital (1742, almshouses
     & chapel)
115. Guisborough Priory (C12 & C14
     remains)
116. Kilton Castle (mediaeval ruin)
117. Boulby Cliff (666 ft)
118. Staithes (fishing village)
119. Lythe Church
120. Saltwick Nab (cliffland) (NT)
121. Whitby (fishing port)
     St. Mary's Church
     Abbey Remains (C12–13)
     Whitby Museum, Panett Park
122. Duck Bridge (packhorse, mediaeval),
     Danby
123. Danby-in-Cleveland Church
124. Beggar's Bridge (1620), Glaisdale
125. Robin Hood's Bay (fishing village)
126. Ravenscar Cliffs (585 ft)
127. Thomason Force (waterfall),
     Beck Hole
128. Mallyan Spout (waterfall), Goathland
129. Nelly Ayre Force (waterfall),
     Wheeldale
130. Roman Road (maintained section),
     Wheeldale
131. Hole of Horcum (natural
     amphitheatre), Saltergate

Map 56

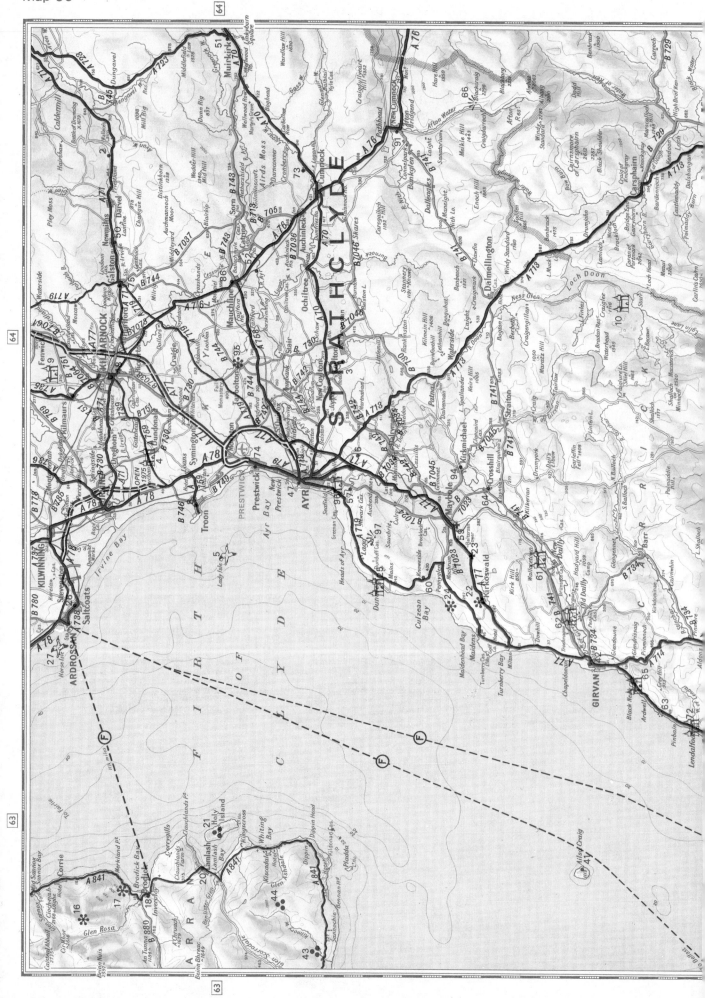

Map 57

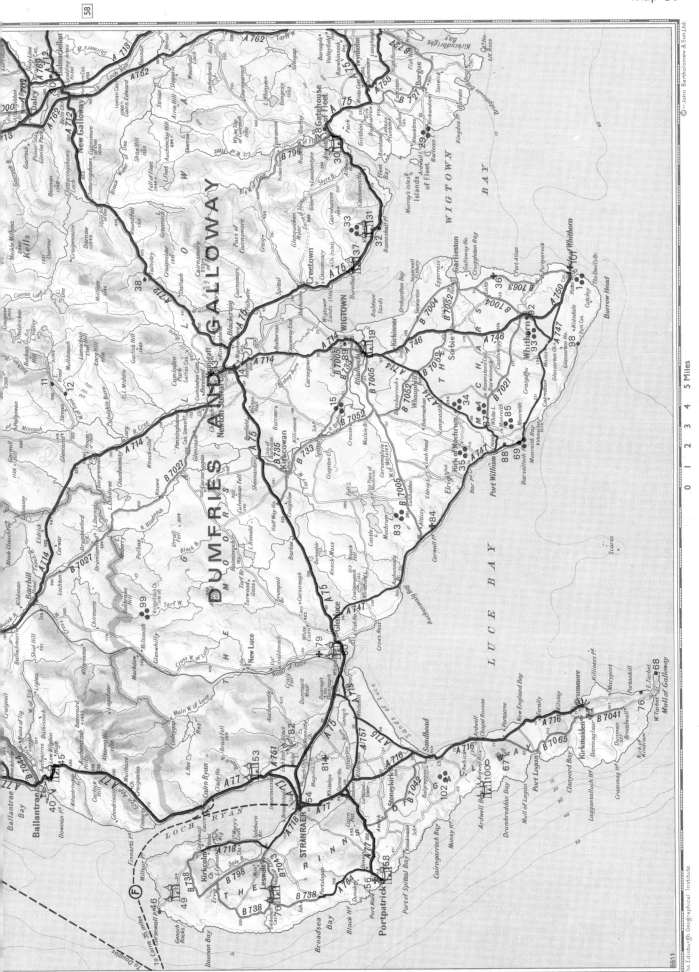

The Edinburgh Geographical Institute

0 1 2 3 4 5 Miles

Gazetteer to Maps 56·57

1. Isle of Whithorn hill-fort (Iron Age)
2. Loudoun Hill Railway Viaduct, thirteen arches (railway abandoned)
3. Coylton *Millmannoch* (fr. C18; mill, three pairsstones)
4. *Dundonald Castle* ((mainly C14; C13 gatehouse; landmark; view from outside)
5. *Lady Isle Bird Sanctuary*
6. Mount Oliphant (Burns association)
7. Kilmaurs Tolbooth 'jougs'
8. Troon Visitor Centre
9. Rowallan Castle (fr. C16; fine mansion (C20); view from outside)
10. Loch Doon Castle (C14; unusual plan: 'transplanted' from mid-loch)
11. Glen Trool Forest Park (135000 acres) (FC)
12. Memorial Stone (Bruce victory, 1306)
13. Minnigaff Church (William Burn, 1836)
14. Newton Stewart Visitor Centre
    Penninghame Church (1840; William Burn: spire)
    Woollen Mills
15. Torhouse Standing Stones (Br. Age?)
16. Goat Fell (NTS)
17. Brodick Castle and Gardens (art collection; gardens; view) (NTS)
18. Brodick Visitor Centre
19. Baldoon Castle (C17; ruins)
20. Lamlash Visitor Centre
21. Holy Island (Runic cave inscriptions)
22. Kirkoswald Souter Johnnie's House (Burnsiana) (NTS)
23. Crossraguel Abbey (1244, gatehouse; dovecot; tower C15
24. Culzean Castle and Country Park (Visitor Centre; C18 Adam elegance: garden/nature walks in 565-acre grounds) (NTS)
25. Dunure Castle, Kennedy, stronghold; ruin
26. Saltcoats Visitor Centre
    North Ayrshire Museum
    Old Custom House Museum (maritime)
27. Ardrossan *Horse Isle Nature Reserve* (RSPB)
28. Gatehouse of Fleet Visitor Centre
    C18 planned village: remains cotton mills
    Murray Forest Centre (FC)
29. Castle Haven (D-shaped galleried dun; view)
30. Cardoness Castle (C15; tower-house; fireplaces; view)
31. Barholm Castle (ruins)
32. Dirk Hatteraick's Cave ('Guy Mannering')
33. Cairn Holy (Keats' Meg Merrilees' camp?)

34. Drumtroddan Stones (Br. Age; cup-and-ring markings)
35. Druchtag Motehill (Med.; earthwork, traces buildings)
36. *Cruggleton Church* (Norman)
37. Carsluith Castle (C16; roofless tower-house)
38. Murray's Monument (to Oriental languages scholar)
39. Bennane Head
40. Ballantrae Nature Reserve (SWT)
41. Ailsa Craig ('Paddy's Milestone'; 1113 ft. Seabirds, granite quarries for curling-stones; lighthouse, 1868)
42. Girvan Visitor Centre
    Bridge Mill five-storey grain mill
    Grant's Distillery
43. Kilmory Torr a'Chaisteal (buried Iron Age fort)
    Torrylin Cairn (Neolithic) chambered cairn
44. Carn Ban (renowned Neolithic long cairn)
45. Glenapp Castle and Gardens
46. Corsewall Lighthouse (1815, Stevenson)
47. Ayr Visitor Centre
    'Auld Brig' (med., now footbridge)
    Loudoun Hall (C16, restored)
    Rozelle Nature Trails (two) (SWT)
48. Kilmarnock *Burns Museum* (1st editions etc.; views from tower)
    Dick Institute (museum, art gallery, library)
49. Corsewall Castle (ruin)
50. Newmilns *Ladeside Flour Mill* (fr. C16)
    26-arch Railway Viaduct (1894)
51. Muirkirk McAdam Cairn (foundations tar kilns)
    Ironworks (1787; remains; works canal)
52. Ballochmyle Railway Viaduct (1848; graceful)
53. Craigcaffie Castle (C16; ruin)
54. Stranraer Visitor Centre
    Castle (fr. C16)
    County Museum and Library
55. View
56. Portpatrick Church (tower, 1628)
57. Alloway Kirk (Burns associations)
    Brig o'Doon
58. Dunskey Castle (C16; ruins)
59. *Maybole Collegiate Church* (C15; ruin; view from street)
60. 'Electric Brae'
61. New Dailly Dalquharran Castle (C15; 1790)
62. Girvan Killochan Castle (1586; mansion, notably unchanged)
63. Kennedy's Pass
64. Crosshill weavers' cottages (early C19)

65. Girvan Ardmillan House (C16; Queen Mary associations)
66. Afton Water (view)
67. Logan Gardens (sub-tropical plants; trees; tidal fish-pond; C18)
68. Mull of Galloway Lighthouse (1828; most S. Scots)
69. Barsalloch Fort 'horseshoe' 12 ft deep, 33 ft wide
70. Lochnaw Castle
71. Pinwherry Castle (in pleasant valley)
72. Lendalfoot Carleton Castle (imposing ruin)
73. Cumnock (Lugar) *Bello Mill* (also birth-place gas-lighting pioneer Murdoch)
74. Prestwick Visitor Centre
75. Galston Grain Mill (fr. C18)
76. St. Medan's Cave
77. Drummore (view)
78. Lochinvar Castle (ruin; 'Young Lochinvar's' home?)
79. Glenluce Abbey (1192; vaulted chapter-house, C15)
80. *Castle of Park* (1590; entire castellated mansion)
81. Soulseat Abbey (C12 site?)
82. *Castle Kennedy and Lochinch Gardens* (laid out fr. C17)
83. Doon of May (vitrified fort)
84. Chapel Finian (C10–11)
85. 'Wren's Egg' Stone Circle
86. Mauchline Burns Memorial (museum; tower)
    Crossroads *Horse-Mill* (c. 1800)
87. Big Balcraig Stones (Br. Age; cup-and-ring engravings)
88. Monreith Cross (wheel-headed)
89. Wigtown Martyr's Monument (Covenanters)
90. Balmaclellan 'Old Mortality' (monument)
91. New Cumnock Visitor Centre (near) Craigdullyeart Lime Works
    Mill (meal water-mill)
92. Whithorn Museum (C5 Latinus Stone)
    Priory (C12; site first Scots Christian church, C5?)
93. Whithorn Rispain Camp
94. Kirkmichael (early C19 weavers' cottages)
95. Tarbolton Bachelors Club (C17; Burns; inc. small museum) (NTS)
96. Alloway Burns' birthplace
97. Brown Carrick Hill (940 ft; view)
98. St. Ninian's Cave
99. Laggangarn Standing Stones
100. Doon Castle (broch? ruins)
101. Isle of Whithorn St. Ninian's Kirk (C13; ruins)
102. Kirkmadrine Stones (C5–6; Christian)

Map 58

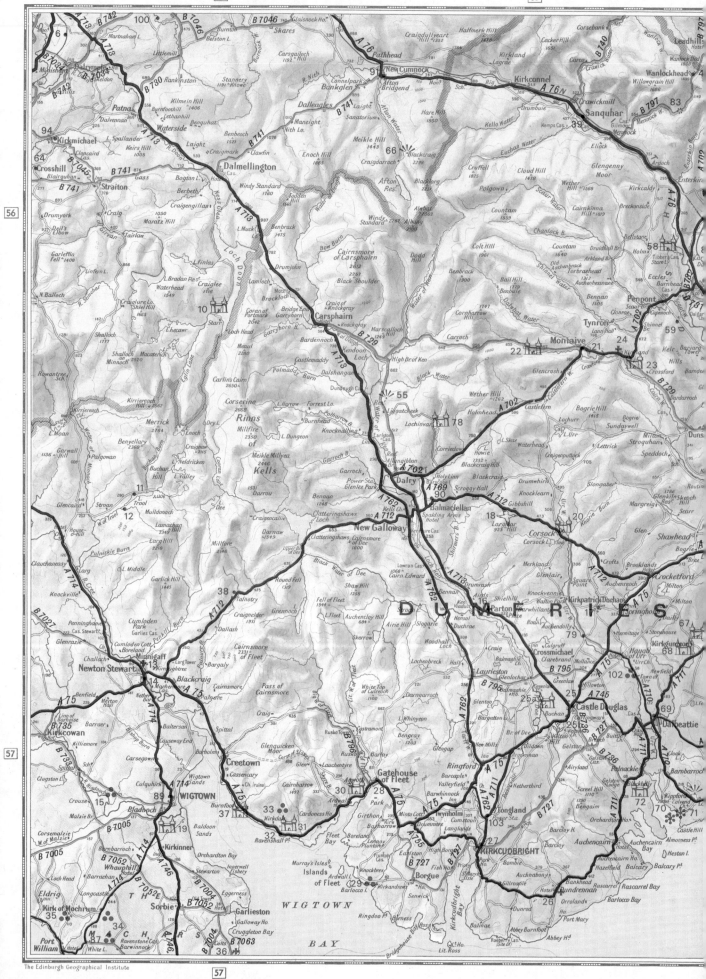

Map 59

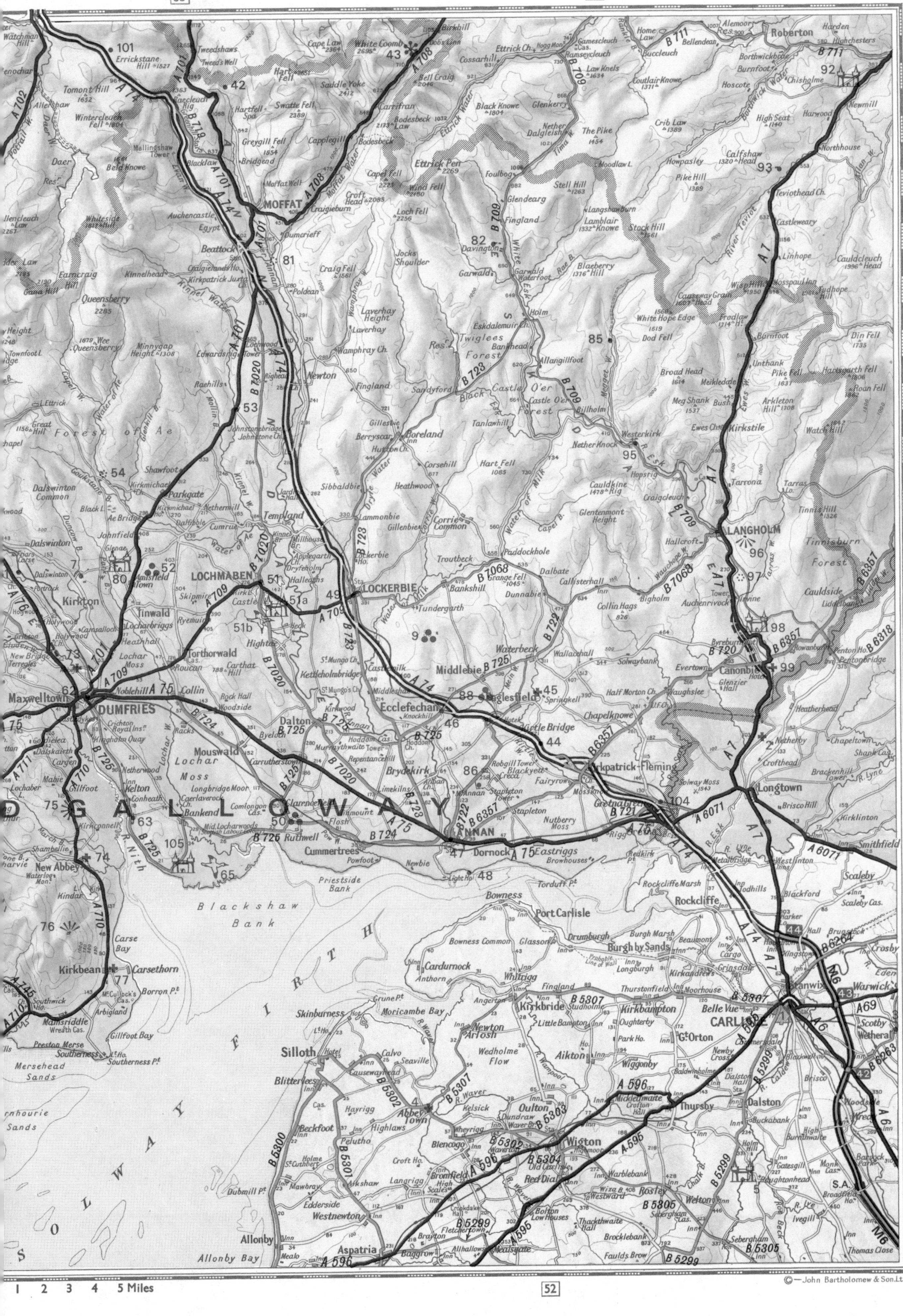

1 2 3 4 5 Miles

1. Carlisle Cathedral
   Carlisle Castle (C12–14;
   Regimental Museum)
   City Walls
   Market Cross (1682)
   Town Hall (1717)
   Tullie House (C17; museum)
2. Kirkandrews-on-Esk Church
3. Wetheral Abbey Gatehouse (C12)
   Corby Castle (C13–17)
4. Holme Cultram Abbey Church
5. Rose Castle (C13–17)
6. Mount Oliphant (Burns association)
7. Duncow Windmill (mid C18)
8. View
9. Birrenswark (six earthworks;
   Roman camp; view)
10. Loch Doon Castle (C14; unusual
    plan; 'transplanted' from mid-loch)
11. Glen Trool Forest Park
    (135000 acres) (FC)
12. Memorial Stone (Bruce victory, 1306)
13. Minnigaff Church (William Burn,
    1836)
14. Newton Stewart Visitor Centre
    Penninghame Church (1840;
    William Burn; spire)
    Woollen Mills
15. Torhouse Standing Stones (Br. Age?)
16. Parton Kirk (1834; inc. 1592
    fragments)
17. Kirkpatrick-Durham
    (C18; planned village)
18. *Knowetop Lochs Nature Reserve*
    (SWT)
19. Baldoon Castle (C17; ruins)
20. *Corsock House Gardens*
    (shrubs; water garden; view)
21. Moniaive Mercat Cross (C17)
22. *Craigdarroch House* (fr. C18;
    house of 'Annie Laurie')
23. *Maxwelton House* (fr. C15,
    restored; chapel; museum;
    boudoir)
24. Glencairn Church (grave of
    'Annie Laurie' and husband)
25. Castle Douglas Visitor Centre
25a. *Threave Castle* (C14; four
    storeys; access by boat)
25b. Threave Gardens (NTS);
    Visitor Centre; gardeners'
    training school; *wildfowl refuge*
26. Dundrennan Abbey (1142)
27. Kirkcudbright Visitor Centre
    Broughton House Museum (C18;
    Hornels; library; garden)
    MacLellan's Castle (C16)
    Stewartry Museum
28. Gatehouse of Fleet Visitor Centre
    C18 planned village; remains
    cotton mills
    Murray Forest Centre (FC)
29. Castle Haven (D-shaped
    galleried dun; view)
30. Cardoness Castle (C15;
    tower-house; fireplaces; view)
31. Barholm Castle (ruins)
32. Dirk Hatteraick's Cave
    ('Guy Mannering')

33. Cairn Holy (Keats' Meg Merrilees'
    camp?)
34. Drumtroddan Stones (Br. Age;
    cup-and-ring markings)
35. Druchtag Motehill (Med.;
    earthwork; traces buildings)
36. *Cruggleton Church* (Norman)
37. Carsluith Castle (C16;
    roofless tower-house)
38. Murray's Monument (to Oriental
    languages scholar)
39. Sanquhar Covenanters' Monument
40. Wanlockhead highest Scots village
    (1380 ft); C18 lead workings;
    good (1770) beam engine
42. Devil's Beef Tub (500 ft, hollow)
43. Grey Mare's Tail (waterfall over
    'hanging valley' in 2000 acres
    access land; wild goats; flowers)
    (NTS)
44. Kirkpatrick-Fleming Merkland
    Cross (C15)
45. Eaglesfield Kirkconnel Churchyard
    (ruined chapel, Med. cross;
    grave 'Fair Helen')
46. Ecclefechan 'Arched House'
    (1791; Carlyle's birthplace) (NTS)
    C18 street village
47. Annan Burgh Museum local
    (Carlyle associations)
    Kinmount House
48. Annan (Seafield; remains 1869
    Solway Viaduct)
49. Lockerbie Visitor Centre
50. Ruthwell *Cross* (late C7;
    renowned, richly figured, Runic)
51. Lochmaben Visitor Centre
51a. Lochmaben Castle (Bruce's
    birthplace 1274?; ruins)
51b. Hightae Lochs Nature
    Reserve
52. Barr's Hill hill-fort
53. St. Ann's Bridge (C18)
54. Ae Forest Walks (FC)
55. View
56. Dalveen Pass
57. Durisdeer Church (C17;
    'Queensberry Marbles', C18
    effigies)
58. Drumlanrig *Castle* (late C17)
59. Keir Mill (1771; meal-mill)
60. Auldgirth Bridge (C18)
61. Ellisland Burns' Farm
    ('Tam o'Shanter' Walk)
62. Dumfries Visitor Centre
    Burns' House, *Mausoleum*
    Devorgilla Bridge (mainly C15)
    Fountainbleau and Ladypark Reserve
    (SWT)
    Mid Steeple (early C18; Scots ell
    measure)
    Museum and Camera Obscura
    (inc. 1797 tower windmill)
    Old Bridge House Museum
    (C17; period rooms)
63. Glencaple village (C18–19 port)
64. Crosshill weavers' cottages
    (early C19)

65. *Caerlaverock Nature Reserve*
    (wildfowl; salt marsh; sand) (NC)
66. Afton Water (view)
67. Drumcoltran Tower (mid-C16;
    three storeys)
68. Corra Castle (ruins)
69. Dalbeattie Visitor Centre
70. *Rough Island Bird Sanctuary* (NTS)
71. Rockcliffe Mote of Mark
    (hill-fort) (NTS)
    Muckle Lands and Jubilee Path
    (NTS) (coast walk)
72. Orchardton Tower (mid-C15;
    unique)
73. Dumfries Lincluden Abbey
    (fr. 1164; decorated C15 church;
    motte; tomb)
74. New Abbey Sweetheart Abbey
    (fr. 1273, mostly C14;
    impressive wall; church tower)
75. Whinny Hill (view)
76. Criffell (1866 ft; easy climb;
    panorama)
77. Kirkbean Church
    Paul Jones memorial
78. Lochinvar Castle (ruin;
    'Young Lochinvar's' home?)
79. Old Bridge of Urr (mid-C18)
80. *Amisfield Tower* (c. 1600)
81. Moffat 'Three Waters Meet'
82. Eskdalemuir *Observatory*
83. Mennock Pass
84. Morton Castle (C11; ruins)
85. Jamestown (former antimony
    miners' village)
86. Annan *Chapelcross Nuclear
    Power Station*
87. Big Balcraig Stones (Br. Age;
    cup-and-ring engravings)
88. Eaglesfield Roman Camp
89. Wigtown Martyr's Monument
    (Covenanters)
90. Balmaclellan 'Old Mortality'
    (monument)
91. New Cumnock Visitor Centre
    (near) Craigdullyeart Limeworks
    Mill (meal water-mill)
92. *Branxholm Tower* (fr. C16)
93. Memorial cairn Riddell (C19 poet)
94. Kirkmichael (early C19 weavers'
    cottages)
95. Westerkirk Telford Memorial
    (1757–1834, engineer)
96. Langholm Monument (to Sir J.
    Malcolm C19; landmark)
97. Tarras
98. Gilnockie Holehouse Tower
    (C16 Armstrong peel tower)
99. *Canonbie Church* (1822; by Scott's
    architect, Atkinson)
100. Coylton Millmannoch (fr. C18;
    mill, three pairs stones)
101. Beattock Summit (1014 ft)
102. Mote of Urr
103. Tongland Bridge (1808; Telford)
104. Gretna Green (blacksmith's shop
    venue former runaway weddings)
105. Caerlaverock Castle (fr. 1290;
    remarkable triangular structure)

Map 60

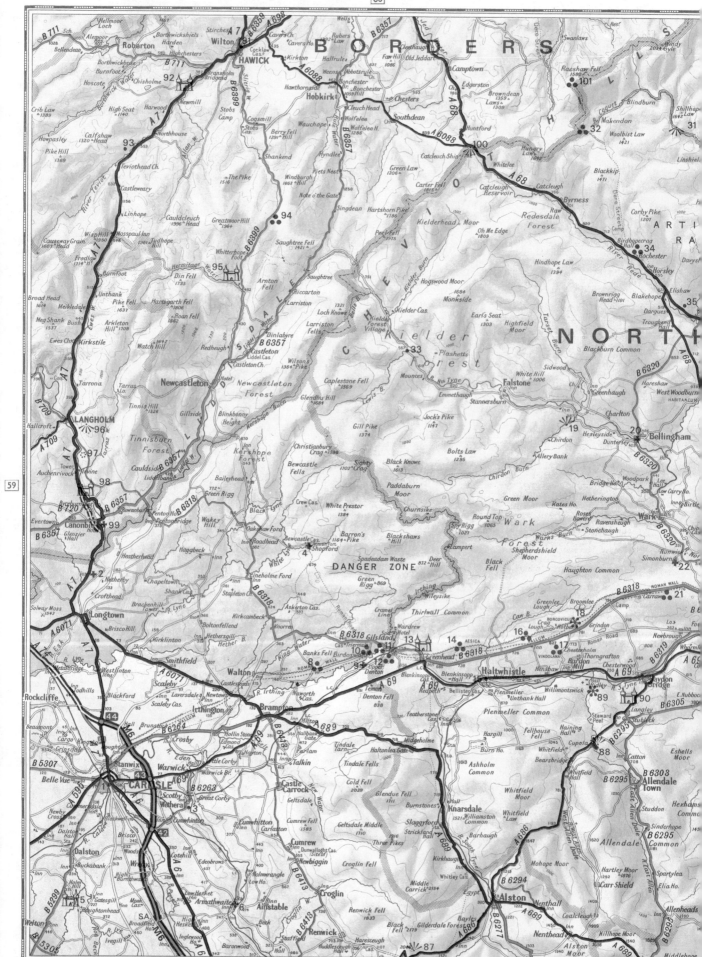

Map 61

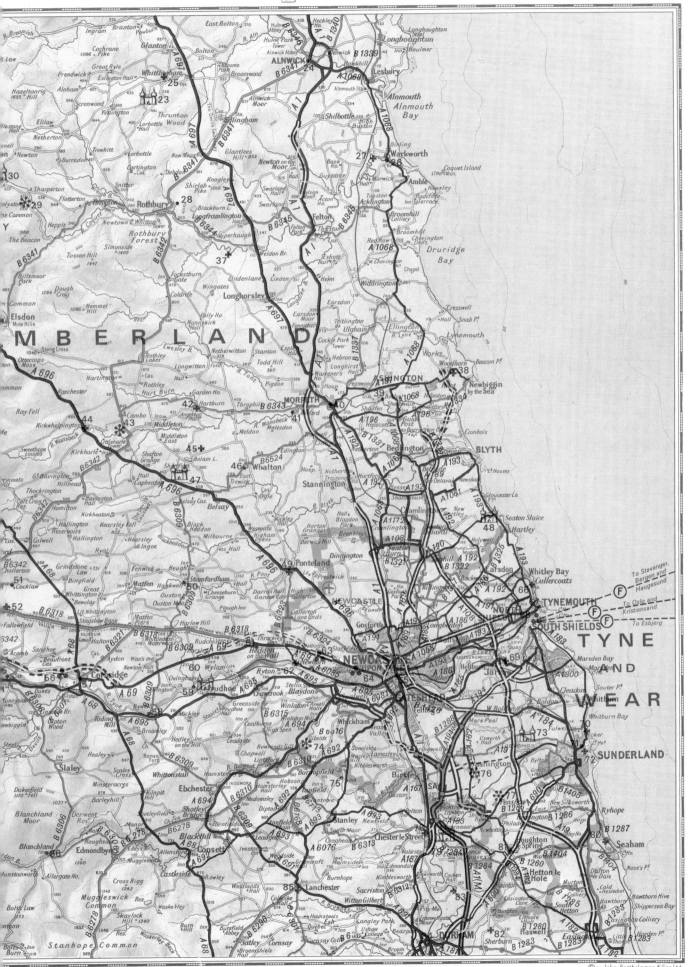

1 2 3 4 5 Miles

©—John Bartholomew & Son Ltd.

Gazetteer to Maps 60·61

1. Carlisle Cathedral
   Carlisle Castle (C12–14; *Regimental Museum*)
   City Walls
   Market Cross (1682)
   Town Hall (1717)
   Tullie House (C17; museum)
2. Kirkandrews-on-Esk Church
3. Wetheral Abbey Gatehouse (C12)
   Corby Castle (C13–17)
4. Churchyard Cross (C7), Bewcastle
5. Rose Castle (C13–17)
6. Armathwaite Church
7. Lanercost Priory (C12; remains) & Church
   Irthing Bridge (C17?)
8. Banks East Turret, Hadrian's Wall
9. Over Denton Church (Saxon)
10. Harrow's Scar Mile Castle, Hadrian's Wall
    Birdoswald Fort
11. Willowford Bridge Abutment, Hadrian's Wall
    Section of Wall in Vicarage garden
12. Poltross Burn Mile Castle, Hadrian's Wall
13. Thirlwall Castle (C14; ruin)
14. Walltown Crags Turret, Hadrian's Wall
15. Holy Cross Church, Haltwhistle
    Haltwhistle Tower (C15)
16. Winshields Mile Castle, Hadrian's Wall
    Section of Wall (410 yds)
17. Chesterholm Fort & Milestone, Hadrian's Wall
18. Housesteads Fort & *Museum* (NT), Hadrian's Wall
19. Dally Castle (C13; ruin, view)
20. Bellingham Church
21. Procolitia (Roman fort & Mithraic temple), Hadrian's Wall
22. Simonburn Church
23. *Callaly Castle & Gardens*
24. *Alnwick Castle*
    St. Michael's Church
    Hotspur Gate (1450)
    Town Hall (1771)
    Northumberland Hall (1826)
    Lion Bridge (John Adam, 1773)
    Alnwick—Rothbury Road (views)
25. Whittingham Church
26. Warkworth Castle (C11–14)
    Warkworth Church
    Mediaeval Bridge & Tower
27. *Warkworth Hermitage* (C14; rock chapel)
28. *Cragside Grounds*, Rothbury
29. Lady's Well (St. Ninian's) (NT), Holystone
30. Harbottle Castle (C12; remains), Coquetdale
31. Road to Blindburn (views)
32. Chew Green (Roman station), Cheviot Hills
33. *Border Forest Museum*, Kielder
34. Bremenium (Roman station), Rochester
35. Percy Cross (battle monument), Otterburn
36. Elsdon Church
    Fortified Rectory (C14)
    Norman Motte & Bailey

37. Brinkburn Priory Church
38. Woodhorn Church
39. Bothal Church & Castle (C14 tower)
40. St. Mary's Church, Morpeth
    Clock Tower (C15)
    Town Hall (Vanbrugh, 1714)
41. Mitford Church
    Norman Castle Ruin
42. Hartburn Church
43. *Wallington Hall & Gardens* (NT), Cambo
44. Kirkwhelpington Church
45. Bolam Church
46. Whalton Church & Village
47. *Harnham Hall* (mediaeval & C17)
48. *Seaton Delaval Hall*
    Our Lady's Church
49. Ponteland Church
50. Stamfordham Church
    Market Cross (1736)
51. Cocklaw Tower (C15 ruin)
52. St. Oswald's Church
53. Brunton Turret, Hadrian's Wall
    Chollerford Bridge (c. 1772)
54. *Chesters Fort & Bath House* (Roman museum), Hadrian's Wall
    Chesters Bridge Abutment
    Chesters—Greenhead Road (views)
55. Hexham Priory Church
    Old Prison (1330)
    Moot Hall (C15 tower)
    Old Grammar School (C17)
    Hexham Bridge (Mylne, 1788; view)
56. *Corstopitum* (Roman station remains & museum)
57. St. Andrew's Church, Corbridge
    Fortified Vicarage (1318)
    Tyne Bridge (1674)
58. Bywell Castle (C15) & Village
    St. Andrew's Church
    St. Peter's Church
59. Ovingham Church
    Packhorse Bridge (Whittle Burn)
60. Prudhoe Castle (C12 remains)
61. Heddon-on-the-Wall Church
    Hadrian's Wall (280 yd section)
    Frenchmen's Row (cottages, 1796)
62. Newburn Church
63. Denton Hall Turret, Hadrian's Wall
64. Roman Temple & Causeway, Hadrian's Wall, Benwell
65. *Newcastle upon Tyne Castle* (C12; museum)
    The Black Gate (C13 gatehouse; museum)
    St. Nicholas' Cathedral
    St. Andrew's Church & Town Walls (mediaeval remains)
    St. John Baptist's Church
    All Saints Church
    St. Ann's Church
    Jesus Hospital (almshouses, 1683)
    Guildhall & Exchange (1658)
    Surtees House (C17), Sandhill
    Eldon Square (Dobson, 1826)
    Leazes Terrace (Oliver, 1829)
    Grey Street (Dobson, 1835–39)
    Central Station (Dobson, 1850)
    University Physics Building (C20)
    High Level Tyne Bridge (R. Stephenson, 1849)
    Tyne Road Bridge (steel arch, 1930)

    Laing Art Gallery & Museum
    Museum of Antiquities, King's College
    Museum of Science & Engineering
66. Cullercoats Church
67. Tynemouth Priory & Castle (C12–14)
    Christ Church
68. *Arbeia* (Roman station remains & museum), South Shields
69. St. Paul's Church (part C7) & Monastic Remains, Jarrow
70. St. Andrew's Church, Roker
71. St. Peter's Church, Monkwearmouth
    Railway Station (1848)
72. Holy Trinity Church, Sunderland
73. Hylton Castle (c. 1400)
74. Gibside Chapel (Paine, 1760) & Grounds (NT)
75. Causey Arch (earliest railway bridge, 1727), Tanfield
76. *Washington Old Hall* (NT)
77. Penshaw Monument (temple, 1844) (NT)
78. Chester-le-Street Church
79. *Lumley Castle* (C14)
80. St. Mary's Church, Seaham
81. Houghton-le-Spring Church
82. Pittington Church
83. Finchdale Priory (C13 remains)
84. Durham Cathedral
    St. Mary-le-Bow Church
    Durham Castle (Norman & later; university)
    Kepier Hospital (gatehouse, 1341)
    Bishop's Hospital (1666), Palace Green
    Bishop Cosin's Hall (C18)
    North & South Bailey (C18 houses)
    Elvet Bridge (C14)
    Framwellgate Bridge (C15)
    Prebends' Bridge (1777, view)
85. Lanchester Church
86. Blanchland (C18 planned village)
    St. Mary's Church
    Churchyard Cross
87. Hartside Height (view)
88. Staward (view & castle ruins)
89. The Allen Banks (hill & river walks) (NT), Ridley
90. *Langley Castle*
91. Hawick Visitor Centre
    Mote Hill mediaeval court meeting place?
    Wilton Lodge Museum
92. Branxholm Tower (fr. C16)
93. Memorial cairn Riddell (C19 poet)
94. Limekilnridge Catrail 20 ft wide ditch, Peel Fell—Galashiels
95. Hermitage Castle (fr. C14, restored C19) Mary Queen of Scots associations
96. Langholm Monument (to Sir J. Malcolm C19); landmark
97. Tarras
98. Gilnockie Holehouse Tower (C16 Armstrong peel tower)
99. *Canonbie Church* (1822 by Scott's architect, Atkinson)
100. Carter Bar panorama Border Site of last Scots–English Border battle (1575)
101. Woden Law fort, Roman siege works (for training?)

Map 62

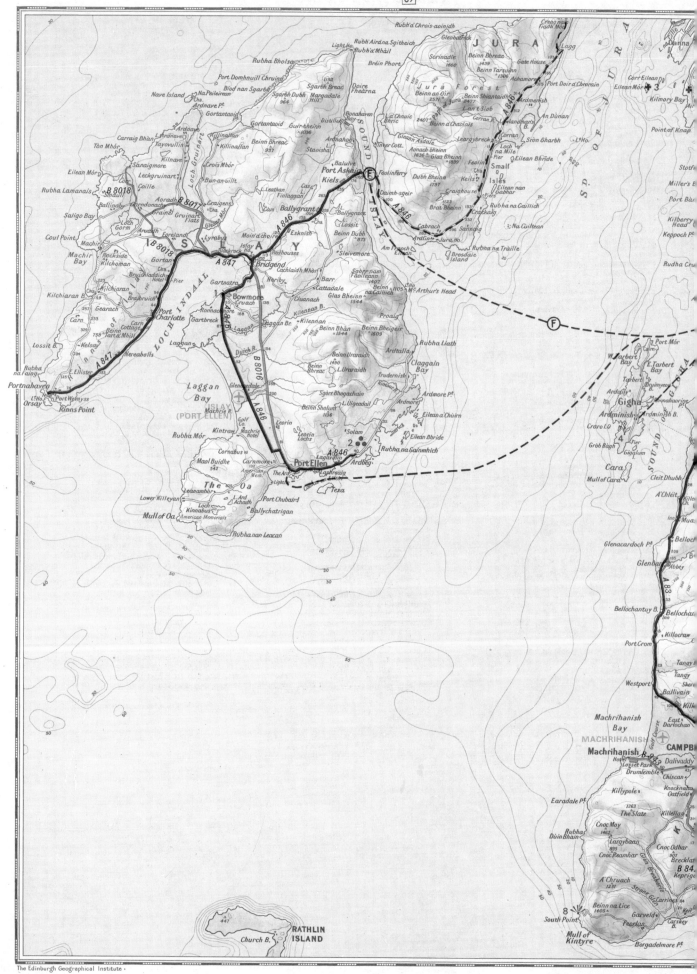

Map 63

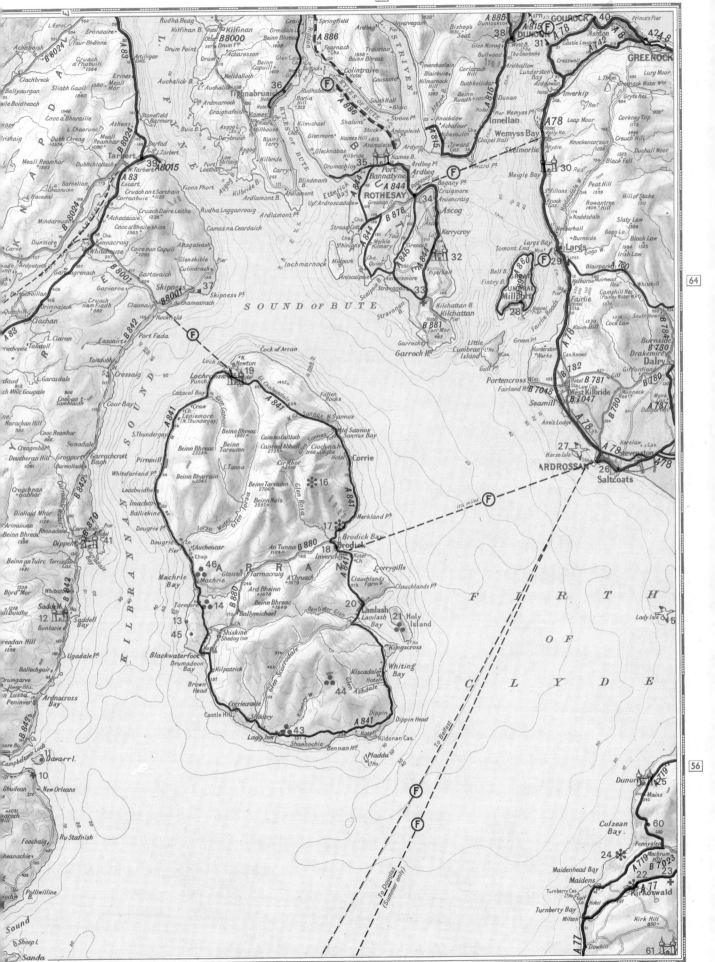

1 2 3 4 5 Miles

©—John Bartholomew & Son,Ltd.

Gazetteer to Maps 62·63

1. Bowmore Visitor Centre
2. Kildalton two Celtic crosses
3. Eilean Mor *St. Cormac's Chapel* nave, vaulted chancel (access difficult)
4. Gigha *Achamore House Gardens*
5. *Lady Isle Bird Sanctuary*
6. Killean Tangy Mill (C18; good condition water-mill)
7. Kilberry Castle sculptured stones (late mediaeval)
8. Mull of Kintyre (lighthouse; view)
9. Campbeltown Visitor Centre Museum
10. *St. Kieran's Cave* earliest Christian chapel in Scotland? (Access difficult)
11. Davarr Island cave painting (C19)
12. Saddell Castle (1508; ruins; also Cistercian monastery ruins, grave-slabs, C13)
13. King's Cave (Bruce associations)
14. Blackwaterfoot, Moss Farm Road Stone Circle
15. Castle Sween (C12; ruin)
16. Goat Fell (NTS)
17. Brodick Castle and Gardens (art collection; gardens; view) (NTS)
18. Brodick Visitor Centre
19. Lochranza Castle (prob. C16; ruins)
20. Lamlash Visitor Centre
21. Holy Island (Runic cave inscriptions)

22. Kirkoswald *Souter Johnnie's House* (Burnsiana) (NTS)
23. Crossraguel Abbey (1244 gatehouse; dovecot; tower, C15)
24. Culzean Castle and Country Park (C18 Adam elegance; visitor centre; garden/nature walks in 565-acre grounds) (NTS)
25. Dunure Castle, Kennedy stronghold, ruin
26. Saltcoats Visitor Centre North Ayrshire Museum Old Custom House Museum (maritime)
27. Ardrossan *Horse Isle Nature Reserve* (RSPB)
28. Millport Visitor Centre Aquarium (Clyde marine life) Robertson Museum (natural history)
29. Largs Visitor Centre Bowen Craig (tower commemorating 1263 battle) Skelmorlie Aisle (1639, Italianate mausoleum)
30. Skelmorlie Castle (1502)
31. *Cloch Lighthouse* (Clyde landmark)
32. *Mount Stuart House* (1877, *grounds*)
33. Kingarth St. Blane's Church (monastic site fr. C6) 'Devil's Cauldron' (32 ft wide)
34. Rothesay Visitor Centre Bute Museum Nature Trails (seven, inc. motorist's) Castle (C14; ruins: circular courtyard, curtain walls)
35. Kames Castle (C14; ruined tower)

36. Tighnabruaich Visitor Centre Wildlife Centre and Forest Trail (1½ miles scenic trail) (FC)
37. Skipness (view Arran; castle ruins; St. Columba church ruins)
38. Dunoon Visitor Centre
39. Tarbert Visitor Centre C14 castle ruins
40. Gourock Visitor Centre
41. Carradale *House* (shrubs; view)
42. Greenock Free French Memorial Lyle Hill McLean Museum (Watt's tools) & Art Gallery *Mid Kirk* (1787) Victoria Tower (245 ft) *West Kirk* (windows Burne-Jones, Morris)
43. Kilmory Torr a'Chaisteal (buried Iron Age fort) Torrylin Cairn (Neolithic chambered cairn)
44. Carn Ban (renowned Neolithic long cairn)
45. Drumadoon (1m N. of) raised caves, sea level now lower
46. Blackwaterfoot Auchagallon Stone Circle (Bronze Age; fifteen stones)
47. Kilmory Knap Chapel (typical W. Highland; late mediaeval sculptured stones, Macmillan s Cross)
60. 'Electric Brae'
61. New Dailly Dalquharran Castle (C15; 1790)

Map 64

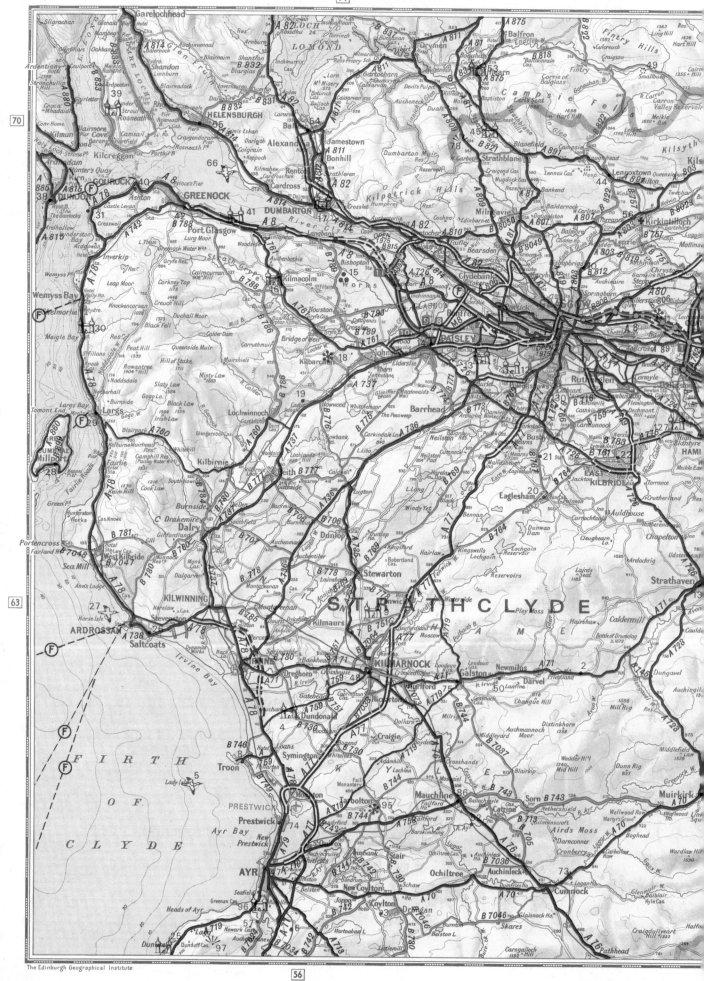

Map 65

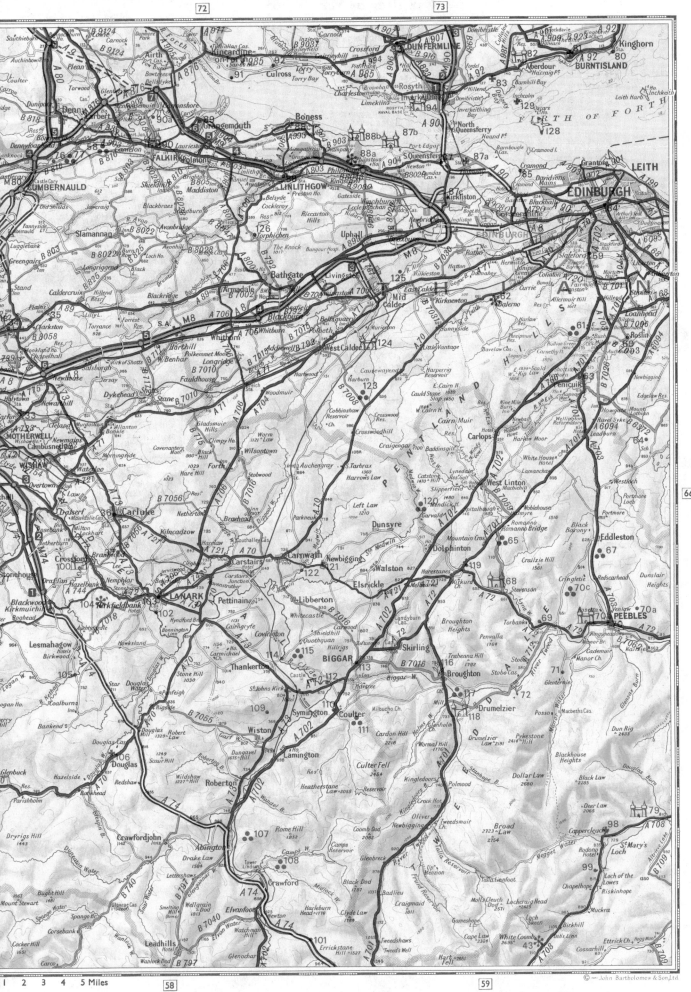

1 2 3 4 5 Miles

5

© — John Bartholomew & Son, Ltd.

Gazetteer to Maps 64·65

1. Glasgow Visitor Centre
   Botanic Gardens (fr. 1817;
      42 acres great variety; Kibble
      Palace glass-houses, rare tree ferns)
   Caledonia Road Church (1857;
      'Greek' Thomson)
   Camphill Museum, Queen's Park
      (paintings, part of Burrell
      Collection)
   Cathedral (fr. C12; most complete
      med. Scots cathedral; crypt
      vaulting, C14 timber roof;
      C15 pulpitum)
   Children's Nature Trails in
      Dawsholm Park, Kelvingrove
      Park, Rosshall Park &
      Springburn Park
   Egyptian Halls (1873) Union St.;
      'Greek' Thomson
   Free Church College (1856; Wilson)
   Gardner's Jamaica St. (1856;
      Baird; early cast-iron building)
   Great Western Road ('Greek'
      Thomson terraces)
   Haggs Castle (1585; restored 1860)
   Hampden Park football stadium
      (163000 capacity)
   Hunterian Museum (fr. 1807;
      1st Glasgow museum; notable)
   Kelvingrove Art Gallery (wide
      collection, esp. French
      Impressionists, Dali 'Christ') &
      Museum (armour; ship models;
      nat. history)
   Mitchell Library (inc. 3500 vols.
      Burnsiana)
   People's Palace (Old Glasgow
      museum; domestic, various inc.
      Lipton relics)
   Provand's Lordship (1471; oldest
      Glasgow house; museum, inc.
      C17 furniture)
   Queen's Cross Church, Garscube
      Rd. (1899; Mackintosh)
   Royal Exchange Square (precinct
      inc. Stirling's Library fr. 1778,
      enlarged 1832 Hamilton)
   St. Vincent St. Church (1859;
      'Greek' Thomson)
   School of Art (1897; Mackintosh)
   Stock Exchange (1875; Burnet;
      Venetian gothic)
   Templeton's Carpet Factory,
      Glasgow Green (1889; Leiper;
      romantic Venetian gothic)
   Tolbooth Steeple (1626)
   Transport Museum, Eglinton Toll
      (gamut Scottish transport)
   University (fr. 1451, at Kelvingrove
      1870; Scott; view)
   Victoria Park, Whiteinch (Fossil
      Grove; fossilised trees)
2. Loudoun Hill Railway Viaduct
   (thirteen arches; railway
   abandoned)
3. Coylton *Millmannoch* (fr. C18;
   mill, three pairs stones)
4. *Dundonald Castle* (mainly C14;
   C13 gatehouse; landmark; view
   from outside)
5. *Lady Isle Bird Sanctuary*
6. Mount Oliphant (Burns association)
7. Kilmaurs Tolbooth 'jougs'
8. Troon Visitor Centre
9. Rowallan Castle (fr. C16; fine
   mansion (C20); view from outside)
10. Bishopbriggs Visitor Centre
11. *Provan Hall* (C15; mansion, well
    restored; best Scots pre-
    Reformation house) (NTS)
12. Pollok House (1752; Adam; large
    art collection inc. Spanish,
    Blake; grounds)
13. Crookston Castle (C15 tower;
    earlier defensive ditch
14. Paisley *Abbey* (1499 chapel; nave
    parish church)
    Glen Nature Trail (children's)
    Museum & Art Gallery
       (esp. Paisley shawls)

Thomas Coats Memorial Church
   (1894; Blanc; cruciform; tower)
15. Barochan Cross (Celtic) sculptured,
    11 ft.
16. Kilmacolm, Windyhill House
    (1901; Mackintosh; view from
    outside)
17. Dumbarton Castle (on 240 ft high
    rock; Queen Mary associations)
    Castlehill monument (1937; to
    Cunninghame Graham (NTS)
18. Kilbarchan *Weaver's Cottage*
    (1723; typical; summer weaving)
    (NTS)
19. Lochwinnoch *Castle Semple
    Collegiate Church* (rectangular;
    view from outside)
    Castle Semple Loch (200 acres;
    boating; birds)
    Muirshiel Country Park
    (varied facilities)
20. Eaglesham (traditional C18
    planned village)
21. Waterfoot Mill (fr. 1761; internal
    water-wheel; in use)
22. East Kilbride *St. Bride's Church*
    (1963; Coia)
    Mains Castle (tower)
23. Hamilton *Burgh Museum* (fr. C15)
    Cameronians Regimental Museum
    Mausoleum (1855; various marbles;
    six-second echo)
    Neilsland Park Nature Trail
    (woodland)
    Parish Church (1732; Adam)
24. Hamilton Avon Bridge (1820;
    Telford; small toll-house)
    Barncluith House (1583;
    Dutch terraced gardens)
    Cadzow Castle (C12; ruins;
    Queen Mary associations;
    white cattle in park)
    Chatelherault Lodge (1732; Adam)
25. Dunure Castle, Kennedy
    stronghold; ruin
26. Saltcoats Visitor Centre
    North Ayrshire Museum
    Old Custom House Museum
    (maritime)
27. Ardrossan *Horse Isle Nature
    Reserve* (RSPB)
28. Millport Visitor Centre
    Aquarium (Clyde marine life)
    Robertson Museum (natural
    history)
29. Largs Visitor Centre
    Bowen Craig (tower commemorating
    1263 battle)
    Skelmorlie Aisle (1639;
    Italianate mausoleum)
30. Skelmorlie Castle (1502)
31. *Cloch Lighthouse* (Clyde landmark)
32. Bothwell Bridge (C18 arches,
    widened 1826; fine cast-iron;
    1679 battle site)
    Castle (C13–15; was largest Scots
    castle; cylindrical keep;
    fine situation)
    Church (C15)
    Orbiston Glen Nature Trail
33. Carfin Grotto (1922; to Our Lady
    of Lourdes; garden)
34. Airdrie Visitor Centre
    Library & Museum
35. Brownieside Mill (fr. 1803;
    two-storey meal mill, inc.
    part flax mill; in use)
36. Carluke Windmill (fr. 1797;
    best-preserved Scots; 35 ft high,
    two storeys; machinery, stack,
    engine-house, C19)
37. Braidwood Fiddler's Bridge Toll
    (c. 1821; Telford; bow-fronted)
38. Dunoon Visitor Centre
39. Knockderry Castle (now hostel;
    includes dungeon)
40. Gourock Visitor Centre
41. Port Glasgow, *Newark Castle*
    (fr. C16; hall; courtyard;
    stepped gables)

42. Greenock Free French Memorial
    Lyle Hill
    McLean Museum (Watt's tools)
    & Art Gallery
    Mid Kirk (1787)
    Victoria Tower (245 ft)
    West Kirk (windows Burne-Jones,
    Morris)
43. Grey Mare's Tail
    (waterfall over 'hanging valley'
    in 2000 acres access land;
    wild goats; flowers) (NTS)
44. Lennoxtown (red alum waste-heaps)
45. Strathblane *Duntreath Castle*
    (partly C15; dungeons; stocks)
46. Kilsyth *Colzium House*
    (Covenanters' museum; gardens)
47. Ayr Visitor Centre
    'Auld Brig' (med.; now footbridge)
    Loudoun Hall (C16; restored)
    Rozelle Nature Trails (two) (SWT)
48. Kilmarnock *Burns Museum*
    (1st editions etc.; views from tower)
    Dick Institute (museum;
    art gallery; library)
49. Loup of Fintry (90 ft waterfall)
50. Newmilns *Ladeside Flour Mill*
    (fr. C16)
    26-arch Railway Viaduct (1894)
51. Muirkirk McAdam Cairn
    (foundations tar kilns)
    Ironworks (1787; remains;
    works canal)
52. Ballochmyle Railway Viaduct
    (1848; graceful)
53. Killearn *Knowe Head* (1803;
    restored house)
54. Balloch Visitor Centre
    Loch Lomond Bear Park (plus
    gardens; *Smollett museum*)
    Nature Trail (especially for children)
55. Helensburgh *Glenarn Gardens*
    (rhododendrons)
    Hermitage Park (Henry Bell
    anvil; flywheel)
56. Kirkintilloch *Old St. Mary's Church*
    (1644; museum)
57. Alloway Kirk (Burns associations)
    Brig o'Doon
58. Bonnybridge (High) Rough Castle
    Roman fort; (A.M. & NTS)
    Antonine Wall (rampart, ditch;
    notable)
59. Hermitage & Blackford Nature Trail
60. Roslin Castle (C14; ruins)
    Chapel (C15; 'Prentice Pillar';
    still used collegiate church)
61. *Castlelaw Fort* (Iron Age)
62. Balerno, *Malleny Garden* (NTS)
63. Penicuik *House* (C18 facade;
    rebuilt separately after fire)
    Valleyfield Mill (fr. 1709; housed
    French prisoners, Napoleonic wars)
64. Temple, Gladhouse Lime Kilns
    (fr. C18)
65. Romanno Bridge ('cultivation'?
    terraces)
66. Ardmore *Nature Reserve* (access
    foreshore, permit for reserve) (SWT)
67. Eddleston *Milkieston Rings Fort*
    (Iron Age)
68. Drochil Castle (to 1581;
    fortress/manor)
69. Lyne *Church* (early C17;
    pleasant situation)
    Roman Fort
70. Peebles Visitor Centre
    Bridge (fr. C15)
    Cademuir Hill (two forts; Iron Age)
    Chambers Institution (library;
    museum; art gallery)
    Cross Kirk (1261; nave, west tower
    of friary)
70a. Glentress Forest (Scotland's
    oldest state forest; walks;
    viewpoint 1500 ft) (FC)
70b. *Neidpath Castle* (C15; well-
    preserved tower; picturesque)
70c. *White Meldon* cairn (Br. Age);
    fort (Iron Age); platform
    settlements

71. Black Dwarf's Cottage
 (Scott associations)
72. *Dawyck Gardens* (trees; shrubs)
73. Cumnock (Lugar) *Bello Mill* (also
 birthplace gas-lighting pioneer
 Murdoch)
74. Prestwick Visitor Centre
75. Galston Grain Mill (fr. C18)
76. Cumbernauld, Forth & Clyde Canal
 (fr. 1790); Wynford Lock;
 bascule bridge; cottage etc.
77. Bonnybridge (High) Seabegs Wood
 (A.M. & NTS) Antonine Wall
 (rampart; ditch)
78. Auchineden 'Queen's View'
 (panorama)
 The Whangie (chasm)
 (NTS-marked route)
79. Dryhope Tower (ruins;
 home Scott ancestor)
80. Kinghorn monument to Alexander III
81. Burntisland *St. Columba's Church*
 (fr. 1592; octagonal; belfry, 1749)
82. Aberdour Castle (fr. C14; ruin;
 dovecot, Norman church nearby)
83. Dalgety St. Bridget's Church
 (E. part, roofless, fr. C13)
84. Edinburgh Visitor Centre
 Ann Street (Raeburn;
 romantic-classic)
 Barclay Bruntsfield Church (1862;
 Gothic picturesque)
 Calton Hill (easy road; view;
 monuments)
 Charlotte Square (N. side) (Adam;
 official residences; NTS HQ)
 City of Edinburgh Art Gallery
 (former Royal High School)
 (Hamilton; fine 'Greek revival')
 Craigmillar Castle (fr. C14;
 Queen Mary associations)
 Dean Bridge (1831; Telford; best
 viewed from Dean Village)
 George Heriot's School (fr. 1628;
 Wallace/Aytoun/Playfair)
 Greyfriars Kirk (National
 Covenant (1638) associations
 (museum within); 'Greyfriars
 Bobby' (famous dog) statue nearby
 Holyrood Park (inc. Arthur's Seat
 822 ft; volcanic, columnar
 basalt S. side, Dunsapie Loch)
 Lamb's House, Leith (C16) (NTS)
 National Library of Scotland
 (very extensive collection)
 National Museum of Antiquities
 (collections; national treasures)
 New Town (1770–1800's; George
 Street—Fettes Row; world's best
 example of Georgian town-
 planning)
 Register House (East) (Adam, 1774;
 archives)
 Register House (West) (former
 church; Reid 1811 archives,
 museum)
 Royal Botanic Garden (notable
 collections; plant houses; inc.
 Scottish National Gallery of
 Modern Art)
 Royal Commonwealth Pool
 (Matthew & Johnson-Marshall)
 Royal Mile, rich in history, includes
 Acheson House (C17; craft centre)
 Canongate Kirk (c. 1690; James
 Smith; restored)
 Canongate Tolbooth (fr. 1591;
 tartan collection)
 Castle (C17–18; some med.;
 Crown Jewels of Scotland;
 Great Hall; Scottish National
 War Memorial; Scottish United
 Services Museum; St.
 Margaret's Chapel (Norman)
 tiny)
 Gladstone's Land (1620; painted
 ceiling, walls) (NTS)
 Holyrood Abbey (fr. C13)
 Holyrood Palace (mainly C17;
 official Royal residence;
 picture gallery; state apartments)

Huntly House (fr. 1570; local
 history; silver, glass, pottery)
John Knox's House (C15)
Lady Stair's House (fr. 1622;
 literary relics)
Museum of Childhood
Parliament House (fr. 1639; fine
 hall; Scots parliament here
 pre-1707)
St. Giles, High Kirk of
 Edinburgh (fr. C14; national
 church; crown steeple)
St. James' Court (Boswell, Hume,
 Geddes associations)
Royal Scottish Museum, Chambers St.
Transport Museum (trams; buses;
 uniforms)
University of Edinburgh, Old
 Quadrangle (C18–19; Adam plans)
85. Cramond, Eagle Rock (Hunter's
 Craig; carving–Roman?)
 Lauriston Castle (C16; furniture,
 antiques)
 Roman fort (N. end of Dere Street)
86. Mauchline Burns Memorial
 (museum, tower)
 Crossroads *Horse-Mill* (c. 1800)
87. South Queensferry Abercorn
 Church (Norman door;
 sculptured stone)
 Forth Railway Bridge (1890;
 cantilevered)
 Forth Road Bridge (1964; suspension,
 1¼ m long)
 Plewlands House (fr. C17; view from
 outside) (NTS)
87a. *Dalmeny Church* (C12;
 well restored)
87b. *Hopetoun House* (Bruce/Adam;
 pictures, furnishings; deer;
 St. Kilda sheep; museum;
 viewpoint; Nature Trail)
87c. Kirkliston three railway viaducts
 (1842)
 Church (C12; Romanesque door)
88. Linlithgow *Palace* (fr. 1400;
 majestic ruin)
 St. Michael's Church (C15; in use)
 'Little Houses' (C16–17; view from
 outside only) (NTS)
 St. Magdalene Distillery (c. 1800;
 fine early example, kilns classic)
 Avon Railway Viaduct (1842)
88a. *The House of The Binns* (C17
 mansion; fine plaster ceilings) (NTS)
88b. Blackness Castle (fr. C15;
 sea-fortress)
88c. Bo'ness *Kinneil House* (C16–17;
 decorated ceiling, murals;
 Roebuck–Watt steam engine, 1765)
89. Grangemouth, Forth & Clyde
 Canal terminus (vestiges)
 oil-refining complex
90. Falkirk *Callendar House* (C14–19;
 Parish Church (1811, inc. 1734
 Adam tower)
 Scottish Railway Preservation Depot
 (locos, rolling-stock)
 Steeple (1813; 146 ft)
90a. Carron Ironworks (fr. 1759;
 associations Roebuck, Watt,
 John Adam; 'Carronade' cannon;
 pioneers electric cookers)
91. Kincardine-on-Forth *Longannet
 Power Station*, 595 ft chimney
92. Culross (C16–17; prototype Scots
 300-year-old burgh) (NTS)
 Abbey (fr. C13; choir now
 parish church Bruce mon. c. 1642)
 Ark, Nunnery, Study (early
 Culross) (NTS)
 Dunimarle Castle (Napoleon treasures)
 St. Mungo's Chapel (1503; ruins) (NTS)
 The Palace (early C17; mansion
 with fine painted ceilings)
93. Dunfermline Visitor Centre
 Andrew Carnegie Birthplace (relics)
 Museum (Viewfield) (local, folk)
 Palace (ruins; royal;
 impressive S. wall)

Pittencrieff House Museum
 (C17; mansion; costume gallery;
 lawns; hot-houses; grounds in
 glen overlooked by Malcolm
 Canmore's Tower (C11; ruin)
94. *Rosyth Castle* (C16; tower;
 dovecot) (SDD)
95. Tarbolton Bachelors Club (C17;
 Burns; inc. small museum) (NTS)
96. Alloway Burns' Birthplace
97. Brown Carrick Hill (940 ft; view)
98. *St. Mary's Kirk* (1292?)
99. St. Mary's Loch statue James Hogg
 Tibbie Shiel's Inn
 (literary associations)
100. Craignethan Castle (C16; tower-
 house, well preserved, ornate)
101. Beattock Summit (1014 ft)
102. New Lanark (c. 1800; Owen's
 model factory village)
103. Lanark Visitor Centre
 Cartland Crags (mile-long chasm)
 Corra Linn (90 ft waterfall)
 *Corehouse (Falls of Clyde) Nature
 Reserve* (two trails) (SWT)
104. Blackhill Stonebyres (view) (NTS)
105. Auchlochan Bridge (c. 1790;
 graceful single-arch)
106. Douglas St. Bride's Church (fr.
 C12; remains inc. three
 altar-tombs)
107. Abington *Arbory Hill fort* (Iron
 Age; 140 ft across, overlooking
 Roman road)
108. Crawford *Normangill* (Neolithic;
 henge monument)
109. Fatlips Castle (C16; ruins
 tower-house; view)
 Tinto Hill (2335 ft; dome-shaped
 felsite intrusion)
110. Coulter Mill (fr. 1800;
 three-storey grain mill)
111. *Cowcastle Fort* (Iron Age; two
 settlements; hut-bases)
112. Coulter Motte Hill (med.; castle
 mound, once moated)
113. Biggar Visitor Centre
 Cadger's Bridge (C15?; pack-bridge)
 coaching inn (C18)
 Collegiate Church (founded 1545)
 Gladstone Court Museum (C19
 trades, crafts)
114. Thankerton Bridge (fr. 1778;
 two arches)
115. Thankerton *Quothquan Law* fort
 (Iron Age)
116. Broughton Place *garden*
 (herbaceous; views)
117. Broughton *Dreva Fort* (Iron/Dark
 age)
118. Drumelzier Tinnis Castle (1592
 ruins, high above Tweed)
119. Blyth Bridge mill (fr. 1812)
120. North Muir round cairns (Br. Age)
121. Newbigging (C18; weavers' village;
 green, smithy, market cross)
122. Carnwath Mill (fr. C18–1946;
 good wheel, kiln)
123. Castle Greg (small Roman fort)
124. *Linhouse* (C16; castellated domestic)
125. East Calder, Almondell Country
 Park ('Man & Almondell' nature
 trail; 90 acres; river; canal; woods)
126. Torphichen Preceptory (C15;
 main Scots seat Knights
 Hospitallers; nave rebuilt (C18)
 now parish church)
 Cairnpapple Hill (Neo./Early Br.
 Age; burial sanctuary complex)
127. High Blantyre David Livingstone
 National Memorial (birthplace
 1813; relics)
128. Inchmickery *Nature Reserve*
 (island; terns) (RSPB)
129. Inchcolm Abbey (island; inc. C13
 chapter house)
130. Cathcart, Linn Park (200 acres)
 Nature Trail (designed for
 schools; river; woods; C14
 castle; zoo; nature centre)
131. Strathaven *John Hastie Museum*

Map 66

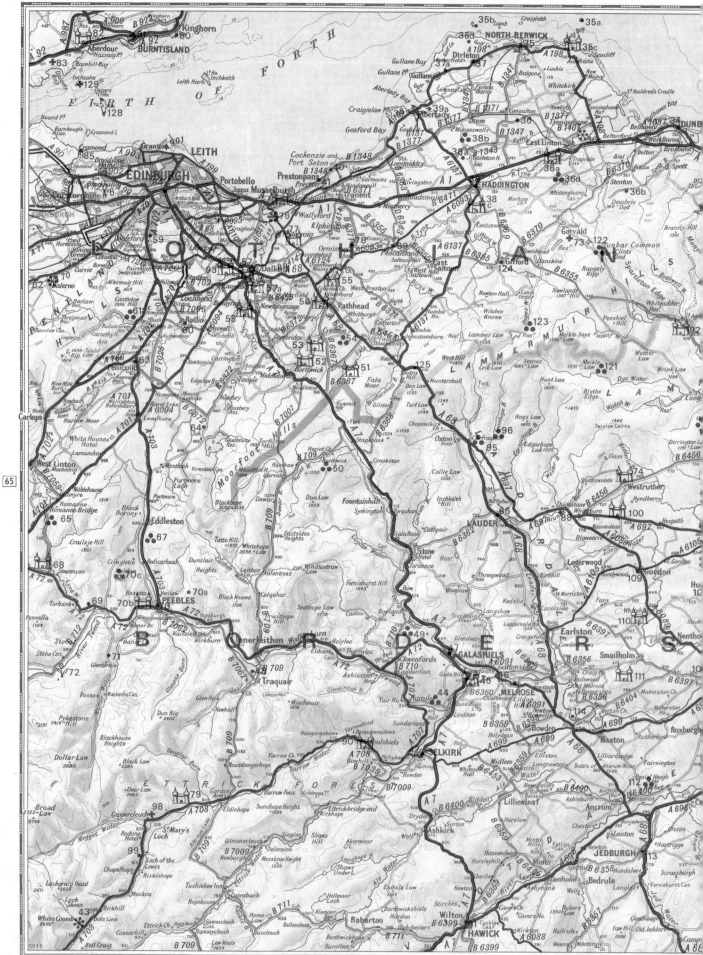

Map 67

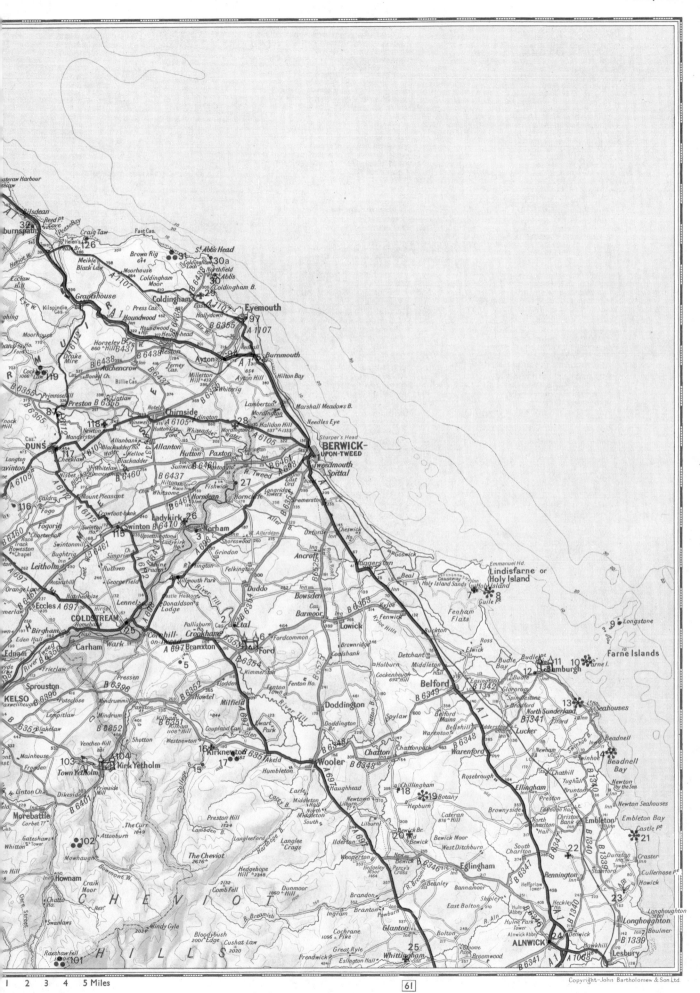

1   2   3   4   5 Miles

Copyright-John Bartholomew & Son.Ltd.

1. Berwick-on-Tweed (town)
   Castle (C12 remains)
   Town Walls (mediaeval, rebuilt 1555)
   Holy Trinity Church
   Barracks (1719)
   Town Hall (1757)
   Old Bridge (1610–34)
   Royal Border Railway Bridge (R. Stephenson, 1847)
   Museum & Art Gallery
2. Etal (village)
3. Norham Castle (C12 keep)
   St. Cuthbert's Church
4. Twizel Bridge (c. 1500)
5. Flodden Field (site of battle 1513)
6. Ford Castle (part C14)
7. St. Mary's Church, Holy Island
   Lindisfarne Priory (C11–14 remains)
8. *Lindisfarne Castle* (C16) (NT), Holy Island
9. Longstone Lighthouse (Grace Darling's home)
10. Farne Islands (seabirds & seals) (NT)
    C14 Chapel & Peel Tower, Inner Farne
11. *Bamburgh Castle* (C12 & later)
12. Bamburgh Church
    Grace Darling Museum
13. Shoreston Dunes (NT), Seahouses
    Monk's House Bird Observatory (BTO)
14. Beadnell Lime Kilns (C18) (NT)
15. Hethpool Pele Tower (C14)
16. Kirknewton Church
17. Yeavering Bell Camp (Iron Age hill-fort)
18. Chillingham Church, Castle (mainly C17) & White Cattle
19. Ros Castle (earthwork, view) (NT)
20. Chapel of the Holy Trinity (Norman), Old Bewick
21. Dunstanburgh Castle (C14 remains) (NT)
22. Roch Church
23. *Howick Hall Gardens*
24. *Alnwick Castle*
    St. Michael s Church
    Hotspur Gate (1450)
    Town Hall (1771)
    Northumberland Hall (1826)
    Lion Bridge (John Adam, 1773)
    Alnwick—Rothbury Road (views)
25. Coldstream Visitor Centre
    Dundock Wood (The Hirsel) (shrubs; old trees; bird sanctuary)
    Museum (site 1650 Guards-raising) (inc. military)
    Tweed Bridge (1766; Smeaton; five arches)
26. Ladykirk Church (fr. 1500)
27. Union Bridge (1820)
28. Foulden *Tithe Barn* for church (1786; view from roadside)
29. Coldingham Priory (C11; ruins; site parish church; choir, C13)
30. St. Abb's fishing village, harbour (1833)
30a. St. Abb's Head (300 ft cliffs; smugglers' caves)
    Lighthouse (1862)
31. *Earns Heugh fort* (Iron Age)
32. Cockburnspath Cove Harbour (C17; smugglers' caves; wave-cut platform in calciferous sandstone)
    Dunglass Collegiate Church (fr. 1450) rich interior
33. Innerwick *East Lammermuir Deans*

Nature Reserve (limestone valleys (four); flora) (SWT)
34. Dunbar Visitor Centre
    Church (rebuilt 1821) (inc. Home Monument)
    Harbour (fr. 1650)
    Myreton Motor Museum (branch of)
    Nature Trail (two miles)
    Town House (C17; three-storied tower)
    White Sands & Barns Ness (limestone coastal area: fossils, plants; restored limekiln, C18)
35. North Berwick Visitor Centre
35a. Bass Rock (350 ft; volcanic plug, gannetry)
35b. Fidra, Eyebroughty, Lamb Islands (seabird sanctuaries, view from boat/shore) (RSPB)
35c. Tantallon Castle (C14; coastal landmark)
35d. Yellowcraig Nature Trail (mixed woodland/coastal)
36. East Fortune Monument (to double Atlantic crossing, airship, 1919)
36a. Hailes Castle (ruin, fortified mansion; good chapel, C16)
36b. Pressmennan Wood Nature Trail (viewpoint) (FC)
36c. Preston Mill (picturesque working water mill and Phantassie Doocot nearby) (NTS)
36d. *Traprain Law* (early Iron Age fortress-capital; ex-treasure site)
37. Dirleton Castle (beautiful ruin, destroyed 1650); bowling green (C17)
    Church (Archerfield Aisle, 1664)
37a. *Muirfield Golf Course* (venue world's oldest golf club, 1744)
38. Haddington
    St. Mary's Church (from C15; 'Lamp of Lothian'; tower landmark)
    Adam houses (esp. *bank*)
    St. Martin's Church (ruined Romanesque nave, altered C13)
    Town House (Adam/Graham)
38a. Hopetoun Monument (C19; landmark)
38b. *Chesters Fort* (Iron Age; well defined)
39. Aberlady Bay Nature Reserve (waders; wildfowl)
39a. *Luffness House* (late C16)
    Myreton Motor Museum (cars; motor-cycles; cycles)
40. Cockenzie Power Station (notable modern landmark)
41. Seton Collegiate Church (C15–16; fine mural monuments)
    Prestonpans *Hamilton House* (c. 1628) (NTS)
    Market Cross (C17; at Preston)
    Northfield House (c. 1600; substantially unchanged)
    Prestongrange Beam Engines (1874–1954) restored; basis mining museum (venue Britain's earliest recorded coal-mine)
42. Selkirk Visitor Centre
    Court Room (Scott/local relics)
    Halliwells Museum (ironmongery relics)
    Tannery (1770; in use)
    woollen mills (C19)

43. Grey Mare's Tail (waterfall over 'hanging valley' in 2000 acres access land; wild goats; flowers) (NTS)
44. *The Rink fort* (Iron Age)
45. *Abbotsford* (Scott's home; library; relics)
    Darnwick Tower (C16; tower-house)
46. Melrose Visitor Centre
    Abbey (fr. 1136; destroyed 1544; renowned; figure sculptures; museum)
    Eildon Hill North (large fort, Iron Age, with Roman signal-post)
    Eildon Walk (inc. part of Dere Street Roman)
47. Galashiels Visitor Centre
    Old Gala House (fr. C16; painted ceilings)
    woollen mills (C19)
48. Innerleithen *Traquair House* (fr. C10; mostly C17; many associations Scots royalty; oldest? inhabited Scots house. *Brewhouse*, fr. 1730, still working)
    Traquair Mill (1802)
49. *Torwoodlee broch, fort* (Iron Age)
50. Heriot *Corsehope Rings Fort* (Iron Age)
51. Cakemuir Castle (C16; tower-house)
52. Middleton *Borthwick Castle* (C15; tower-house; Queen Mary associations; view from footpath)
53. Crichton Castle (C14–16; large, fine; Italianate wing, c. 1590)
54. Crichten Mains *earth-house* (Roman sculptured stone)
55. Pathhead *Preston Hall* (c. 1794; handsome)
56. Pathhead *Ford House* (1680; almost unaltered)
57. Dalkeith *Palace* (C12 hunting-lodge; rebuilt 1700; Vanbrugh)
    Hawthornden (rebuilt 1638; Drummond) mansion
57a. Newbattle Abbey (mansion on abbey site ; now college; C18 ceilings; C19 drawing room)
58. Dalhousie Castle (fr. C12; much altered)
59. Hermitage & Blackford Nature Trail
60. Roslin Castle (C14; ruins)
    Chapel (C15; 'Prentice Pillar'; still used collegiate church)
61. *Castlelaw Fort* (Iron Age)
62. Balerno, *Malleny Garden* (NTS)
63. Penicuik *House* (C18 facade; rebuilt separately after fire)
    Valleyfield Mill (fr. 1709; housed French prisoners, Napoleonic wars)
64. Temple, Gladhouse Lime Kilns (fr. C18)
65. Romanno Bridge 'cultivation'? terraces)
66. Lauder Visitor Centre
    Church (C16; octagonal spire)
    Thirlestane Castle (fr. C16; exhibits)
    Tolbooth
67. Eddleston *Milkieston Rings Fort* (Iron Age)
68. Drochil Castle (to 1581; fortress/manor)
69. Lyne *Church* (early C17; pleasant situation)
    Roman Fort

70. Peebles Visitor Centre
Bridge (fr. C15)
Cademuir Hill (two forts; Iron Age)
Chambers Institution (library;
museum; art gallery)
Cross Kirk (1261; nave, west
tower of friary
70a. Glentress Forest (Scotland's oldest
state forest; walks; viewpoint
1500 ft) (FC)
70b. *Neidpath Castle* (C15; well-
preserved tower; picturesque)
70c. *White Meldon* cairn (Br. Age);
fort (Iron Age); platform settlements
71. Black Dwarf's Cottage (Scott
associations)
72. *Dawyck Gardens* (trees; shrubs)
73. Garvald, Nunraw Abbey (fr. 1952)
74. Westruther (coaching inn; 1721)
75. Burnmouth (picturesque cliff-foot
fishing village)
76. Inveresk Lodge *Garden* (features
plants for small gardens) (NTS)
77. *Carberry Tower* (fr. C16; extended
to mansion)
78. Ormiston Market Cross (C15;
free-standing)
79. Dryhope Tower (ruins; home
Scott ancestor)
80. Kinghorn monument to Alexander III
81. Burntisland *St. Columba's Church*
(fr. 1592; octagonal; belfry, 1749)
82. Aberdour Castle (fr. C14; ruin;
dovecot, Norman church nearby)
83. Dalgety St. Bridget's Church (E.
part, roofless, fr. C13)
84. Edinburgh Visitor Centre
Ann Street (Raeburn; romantic-
classic)
Barclay Bruntsfield Church (1862;
Gothic picturesque)
Calton Hill (easy road; view;
monuments)
Charlotte Square (N. side) (Adam;
official residences; NTS HQ)
City of Edinburgh Art Gallery
(former Royal High School;
Hamilton; fine 'Greek revival')
Craigmillar Castle (fr. C14; Queen
Mary associations)
Dean Bridge (c. 1831; Telford;
best viewed from Dean Village)
George Heriot's School (fr. 1628;
Wallace/Aytoun/Playfair)
Greyfriars Kirk (National Covenant
(1638), associations; (museum
within) Greyfriars Bobby (famous
dog) statue nearby)
Holyrood Park (inc. Arthur's
Seat 822ft; volcanic, columnar
basalt S. side Dunsapie Loch)
Inchmickery Nature Reserve (island;
terns) (RSPB)
Lamb's House, Leith (C16) (NTS)
National Library of Scotland (very
extensive collection)
National Museum of Antiquities
(collections; national treasures)
New Town (1770–1800's; George
St.—Fettes Row; world's best
example of Georgian town-
planning)
Register House (East) (Adam;
1774; archives)
Register House (West) (former

church; Reid 1811; archives;
museum)
Royal Botanic Garden (notable
collections; plant houses; inc.
Scottish National Gallery of
Modern Art)
Royal Commonwealth Pool
(Matthew & Johnson-Marshall)
Royal Mile, rich in history, includes
Acheson House (C17; craft centre)
Canongate Kirk (c. 1690; James
Smith; restored)
Canongate Tolbooth (fr. 1591;
tartan collection)
Castle (c17–18; some med.;
Crown Jewels of Scotland;
Great Hall; Scottish National
War Memorial; Scottish United
Services Museum; St. Margaret's
Chapel (Norman) tiny)
Gladstone's Land (1620; painted
ceiling, walls) (NTS)
Holyrood Abbey (fr. C13)
Holyrood Palace (mainly C17;
official Royal residence; picture
gallery; state apartments)
Huntly House (fr. 1570; local history;
silver, glass, pottery)
John Knox's House (C15)
Lady Stair's House (fr. 1622;
literary relics)
Museum of Childhood
Parliament House (fr. 1639; fine
hall; Scots parliament here
pre-1707)
St. Giles, High Kirk of Edinburgh,
(fr. C14; national church; crown
steeple, C15)
St. James' Court (Boswell, Hume,
Geddes associations)
Royal Scottish Museum, Chambers St.
Transport Museum (trams; buses;
uniforms)
University of Edinburgh, Old
Quadrangle (C18–19; Adam
plans)
85. Cramond, Eagle Rock (Hunter's
Craig; carving-Roman?)
Roman Fort (N. end of Dere St.)
Lauriston Castle (C16; furniture;
antiques)
86. Musselburgh *Pinkie House* (fr. 1613;
tower, 1390; fine painted ceiling;
part of Loretto School)
87. Preston Bridge (fr. 1770; three-
arched)
88. Dod Mill (traditional, pantiled)
89. Pencaitland Bridge (fr. 1510)
Winton House (notable Jacobean
architecture; ceilings; furniture)
90. Newark Castle (fr. 1423?; tower-
house)
91. Hawick Visitor Centre
Mote Hill (mediaeval court meeting-
place)
Wilton Lodge Museum
92. Cranshaws Castle (tower-house)
93. Melville Castle (1786; Playfair)
94. Ayton Castle (1851; red sandstone
baronial Victoriana)
Village (C18; planned)
95. *West Addinston Fort* (Iron Age)
96. *Longcroft Fort* (Iron Age)
97. Eyemouth, *Gunsgreen House*
(1764; built by wealthy smuggler)
Harbour (fr. 1770; Smeaton)
98. *St. Mary's Kirk* (1292?)

99. St. Mary's Loch statue James Hogg
Tibbie Shiel's Inn (literary
associations)
100. Houndslow Toll (traditional)
101. Woden Law fort (Roman siege
works-for training?)
102. Hownam Law Fort (Iron Age)
103. Yetholm Loch *Nature Reserve*
(wildfowl; marsh plants) (SWT)
104. Kirk Yetholm Gipsy 'Palace' (last
'royal' gipsy, 1883)
105. Kelso Visitor Centre
Abbey (C12; destroyed 1545;
N. transept; transitional)
Bridge (1803; Rennie; model old
Waterloo Bridge)
Court House (C18)
Mill fr. C15; monastic; wall; lade)
106. *Floors Castle* (1718) *Gardens*
107. *Newton Don*
108. Hume Castle (C13; restored 1794
'antique'; view)
109. *Gordon Moss Nature Reserve* (SWT)
Greenknowe Tower (C16; tower-
house; iron 'yett')
110. *Mellerstain House* (Adams'; ceilings;
furniture; library; paintings;
Italian garden)
111. Smailholm Tower (C16; keep; view)
112. Peniel Heugh *forts* (Iron/Dark Ages)
monument (Waterloo)
113. Jedburgh Visitor Centre
Abbey (fr. 1118, burnt 1523; very
fine; museum)
Castle (former 1823 prison on
mediaeval site)
Dunion Hill (view)
Queen Mary's House (late C16; relics)
114. St. Boswells Dryburgh Abbey
(C12; Haig's, Scott's graves)
'Scott's View', Bemersyde
115. Swinton (coaching inn, village
green, weavers' cottages; windmill,
C18, remains)
116. Polwarth *Church* (1703)
Marchmont House (C18; Adam)
117. Duns *Castle* (modern; C14 tower;
avenue lime trees)
Nature Reserve (SWT)
Jim Clark Memorial (County
Library & Museum)
Covenanters' Monument (view;
Duns Law)
118. Edrom Church (Norman door to
burial vault)
119. Edinshall Broch (Iron Age; large
fort)
120. Dirrington Great Law three cairns
(Br. Age; on summit (1309 ft)
121. Mutiny Stones long cairn (Neolithic)
122. White Castle fort (Iron Age)
123. The Hopes fort (Iron Age)
124. Gifford *Church* (1710; bell, C15;
pulpit, C17)
Yester Castle (ruins, inc. 'Goblin
Ha' '; vaulted underground
chamber)
Yester House (1745; Adam) *Gardens*
125. Soutra view
Roman Road (Dere Street) Turf
Law
126. Siccar Point (geol. unconformity)
127. Greenlaw Kirk (tower prob. C15)
128. *Inchmickery Nature Reserve* (island;
terns) (RSPB)
129. Inchcolm Abbey (island; inc. C13
chapter house)

Map 68

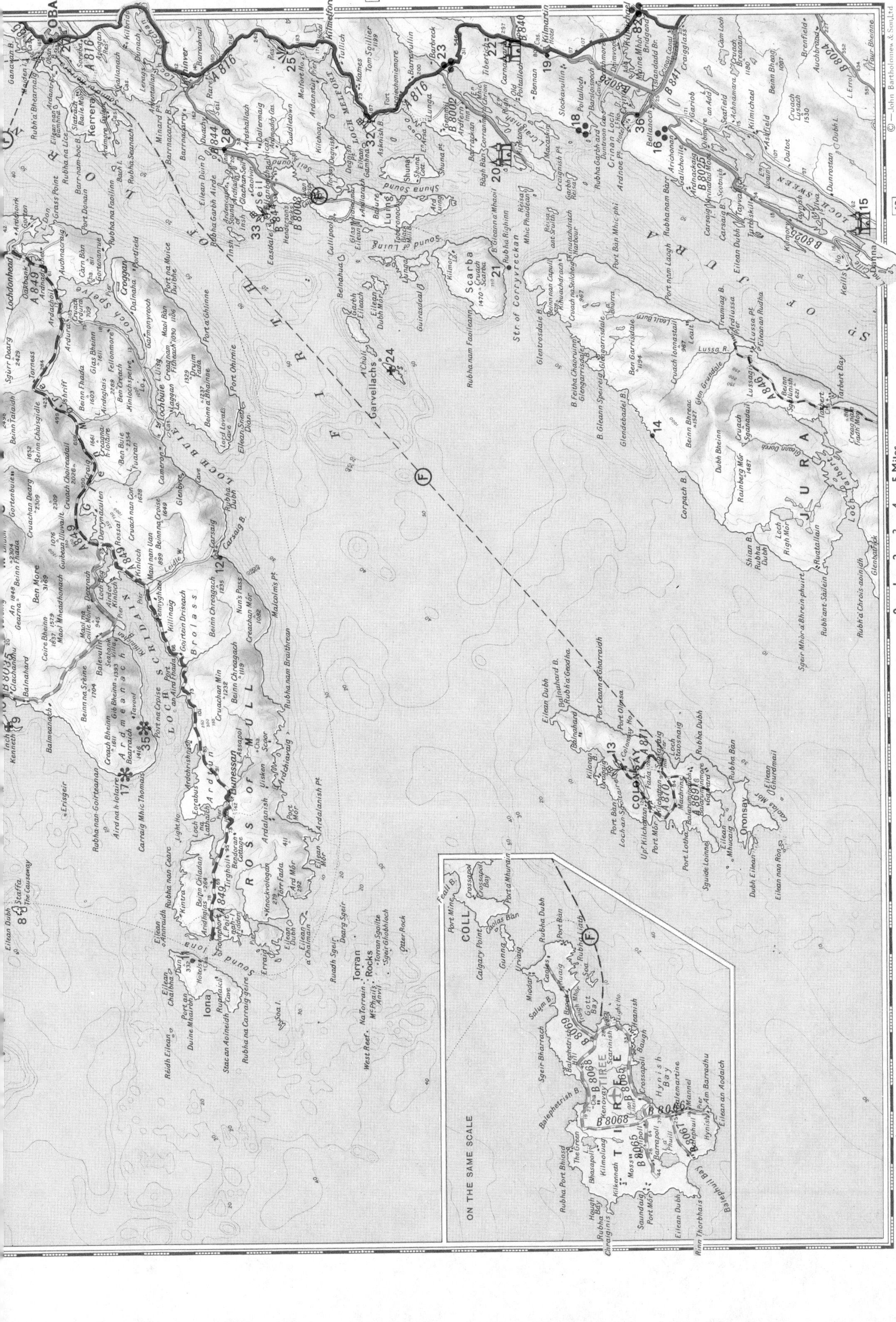

Map 69

OBAN

A 816

A 849

ROSS OF MULL

LOCH BUIE

FIRTH OF LORN

JURA

COLONSAY

Oronsay

Staffa

Iona

TIREE

COLL

LOCH MELFORT

Garvellachs

Scarba

Str. of Corryvreckan

ON THE SAME SCALE

0 1 2 3 4 5 Miles

© — John Bartholomew & Son, Ltd.

The Edinburgh Geographical Institute

Gazetteer to Maps 68·69

1. Eigg Camas Sgiotaig Bay ('musical sands')
2. Eigg Sgurr of Eigg (landmark; 1289ft)
3. Ardnamurchan Point (most W. mainland Britain) lighthouse (1848; Stevenson)
4. Mingary Castle (imposing ruin)
5. Tobermory Visitor Centre
   Aros House Gardens
6. Ardtornish Castle (C14; cliffs; waterfalls)
7. Loch Aline (silica sands)
8. Staffa Fingal's Cave (impressive cavern in basalt)
9. Inch Kenneth Chapel (mediaeval churchyard monuments)
10. Gribun Rocks (overhanging cliffs)
11. Iona Cathedral (fr. 1203, restored C20)
    MacLean's Cross (C15; Hebridean)
    St. Columba's Cell
    St. John's Cross (C9)
    St. Martin's Cross (C10; Runic)
    St. Oran's Cemetery (c62 kings buried)
12. Carsaig Arches (basaltic tunnels, sea-wrought)
13. Colonsay *Kiloran Gardens*
14. Jura (raised beaches)
15. Castle Sween (C12; ruin)
16. Druim An Duin (galleried dun)
17. MacCulloch's tree (fossil 50ft. tall; arduous walk from Burg) (NTS)
18. Ardifuir Dun (Iron Age)
19. Kilmartin Churchyard (C16 slabs; crosses)
    Glebe Cairn (Br. Age)
20. Craignish *Castle* (C16 keep) *gardens*
21. Corryvreckan (whirlpool)
22. Carnassarie Castle (C16; semi-ruined)
23. Kintraw cairns, standing stones
24. Garvellachs (beehive cells)
    Eileach an Naoimh (Celtic monastic remains)
25. Pass of Melfort (view)
26. Seil Clachan Bridge ('spans' Atlantic)
27. Oban Visitor Centre
    McCaig's Folly (incomplete, over-looks town)
    Pulpit Hill (viewpoint)
28. Torosay Castle (C19)
29. *Duart Castle* (ruined C18; restored C20; fine setting)
30. Strontian Ariundle Oakwood (NC and DAFS)
    Glen Nature Trail (oaks; moors; leadmines)
31. Morar (white sands)
32. *Arduaine House Gardens* interesting shrubs
33. Easdale *An Cala Gardens*
34. *Calgary House Gardens*
35. Burg (2000 acres) (NTS)
36. Crinan Canal (1801)
82. Kilmichael Glassary rock engravings (c. 2000 BC)
    Auchnahoish Cairn
    Dunadd Fort (Dark Age; walled)

Map 70

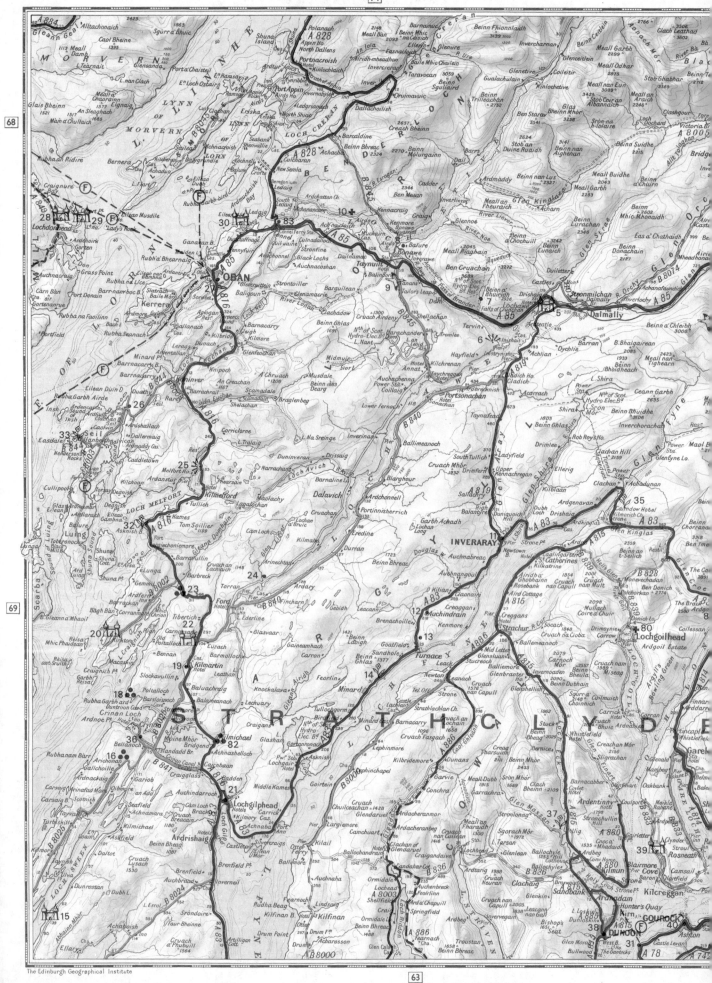

Map 71

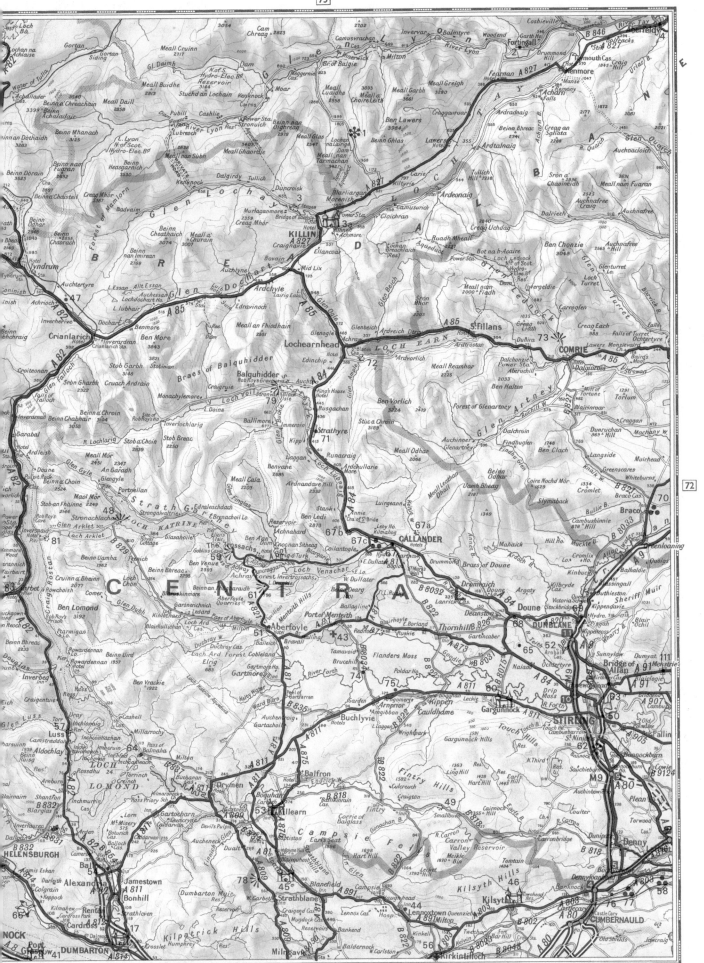

1   2   3   4   5 Miles

Gazetteer to Maps 70·71

1. Ben Lawers (Visitor Centre; Nature Trail; viewpoint (NTS)
2. Fortingall (thatched houses; old yew)
   Glen Lyon to W. (30 m long)
   Roman Camp (Pilate's birthplace?)
3. Killin Falls of Lochay (fish-pass)
3a. Finlarig Castle (1629 ruins; beheading pit)
4. Aberfeldy Visitor Centre
   'Birks', (Nature Trail; picnic site)
   Drummond Hill Forest Walks (four, varied) (FC)
   Falls of Moness
   Strathtay History Trails (four)
   Tay Bridge (1733; Wade)
5. Kilchurn Castle (C15; landmark; view from outside only)
6. Ardanaiseig Gardens (shrubs; view)
7. Cruachan Power Station Visitor Centre
   R. Awe (runs along deep fault)
8. Lorn Furnace (C18; ironworks complex)
9. Taynuilt *Glen Nant* (fine mixed woodland) (FC & NC)
10. Ardchattan Priory (1230 ruins)
11. Inveraray Visitor Centre
    Bell Tower (view)
    Castle (armoury, C18 furniture)
    Church (C18; Mylne; 'double')
12. Auchindrain Museum of Farming Life (C18–19 furnished steadings)
13. Furnace Craleckan Furnace (C18; disused charcoal ironworks)
14. Crarae Forest Garden (rare trees; conifers) (FC)
    Lodge Garden
15. Castle Sween (C12 ruin)
16. Druim An Duin (galleried dun)
17. Dumbarton Castle (on 240 ft high rock; Queen Mary associations)
    Castlehill monument (1937; to Cunninghame Graham; (NTS)
18. Ardifuir Dun (Iron Age)
19. Kilmartin Churchyard (slabs; crosses, C16)
    Glebe Cairn (Br. Age)
20. *Craignish Castle* (keep C16;, *gardens*)
21. Lochgilphead Visitor Centre
    Knapdale Forest Walks (various) (FC)
22. Carnassarie Castle (C16; semi-ruined)
23. Kintraw cairns, standing stones
24. Loch Awe Nature Trail, Forest Walks (FC)
25. Pass of Melfort (view)
26. Seil Clachan Bridge ('spans' Atlantic)
27. Oban Visitor Centre
    McCaig's Folly (incomplete, overlooks town)
    Pulpit Hill (viewpoint)
28. Torosay Castle (C19)
29. *Duart Castle* (ruined C18; restored C20; fine setting)
30. *Dunstaffnage Castle* (C13 ruins; curtain wall; *grounds* only)
31. *Cloch Lighthouse* (Clyde landmark)
32. *Arduaine House Gardens* interesting shrubs
33. Easdale *An Cala Gardens*

34. Ben Lui Nature Reserve (geology) (NC)
35. Cairndow Gardens
36. Crinan Canal (1801)
37. Benmore Younger Botanic Garden *Eckford Gardens*
38. Dunoon Visitor Centre
39. Knockderry Castle (now hostel; includes dungeon)
40. Gourock Visitor Centre
41. Port Glasgow *Newark Castle* fr. C16; hall; courtyard; stepped gables)
42. Greenock Free French Memorial Lyle Hill
    McLean Museum (Watt's tools) & Art Gallery
    Mid Kirk (1787)
    Victoria Tower (245 ft)
    West Kirk (windows Burne-Jones, Morris)
43. *Inchmahome Priory* (fr. 1238; good C13 remains)
44. Lennoxtown (red alum waste-heaps)
45. Strathblane *Duntreath Castle* (partly C15; dungeons; stocks)
46. Kilsyth *Colzium House* (Covenanters' museum; gardens)
47. St. Fillan's Pool (mediaeval 'cure' for lunatics)
48. Loch Katrine (viewpoint)
49. Loup of Fintry (90ft. waterfall)
50. Stirling Visitor Centre
    Argyll Lodging (C17; town mansion)
    Cambuskenneth Priory (C12; C14 bell-tower)
    Castle (C15, restored) 'King's Knot' (early garden); 'Queen Victoria's Look-out' (views); regimental museum
    Church of the Holy Rude (Mary, James VI crowned)
    Cowane's Hospital (C17; almshouse)
    Landmark Centre (exhibition old Stirling)
    Mar's Wark (1570; part ruins; gatehouse sculptures)
    The Old Bridge (1415; very fine)
    Smith Institute
    Touch House (fr. C16; Georgian facade)
51. Aberfoyle Visitor Centre
    Nature Trail (fr. caravan site)
    Queen Elizabeth Forest Park (main centre)
52. *Keir Gardens*
53. Killearn *Knowe Head* (1803; restored house)
54. Balloch Visitor Centre
    Loch Lomond Bear Park (plus gardens, *Smollett museum*)
    Nature Trail (especially for children)
55. Helensburgh *Glenarn Gardens* (rhododendrons)
    Hermitage Park (Henry Bell anvil, flywheel)
56. Kirkintilloch *Old St. Mary's Church* (1644; museum)
57. Luss village
58. Bonnybridge (High) Rough Castle Roman fort; (A.M. & NTS)
    Antonine Wall (rampart; ditch; notable)

59. The Trossachs (viewpoint)
60. *Gargunnock House* (fr. C16–18; mansion)
61. Viewpoint
62. Bannockburn Monument (Visitor Centre; equestrian statue; 'Forging of a Nation' exhibition; rotunda) (NTS)
63. Causewayhead Stirling University Wallace Monument (1869; 220 ft landmark; museum; panorama)
64. Balmaha *Inch Cailleach Nature Trail* (NC)
65. Blair Drummond *House, gardens* Kincardine Church (1816; brass, C17)
    Safari Park
66. Ardmore *Nature Reserve* (access foreshore,) permit for reserve (SWT)
67. Callander Visitor Centre
67a. Falls of Bracklinn
67b. Pass of Leny
67c. Roman Camp, Bochastle Farm
68. Doune *Castle* (C15, restored 1883) *Motor Museum*
    Park Gardens (early C19; varied)
69. Dunblane Cathedral (fr. C13, restored 1895, beech walk; museum)
70. Braco *Ardoch Roman Camp* earthworks of camp for c. 40 000 men)
71. Strathyre Forest Centre (walk; picnic site) (FC)
72. Loch Earn Edinample Falls
73. Comrie Melville Monument (view; Falls of Lednock & Devil's Cauldron)
74. Cardross Bridge (1774)
75. Kippen Laraben Dovecot
76. Cumbernauld, Forth & Clyde Canal (fr. 1790); Wyndford Lock; bascule bridge, cottage etc.
77. Bonnybridge (High) Seabegs Wood (A.M.& NTS) Antonine Wall (rampart; ditch)
78. Auchineden 'Queen's View' (panorama)The Whangie (chasm) (NTS-marked route)
79. Balquhidder bridge (view Ben Vorlich, Braes, Loch Voil)
80. Lochgoilhead *Church* (restored 1955; 1512 altar; C17 memorial, pulpit)
81. Inversnaid (waterfall; view; Wordsworth association)
82. Kilmichael Glassary (rock engravings c. 2000 BC)
    Auchnahoish Cairn
    Dunadd Ford (Dark Age; walled)
83. Connel Loch Etive Bridge (long cantilever)
    Falls of Lora (sea-cataract)
84. Argyll Forest Park (60000 acres in three forests) (FC)
    scenic variety, mountains, 'Rest-and-be-Thankful'
    Visitor Centre, camping site Ardgartan
111. Menstrie (main road runs along Ochil Fault)
    Castle ('Nova Scotia' rooms)

Map 72

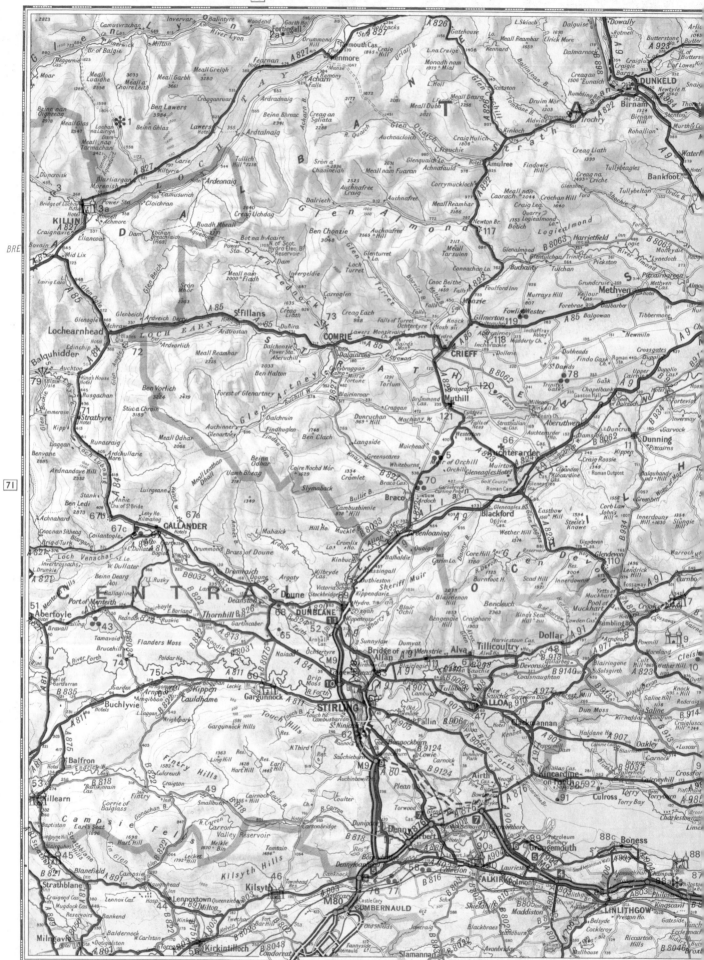

Map 73

1 2 3 4 5 Miles

© —John Bartholomew & Son Ltd.

1. Ben Lawers (Visitor Centre; Nature Trail; viewpoint) (NTS)
2a. Fortingall (thatched houses; old yew)
   Roman Camp (Pilate's birthplace?) 30 m of Glen Lyon to W.
2b. Dunkeld Visitor Centre
   Cathedral (fr. C15; choir now parish church)
   Craigvinean Walks (three; viewpoint) (FC)
   Hermitage (c18; folly above waterfall; woodland walk) (NTS)
   'Little Houses' (extensive restoration of C17 houses) (NTS)
3. Killin Falls of Lochay (fish-pass)
3a. Finlarig Castle (1629 ruins; beheading pit)
4. Crieff Visitor Centre
   Drummond Castle (gardens)
   Falls of Turret
5. Kaims Castle (Roman Fort)
6. Alva (silver mill; tweed mill, 1820; now warehouse)
7. Crook of Devon Tullibole Castle (1608)
8. Rumbling Bridge (gorge, waterfall, 1713 bridge below modern one)
9. Aldie Castle (fr. C16; tower)
10. Dumglow Fort (Iron Age)
11. Dunning Church (c. 1200)
12. Kinross Visitor Centre
   House (late C17; gardens)
   Tolbooth (C17; Adam decorations)
13. Perth Visitor Centre
   Art Gallery & Museum
   Balhousie Castle (C17) Black Watch Museum
   Branklyn Garden (fine two acres) (NTS)
   Bridge (1771; Smeaton)
   Elcho Castle (C16; intact fortified mansion)
   Fair Maid's House (fr. C14; crafts centre)
   Forgandenny Fort (Iron Age)
   Huntingtower (C15–16; fine castellated mansion)
   Kinnoull Hill Nature Trail
   St. John's Kirk (C15)
   Scone Palace (mainly 1803; inc. 1580 part; furniture, china, C16 needlework; pinetum; woodland garden)
   Waterworks (1832; disused; outstanding)
14. Stanley (fr. 1785; former cotton-mills village)
15. Abernethy Castle Law Fort (Iron Age)
   Round Tower (C11; nearby Pictish symbol stone)
16. Auchtermuchty Tolbooth (1729)
   Weavers' cottages (1770; thatched)
17. Falkland Visitor Centre
   Bruce's Mill (fr. 1734)
   'Little Houses' (inc. weavers' cottages, 1800)
   Palace & Garden (fr. C15; Stuart hunting-lodge; facade notable renaissance architecture) (NTS)
   The East Lomond Fort (Iron/Dark Age)
18. Dogton Stone (weathered Celtic cross)
19. Lochgelly Visitor Centre (NTS)
20. Kirkcaldy Dunnikier Park Nature Trail (local) (SWT)
   Museum & Art Gallery (Scots artists; coal carvings)
   Ravenscraig Castle (C15; ruin; masonry notable)
   Ravenscraig Park Nature Trail (exotic trees)
   'Sailor's Walk' houses (C15–17) (NTS)
20a. Dysart fishermen's houses (restored by NTS)
21. Glenrothes Visitor Centre
   Balbirnie Stone Circle (Neo./Br. Age)
22. East Wemyss cave carvings (pre-historic)
23. Leven Visitor Centre
24. Lower Largo (Alexander 'Crusoe' Selkirk statue)

25. Ceres Bankhead Moss Nature Reserve (peat) (SWT)
   Bishop's Bridge (C17; pony bridge; Ceres Burn)
   Clushford Tollhouse (1820)
   Fife Folk Museum (inc. C17 tolbooth)
   Weavers' cottages (C18)
26. Cupar Parish Church tower (fr. 1415)
   Tollhouses (1820; two)
26a. Hill of Tarvit (1700; 1906 Lorimer rest. porcelain; tapestries; furniture; paintings) (NTS)
26b. Scotstarvit Tower (C16)
27. Letham Bakehouse (fr. 1691)
   Melville House (1701; architect James Smith)
   Weavers' cottages (1810)
28. Balmerino Abbey (C13; ruins) (NTS)
29. Creich Norman's Law Fort (Iron/Dark Age)
   Weavers' cottages (1805)
30. Newburgh Lindores Abbey (ruins)
31. Strathmiglo weavers' cottages (fr. 1780)
32. Meikleour beech hedge (1746; 580 yds long)
33. Megginch Castle gardens (formal)
34. Meigle Belmont Estate Nature Trail (for children)
   Museum (25 Celtic (Christian) sculptured stones)
35. North Berwick Visitor Centre
35a. Bass Rock (350 ft; volcanic plug, gannetry)
35b. Fidra, Eyebroughty, Lamb Islands (seabird sanctuaries) (view from boat/shore) (RSPB)
35c. Tantallon Castle (C14; coastal landmark)
35d. Yellowcraig Nature Trail (mixed woodland/coastal)
36. East Fortune Monument (to double Atlantic crossing, airship, 1919)
36a. Hailes Castle (ruin; fortified mansion; good chapel, C16)
36b. Pressmennan Wood Nature Trail (viewpoint) (FC)
36c. Preston Mill (picturesque working water-mill and Phantassie Doocot nearby) (NTS)
36d. Traprain Law (early Iron Age fortress capital; ex-treasure site)
37. Dirleton Castle (beautiful ruin, destroyed 1650; bowling green) (C17)
   Church (Archerfield Aisle, 1664)
37a. Muirfield Golf Course (venue world's oldest golf club, 1744)
38. Haddington
   St. Mary's Church (from C15; 'Lamp of Lothian'; tower landmark)
   Adam houses (esp bank)
   St. Martin's Church (ruined Romanesque nave, altered C13)
   Town House (Adam/Graham)
38a. Hopetoun Monument (C19; landmark)
38b. Chesters Fort (Iron Age; well defined)
38c. Lennoxlove (C14 tower, with C17 wing)
39. Aberlady Bay Nature Reserve (waders; wildfowl)
39a. Luffness House (late C16)
   Myreton Motor Museum (cars; motor-cycles; cycles)
40. Cockenzie Power Station (notable modern landmark)
41. Seton Collegiate Church (C15–16; fine mural monuments)
   Prestonpans Hamilton House (c 1628) (NTS)
   Market Cross (C17; at Preston)
   Northfield House (c. 1600; substantially unchanged)
   Prestongrange Beam Engine (1874–1954) restored; basis mining museum (venue Britain's earliest recorded coal-mine)
42. Isle of May Nature Reserve (bird observatory, 1947;

field station; boat from Crail) (NC)
   Lighthouse tower (1636)
43. Inchmahome Priory (fr. 1238; good C13 remains)
44. Lennoxtown (red alum waste-heaps)
45. Strathblane Duntreath Castle (partly C15; dungeons; stocks)
46. Kilsyth Colzium House (Covenanters' museum; gardens)
47. Alloa Clackmannan Tower (fr. C14; miners' view from outside) houses (C18)
48. Dollar Academy (1820, Playfair)
   Castle Campbell (C15; head of Dollar Glen; panorama)
   Dollar Glen (NTS)
49. Loup of Fintry (90 ft waterfall)
50. Stirling Visitor Centre
   Argyll Lodging (C17; town mansion)
   Cambuskenneth Priory (C12; C14 bell-tower)
   Castle (C15, restored)
   'King's Knot' (early garden); 'Queen Victoria's Look-out' (views); regimental museum
   Church of The Holy Rude (Mary, James VI crowned)
   Cowane's Hospital (C17; almshouse)
   Landmark Centre (exhibition old Stirling)
   Mar's Wark (1570; part ruins; gatehouse sculptures)
   The Old Bridge (1415; very fine)
   Smith Institute
   Touch House (fr. C16; Georgian facade;
51. Aberfoyle Visitor Centre
   Nature Trail (fr. caravan site)
   Queen Elizabeth Forest Park (main centre)
52. Keir Gardens
53. Killearn Knowe Head (1803; restored house)
54. Arbroath Visitor Centre
   Abbey (fr. C12; ruins; William the Lion's tomb)
   Abbot's House (fr. C12; folk museum)
   Cliffs Nature Trail (SWT)
55. St. Vigeans Museum (c40 sculptured stones, Early Christian-mediaeval)
56. Kirkintilloch Old St. Mary's Church (1644; museum)
57. Tealing Dovecot (C16)
   Earth House (Iron Age)
58. Bonnybridge (High) Rough Castle Roman fort (A.M. & NTS)
   Antonine Wall (rampart; ditch; notable)
59. Glamis Castle (mainly C17; china; furniture; tapestry)
   Kirkwynd Cottages (C17; now Angus Folk Museum) (NTS)
60. Gargunnock House (fr. C16–18; mansion)
61. Glamis Milton Corn Mill (1780; working order)
62. Bannockburn Monument (Visitor Centre; equestrian statue; 'Forging of a Nation' exhibition; rotunda) (NTS)
63. Causewayhead Stirling University
   Wallace Monument (1869; 220 ft landmark; museum; panorama)
64. Blairgowrie Visitor Centre
   brewery (c. 1780)
65. Blair Drummond House, gardens
   Kincardine Church (1816; brass, C17)
   Safari Park
66. Tullibardine Chapel (1446; unaltered)
67. Callander Visitor Centre
67a. Falls of Bracklinn
67b. Pass of Leny
67c. Roman camp, Bochastle Farm
68. Doune Castle (C15; restored 1883)
   Motor Museum
   Park Gardens (early C19; varied)
69. Dunblane Cathedral (fr. C13; restored 1895; beech walk; museum)

70. Braco *Ardoch Roman Camp* (earthworks of camp for c. 40 000 men)
71. Strathyre Forest Centre (walk; picnic site) (FC)
72. Loch Earn Edinample Falls
73. Comrie Melville Monument (view; Falls of Lednock & Devil's Cauldron)
74. Cardross Bridge (1774)
75. Kippen Laraben Dovecot
76. Cumbernauld, Forth & Clyde Canal (fr. 1790); Wyndford Lock; bascule bridge; cottage etc.
77. Bonnybridge (High) Seabegs Wood (A.M. & NTS) Antonine Wall (rampart; ditch)
78. Gask Ridge (*Roman road and signal-stations*)
79. Balquhidder bridge (view Ben Vorlich, Braes, Loch Voil)
80. Kinghorn monument to Alexander III
81. Burntisland *St. Columba's Church* (fr. 1592; octagonal; belfry, 1749)
82. Aberdour Castle (fr. C14; ruin; dovecot, Norman church nearby)
83. Dalgety St. Bridget's Church (E. part, roofless, fr. C13)
84. Edinburgh Visitor Centre
    Ann Street (Raeburn; romantic-classic)
    Barclay Bruntsfield Church (1862; Gothic picturesque)
    Calton Hill (easy road; view; monuments)
    Charlotte Square (N. side) (Adam; official residences; NTS HQ)
    City of Edinburgh Art Gallery (former Royal High School; Hamilton; fine 'Greek revival')
    Craigmillar Castle (fr. C14; Queen Mary associations)
    Dean Bridge (1831; Telford; best viewed from Dean Village)
    George Heriot's School (fr. 1628; Wallace/Aytoun/Playfair)
    Greyfriars Kirk (National Covenant (1638) associations (museum within); 'Greyfriars Bobby' (famous dog) statue nearby)
    Holyrood Park (inc. Arthur's Seat 822 ft; volcanic, columnar basalt S. side, Dunsapie Loch)
    Lamb's House, Leith (C16) (NTS)
    National Library of Scotland (very extensive collection)
    National Museum of Antiquities (collections; national treasures)
    New Town (1770–1800's; George St.—Fettes Row; world's best example of Georgian town-planning)
    Register House (East) (Adam; 1774; archives)
    Register House (West) (former church; Reid 1811; archives; museum)
    Royal Botanic Garden (notable collections, plant houses; includes Scottish National Gallery of Modern Art)
    Royal Commonwealth Pool (Matthew & Johnson-Marshall)
    Royal Mile, rich in history, includes Acheson House (C17; craft centre)
    Canongate Kirk (c. 1690; James Smith; restored)
    Canongate Tolbooth (fr. 1591; tartan collection)
    Castle (C17–18: some med.; Crown jewels of Scotland; Great Hall; Scottish National War Memorial; Scottish United Services Museum; St. Margaret's Chapel (Norman) tiny)
    Gladstone's Land (1620; painted ceiling, walls) (NTS)
    Holyrood Abbey (fr. C13)
    Holyrood Palace (mainly C17; official Royal residence; picture gallery; state apartments)

    Huntly House (fr. 1570; local history; silver. glass, pottery)
    John Knox's House (C15)
    Lady Stair's House (fr. 1622; literary relics)
    Museum of Childhood
    Parliament House (fr. 1639; fine hall; Scots parliament here pre-1707)
    St. Giles, High Kirk of Edinburgh, (fr. C14; national church; crown steeple, C15)
    St. James' Court (Boswell, Hume, Geddes associations)
    Royal Scottish Museum, Chambers St.
    Transport Museum (trams; buses; uniforms)
    University of Edinburgh, Old Quadrangle (C18–19; Adam plans)
85. Cramond, Eagle Rock (Hunter's Craig; carving-Roman?)
    Lauriston Castle (C16; furniture; antiques)
    Roman fort (N. end Dere Street)
86. Musselburgh *Pinkie House* (fr. 1613; tower, 1390; fine painted ceiling; part of Loretto School)
87. South Queensferry Abercorn Church (Norman door; sculptured stone)
    Forth Railway Bridge (1890; cantilevered)
    Forth Road Bridge (1964; suspension, 1½ m long)
    Plewlands House (fr. C17; view from outside) (NTS)
87a. *Dalmeny Church* (C12; well restored)
87b. *Hopetoun House* (Bruce/Adam; pictures; furnishings; deer; St. Kilda sheep; museum; viewpoint; Nature Trail)
87c. Kirkliston three railway viaducts (1842)
    Church (C12; Romanesque door)
88. Linlithgow *Palace* (fr. 1400; majestic ruin)
    St. Michael's Church (C15; in use)
    'Little Houses' (C16–17; view from outside only) (NTS)
    St. Magdalene Distillery (c. 1800; fine early example, kilns classic)
    Avon Railway Viaduct (1842)
88a. *The House of The Binns* (C17; mansion; fine plaster ceilings) (NTS)
88b. Blackness Castle (fr. C15; sea-fortress)
88c. Bo'ness *Kinneil House* (C16–17; decorated ceiling, murals; Roebuck-Watt steam engine, 1765)
89. Grangemouth, Forth & Clyde Canal terminus (vestiges) oil-refining complex
90. Falkirk, *Callendar House* (C14–19)
    Parish Church (1811; inc. 1734 Adam tower)
    Scottish Railway Preservation Depot (locos, rolling-stock)
    Steeple (1813; 146 ft)
90a. Carron Ironworks (fr. 1759; associations Roebuck, Watt, John Adam; 'Carronade' cannon; pioneers electric cookers)
91. Kincardine-on-Forth *Longannet Power Station*, 59 ft chimney)
92. Culross (C16–17; prototype Scots 300-year-old burgh) (NTS)
    Abbey (fr. C13; choir now *parish church*; Bruce mon. c. 1642)
    Ark, Nunnery, Study (early Culross) (NTS)
    Dunimarle Castle (Napoleon treasures)
    St. Mungo's Chapel (1503; ruins) (NTS)
    The Palace (early C17; mansion with fine painted ceilings)
93. Dunfermline Visitor Centre
    Andrew Carnegie Birthplace (relics)
    Museum (Viewfield) (local; folk)
    Palace (ruins; royal; impressive S. wall)
    Pittencrieff House Museum (C17; mansion; costume gallery; grounds in glen; lawns,

    hot-houses, overlooked by Malcolm Canmore's Tower (C11; ruin)
94. *Rosyth Castle* (C16; *tower*; dovecot) (SDD)
95. Elie Visitor Centre
    Castle (C16–17; domestic)
    Kincraig Hill (W. side; rock shelves, sea-cut)
    Ladies' Tower (ruin)
96. St. Monance Visitor Centre
    Ardross Castle
    Church (C13)
    'Little Houses' (view from outside) (restored by NTS)
97. Pittenweem cave-shrine (near harbour)
    Kellie Castle & Garden (C16–17; domestic; Victorian walled garden) (NTS)
    'Little Houses' (restored by NTS)
98. Anstruther Scottish Fisheries Museum
    'Little Houses' (restored by NTS)
99. *Lochty Private Railway* (steam)
100. Crail *Collegiate Church* (1517)
    'Little Houses' (view from outside) (restored by NTS)
    Town House (Dutch tower)
101. Collessie weavers' cottages (C18)
102. St. Andrews Visitor Centre
    Castle (C14; ruins; bottle dungeon; secret passages)
    Cathedral (1318; ruins)
    Harbour (med.-1820)
    Queen Mary's House
    'Royal & Ancient' Golf Club (fr.1754)
    Old Course (C15; world's oldest)
    St. Rule's Tower (108 ft)
    University (founded 1412)
103. Leuchars Church (fr. C12; C17 tower; notable)
    Earlshall Mansion (C16; Lorimer 1891 restoration)
104. *Tentsmuir Point Nature Reserve* (dunes; marsh) (NC)
105. Newport-on-Tay Visitor Centre
106. Tayport *Morton Lochs Nature Reserve* (NC)
    Forest Walks
107. Carnoustie Visitor Centre
108. Monifieth Visitor Centre
    Ardestie & Carlungie Earth-Houses
109. Dundee Visitor Centre
    Barrack Street Museum (ships)
    Camperdown Park (nature trails; children's zoo)
    City Museum & Art Gallery
    Law view (571 ft)
    Mills Observatory
    Old Steeple (C15; over three churches)
    Orchar Art Gallery (C19; Scots mainly)
    St. Mary's Tower (C15; bells)
    Spalding Golf Museum
109a. Claypotts Castle (C16; picturesque Z-plan; angle towers)
110. Glendevon
111. Menstrie (main road runs along Ochil Fault)
    Castle ('Nova Scotia' rooms)
112. Burleigh Castle (c. 1500; roofless tower house)
113. Loch Leven Castle (C15; island ruins; Queen Mary's prison)
114. Loch Leven *Nature Reserve* (wildfowl) (NC)
115. Vane Farm Nature Centre (trail) (RSPB)
116. Kinnesswood, Michael Bruce's cottage (mid-C18; museum)
117. Sma' Glen
118. Abercairney *Gardens* (shrubs; views)
119. Fowlis Wester (Pictish sculptured stone)
120. Innerpeffray *Library* (1691; 2nd oldest public library in Scotland)
    Church (fr. 1508)
121. Muthill Church (C15; ruins; tower, C12)
128. Inchmickery *Nature Reserve* (island; terns) (RSPB)
129. Inchcolm Abbey (island; inc. C13 chapter house)

Map 74

80

9
Mam nan Gleann Beag
Uranan
Balvraid
Meall Buidhe 1594
Meall a'Chapuill 2421
3196
Ben Screel 2536 Beinn nan Caorach 1799
The Saddle 3082 3317
Dhomhuill Bhric
Spidean Mialach
Sgurr na Sgine
Sgurr na h-Aide
Sgurr a'Gharg Gharaidh
Sgurr a'Bhealaich Dheirg
Sgurr na Ciste Duibhe
A'Chralaig 3673
Sgurr nan Conbhairean
Ceannacroc Forest
Ceannacroc Br
Power Sta.
R. Doe
Dundreggan Lo
Lagganbane
Torgyle
Torgyle Br
Inver
A 887
Dalchreichart
Achlain
Wades Military
Inchnacardoch Fo
Carn Mhic Raonuill

Arnisdale
Corran
Dubh Lochain
Glen Arnisdale Ho
Glenelg
Druim Fada
Loch Hourn
Runival
Skiary
Kinloch Hourn
Barrisdale
Ladhar Bheinn 3343
Barrisdale Bay
Carn Mairi
Gleann Cosaidh
Sgurr Sgiath Airidh
Glen Barrisdale
Slat Bheinn
Meall nan Eun
Coire Shubh
Cluanie Br
L. Cluanie (Reservoir)
Glen Cluanie
Loch Quoich
Gleouraich
Spidean Mialach
Tomdoun Hotel
Beinn Loinne
Bunloinne
Forest
Loch Loyne
Mullach Coire
Ard Achaidh
L. a'Bhainne
Loch Garry
Inchlaggan
Greenfield
Glengarry Forest
Ben Tee 2956
Laggan Locks
South Laggan
Laggan
Leacann Doire Bainneir
A 82

Knoydart
Ladhar Bheinn
Aonach Sgoilte
Luinne Bheinn
Ben Aden
Sgurr Mor
Sgurran Fhuaran
Glen Kingie
R. Kingie
Sgurr nan Coireachan
Druim a'Chuirn
Sgurr Mhurlagain
Sourlies
Gleann Meadail
Sgurr na Ciche
Meall Buidhe
Carnoch
Loch Nevis
Sgurr na h-Aide
Finiskaig
Kylesmorar
Sgurr Breac
Kinlochmorar
Carn Mor
Monadh Gorm
Glen Pean
R. Pean
Kinlocharkaig
Loch Arkaig
Inver Mallie
Clunes
Mile Dorcha
Achnasaul
Glenfintaig Lo
A 82

Morar
Druim a'Chuirn
An Stac
Sgurr an Ursainn
Meith Bheinn
Meoble
Loch Beoraid
Sgurr an Utha
Streap
Sron Liath
Gulvain
Beinn Bhan
Glen Mallie
Kinlochbeoraid
Mullach Coire nan Geur-oirean
Locheil Forest
Achnacarry
Gairlochy
A 82

Glenfinnan Sta.
A 830
Kinlocheil Sta.
Loch Eil
Loch Eil
Corpach
Banavie
Kilmonivaig Ch.
Spean Bridge
Tirandrish
Roy Br
Spean
Glen Loy
Glen Roy
22
21
A 86
A 82

32
Drumfern
A 861
Garvan
Duisky
Blaich
Achaphubuil
Camusnagaul
Trislaig
Ceann Caol
Ardgour
28
20
Fort William
Aluminium Works
Ben Nevis
Ben Nevis 4406
Carn Mor Dearg
Aonach Mor
Aonach Beag
Stob Choire Claurigh
Stob Ban
Stob Coire Easain
36

Conaglen
Druim Leathad nam Fias
Glen Scaddle
Inverscaddle
Coruanan
Achriabhach
Mamore Forest
Stob Ban
Sgor an Fhuarain
Binnein Mor
Sgurr Eilde Mor
L. Eilde Mor
Glas Bheinn
35
29

Ardgour
Glen Gour
Kingairloch
Tigh Ghlinnegabhair
Sallachan
Ardgour Hotel
Corran
Onich
North Ballachulish
Callert
Kinlochleven
Aluminium
River Leven
Blackwater Res
30
F

L. Sunart
Glen Tarbert
Inversanda
Strontian
A 861
A 884
Achleek
Ballachulish
Ballachulish Ho
Loch Leven
Pap of Glencoe
Bridge of Coe
Glen Coe
Devil's Staircase
Beinn a'Bheithir
A 82
68
F

Glen Gour
Kentallen
Duror
Cuil Bay
Achindarroch
Sgorr Dhearg
Sgorr Dhonuill
Meall Mor
Sgorr na Choise
Bidean nam Bian 3766
Beinn Fhada
Ossians Cave
Altnafeadh
King's House Hotel
19
A 82

Appin
Portnacroish
Airds Bay
Castle Stalker
North Shian
Inver
Port Appin
Airds Ho
Beinn a'Bheithir
Salachail
Meall Lighiche
Sgorr na h-Ulaidh
Beinn Maol Chaluim
Beinn Fhionnlaidh
Invercharnan
Glen Etive
River Etive
Royal Forest
Buachaille Etive Mor
Buachaille Etive Beag
18
34

Morvern
Eignaig
Lynn of Lorn
Barcaldine
Creach Bheinn
Ben Starav
Glas Bheinn Mhor
Stob Coire an Albannaich
Stob Ghabhar
Black Mount
Loch Tulla
Victoria Br
A 828
A 82

70

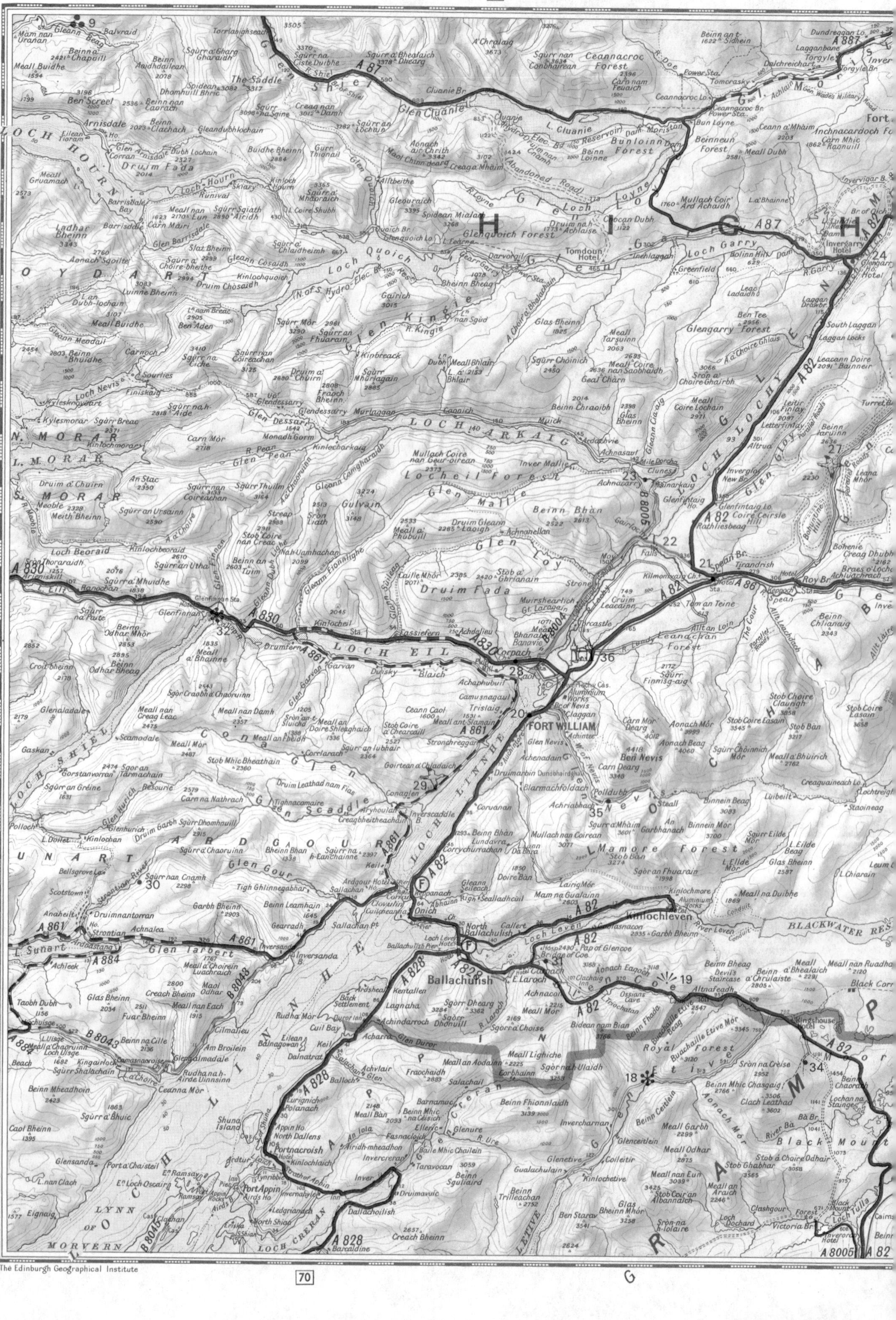

The Edinburgh Geographical Institute

79
27
68
G

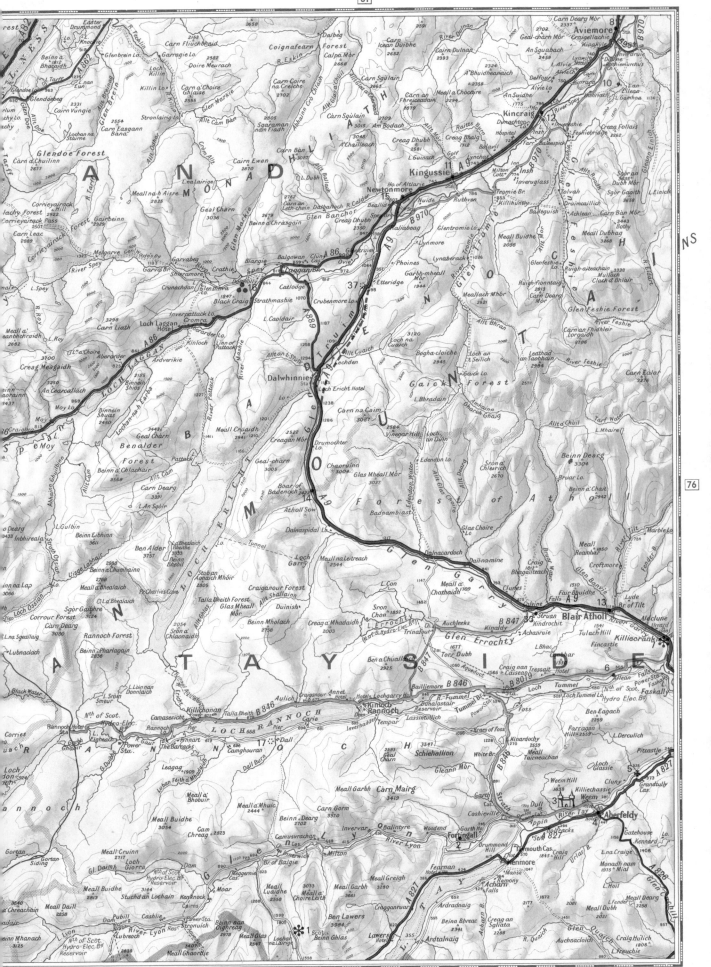

Map 75

1 2 3 4 5 Miles

Gazetteer to Maps 74·75

1. Ben Lawers (Visitor Centre; Nature Trail; viewpoint) (NTS)
2. Fortingall (thatched houses; old yew) Glen Lyon to W. 30 m long Roman Camp (Pilate's birthplace?)
3. Aberfeldy Castle Menzies (1571 baronial mansion)
4. Aberfeldy Visitor Centre Drummond Hill Forest Walks (four, varied) (FC)
   'Birks' (Nature Trail; picnic site) Tay Bridge (1733; Wade) Falls of Moness Strathtay History Trails (four)
5. Grandtully St. Mary's Church (C16; painted ceiling)
6. Loch Tummel Visitor Centre Linn of Tummel 'Queen's View' (geol. interest; metamorphics, to quartzite of Schiehallion)
7. Pass of Killiecrankie (Visitor Centre; viewpoint, 'Soldier's Leap'; nature trail) (NTS)
8. Aviemore Visitor Centre *Cairngorms Nature Reserve* (very large & varied) (NC) Ski Centre, Cairngorms

9. Glenelg two Brochs (30 ft walls)
10. Loch an Eilean Castle and Visitor Centre; Nature Trail
11. Kingussie Visitor Centre 'Am Fasgadh' (Highland Folk Museum) Ruthven Barracks (burnt 1746)
12. Kincraig Highland Wild Life Park Insh Church (fr. C6; old bell)
13. Blair Atholl *Blair Castle* (C13 tower, C18 altered; 32 rooms displays) railway viaduct (1862; Mitchell)
14. Dalnaspidal Station (2 m beyond; railway at 1484 ft)
15. Newtonmore Visitor Centre *Clan Museum*
16. Dun-na-Lamb (prehistoric hill fort, slate-walled)
17. Black Wood of Rannoch (pines)
18. Dalness Glen Etive (rapids) (NTS)
19. 'The Study' (rocky viewpoint)
20. Fort William Visitor Centre West Highland Museum
21. Spean Bridge (1736; Wade) Commando Memorial
22. Gairlochy Falls of Mucomir
23. Achnacarry House (*beech avenue*)
24. Invergarry, Loch Oich 'Well of the Heads'

25. Fort Augustus Visitor Centre Abbey (C19) Fort (1715) Inchnacardoch Forest Trail (FC)
26. Great Glen Exhibition
27. Glen Roy Nature Reserve ('parallel roads') (NC)
28. Corpach 'Neptune's Staircase' (eight canal locks; view)
29. Corran Ferry *Doire Donn Nature Reserve* (oaks) (SWT)
30. Strontian Ariundle Oakwood (NC & DAFS) Glen Nature Trail (oaks; moors; leadmines)
31. Glencoe Visitor Centre (NTS) Folk Museum Forest Walks (two trails) (FC)
32. Glenfinnan Visitor Centre (NTS) Monument (to 1745 standard-raising) (NTS)
33. Struan Clan Museum
34. Kingshouse (near) ski tow
35. Glen Nevis waterfall
36. Inverlochy *Castle* (C13; view from outside)
37. Falls of Truim

Map 76

81 82

CAIRNGORM MOUNTAINS

Aviemore
Craigellachie
Coylumbridge
Rothiemurchus
Forest
Queen's Forest

Cairn Gorm 4084
Braeriach 4248
Ben Macdui 4300
Cairn Toul 4241
The Devils Point 3303

Glen Feshie Forest

Beinn a'Bhùird 3924
North Top
Beinn a'Bhùird South Top 3860
Càrn Eàs 3556

GRA

Cock Bridge
Corgarff
River Don
Glenfenzie
Brown Cow 2721
Mona Gowan 2456
Morven 2862

Ballater
Bridgend
Glenmuick

Braemar
Invercauld Forest
Invercauld
Balmoral Forest

Beinn Chiochan (Lochnagar) 3786
Lochnagar
White Mounth

Mar Forest

Glen Ey Forest

Spittal of Glenshee

Glen Clunie

Glas Maol 3502
Monega Hill 2917

Glen Clova
Clova
Glen Prosen
Glen Isla

Beinn a'Ghlo
Glen Tilt

Blair Atholl
Killiecrankie
Ben Vrackie 2757

Pitlochry
Moulin

Kirkmichael
Strathardle

Forest of Alyth

Aberfeldy
Grandtully Cas.
Logierait
Ballinluig

Dowally
Butterstone

BLAIRGOWRIE
Rattray
New Alyth
Meigle
Newtyle
Coupar Angus

DUNKELD
Birnam
Birnam Hill
Caputh

Murthly
Waterloo

Glen Shee
A 93
A 9
A 924
A 926
A 94
A 984
A 923
A 822
A 826
A 827

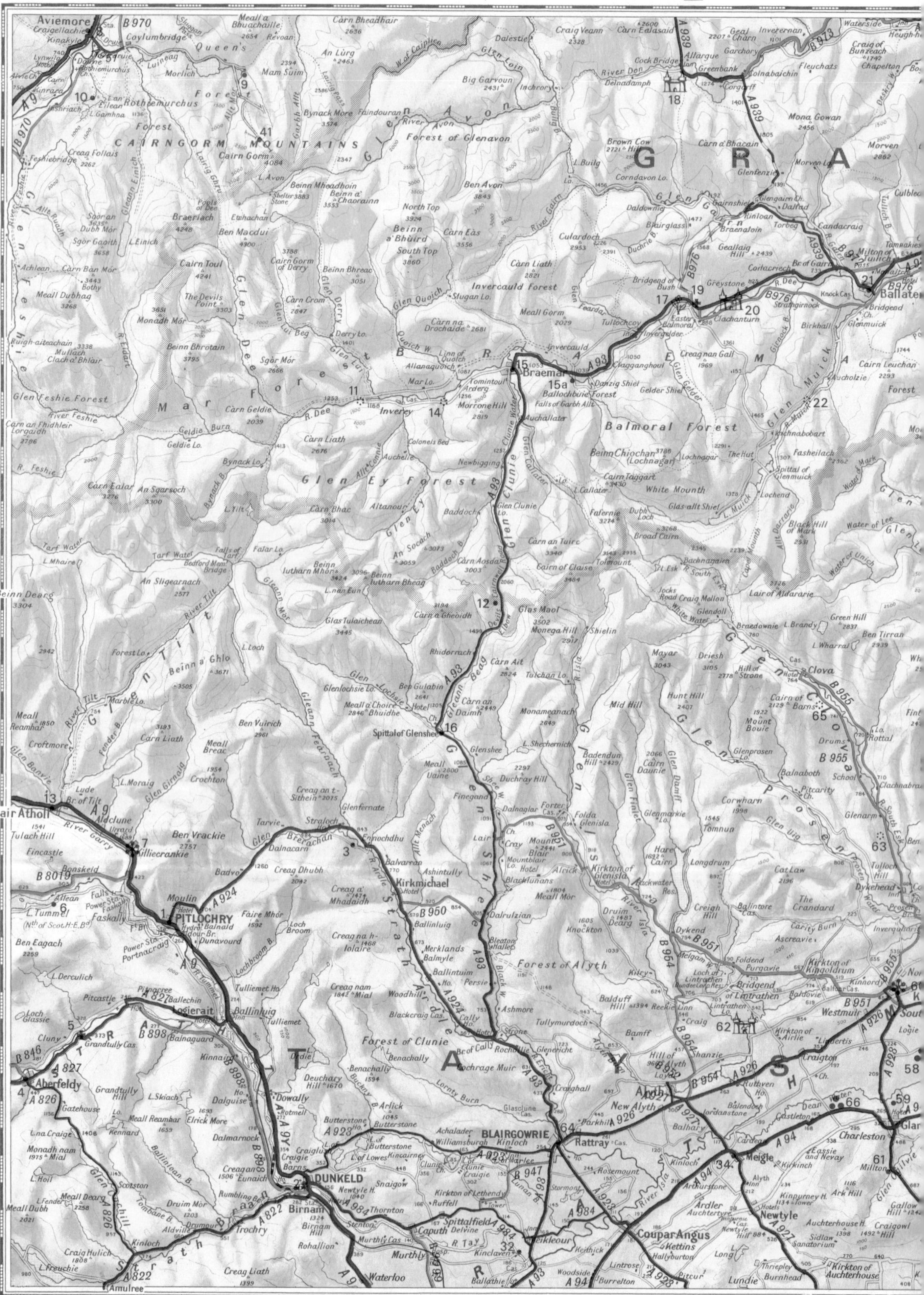

The Edinburgh Geographical Institute

Map 77

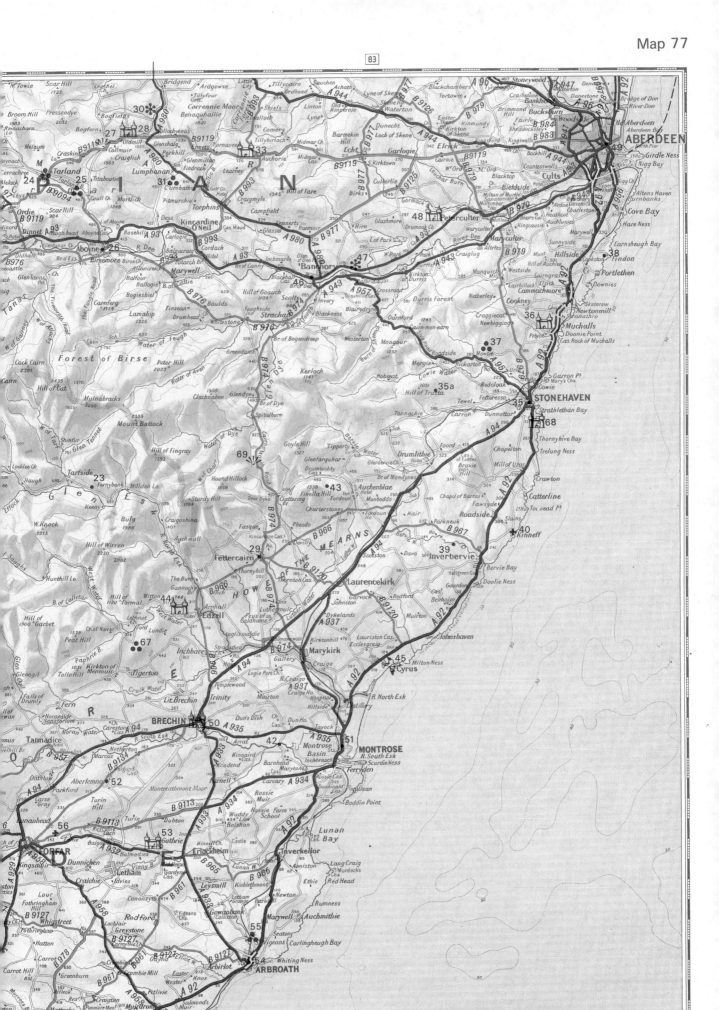

© — John Bartholomew & Son, Ltd.

Gazetteer to Maps 76·77

1. Pitlochry Visitor Centre
   Craigower hill (1300 ft; views) (NTS)
   Dunfallandy Stone (C8; Pictish)
   Linn of Tummel nature trail (waterfall; woods) (NTS)
   Loch Faskally (salmon ladder; observation chamber)
   Moulin, railway viaduct (1864; Mitchell)
   Tummel Forest Walks and Trails (five, varied) (FC)
2. Dunkeld Visitor Centre
   Cathedral (fr. C15; choir now parish church)
   Craigvinean Walks (three; viewpoint) (FC)
   Hermitage (C18 folly above waterfall; woodland walk) (NTS)
   'Little Houses' (extensive restoration of C17 houses) (NTS)
3. Kindrogan Field Centre (naturalists' courses; two trails) (SFSA)
4. Aberfeldy Visitor Centre
   'Birks' (Nature Trail; picnic site)
   Drummond Hill Forest Walks (four, varied) (FC)
   Strathtay History Trails (four)
   Tay Bridge (1733; Wade)
   Falls of Moness
5. Grandtully St. Mary's Church (C16; painted ceiling)
6. Loch Tummel Visitor Centre
   Linn of Tummel
   'Queen's View' (geol. interest; metamorphics, to quartzite of Schiehallion)
7. Pass of Killiecrankie (Visitor Centre; viewpoint 'Soldier's Leap'; nature trail) (NTS)
8. Aviemore Visitor Centre
   Cairngorms Nature Reserve (very large and varied) (NC)
   Ski Centre, Cairngorms
9. Glenmore Forest Park (Highland fauna; ancient pines; mountains; sailing; forest trails)
10. Loch an Eilean Castle and Visitor Centre;
    Nature Trail
11. Linn of Dee (gorge)
12. Cairnwell Pass (2199 ft; Devil's Elbow near)
    Ski chairlifts
13. Blair Atholl *Blair Castle* (C13 tower; C18 altered; 32 room displays)
    railway viaduct (1862; Mitchell)
14. Linn of Corriemulzie (waterfall)
15. Braemar Visitor Centre
    Castle (1628; rebuilt 1748)
15a. Old Bridge of Dee (1752)

16. Spittal of Glenshee Visitor Centre
    Ski Centre
17. *Balmoral Castle Gardens*
18. Cock Bridge *Corgarff Castle* (C16; ruin; view from outside)
19. Crathie *Kirk* (C19)
20. Abergeldie Castle (fr. C17)
21. Ballater Visitor Centre
22. Linn of Muick waterfall
23. Glenesk *Folk Museum* (library)
24. Tarland Culsh Earth-House (Iron Age)
25. Tarland Tomnaverie Stone Circle
26. Aboyne Visitor Centre
27. Slack of Tillylodge (viewpoint)
28. Corse Castle
29. Fettercairn *Balbegno Castle* (fr. C16; Cross, C17; 'ell' measure)
30. *Craigievar Castle* (1626; notable L-plan (modified) baronial; plaster ceilings) (NTS)
31. Lumphanan Peel Ring (med.; earthwork)
32. Meikleour *beech hedge* (1746; 580 yds long)
33. *Drumlasie Toll* (1820)
34. Meigle Belmont Estate Nature Trail (for children)
    Museum (25 Celtic Christian sculptured stones)
35. Stonehaven Visitor Centre
    Tolbooth (C16)
35a. Fetteresso Forest
36. *Muchalls Castle* (C17; fireplaces; ceilings)
37. Camp of Raedykes (Roman)
38. Findon *Mill* (C18; used occasionally)
39. Inverbervie Arbuthnott Church (C13, 15)
    Castle of Allardyce
40. Kinneff Church (1738)
41. Cairngorn *ski chairlift*
42. Bridge of Dun (1787; Stevens)
43. Laurencekirk Drumtochty Forest (FC)
44. Edzell Castle (C16; unique 1604 walled garden, sculptured panels)
45. St. Cyrus *Nature Reserve* Nature Trail (NC)
46. Banchory Visitor Centre
    Bridge of Feuch (rapids)
    Lavender Water Factory
47. Crathes *Castle* (C16; and Gardens; dramatic baronial architecture, informal garden; painted ceilings) (NTS)
    Nature Trail (through woods)
48. Drum *Castle* (C17; C13 tower) and *Grounds*
49. Aberdeen Visitor Centre
    Art Gallery and Museum
    Bridge of Balgownie (C14)

Bridge of Dee (C16)
Hazlehead Nature Trail (in park)
King's College (C16–17)
Marischal College (C19; fine granite building)
Mercat Cross (C17)
Provost Ross's House (C16) (NTS)
Provost Skene's House (C16; museum)
Rubislaw Granite Quarry (view; hole)
St. Machar's Cathedral (mainly C15)
Seaton Park (inc. tower-house, C17)
West St. Nicholas Church (C12–18)
50. Brechin *Maison Dieu Chapel* (C13)
    Round Tower (C11; Irish; view from churchyard)
51. Montrose Visitor Centre
    Library (four pre-1501 books)
    Old Church: 'Big Peter' bell (1676) 'hearse' chandelier (1627)
52. Aberlemno Finavon (vitrified fort, wall 16 ft. high)
    Sculptured Stones (Pictish)
    Turin Hill 'Kemp's Castle' (hill forts)
53. Guthrie Castle (1468) *grounds, garden*
54. Arbroath Visitor Centre
    Abbey (fr. C12; ruins; William the Lion's tomb)
    Abbot's House (fr. C12; folk museum)
    Cliffs Nature Trail (SWT)
55. *St. Vigeans Museum* (c. 40 sculptured stones, Early Christian-mediaeval)
56. Forfar Restenneth Priory (ruins inc. tower, C9?)
57. Tealing Dovecot (C16)
    Earth House (Iron Age)
58. Glamis St. Orland's Stone (early Christian sculpture)
59. Glamis *Castle* (mainly C17; china; furniture; tapestry)
    Kirkwynd Cottages (C17; now *Angus Folk Museum*) (NTS)
60. Kirriemuir Barrie's Birthplace (NTS)
61. Glamis *Milton Corn Mill* (1780; working order)
62. *Airlie Castle* (fr. 1431, restored fr. 1792; 'Waterloo' topiary)
63. Glen Clova
64. Blairgowrie Visitor Centre brewery (c. 1780)
65. Glen Clova
66. Eassie Sculptured Stone (early Christian)
67. Brechin The Caterthuns (two well-preserved hill-forts; Iron Age)
68. Dunnottar Castle (C14, 16; on 160 ft headland; geol. interest)
69. Cairn o'Mount

Map 78

Map 79

SKYE

LOCH ALSH

LOCH HOURN

KNOYDART

NORTH MORAR

SOUTH MORAR

LOCH MORAR

SLEAT

SOUND OF SLEAT

LOCH BRACADALE

Cuillin Hills

Strathaird

LOCH SCAVAIG

SOAY SOUND

Soay

CUILLIN SOUND

RUM

EIGG

CANNA

SANDAY

SOUND OF CANNA

SOUND OF RUM

Kyle of Lochalsh

Broadford

Mallaig

Portree

A 850

A 851

A 852

A 830

A 87

A 863

A 881

B 8009

0 1 2 3 4 5 Miles

Gazetteer to Maps 78·79

1. Eigg Camas Sgiotaig Bay ('musical sands')
2. Rum *Nature Reserve* (two trails) (NC)
3. Canna 'Compass Hill' (viewpoint)
4. Mallaig Visitor Centre View
5. Armadale Castle (Gothic; grounds)
6. Knock Castle (ruins)
7. *Spar Cave* (stalagmites)
8. Elgol (view Cuillins)
9. Glenelg two Brochs (30 ft walls)
10. Broadford Visitor Centre
11. Pabay (fossils)
12. Kyleakin Castle Moil (picturesque ruin)
13. Kyle of Lochalsh Visitor Centre
14. Balmacara Visitor Centre (NTS)
15. Drumbuie (typical crofting township)
16. Plockton (pleasant village)

Eilean Na Creige Duibhe Nature Reserve (SWT)
17. Strome Castle (ruin 1603) (NTS)
18. Loch Kishorn Rassal Ashwood Nature Reserve (NC)
19. Applecross (scenic 2054 ft pass approach) Church (C7; ruins)
20. Gairloch Visitor Centre
21. Loch Maree Slattadale Forest Walks (FC) islands; Nature Reserve
22. Inverewe (sub-tropical gardens; camping site) (NTS) Visitor Centre
23. MacLeod's Maidens (three stacks)
24. Quiraing rock towers (inc. 'The Needle', 120 ft)
25. Monument to Flora Macdonald Skye Cottage Museum, Kilmuir

26. Stack of Skudiburgh
27. *Dunvegan Castle* (fr. C15; 'Fairy Flag')
28. Dornie *Eilean Donan Castle* (fr. 1220, restored C20)
29. Staffin Bay (view)
30. Kilt Rock
31. Morar (white sands)
32. Falls of Mealt
33. Falls of Lealt
34. The Storr (square-topped 2360 ft) Old Man of Storr (160 ft needle)
35. Colbost Folk Museum
36. Glendale (C18 water-mill)
37. Prince Charles' Cave
38. Portree Visitor Centre Nature Trail (riverside)
39. Cuillins (spectacular; challenging climbs)
40. Blaven (3042 ft mass of serrated rock)

Map 80

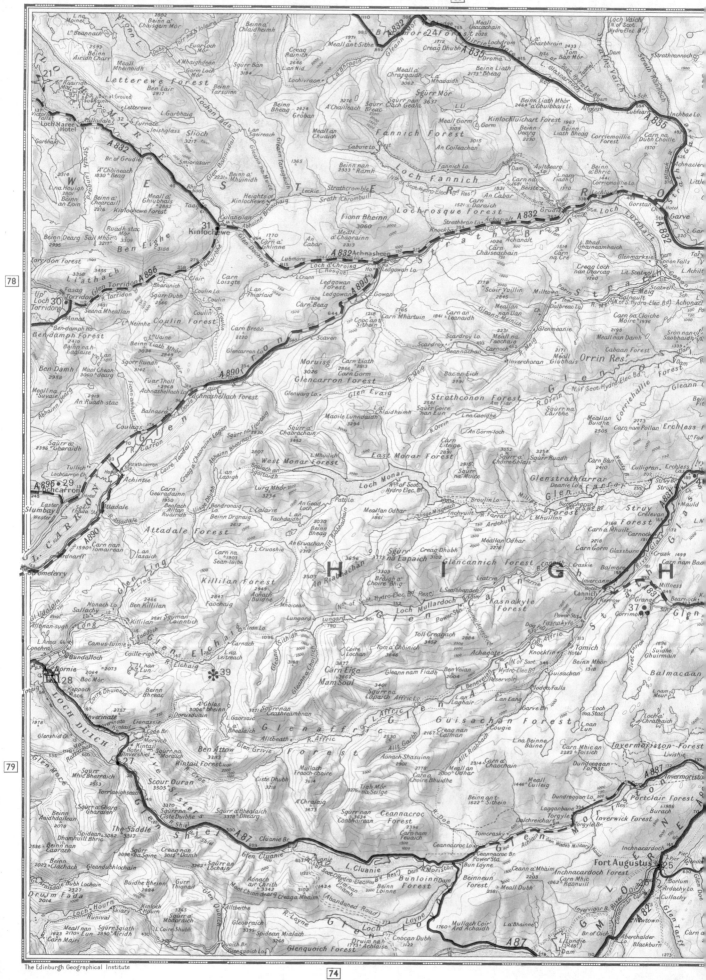

Map 81

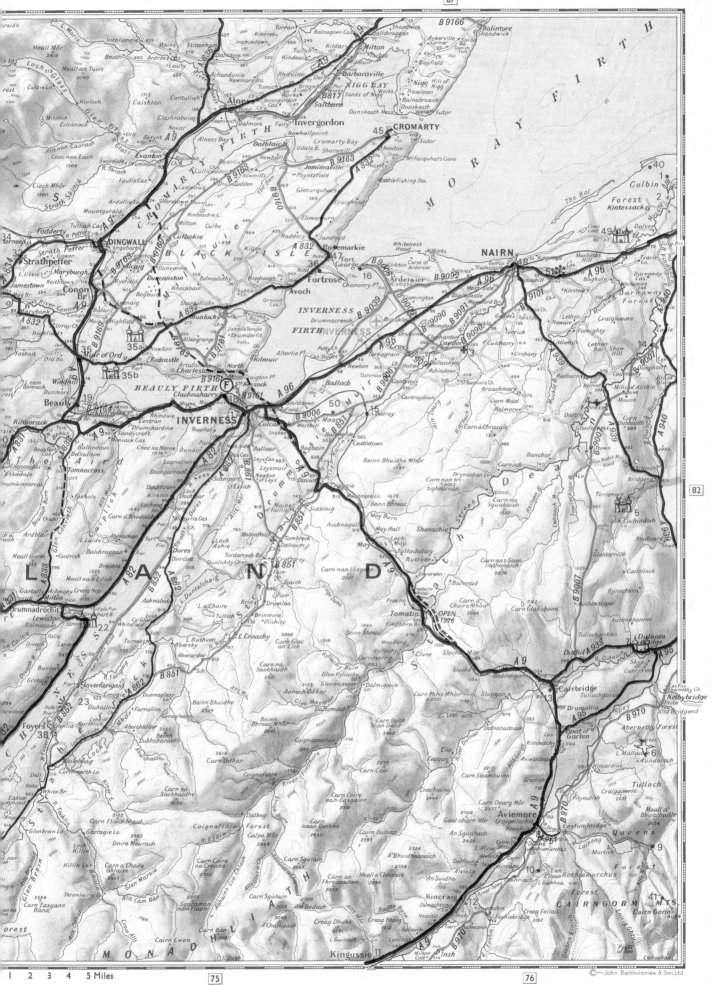

1 2 3 4 5 Miles

Gazetteer to Maps 80·81

1. Culbin Sands (reclamation by tree-planting)
2. *Kincorth Gardens*
3. Cawdor Kirk (C14 and later)
4. Ardclach Bell Tower (C17)
5. Lochindorb Castle (C13)
6. *Loch Garten Nature Reserve* (ospreys) (RSPB)
7. Muckrach Tower (C16)
8. Aviemore Visitor Centre
   Cairngorms Nature Reserve (very large and varied) (NC)
   Ski Centre, Cairngorms
9. Glenmore Forest Park (Highland fauna; ancient pines; mountains; sailing; forest trails)
10. Loch an Eilean Castle and Visitor Centre; Nature Trail
11. Kingussie Visitor Centre
    'Am Fasgadh' (Highland Folk Museum)
    Ruthven Barracks (burnt 1746)
12. Kincraig Highland Wild Life Park
    Insh Church (fr. C6; old bell)
13. Carrbridge Landmark Visitor Centre (exhibition)
14. Randolph's Leap
15. Croy/Dalcross Nairn railway viaduct (1898; large)
16. Fort George (fr. 1748)
    Regimental Museum;
    Chapel (1767; three-decker pulpit)
17. Inverness Visitor Centre
    Abertarff House (C16) (NTS)
    Craig Phadrig Forest Walk (to vitrified fort) (FC)
    Knocknagael Boar Stone
    Tomnahurich ('Hill of the Fairies')

18. Clachnaharry (N. exit Caledonian Canal)
19. Beauly Priory (1230)
    Reelig Glen Forest Walk (FC)
20. Druim Pass (picturesque)
21. Loch Maree Slattadale
    Forest Walks (FC)
    islands; Nature Reserve
22. Drumnadrochit Urquhart Castle (large; historically strategic)
23. Farigaig Forest Walk (view L. Ness) (FC)
24. Braemore Lael Forest Garden (FC)
    Corrieshalloch Gorge; Falls of Measach (150 ft) (NTS)
    Corrieshalloch Nature Reserve (NC)
25. Fort Augustus Visitor Centre
    Abbey (C19)
    Fort (1715)
    Inchnacardoch Forest Trail (FC)
26. Great Glen Exhibition
27. Shiel Bridge Visitor Centre
    'Five Sisters of Kintail' (NTS)
28. Dornie *Eilean Donan Castle* (fr. 1220, restored C20)
29. Lochcarron Visitor Centre
    Allt Nan Carnan Nature Reserve (gorge) (NC)
30. Torridon Visitor Centre
    estate (mountains; fauna; flora) (NTS)
31. Kinlochewe Visitor Centre
    Beinn Eighe Nature Reserve (Caledonian pines; plants; geology; two trails; picnic sites; field station) (NC)
32. Strathpeffer Visitor Centre

   Castle Leod (*gardens*)
   Torrachilty Forest Walk (FC)
33. Rogie Falls (salmon leap)
34. Raven Rock (picturesque)
35. Muir of Ord Visitor Centre
35a. *Kilcoy Castle* (C17)
35b. *Tarradale House* (library; museum)
36. Fortrose Cathedral (C14 parts extant)
    Chanonry Point (three-tiered raised beach nearby)
37. Corrimony Cairn (chambered; stone circle)
38. Falls of Foyers
39. Falls of Glomach (350 ft; long walk) (NTS)
40. Buckie Loch (aquatic plants)
41. Cairngorm *ski chairlift*
45. Cromarty *Hugh Miller's Cottage* (museum) (NTS)
    Harbour (1785)
46. Strath Glass, R. Glass meanders (ox-bow lakes) along line of fault
47. Rosemarkie churchyard (Pictish symbol stone)
    The Dens (earth-pillars eroded by Rosemarkie Burn)
48. Nairn Visitor Centre
    viewpoint of battlefield (1645) (NTS)
49. *Brodie Castle* (C15 to C19)
50. Culloden Visitor Centre
    Battlefield (clan graves; museum) (NTS)
    Clava Cairns (Neo/Bronze; in stone rings)
    Forest Walk (trees; history) (FC)
51. Boath Doocot Auldearn (NTS)

Map 82

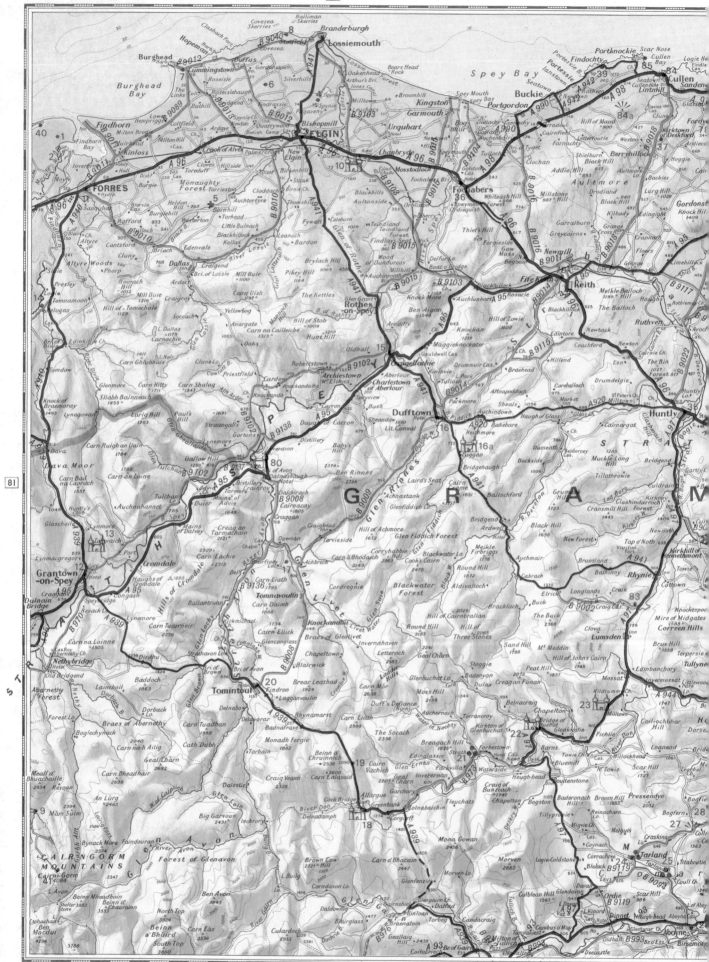

Map 83

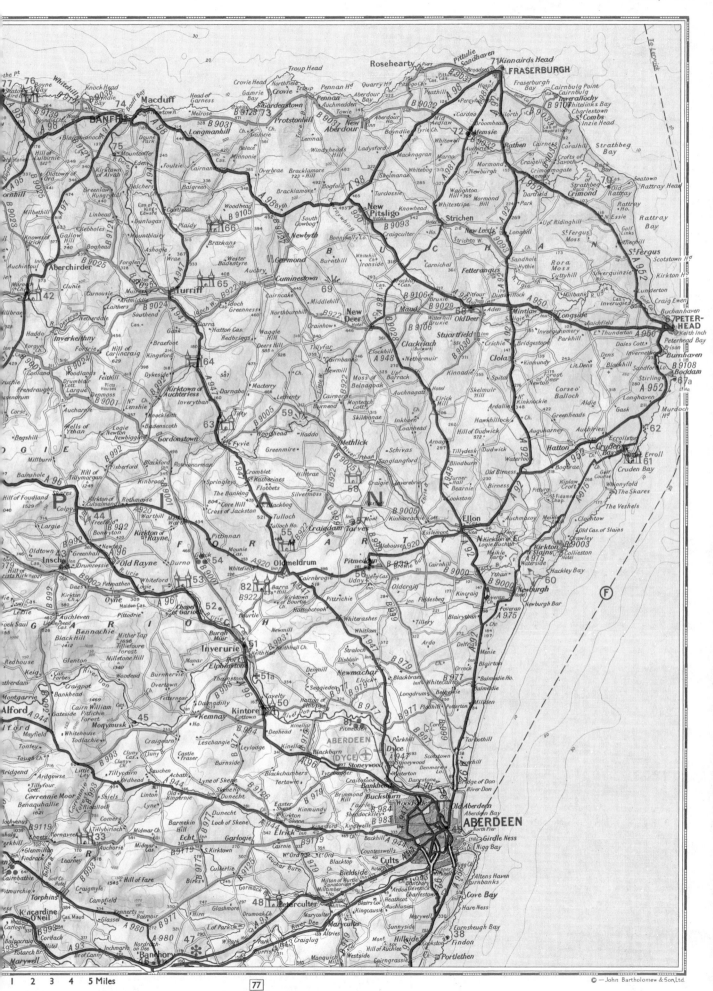

© — John Bartholomew & Son, Ltd.

1 2 3 4 5 Miles

Gazetteer to Maps 82·83

1. Culbin Sands (reclamation by tree-planting)
2. *Kincorth Gardens*
3. Elgin Visitor Centre
   Cathedral (founded 1236, burned 1390; imposing ruin)
   Grant Lodge Library (Georgian)
   Gray's Hospital (1819; Gillespie)
   Greyfriars Chapel (C15; restored)
   Museum
   St. Giles' Church (1828; Simpson)
4. Spynie Canal (fr. 1812; restored; Telford)
   Palace (C15; ruins bishops' fortress)
5. Pluscarden *Priory* (founded 1236, destroyed 1390; restored)
6. Duffus Castle (motte and bailey)
   St. Peter's Church (fr. C14–16) and Cross (C14)
7. Burghead Well (early Christian baptistry)
8. *Covesea Skerries Lighthouse* (1844; Stevenson)
9. Glenmore Forest Park (Highland fauna; ancient pines; mountains; forest trails; sailing)
10. Coxton Tower
11. Forres Visitor Centre
    Falconer Museum (fossils; miscellaneous)
    Nelson Tower (view)
    Sueno's Stone (Pictish cenotaph, C9–10)
12. Grantown-on-Spey Visitor Centre (C18 planned town)
13. Castle Grant (C16–18)
14. Randolph's Leap
15. Craigellachie Bridge (1815; restored; Telford)
16. Dufftown Visitor Centre
16a. *Auchindown Castle* (med.; massive ruin within prehistoric earthworks; view from outside)
    Balvenie Castle (C15–16; iron 'yett')
    Glenfiddich Distillery (tours; museum)
    Mortlach Kirk (C12; restored; ancient tombstones)
17. Blairfindy Castle
    Glenlivet Distillery
18. Cock Bridge *Corgarff Castle* (C16; ruin; view from outside)
19. Lecht Road (1752, military; ascending to 2090 ft)
20. Tomintoul Visitor Centre
21. Doune of Invernochty (40 ft; once castle site)
22. *Glenbuchat Castle* (1590; Z-plan; view from outside)
23. Kildrummy Castle (most complete secular building of C13)
24. Tarland Culsh Earth-House (Iron Age)
25. Tarland Tomnaverie Stone Circle
26. Aboyne Visitor Centre
27. Slack of Tillylodge (viewpoint)
28. Corse Castle
29. Alford Pitfichie Forest (to E.) (FC)

30. *Craigievar Castle* (1626; notable L-plan (modified) baronial; plaster ceilings) (NTS)
31. Lumphanan Peel Ring (med.; earthwork)
32. Suie Hill (viewpoint)
33. *Drumlasie Toll* (1820)
34. Kennethmont *Leith Hall* (fr. 1650) *Garden* (NTS)
35. Huntly Visitor Centre
    Castle (fr. C15; interesting ruins)
    Clashindarroch Forest (to South) (FC)
36. Fochabers Visitor Centre
37. Deskford Church (C16; ruin; sacrament house)
    Berryhillock Mill (c. 1800; working)
38. Findon *Mill* (C18; used occasionally)
39. Findochty (early C18 village)
40. Buckie Loch (aquatic plants)
41. Cairngorm *ski chairlift*
42. Kinnairdy Castle (C17)
43. Insch Dunnideer Hill (vitrified fort)
    Picardy Stone (Pictish symbols)
44. Williamston House *Gardens*; St. Michael's Well nearby
45. Monymusk *Church* (C13) *House* (C15–17)
46. Banchory Visitor Centre
    Bridge of Feuch (rapids)
    Lavender Water Factory
47. Crathes *Castle* (C16; and Gardens; dramatic baronial architecture, informal garden; painted ceilings)
    Nature Trail (through woods) (NTS)
48. Drum *Castle* (C17; C13 tower) and *Grounds*
49. Aberdeen Visitor Centre
    Art Gallery and Museum
    Bridge of Balgownie (C14)
    Bridge of Dee (C16)
    Hazlehead Nature Trail (in park)
    King's College (C16–17)
    Marischal College (C19; fine granite building)
    Mercat Cross (C17)
    Provost Ross's House (C16) (NTS)
    Provost Skene's House (C16; museum)
    Rubislaw Granite Quarry (view; hole)
    St. Machar's Cathedral (mainly C15)
    Seaton Park (inc. tower-house, C17)
    West St. Nicholas Church (C12–18)
50. Kintore *Balbithan House & Garden* (C17)
    Tolbooth (C18)
51. Inverurie Bennachie Forest (to W.) (FC)
    Brandsbutt Stone (Pictish; inscribed)
    East Aquhorthies Stone Circle (Br. Age; almost complete)
51a. Kinkell Church (C16; ruins; 1524 sacrament house)
    Maiden Stone (early Christian; legendary)

52. Harlaw Monument
53. Pitcaple Castle (C15–19)
54. Daviot Loanhead Stone Circle
55. Meldrum House
56. Pitmedden *Garden* (C17; elaborate) (NTS)
    Tolquhon Castle (C16; gatehouse; gun-loops)
57. Tarves, Mediaeval Tomb
    Prop of Ythsie (C19; monument)
58. *Haddo House* (1735; Adam; paintings, chapel)
59. Gight Castle (view)
60. Sands of Forvie (*nature reserve*; dunes; wildfowl; seabirds) (NC)
61. Cruden Bay Slains Castle (ruin)
62. Bullers of Buchan (dramatic rock-hollow 200 ft deep, 50 ft wide)
63. *Fyvie Castle* (C15–18; castellated mansion)
64. *Towie Castle* (C16; tower)
65. *Delgatie Castle* (C16; painted ceilings)
66. *Craigston Castle* (C17; little altered)
67. Peterhead Arbuthnot Museum and Art Gallery (fishing)
    Bell Tower (1592)
    St. Peter's Church (1132; ruin)
67a. Buchan Ness (most E. Scotland; granite quarries near)
68. Deer Abbey (C13; ruin)
69. Hill of Corsegight Crossroads (viewpoint)
70. *Loch of Strathbeg* (wildfowl)
71. Fraserburgh Visitor Centre
    Kinnairds Head Lighthouse (1786)
    Wine Tower (C15)
72. Memsie Burial Cairn (c. 1500 BC)
73. Gardenstown Village (cliff-side)
74. Banff Visitor Centre
    Bridge of Banff (1779; widened 1881; Rennie)
    Duff House (1739; Adam; view from outside)
    Houses (C17–18)
75. Alvah *Brydoch Mill* (1810) working
    Bridge of Alvah
76. Boyne Castle (C15; ruin)
77. Portsoy harbour, warehouses (C18)
78. Fordyce Castle (C16)
79. Keith Visitor Centre
80. Ballindalloch Castle (baronial)
81. Dyce Symbol Stones (Pictish; two)
82. Barra *Castle* (C16–17)
83. Auchindoir *Druminnor Castle* (fr. C15; restored; inc. small domestic museum)
    St. Mary's Church (med.; very fine C16 sacrament house)
84. Cullen Visitor Centre
    Church (C15; inc. tabernacle)
    House (early C19; castellated; painted ceilings)
84a. Bin of Cullen (1050 ft viewpoint)
85. Portknockie, The Bow Fiddle (sea-arch in inclined quartz-schist; similar formations on land)

Map 84

Map 85

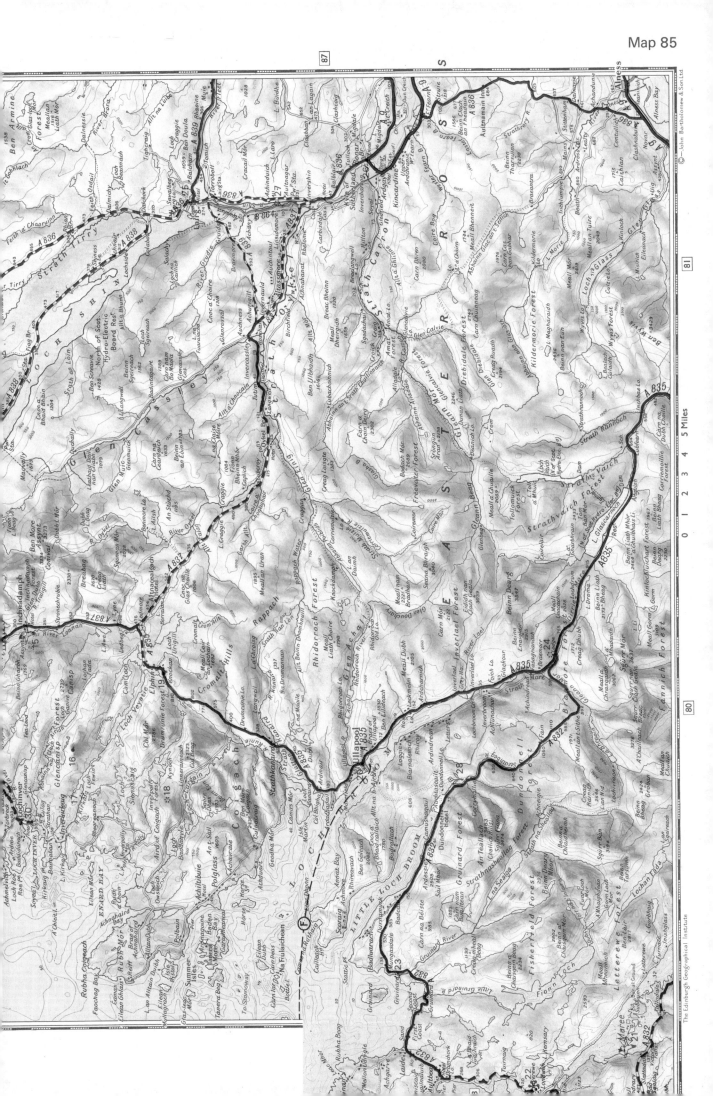

Gazetteer to Maps 84·85

1. Tongue Castle Varrich (Norse ruin?)
2. Altnaharra (brochs)
3. Dornadilla Broch
4. Loch Eriboll (picturesque)
5. Durness (Smoo Cave)
6. Durness Visitor Centre
   Church (C17)
7. Cape Wrath (cliffs; view)
8. Kinlochbervie (crimson sands)
9. *Handa Nature Reserve*
   (bird sanctuary) (RSPB)
10. Scourie palm trees (most northerly)
11. Loch Stack (white quartzite screes)
12. Unapool (view)
13. Stoer (view)
14. Loch Glencoul (1½ m); Eas Coul
    Aulin (600 ft waterfall)

15. *Inchnadamph Nature Reserve*
    (varied interests) (NC)
16. Suilven (2399 ft; 'Sugar loaf')
17. Falls of Kirkaig
18. Stac Polly (impressive 2009 ft)
19. Inverpolly Nature Reserve
    (varied) (NC)
    Knockan Visitor Centre,
    (motor trail)
20. Ullapool Visitor Centre
    Loch Broom Museum
21. Loch Maree Slattadale Forest
    Walks (FC); islands; Nature
    Reserve
22. Inverewe (sub-tropical gardens;
    camping site; Visitor Centre)
    (NTS)

23. Gruinard Bay (pink sand)
24. Braemore Lael Forest Garden (FC)
    Corrieshalloch Gorge;
    Falls of Measach (150 ft) (NTS)
    Corrieshalloch Nature Reserve (NC)
25. Lairg Visitor Centre
26. Bonar Bridge Visitor Centre
    Forest Walks (four, with
    viewpoints) (FC)
    cairns, circles
    Telford Bridge (1812; restored)
27. Falls of Shin (salmon leap)
28. *Dundonnell House* (C18;
    gardens only)
29. Ardvreck Castle (C18; ruins)
30. Lochinver Visitor Centre

89

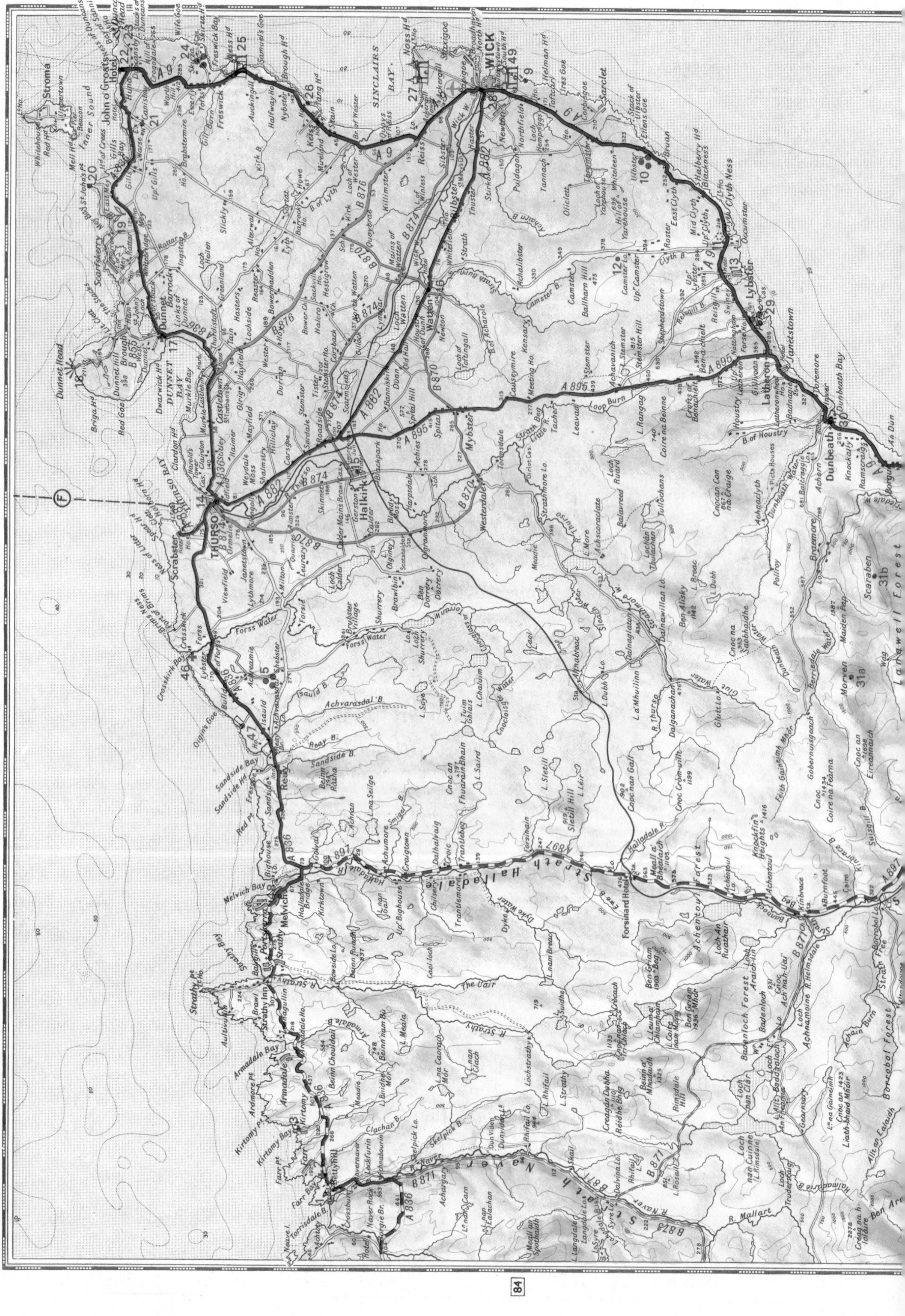
Stroma
Inner Sound
John o' Groats
Duncansby Head
Dunnet Head
Dunnet
DUNNET BAY
THURSO BAY
THURSO
Scrabster
Castletown
SINCLAIRS BAY
WICK
Keiss
Watten
Halkirk
Lybster
Latheron
Dunbeath
Reay
Melvich
Strathy
Armadale
Bettyhill
Forsinard Hotel
Strath Halladale
Scaraben
Morven
Langwell Forest
Kinbrace
Borrobol Forest

84

Map 87

Gazetteer to Maps 86·87

1. Bettyhill Invernaver Nature
    Reserve (NC)
2. Farr Church (1774; sculptured
    stone outside)
3. Kirtomy Bridge (sea-tunnelled rocks)
4. Spynie Canal (fr. 1812; restored;
    Telford)
    Palace (C15; ruins bishops' fortress)
5. Reay, Cnoc Freiceadain
    (Neolithic long-horned cairns)
6. Duffus Castle (motte and bailey)
    St. Peter's Church (fr. C14–16)
    and Cross (C14)
7. Burghead Well (early Christian
    baptistry)
8. *Covesea Skerries Lighthouse*
    (1844; Stevenson)
9. Brig o'Tram (cliff arch)
10. Ulbster, Cairn of Get
    (Neolithic; 'short-horned')
11. Trollie Pow Waterfall (nr. Clyth)
12. Camster Cairns
    Hill o' Many Stanes (200 in 22
    parallel rows)
13. Lybster (sandstone cliffs)
14. Thurso Visitor Centre
    Bishop's Palace (med.; ruins)
    Bridge (1798)
    Harold's Tower (C19; monument
    to 1196 Earl)
    Meal Mill, Foundry (from C17)
    St. Peter's Church (C17; ruins;
    Runic cross)

St. Peter's (1833)
15. Halkirk (symmetrical village,
    castle walls 10 ft thick)
16. Watten Greystones Bridge
    (Telford; 1817)
    Toll (C18)
17. Dunnet Church (fr. mediaeval)
18. Dunnet Head (northernmost
    mainland; view; *lighthouse*; dunes)
19. *Castle of Mey* (C16; restored;
    royal; *gardens only*)
20. Merry Men of Mey (reef)
21. Canisbay Church (fr. C16; rebuilt;
    most northerly Scots)
    Mill (old)
22. John o' Groats (popular but not
    actual northernmost village)
23. Duncansby Head (view; stacks)
24. Skirza (cliff-top broch)
25. Bucholly Castle (C12; ruins; scenic)
26. Keiss Old Keiss Castle
    (C18 fishermen's houses)
27. Castle Sinclair (ruins)
    Castle Girnigoe (ruins)
28. Wick Visitor Centre
29. Forse (Iron Age type village)
30. Dunbeath Visitor Centre
    Castle (from C15; cliffs)
    Harbour; Bridge; Meal Mill
31a. Morven (2313 ft) landmark
31b. Scaraben (2054 ft) landmark
32. Langwell (ancient homestead
    structures)

33a. b. Ousdale (views)
34. Ousdale Broch (good condition)
35. Ord of Caithness (view)
36. Helmsdale Castle
37. Cinn Trolla (broch)
    Kilphedir (broch)
38. Loch Brora, Carrol Rock (cliff)
39. Brora Visitor Centre
    early industrial village; coal mines
    fr. C16
40. Golspie *Dunrobin Castle*
    (from C13; *gardens*)
41. Golspie (C18; planned village)
    Church (C18; loft; canopied pulpit)
42. *Loch Fleet Nature Reserve* (SWT)
43. Dornoch Castle (tower only)
    Bishop's Palace
    Cathedral (from C13)
43a. *Skibo Castle*
44. Tain St. Duthus Chapel (C13; ruins)
    St. Duthus Church (C14)
    Morangie Forest Walk
    Tolbooth (rebuilt C18)
45. Cromarty *Hugh Miller's Cottage*
    (museum) (NTS)
    Harbour (1785)
46. Crosskirk St. Mary's Chapel (C12)
47. Dounreay Visitor Centre
    atomic engrgy plant; museum
48. Melvich Visitor Centre
    Cliffs at Portskerra and Bighouse
49. *Castle of Old Wick* (C12; ruined
    tower)

Map 88

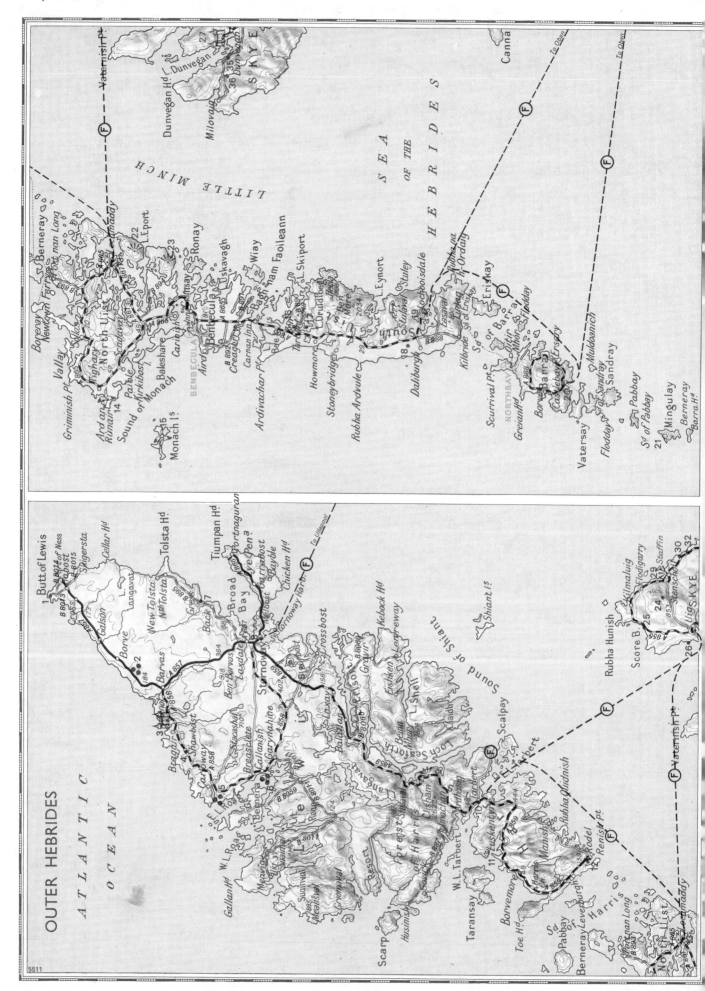

OUTER HEBRIDES

Map 89

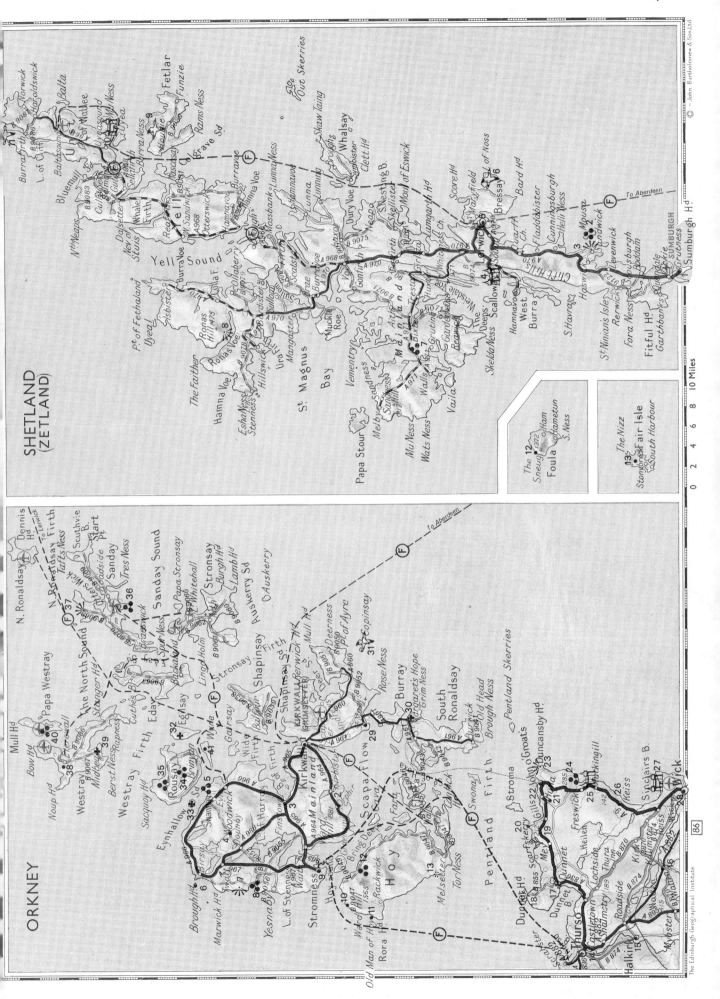

SHETLAND
(ZETLAND)

ORKNEY

© —John Bartholomew & Son,Ltd

The Edinburgh Geographical Institute

86

0   2   4   6   8   10 Miles

Gazetteer to Maps 88·89

1. Butt of Lewis Lighthouse views
   Temple of St. Molva
   (C13; restored)
2. Barvas Stein-a-cleit Cairn and
   Stone Circle (2000 BC)
3. *Black House, No. 43 Arnol*
   (traditional dwelling)
4. Shawbost Museum and Mill
5. Carloway Broch (30 ft high)
6. Callanish Standing Stones
   (47 cruciform)
7. Gress Seal Cave
8. Stornoway Visitor Centre
   Lewis Castle (grounds only)
9. Loch Seaforth (views)
10. Tarbert Visitor Centre
11. Luskentyre (beaches)
12. Rodel St. Clement's Church
    (1500; restored; richly
    ornamented)
13. Lochmaddy Visitor Centre
14. *Balranald Nature Reserve* (flowers;
    rednecked phalaropes) (RSPB)
15. *Monach Isles Nature Reserve*
    (wildfowl; seals) (NC)
    Lighthouse (150 ft; 1864)
16. Statue 'Our Lady of the Isles'
    (125 ft)
17. *Loch Druidibeg Nature Reserve* (NC)
    South Uist Cottage Museum
18. Milton (Flora Macdonald's
    birthplace)
19. Lochboisdale Visitor Centre
20. Castlebay Visitor Centre
    Kiessimul Castle (C12; restored
    1956)
21. Mingulay cliffs (700 ft–900 ft;
    flowers)
22. Viewpoint
23. Viewpoint
24. Quiraing rock towers
    (inc. 'The Needle', 120 ft)
25. Flora Macdonald Monument
    Skye Cottage Museum, Kilmuir
26. Stack of Skudiburgh
27. *Dunvegan Castle* (fr. C15;
    'Fairy Flag')
29. Staffin Bay (view)
30. Kilt Rock
32. Falls of Mealt
35. Colbost Folk Museum
36. Glendale (C18 water-mill)

1. Sumburgh Jarlshof (remains
   villages, Br. Age–Viking)
   Ness of Burgi (Iron Age structure)
   Dunrossness Croft House Museum
   (inc. click mill)
2. Mousa (notable broch)
3. Sandwick (view)
4. Scalloway Castle (1600)
5. Lerwick Visitor Centre

Clickhimin (Br. Age fort)
Fort Charlotte (C17)
Shetland County Museum
6. *Noss Nature Reserve* (seabird
   cliff 592 ft) (NC, RSPB)
7. Walls Staneydale (1600 BC structure)
8. Ronas Voe (view)
9. *Fetlar Nature Reserve* (RSPB)
10. Muness Castle (C16)
11. Unst Hermaness Nature Reserve
    (NC)
12. *Foula* (seabird cliffs 1220 ft)
13. *Fair Isle* (bird observatory)
    (NTS)

1. Kirkwall Visitor Centre
   Bishop's Palace (C12; ruin)
   St. Magnus Cathedral (fr. C13;
   well preserved; in use)
   Earl Patrick's Palace (Renaissance)
   (Hatston) Grain Earth-House
   (Iron Age)
   Library (1683)
   Rennibister Earth-House (Iron Age)
   Tankerness House (restored;
   C16; museum)
   Wideford Hill Cairn (c. 1800 BC)
2. Orphir Church (round; mediaeval)
   Earl's Bu (ruins Viking Palace)
3. Finstown Cuween Hill Cairn
   (megalithic)
   Dale of Cottasgarth Nature Reserve
   (RSPB)
4. Dounby Click Mill (working)
5. Aikerness Broch of Gurness
   (Iron Age)
6. Birsay *Brough of Birsay* (ruined
   Romanesque Church)
   Earl's Palace (C16; ruin)
7. Skara Brae (N. of) view
8. Skara Brae (well preserved
   c. 1600 BC village)
9. Stromness Visitor Centre
   Maes Howe (finest megalithic
   tomb in Britain)
   Museum
   Ring of Brogar (stone circle)
   Stones of Stenness (remains circle)
   Unstan Cairn (c. 2500 BC
   burial chamber)
10. St. John's Head (1141 ft
    vertical cliff)
11. Old Man of Hoy (pillar 450 ft)
12. Hoy Dwarfie Stane (rock burial
    chamber)
13. Melsetter (coloured cliffs)
14. Thurso Visitor Centre
    Bishop's Palace (med.; ruins)
    Bridge (1798)
    Harold's Tower (C19; monument
    to 1196 Earl)

Meal Mill, Foundry (from C17)
St. Peter's Church (C17; ruins;
Runic cross)
St. Peter's (1833)
15. Halkirk (symmetrical village;
    castle walls 10 ft thick)
16. Watten Greystones Bridge
    (Telford; 1817)
    Toll (C18)
17. Dunnet Church (fr. mediaeval)
18. Dunnet Head (northernmost
    mainland; view;
    lighthouse; dunes)
19. *Castle of Mey* (C16; restored;
    royal; *gardens only*)
20. Merry Men of Mey (reef)
21. Canisbay Church (fr. C16; rebuilt;
    most northerly Scots)
    Mill (old)
22. John o' Groats (popular but not
    actual northernmost village)
23. Duncansby Head (view; stacks)
24. Skirza (cliff-top broch)
25. Bucholly Castle (C12; ruins; scenic)
26. Keiss Old Keiss Castle;
    (C18 fishermen's houses)
27. Castle Sinclair (ruins)
    Castle Girnigoe (ruins)
28. Wick Visitor Centre
29. St. Mary's Holm Churchill
    Causeway (World War II
    defensive enclosure)
30. Lamb Holm Italian Chapel
    (prisoner-built, World War II)
31. Copinsay *James Fisher Memorial
    Nature Reserve*
32. Egilsay St. Magnus Church (tower)
33. Eynhallow Church (C12; ruins)
34. Rousay Blackhammer Cairn
    (seven-stall)
    Know of Yarso Cairn (three-stall)
    Taversoe Tuick Cairn
    (chambered mound)
35. Midhowe Broch (Iron Age;
    encloses other structures)
    Cairn (twelve-stall barrow)
    Wasbister (view)
36. Sanday Quoyness Cairn
    (chambered cairn)
37. Sanday (view)
38. Westray Noltland Castle
    (mid C16; ruin)
    Pierowall Church (C13; ruins)
39. Tuquoy Church (C12; ruins)
40. Holm of Papa Westray Cairn
    (1800 BC; engravings)
    Papa Westray Knap of Howar
    (domestic broch-dwellings)
41. Wyre Cobbie Row's Castle (c. 1145
    earliest Scots stone castle?)
    St. Mary's Chapel (C12; ruin)

Map 90

STATUTE MILES

2   0   2   4   6   8   10

Map 91

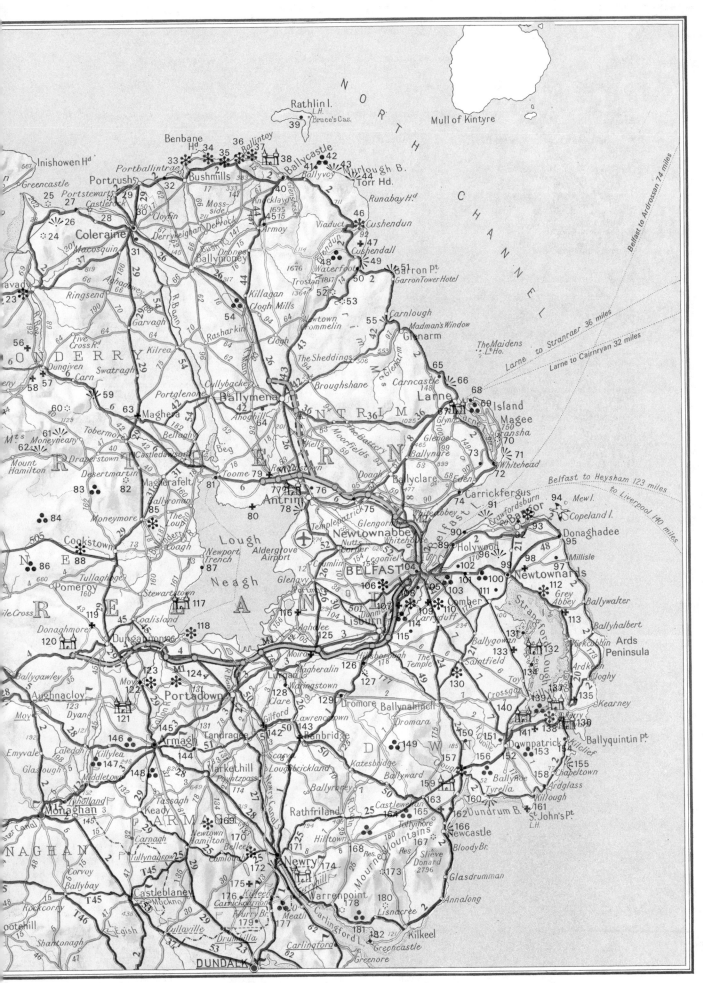

KILOMETRES

2 0 2 4 6 8 10   20   30

Gazetteer to Maps 90·91

1. Aghalurcher Old Church (early Christian ruin)
2. Castle Balfour (C17 ruin), Lisnaskea
3. *Florence Court* (C18) (NT)
4. Belmore Forest
5. *Castlecoole* (C18) (NT)
6. Enniskillen Cathedral Water Gate (C16)
7. *Devenish Abbey, Round Tower & Churches* (early Christian remains)
8. Monea Castle (C17; ruin)
9. Ely Lodge Forest
10. Inishmacsaint Cross (early Christian)
11. Navar Forest, Lower Lough Erne Shore
12. White Island Church (Pagan & early Christian ruins)
13. Old Castle Archdale (C17 ruin)
14. Clogher Cathedral (on early Christian site)
15. *Knockmany Chambered Cairn* (neolithic)
16. Knockmany Forest
17. Errigal Keeroe Cross & Church (C15)
18. Drumskinny Stone Circle (Bronze Age)
19. Lislap Forest
20. Harry Avery's Castle (C14 ruin), Newtownstewart
21. Londonderry Walls (first built 1619) St. Columb's Cathedral First Derry Presbyterian Church Courthouse (1815)
22. *Culmore Fort* (C17 & 1824)
23. Roughfort (earthwork) (NT) Limavady
24. Ballyleighery Forest
25. Magilligan Strand
26. Bishop's Road (views)
27. Downhill Forest (wooded glen) Bishop's Gate (C18) (NT) Mussenden Temple (1783; coastal views) (NT)
28. Castlerock Strand
29. Portstewart Strand
30. Coleraine Church Town Hall (C18)
31. Mountsandel (early Christian & Norman site) Salmon Leap (r. Bann)

32. Whiterocks (limestone cliffs), Portrush *Dunluce Castle* (C13 ruin)
33. Giant's Causeway (basalt rock formation) (NT)
34. Dunseverick Castle (ancient site) (NT)
35. Whitepark Bay (NT)
36. Ballintoy Harbour (NT) & Church (C17)
37. Carrick-a-rede (cable bridge over chasm) (NT)
38. Kenbane Castle (C14 ruin)
39. Rathlin Island (seabird colonies)
40. Ballycastle Church (Boyd Chapel of Ease, 1754) Bonmargy Friary (C16 ruin) Ballycastle Beach (viewpoint)
41. Marconi's House, Fair Head
42. Fair Head Crannog (Bronze Age lake dwelling)
43. Murlough Bay (viewpoint)
44. Torr Head (viewpoint)
45. Armoy Round Tower (C7)
46. Cushendun (village & bay) (NT)
47. Layde Church (C13 ruin)
48. Ossian's Grave (megalithic tomb), Cushendall
49. Cushendall Beach (viewpoint)
50. Waterfoot Beach (viewpoint), Red Bay Red Bay Castle (C16 ruin)
51. Garron Point (viewpoint)
52. Parkmore Forest, Glens of Antrim
53. Glenariff Waterfalls
54. Doey's Cairn (megalithic tomb), Dunloy
55. Carnlough Beach (viewpoint)
56. Bovevagh Church (early Christian ruin)
57. Dungiven Priory (C12 ruins)
58. Banagher Old Church (C11 ruin)
59. Glenshane Pass (viewpoint)
60. Moydamlaght Forest, Sperrin Mountains
61. Craigagh Hill (viewpoint)
62. Crocknakin (viewpoint)
63. Maghera Old Church (C6 & later remains)
64. Gracehill Moravian Church & Village

65. Ballygally Castle (1625; hotel)
66. Drain's Bay Beach (viewpoint)
67. Olderfleet Castle (C16 ruin), Larne
68. Brown's Bay Beach (viewpoint) St. John's Church
69. Ballylumford Dolmen (megalithic tomb)
70. Gobbins Cliffs
71. Black Head (viewpoint)
72. Castle Chichester (C17 tower house ruin), Whitehead
73. Dalway's Bawn (C17 fortified enclosure)
74. Carrickfergus Church (Church of Ireland) Castle & Town Wall (C12)
75. *Castle Upton Mausoleum* (R. Adam), Templepatrick
76. Antrim Round Tower (C7)
77. Antrim Castle (C18), Norman Motte & Gardens
78. Antrim Bay (viewpoint), Lough Neagh
79. Randalstown Barn Church (C17)
80. Cranfield Church (C12 ruin)
81. Toome Eel Fisheries
82. Inniscarn Forest
83. Ballybriest Long Cairn (neolithic)
84. Beaghmore Circles & Cairns (neolithic)
85. *Springhill* (C17) (NT)
86. Creganconroe Cairn (neolithic)
87. Ardboe Cross (C10 or C11)
88. *Wellbrook Beetling Mill* (NT)
89. Holywood Motte Presbyterian Church (non-subscribing)
90. *Ulster Folk Museum*, Cultra Manor
91. Greypoint (viewpoint), Helen's Bay
92. Bangor Tower (C17)
93. Ballymacormick Point (entrance to Belfast Lough) (NT)
94. Copeland Bird Observatory (BTO)
95. Donaghadee Market House (C18)
96. *Helen's Tower* (viewpoint), Conlig
97. *Ballycopeland Windmill* (C18?)
98. Movilla Abbey (mediaeval remains)
99. Newtownards Priory (C13 remains) Town Hall (1770) *Regent House School* (C18)

100. Kempe Stones (megalithic tomb
     Dundonald
101. Dundonald Motte (Norman)
102. Houses of Parliament (1932),
     Stormont
103. Shandon Park Mound (Iron Age
     & later motte site)
104. Presbyterian Church (C17),
     Rosemary Street, Belfast
     Custom House (C18), Donegall Quay
     Charitable Institute (C18),
     Clifton Street
     Transport Museum,
     Newtownards Road
105. Queen's University (C19),
     Belfast
     Botanic Gardens
     Ulster Museum & Art Gallery
106. Collin Glen (NT)
107. Presbyterian Church (non-
     subscribing), Dunmurry
108. Minnowburn Beeches (NT),
     Shaws Bridge
109. Newtownbreda Parish Church
110. Lisnabreeny (glen, waterfall,
     views) (NT)
111. Scrabo Tower (viewpoint)
     Killynether Woods (NT)
112. *Mount Stewart Gardens* (NT)
113. Grey Abbey (C12 remains)
114. The Giant's Ring
     (neolithic earthwork)
115. Drumbo Round Tower (ruin)
116. Middle Church (Presbyterian),
     Lower Ballinderry
117. Mountjoy Castle (C17 ruin)
118. Coney Island (viewpoint) (NT),
     Lough Neagh
119. Donaghmore Cross (early Christian)
120. Castle Caulfield (C17 ruin)
121. Benburb Castle (C17 ruin)
122. Charlemont Fort (C18 gateway)
123. Derryscollop Grove (views) (NT),
     Moy
124. *Ardress House* (C17–18) (NT)
125. Moira Parish Church
126. Hillsborough Gates, Courthouse
     & Church (mid C17)
     Hillsborough Fort (mid C17)
127. Hillsborough Forest

128. Waringstown Parish Church & House
     (C17)
129. Dromore Cross (C9–11)
     Dromore Mound (Norman motte
     & bailey)
130. *Rowallane Gardens* (NT)
131. Nendrum Abbey (early Christian
     ruins), Mahee Island
     Nendrum Castle (Norman & C15
     ruins)
132. Sketrick Castle (C15 ruin),
     Whiterock Bay
133. Presbyterian Church (non-
     subscribing), Killinchy
134. Ringhaddy Motte (C12),
     Church (C13) & Castle (C15)
135. Derry Chapels (C8 or later ruins),
     Portaferry
136. Strangford Castle (C16 ruin)
137. Audley's Castle (C15 ruin)
138. *Castle Ward, House & Grounds* (NT)
139. Audleystown Long Cairn (neolithic)
140. Walshestown Castle (C16 ruin)
141. Raholp Church (C10 or earlier ruin)
142. Presbyterian Church, Gilford
143. Presbyterian Church (non-
     subscribing), Banbridge
144. Hamilton's Bawn (C17 fortified
     enclosure)
145. Armagh City (mainly C18)
     St. Patrick's Cathedral
     (Church of Ireland)
     St. Patrick's Cathedral (RC)
     Archbishop's Palace & Chapel (C18)
     Mall (Georgian houses)
     Bank of Ireland
     (Georgian town house)
     Courthouse (1809)
     County Museum
     Museum of Royal Irish Fusiliers
146. Navan Fort (Bronze Age)
147. Tynan Cross & The Well Cross (C10)
148. Danes Cast (Iron Age earthwork)
     Armagh
149. Legananny Dolmen
     (megalithic tomb)
150. Loughinisland Church (C13 ruins)
     & Lake
151. Downpatrick Mound
     (Norman motte & bailey)

     Inch Abbey (early Christian &
     C13 remains)
152. Struel Wells, Bath Houses & Church
     (Pagan & early Christian)
153. Ballyalton Horned Cairn
154. Kilclief Castle (C15 ruin)
     Kilclief Beach (viewpoint)
155. Ballyhornan Beach (viewpoint)
156. Ballynoe Stone Circle (neolithic)
157. Clough Castle (c. 1200 motte &
     bailey) (NT)
158. Ardtole Church (C15 ruin), Ardglass
     Jordan's Castle (C15 & later remains
     of fortified houses)
159. Dundrum Castle (C12 ruin)
160. Tyrella Beach (viewpoint)
161. St. John's Point Church (C6–11
     remains)
162. Sliddery Ford Dolmen
     (megalithic tomb)
     Murlough Nature Reserve & Beach
     (NT)
163. Maghera Church & Round Tower
     (early Christian remains)
164. Drumena Cashel & Souterrain (C6–13)
165. Tollymore Park Forest
166. Newcastle Beach (viewpoint)
167. Newcastle Forest
168. Goward Dolmen (megalithic tomb)
169. Ballymoyer Forest (NT)
170. *Derrymore House* (C18) (NT)
171. St. Mary's Church, Newry
     Courthouse (1843)
172. Ashton (Newry Canal viewpoint)
173. Spelga Pass, Mourne Mountains
174. *Narrow Water Castle* (C17) & Park
175. Killevy Church (C10 ruin)
176. Slieve Gullion Forest
     Slieve Gullion Passage-grave Cairn
     (neolithic)
177. Clontygora Horned Cairn (neolithic),
     Killeen
178. Rostrevor Forest
179. Kilnasaggart (inscribed stone),
     Jonesborough
     Moyry Castle (C17 ruin)
180. Mourne Park Forest
181. Kilfeaghan Dolmen
     (megalithic tomb)
182. Greencastle (C13 ruin)

Places to Visit

INDEX

St. Anne's, Dumf & Gal, **59** 53

St. Anthony Head, Corn, **2** 77

St. Anthony-in-Roseland, Corn, **2** 76

St. Asaph, Clwyd, **41** 133

St. Augustine's Monument, Kent, **13** 8

St. Bees, Cumb, **52** 42

St. Benet's Abbey, Norf, **39** 54

St. Beuno's Well, Gwynedd, **40** 85

St. Boniface Down, I. of Wight, **10** 307

St. Boswells, Borders, **66** 114

St. Breock, Corn, **3** 64

St. Briavels, Glos, **16** 246

Saintbury, Glos, **27** 314

St. Buryan, Corn. **2** 122

St. Cadfan's Stone, Gwynedd, **32** 42

St. Catherine, Avon, **16** 187

St. Catherine's, I of Wight, **10** 302/3

St. Catherine's Castle, Corn, **3** 47

St. Catherine's Chapel, Surrey, **11** 121

St. Catherine's Hill, Dorset, **9** 264

St. Catherine's Hill, Hants, **10** 36

St. Chloe's Green, Glos, **16** 267

St. Cleer, Corn, **3** 35

St. Clement, Corn, **2** 81

St. Cross, Hants, **10** 35

St. Cyrus Nature Reserve, Tay, **77** 45

St. David's, Dyfed, **22** 71/2

St David's College, Dyfed, **24** 38

St. David's Head, Dyfed, **22** 73

St. Dogmael's, Dyfed, **22** 45

St. Endellion, Corn, **3** 66

St. Fagan's Castle, S. Glam, **15** 33

St. Fillan's Pool, Tay, **71** 47

St. Germans, Corn, **4** 20

St. Giles House, Dorset, **9** 256

St. Govan's, Dyfed, **22** 77

St. Helen's, I. of Wight, **10** 315

St. Helens, Merseyside, **42** 181

St. Ishmael, Dyfed, **23** 19

St. Ives, Cambs, **29** 207/8

St. Ives, Corn, **2** 109

St. John's Head, Orkney, **89** 10

St. John's Jerusalem, Kent, **20** 166

St. John's Point, Down, **91** 161

St. Just, Corn, **2** 125

St. Keverne, Corn, **2** 94

St. Leonard's Tower, Kent, **12** 137

St. Lythan's, S. Glam, **15** 38

St. Margarets, Heref & Worc, **25** 153

St. Margaret's-at-Cliffe, Kent, **13** 66

St. Martha's Chapel, Surrey, **11** 127

St. Martin's Salop, **34** 108

St. Marychurch, Devon, **5** 91

St. Mary-in-the-Marsh, Kent, **13** 87

St. Mary's, Scilly, **2** 135

St. Mary's, W. Sussex, **11** 204

St. Mary's Loch, Borders, **65** 98/99

St. Mawes, Corn, **2** 78

St. Medan's Cave, Dumf & Gal, **57** 76

St. Michael's Island, I. of Man, **46** 134

St Michael's Mount, Corn, **2** 111

St. Monance, Fife, **73** 96

St. Neot, Corn, **3** 42

St. Neots, Cambs, **29** 142

St. Nicholas, S. Glam, **15** 37

St. Nicholas-at-Wade, Kent, **13** 17

St. Ninian's Cave, Dumf & Gal, **57** 89

St. Non's Chapel, Dyfed, **22** 72

St. Olave's, Norf, **39** 33

St. Orland's Stone, Tay, **77** 58

St. Oswald's, N'land, **61** 52

St. Osyth, Essex, **31** 82

St. Paul's Walden, Herts, **29** 248

St. Peri's Well, Gwynedd, **40** 67

St. Radigund's Abbey, Kent, **13** 71

St. Roche Hill, W. Sussex, **11** 254

St. Sampson, Corn, **3** 49

St. Seiriol's Well, Angl, **40** 15

St. Trinian's Chapel, I. of Man, **46** 118

St. Winefride's, Clwyd, **41** 141

Salford, Gtr. Manchester, **42** 197

Salisbury, Wilts, **9** 22/4

Salisbury Hall, Herts, **19** 105

Sall, Norf, **39** 75

Salmestone Grange, Kent, **13** 6

Saltaire, W. Yorks, **48** 160

Saltash, Corn, **4** 19

Saltcoats, S'clyde, **64** 26

Saltergate, N. Yorks, **55** 131

Saltersford, Ches, **43** 213

Saltfleetby, Lincs, **45** 199

Salthouse, Norf, **39** 101

Saltram, Devon, **4** 46

Saltwick Nab, N. Yorks, **55** 120

Saltwood Castle, Kent, **13** 75

Salvington, W. Sussex, **11** 214

Salwick, Lancs, **47** 36

Samlesbury Hall, Lancs, **47** 34

Sampford Courtenay, Devon, **7** 125

Sancreed, Corn, **2** 128

Sanctuary (The), Wilts, **17** 355

Sandal Castle, W. Yorks, **49** 37

Sanday, Orkney, **89** 36/37

Sandbach, Ches. **42** 133

Sandford Orcas, Dorset, **8** 127

Sandham Chapel, Hants, **18** 5

Sandhills, Surrey, **11** 279

Sandhurst, Berks, **18** 421

Sandiacre, Derby, **36** 58

Sandleford Priory, Berks, **18** 4

Sandling Park, Kent, **13** 77

Sandon, Staffs, **35** 194/5

Sandringham, Norf, **38** 122

Sandsfoot Castle, Dorset, **9** 198

Sands of Forvie, Gramp, **83** 60

Sandwich, Kent, **13** 9/10

Sandwich Bay, Kent, **13** 7

Sandwick, Cumb, **52** 35

Sandwick, Shet, **89** 3

Sankey Viaduct, Merseyside, **42** 180

Sanquhar, Dumf & Gal, **58** 39

Santon Downham, Suff, **38** 169

Sapperton, Glos, **16** 265

Sarnesfield, Heref & Worc, **25** 138

Sarratt, Herts, **19** 266

Sarsden, Oxon, **27** 329

Sausthorpe, Lincs, **45** 172

Savernake Forest, Wilts, **17** 365

Savill Gardens, Berks, **18** 415

Sawbridgeworth, Herts, **20** 236

Sawley, Derby, **36** 48

Sawley Abbey, Lancs, **47** 86

Saxby, Lincs, **45** 128

Saxham Hall, Suff, **30** 195

Saxlingham, Norf, **39** 35

Saxstead Green, Suff, **31** 37

Scalloway, Shet, **89** 4

Scampston Hall, N. Yorks, **50** 14

Scamridge Dikes, N. Yorks, **55** 28

Scaraben, H'land, **86** 31

Scarborough, N. Yorks, **55** 26/7

Scarisbrick, Lancs, **47** 10

Scarth Wood, N. Yorks, **54** 57

Scawby, Humberside, **44** 37

Scole, Norf, **39** 11

Scolt Head, Norf, **38** 119

Scord's Wood, Kent, **12** 206

Scorhill, Devon, **4** 110

Scotney Castle, Kent, **12** 240

Scotstarvit Tower, Fife, **73** 26b

Scotter, Lincs, **44** 15

Scottsquar Hill, Glos, **16** 255

Scourie, H'land, **84** 10

Scrabo, Down, **91** 111

Scratchbury Hill, Wilts, **16** 127

Scrubbs (The) Glos, **26** 236

Scunthorpe, Humberside, **44** 40

Scwdeinon Gam, W. Glam, **14** 22

Scwd-yr-Eira, Powys, **15** 98

Seaham, Durham, **61** 80

Seahouses, N'land, **67** 13

Seamer, N. Yorks, **55** 20

Seathwaite, Cumb, **52** 135

Seaton Delaval, N'land, **61** 48

Seckford Hall, Suff, **31** 68

Sedburgh, Cumb, **53** 70

Sedgefield, Durham, **54** 79

Sedgemoor, Som, **8**, 105, 115

Sefton, Merseyside, **42** 5

Segontium, Gwynedd, **40** 64

Seighford, Staffs, **35** 197

Seil, S'clyde, **70** 26

Selborne, Hants, **10** 29/30

Selby, N. Yorks, **50** 56

Selham, W. Sussex, **11** 256

Selkirk, Borders, **66** 42

Selling, Kent, **13** 43

Selly Oak, W. Midlands, **35** 222

Selsfield Common, W. Sussex, **12** 250

Selsley, Glos, **16** 254

Selworthy, Som, **7** 72

Sempringham, Lincs, **37** 160

Sennen Cove, Corn, **2** 126

Seton, Lothian, **66** 41

Settle, N. Yorks, **48** 81

Sevenoaks, Kent, **12** 202

Seven Sisters Cliffs, E. Sussex, **12** 316

Severell's Copse, Surrey, **11** 145

Sewerby, Humberside, **51** 31

Shadoxhurst, Kent, **13** 95

Shaftesbury, Dorset, **9** 43

Shakespeare Cliff, Kent, **13** 70

Shakespeare's Birthplace, Warks, **27** 306

Shaldon, Devon, **5** 97

Shalfleet, I of Wight, **10** 295

Shallowford, Staffs, **35** 196

Sham Castle, Avon, **16** 185

Shandon Park, Down, **91** 103

Shanklin Chine, I. of Wight, **10** 311

Shap, Cumb, **53** 139 142

Shardlow, Derby, **36** 47

Shareshill, Staffs, **35** 83

Sharow, N. Yorks, **49** 125

Sharpenhoe, Beds, **29** 190

Sharpitor, Devon, **4** 70

Sharp Tor, Devon, **4** 115

Sharrow Point, Corn, **4** 23

Shawbost, Outer Isles, **88** 4

Shaws Bridge, Down, **91** 108

Shaw's Corner, Herts, **29** 100

Sheen, Staffs, **43** 218

Sheepwash Bridge, Derby, **43** 272

Sheffield, S. Yorks, **43** 233

Sheffield Park, E. Sussex, **12** 266

Shelland, Suff, **31** 212

Shellingford, Oxon, **17** 306

Shelsley Walsh, Heref & Worc, **26** 161

Shelton, Beds, **29** 199

Shelton, Norf, **39** 21

Shenfield, Essex, **20** 267

Shepperton, Surrey, **19** 175

Shepreth, Cambs, **29** 178

Shepton Mallet, Som, **16** 121

Sherborne, Dorset, **8** 42

Sherburn, Durham, **54** 87

Sherburn-in-Elmet, N. Yorks, **49** 58

Shere, Surrey, **11** 133

U

Y

Z